The Royal Navy and Anti-Submarine Warfare, 1917

Until 1944 U-boats operated as submersible torpedo craft which relied heavily on the surface for movement and charging their batteries. This pattern was repeated in World War II until Allied anti-submarine countermeasures had forced the Germans to modify their existing U-boats with the schnorkel. Countermeasures also pushed along the development of high-speed U-boats capable of continuously submerged operations.

These improved submarines became the benchmark of the post-war Russian submarine challenge. Royal Navy doctrine was developed by professional anti-submarine officers, and was based on the well-tried combination of defensive and offensive anti-submarine measures that had stood the test of time since 1917, notwithstanding considerable technological change.

This consistent and holistic view of anti-submarine warfare has not been understood by most of the subsequent historians of these anti-submarine campaigns, and this book provides an essential and new insight into how Cold War (and indeed modern) anti-submarine warfare is conducted.

Malcolm Llewellyn-Jones served in the Royal Navy for 26 years, mainly in the Fleet Air Arm. After retiring form the Navy he completed an MA and a PhD in War Studies at King's College, London. He is a historian in the Naval Historical Branch, MoD.

Cass series: Naval policy and history
Series Editor: Geoffrey Till

This series consists primarily of original manuscripts by research scholars in the general area of naval policy and history, without national or chronological limitations. It will from time to time also include collections of important articles as well as reprints of classic works.

1. **Austro-Hungarian Naval Policy, 1904–1914**
   Milan N. Vego

2. **Far-Flung Lines**
   Studies in imperial defence in honour of Donald Mackenzie Schurman
   Edited by Keith Neilson and Greg Kennedy

3. **Maritime Strategy and Continental Wars**
   Rear Admiral Raja Menon

4. **The Royal Navy and German Naval Disarmament 1942–1947**
   Chris Madsen

5. **Naval Strategy and Operations in Narrow Seas**
   Milan N. Vego

6. **The Pen and Ink Sailor**
   Charles Middleton and the King's navy, 1778–1813
   John E. Talbot

7. **The Italian Navy and Fascist Expansionism 1935–1940**
   Robert Mallett

8. **The Merchant Marine and International Affairs, 1850–1950**
   Edited by Reg Kennedy

9. **Naval Strategy in Northeast Asia**
   Geo-strategic goals, policies and prospects
   Duk-Ki Kim

10. **Naval Policy and Strategy in the Mediterranean Sea**
    Past, present and future
    Edited by John B. Hattendorf

11. **Stalin's Ocean-going Fleet**
    Soviet naval strategy and shipbuilding programmes 1935–1953
    Jürgen Rohwer and Mikhail S Monakov

12. **Imperial Defence, 1868–1887**
    Donald Mackenzie Schurman: edited by John Beeler

13. **Technology and Naval Combat in the Twentieth Century and Beyond**
    Edited by Phillips Payson O'Brien

14. **The Royal Navy and Nuclear Weapons**
    Richard Moore

15. **The Royal Navy and The Capital Ship in the Interwar Period**
    An operational perspective
    Joseph Moretz

16. **Chinese Grand Strategy and Maritime Power**
    Thomas M. Kane

17. **Britain's Anti-submarine Capability 1919–1939**
    George Franklin

18. **Britain, France and the Naval Arms Trade in the Baltic, 1919–1939**
    Grand strategy and failure
    Donald Stoker

19 **Naval Mutinies of the Twentieth Century**
An international perspective
Edited by Christopher Bell and Bruce Elleman

20 **The Road to Oran**
Anglo–French naval relations, September 1939–July 1940
David Brown

21 **The Secret War against Sweden**
US and British submarine deception and political control in the 1980s
Ola Tunander

22 **Royal Navy Strategy in the Far East, 1919–1939**
Planning for a war against Japan
Andrew Field

23 **Seapower**
A guide for the twenty-first century
Geoffrey Till

24 **Britain's Economic Blockade of Germany, 1914–1919**
Eric W. Osborne

25 **A Life of Admiral of the Fleet Andrew Cunningham**
A twentieth-century naval leader
Michael Simpson

26 **Navies in Northern Waters, 1721–2000**
Edited by Rolf Hobson and Tom Kristiansen

27 **German Naval Strategy, 1856–1888**
Firerunners to Tirpitz
David Olivier

28 **British Naval Strategy East of Suez, 1900–2000**
Influences and actions
Edited by Greg Kennedy

29 **The Rise and Fall of the Soviet Navy in the Baltic, 1921–1940**
Gunnar Aselius

30 **The Royal Navy, 1930–1990**
Innovation and defence
Edited by Richard Harding

31 **The Royal Navy and Maritime Power in the Twentieth Century**
Edited by Ian Speller

32 **Dreadnought Gunnery and the Battle of Jutland**
The question of fire control
John Brooks

33 **Greek Naval Strategy and Policy, 1910–1919**
Zisis Fotakis

34 **Naval Blockades and Seapower**
Strategies and counter-strategies, 1805–2005
Edited by Bruce A. Elleman and Sarah C. M. Paine

35 **The US Pacific Campaign in World War II**
From Pearl Harbor to Guadalcanal
William Bruce Johnson

36 **Anti-Submarine Warfare in World War I**
British naval aviation and the defeat of the U-boats
John J. Abbatello

37 **The Royal Navy and Anti-Submarine Warfare, 1917–49**
Malcom Llewellyn-Jones

The Royal Navy and Anti-Submarine Warfare 1917–49

Malcolm Llewellyn-Jones

Routledge
Taylor & Francis Group

LONDON AND NEW YORK

First published 2006
by Routledge
2 Park Square, Milton Park, Abingdon, Oxfordshire OX14 4RN

Simultaneously published in the USA and Canada
by Routledge
711 Third Avenue, New York, NY 10017

First issued in paperback 2014

Routledge is an imprint of the Taylor & Francis Group, an informa business

© 2006 Malcolm Llewellyn-Jones

Typeset in Times by
HWA Text and Data Management, Tunbridge Wells

All rights reserved. No part of this book may be reprinted or reproduced or utilised in any form or by any electronic, mechanical, or other means, now known or hereafter invented, including photocopying and recording, or in any information storage or retrieval system, without permission in writing from the publishers.

British Library Cataloguing in Publication Data
A catalogue record for this book is available from the British Library

Library of Congress Cataloging in Publication Data
A catalog record for this book has been requested

ISBN 978-0-415-38532-9 (hbk)
ISBN 978-1-138-01042-0 (pbk)

For my beloved Mother and Father

Contents

Preface		xi
List of abbreviations		xiii
	Introduction	1
1	**Echoes from the past, 1917–40**	8
	British anti-submarine warfare, 1917–40 8	
	Convoys and striking forces 12	
	Wartime experience 17	
2	**Mastering the submersible, 1939–43**	25
	U-boats and their tactics, 1939–43 25	
	Methods of detecting and attacking U-boats 28	
	Tactics on gaining contact 35	
	Beating the submersible 39	
3	**Elusive victory: countering the schnorkel, 1944–45**	46
	Introduction of the schnorkel and its effect on anti-submarine operations 46	
	British tactical countermeasures 50	
	Tactics refined from experience 56	
	Coastal Command's response 58	
	Results of the anti-schnorkel campaign 60	
	Prospects of the U-boat war 63	
4	**The dawn of modern anti-submarine warfare, 1944–46**	68
	The problem of the fast U-boat 68	
	HM submarine Seraph *trials 69*	
	Further assessment of the type XXI 75	
	Captain Roberts' interrogation of German U-boat officers 78	

      The thrall of the Walter-Boat   81
      Planning U-boats trials   84
      Type XXI trials and tribulations   88
      New organization and old timers at the Admiralty   91

5 Short-term problems, long-term solutions, 1946–47   93
      Assessments of the Russian threat   93
      Policy review of methods for attacking submerged submarines   98
      The first tranche of doctrine papers   104
      The ability of future submarines to make contact   112

6 New problems, old recipes, 1947–48   119
      Anti-submarine problems of the future and attack-at-source   119
      Submarine tactical and technical development   129
      The joint anti-submarine school's view of anti-submarine tactics   131
      Anti-submarine trials at sea   140

7 Future uncertainties, 1948–49   147
      The 'Iron Curtain' and policy deliberations   147
      British and allied tactical doctrine   150
      A second tranche of doctrine papers   155
      A year of exercises with fast submarines   162
      Technological answers?   165

Conclusion: joining up the dots, 1944–9   170
      The nature of anti-submarine warfare   170
      The nature of the threat   172
      Tactics and technology   172
      The 'defensive' and 'offensive'   173
      Synthesis   175

Notes   177
Bibliography   208

Preface

In my case, the teacher was Mr Weeks who first stimulated my fascination with history. Curiously, however, I followed a different path, via a degree in mathematics to a full career in the Royal Navy's Fleet Air Arm as an anti-submarine specialist. Historical reading remained an obsessive hobby, until frustration at not understanding the 'whys' and 'hows' of events took me towards some serious enquiry which, in turn, led me to postgraduate research. The dawn of modern anti-submarine warfare had always intrigued me, but it was Professor Geoffrey Till, David Waters and the late Commander Richard Compton-Hall, each in their own way, who provided the inspiration and impetus for this particular avenue of research. Sustaining the effort was made easier through the subtle guidance of my supervisor, Professor Andrew Lambert, and by friends who rallied to help and nag during many dinners, especially by George Karger and John Salmon, as well as the 'Ol' Fogies', Bronwyn Fysh, Tony Hampshire, John Ross, Dr Nick Black and Dr Warwick Brown. But special mention must go to Lieutenant Commander Doug McLean, MA, CF (an anti-submarine specialist) and Peter Nash, who each read the whole work in draft, asked many searching questions and corrected innumerable errors of spelling and syntax. Drs Joe Maiolo and Robin Woolven were also kind enough to read the draft.

Every archive I visited provided cheerful and unfailing help in unearthing the primary sources upon which this work is based, though special thanks must go to Kate Tildesley and Jenny Wraight of the Naval Historical Branch and Admiralty Library, and Julie Ash at the National Archives (formerly the Public Record Office) at Kew. Others provided access to private and public papers, of which I would, otherwise, have been unaware. These individuals include Rear Admiral J.H. Adams, CB, LVO, David Lees, K.T. Nethercoate-Bryant (of the Submarine Old Comrades Association, Gatwick), Lieutenant Commander Paul Mallett, SAN(CF), Ret'd, Electrical Sub Lieutenant M. Walford, RNVR, Ret'd, Professor R.D. Keynes and Dr Gary Weir (of the Naval Historical Center, Washington). On a different plane, Michael Whitby, MA, Dr William Glover, Lieutenant Colonel John Abbatiello, PhD, USAF, Lieutenant Commander George Franklin, MPhil, RN, Commander David Stevens, PhD, RAN, Ron Curtis, T.H. Pratt, David Webb and Dr Susan Cunningham all generously shared their research, insights and wisdom, without which this monograph would have been the lesser. I must also thank Captain

Christopher Page, Head of the Naval Historical Branch for allowing me time, amidst my other duties, to pursue the latter stages of my research, though neither he nor the Branch have any responsibility for the conclusions I have drawn.

And, lastly, to the staff of the Whitehall Café in London go my thanks for endless cups of the best espresso in Britain, and the Coffee House in Stow-on-the-Wold for relaxing surroundings and relaxed service, which allowed many thematic connections to be made over a panini and yet more coffee. Clearly, the culinary input to this monograph was crucial to its assembly; it can only be hoped that the result provides the reader with some food for thought. My gratitude goes to everyone for their company and encouragement to follow, what seemed at times, to be a trackless path, but which led to a successful PhD thesis that has been truncated and transformed into this monograph.

Abbreviations

Abbreviations used in archival citations are listed in the Bibliography.

A/A	anti-aircraft
ACAS	Assistant Chief of Air Staff
ACHQ	Area Combined Headquarters
ACI(s)	Admiralty Convoy Instructions
ACNS	Assistant Chief of Naval Staff
ACNS(UT)	Assistant Chief of Naval Staff (U-boats and Trade)
AD(A/S)	Assistant Director (Anti-Submarine) in DTASW
A/D	aircraft direction
AEW	airborne early warning
AIO	Action Information Organization (sometimes AIC – Action Information Centre – or Operations Room, equivalent to the US CIC, or Combat Information Centre)
ARL	Admiralty Research Laboratory
A/S	anti-submarine
Asdic	supersonic echo-ranging equipment (equivalent to US Sonar)
A/SEE	Anti-Submarine Experimental Establishment. See also HMA/SEE – later became HMUDE
ASV	air-to-surface vessel
ASW	anti-submarine warfare
ASWDU	Air Sea Warfare Development Unit
ASWORG	Anti-Submarine Warfare Operations Research Group, Tenth Fleet, USN (a rough equivalent to DNOR)
ATW	ahead throwing weapon (such as, Hedgehog and Squid)
BAD	British Admiralty Delegation, Washington, DC.
BdU	*Befehlshaber der Unterseeboote*, the U-boat High Command
C-in-C	Commander-in-Chief
C-in-C, WA	Commander-in-Chief, Western Approaches
CAFO	Confidential Admiralty Fleet Orders
CAOR	Chief Advisor on Operational Research
CCDU	Coastal Command Development Unit
CNO	Chief of Naval Operations (US Navy)

CoS	Chiefs of Staff
CVE	escort carrier
D of Ops	Director of Operations, Air Ministry
D of P	Director of Plans Division, Admiralty
D of TD	Director of Tactical Division
DASW	Director of Anti-Submarine Warfare Division, Admiralty
DAUD	Director of Anti-U-Boat Division, Admiralty
DAW	Director of Air Warfare
DCNS	Deputy Chief of Naval Staff
DDOps(M)	Deputy Director of Operations (Maritime), Air Ministry
6DF	Sixth Destroyer Flotilla
D/F	direction finder (or finding)
DNC	Director of Naval Construction, Admiralty
DNI	Director, Naval Intelligence
DNOR	Director of Naval Operational Research. [See also CAOR]
DOD	Director of Operations Division, Admiralty
DOR	Director of Operational Research, Admiralty
DSR	Director of Scientific Research
DTASW	Director of Torpedo, Anti-Submarine and Mine Warfare Division, Admiralty
DTM	Director of Torpedoes and Mining, Admiralty
DTSD	Director of Tactical and Staff Duties Division, Admiralty
3EF	Third Escort Flotilla
4EF	Fourth Escort Flotilla
EGx	xth Escort Group
FoC	furthest-on-circle
FOSM	Flag Officer, Submarines
Gnat	German naval acoustic torpedo, otherwise known in Britain as 'Curly', and by the German Navy as *Zaunkönig*
GSR	German search receiver
HE	hydrophone effect
H/F	high frequency radio, sometimes shown as 'HF'
HF/DF	high frequency [radio] direction finding (colloquially known as 'Huff-Duff')
HM	His or Her Majesty's … (ship, submarine, etc.)
HMA/SEE	His Majesty's Anti-Submarine Experimental Establishment, Fairlie. See also A/SEE
HMS	HM ship
HMCS	HM Canadian ship
HMUDE	His Majesty's Underwater Detection Establishment, Portland
HQ	Headquarters
HTP	high test peroxide (otherwise known as hydrogen peroxide – H_2O_2 – or Ingolin, the power source for the Walter turbine)
JASS	Joint Anti-Submarine School, Londonderry
LLSuA	limited lines of submerged approach

LuT	Lage-Unabhängige Torpedo
MAD	magnetic anomaly detector
MLA	mean line of advance
NavTecMisEu	US Naval Technical Mission in Europe
NATO	North Atlantic Treaty Organisation
NELM	North East Atlantic and Mediterranean, USN Command
NID	Naval Intelligence Division
NOIC	Naval Officer-in-Charge
OIC	Operational Intelligence Centre
ORS	Operational Research Section
PNM	pipe noise maker
POBRY	standard 5-sonobuoy pattern (derived from colours assigned to individual buoys: purple, orange, blue, red and yellow; green was also available)
PoW	prisoner(s)-of-war
PPI	plan position indicator (Radar or Asdic display)
QH	radio navigation aid (similar to the RAF radio navigation aid, GEE, and forerunner of modern Decca radio navigation system)
RAAF	Royal Australian Air Force
RAF	Royal Air Force
RAN	Royal Australian Navy
RCAF	Royal Canadian Air Force
RCN	Royal Canadian Navy
RN	Royal Navy
RP	rocket projectile
R/T	radio telephony
SASO	Senior Air Staff Officer, of an RAF Command
SAWC	Joint (Admiralty and Air Ministry) Sea/Air Warfare Committee
SO	Senior Officer (of Escort Group)
σ (sigma)	symbol denoting the statistical measure 'standard deviation'
TDZ	torpedo danger zone
UHF	ultra high frequency (radio)
US	United States
USN	United States Navy
USNR	United States Naval Reserve
UWD	Underwater Weapons Department, Admiralty and USN
VCNS	Vice Chief of the Naval Staff
VHF	very high frequency (radio)
VLF	very low frequency (acoustics)
WATU	Western Approaches Tactical School, Liverpool
W/T	wireless telegraphy

Introduction

As the Second World War came to a close, Korvetten-Kapitan Adalbert Schnee took the new Type XXI U-boat *U-2511* on its first operational patrol. These streamlined boats were capable of high underwater speed and (by use of the schnorkel breathing tube) of continuous submerged operations. Taking *U-2511* to the North of the Shetlands, Schnee, so the literature relates, found himself in an excellent position to attack the cruiser HMS *Norfolk*, screened by a single destroyer. Some accounts suggest that Schnee penetrated the cruiser's destroyer screen and simulated firing a torpedo salvo at point-blank range, while others suggest that by making a 30° alteration of course and increasing speed to 16 knots he passed well outside the British destroyer's detection range and thus avoided contact.[1] Commander Richard Compton-Hall, MBE, RN, himself an experienced submarine commander, spent some time with Schnee to assess his capabilities and concluded that '… without intending (I am sure) to brag, … [he] felt able to run circles round the escorts and attack favourably if he wanted. … He was, I think, way ahead of his contemporaries, and his background doubtless enabled him to see the future, and innovation, with unusual clarity.'[2] Schnee, not a man to camouflage his exploits, felt certain he could have sunk both ships with the greatest of ease. However, he had just received the signal from Dönitz ordering the cessation of hostilities, so he made for his base at Bergen, leaving the British unaware of their narrow escape.[3]

The incident itself seems to have made little impact on contemporary Admiralty action, for by the end of the war the British already had a firm grasp of the nature of this threat and had evolved anti-submarine (A/S) measures to deal with it as best they could with existing equipment. Indeed, the Admiralty were much more confident that they could counter it than is generally supposed in the historiography. In the subsequent literature, however, Schnee's 'attack' is depicted with greater authority than it deserves, for the surviving evidence to support the event is nebulous.[4] Nevertheless, it has entered the folklore of the Battle of the Atlantic as epitomising the power of these new U-boats and the deadly threat they might have posed to British shipping. But most accounts exaggerate the 'new' technical capabilities of the Type XXI, which would have been pitted against the 'out-of-date' British wartime technology, while ignoring the U-boat's tactical limitations. Worse, some authors have claimed that the British were frightened by the impending deployment of the Type XXI, to which there were 'no ready technical or operational answers.'[5] This theme has been tirelessly regurgitated by many historians.[6] There was, of course, a genuine concern in the late 1940s over the potential Russian use of the end-of-war German technology, and the analysis was reinforced by 1948, when the United States Navy (USN) realized that submarines modified to achieve fast underwater speeds were able to penetrate anti-submarine screens and torpedoed the carriers with ease. Subsequent exercises seemed to confirm the power and invulnerability of the new submarine types and to stress the impotence of anti-submarine forces. The arrival of the nuclear submarine in the mid-1950s served only to re-emphasize the problem.

Too many historical accounts provide a jaundiced view of the interwar era, or concentrate on the great convoy battles of the Battle of the Atlantic (apparently made more difficult by supposed inter-Service squabbling, conservatism and incompetence). The depiction of these battles against packs of U-boats attacking on the surface at night leads to an exaggeration of their overall historical importance, for, in many respects, these battles are perturbations in the overall progress of submarine (and hence anti-submarine) warfare. Meanwhile, accounts of the momentous events of the Cold War have overshadowed the strategic cusp between the end of the Second World War and the East-West super power rivalry. For these reasons the period from 1944–49 has been barely examined, yet in it lie many of the seeds that flourished in the Cold War. Nevertheless, there are several valuable and critical analyses of the Battle of the Atlantic, some of which cover the last year of the campaign.[7] However:

> Research on the Battle [of the Atlantic] has tended to focus on either the operational *or* the technological developments. Operational historians have been content simply to add new technology to their discussions of convoy actions. These historians have provided little or no discussion on why and how the new weapons systems were developed, and have ignored any mention of the new tactical doctrine and training programmes introduced to make use of them.[8]

This monograph redresses such narrow accounts by examining a number of wider themes barely touched in the existing literature and, in particular, shows that the inshore anti-U-boat campaign in 1944–45 had a much greater impact on post-war anti-submarine doctrine than the earlier battles against the wolf-packs. In tracing this, and the post-war tactical applications, the Royal Navy, and especially the Admiralty, are shown to be more subtle and forward-thinking organizations than is generally supposed.

The most significant conclusion is over the Royal Navy's approach to defensive and offensive anti-submarine operations. In the mid-1950s, the Admiralty's Historical Section thought they were witnessing a growing acceptance of the 'Convoy is Defensive' school of thought within the Service. A section of naval opinion, the Historians held, viewed the convoy system as '… the embodiment of the defensive,' but this, they added, '… is not substantiated by the facts of war ascertained by rigorous historical research.' Indeed, their analysis revealed that, in both World Wars, '… of all the measures we adopted, the convoy system alone provided the means for waging unremitting and highly remunerative *offensive* action ... .'[9] They drove home their point with a statistical comparison, albeit only up to May 1943, of the effectiveness of 'convoy' forces in destroying U-boats, as opposed to other operations, such as hunting patrols, transit offensives, mining and bombing of bases, that were invariably seen as 'offensive'. The writers claimed that 23 per cent of the U-boats were sunk by 'offensive' operations but 65 per cent were destroyed by convoy escorts and their supports, with the remainder being lost to various other means.[10] Their subsequent Staff History was somewhat more muted but emphasized these same ideas.[11] They were also echoed by the Official Historian, who noted that there was a '... widely held but fallacious belief that [these] so-called "offensive" measures against the U-boats could provide an effective alternative to convoy.'[12] The point has been amplified by later historians, who also point to the concomitant inability of the Admiralty to 'learn from history'.[13] The heresy of dividing the tactical application of anti-submarine warfare into 'defensive' or 'offensive' operations has become widespread and is followed, albeit erratically, in the current *British Maritime Doctrine* Manual.[14] The use of 'offensive' and 'defensive' inconsistently or in odd juxtaposition in most accounts betrays a fundamental misunderstanding of how anti-submarine warfare was viewed by the Admiralty during the Second World War and in its aftermath.

This monograph provides a new interpretation of the Royal Navy's anti-submarine philosophy – one that unequivocally shows that the 'defensive' and 'offensive' operations were consistently visualized (in both peace and war) as interdependent and symbiotic parts of anti-submarine strategy, and not as alternative strategies. This analysis provides a new basis against which to reassess the British approach to anti-submarine warfare in the first half of the twentieth century at a time when advances in submarine technology, the switch of main threat from Germany to Russia and the move from hot to cold war provided great changes in the operational environment. This period is one in which the Royal Navy and, especially, the Admiralty proved to be more subtle, adaptable and forward-thinking organizations than is generally supposed. The narrative is structured around the work of the 'middle management' (that is, the Commanders and Captains) of the Admiralty and Royal Navy commands, who were the main authors of development.

The first hurdle in dealing with anti-submarine warfare is that it is intrinsically difficult, as will be explored in the chapters that follow. Submerged submarines are usually hard to locate – a factor which submariners exploit by optimizing their operations to create swift, decisive attacks from an ambush, and then endeavouring to withdraw amidst the ensuing confusion in order to re-initiate an attack at a time and place where again they hope to enjoy, once more, the advantages of stealth. Anti-submarine forces, conversely, strive for deliberate tactical engagements (often in counter-attacks) with submarines where their advantages of superior tactical coordination and numbers can be brought to bear. Submarines have tried to emulate the escort advantage of mass, by bringing more submarines into the area of a specific convoy battle. But in doing so they normally sacrifice the benefit of stealth by having to move at speed and to communicate with each other. In these circumstances, or when in transit to their allotted operational areas, submarines become vulnerable to offensive anti-submarine forces. These tactical preferences of the opponents therefore force anti-submarine forces to employ a cocktail of defensive and offensive measures. They also provide a basic underpinning of the continuity in anti-submarine warfare tactical concepts.[15]

It has been suggested that when the British realized the scale of the new threat they inexorably abandoned their war-winning, but 'defensive', convoy strategy and replaced it with an 'offensive' one. This strategic philosophical shift was reinforced by the Royal Navy's supposed ambivalence about convoy and institutional bias towards aggressive methods. These arguments, however, are not supported by the primary evidence. They are also a reflection of the influence of later Cold War operations which emphasized area surveillance and stealth employing long-range acoustic listening devices. Although the incipient threat of engagements was ever present, and practised against, the stress during operations was on detection and tracking the enemy, preferably without alerting him to the presence of friendly forces. These were not the primary tactical drivers in the 1940s. Anti-submarine tactics in the 1940s were not, however, homogeneous. For a major change in submarine warfare occurred in 1944 when the Germans began to operate U-boats on war patrols during which they remained submerged throughout, made possible by the introduction of the schnorkel. In parallel the enemy was developing new U-boat types capable of high submerged speed. Thus 1944 marks the dawning of modern anti-submarine warfare, though contemporary opinions were divided on whether this represented a revolution or simply the evolution of methods used to deal with older submarines. Technological remedies, by and large, did not to appear until the 1950s and the equipment itself was in part an amalgam of gear initially developed to meet a different requirement together with wholly new concepts which, however, did not become operationally effective for another decade. This monograph shows that, contrary to most expectations, the Admiralty proved to be an adaptive and innovative institution, and the operational parts of the Royal Navy approached the problem of the fast submarine in the post-war era by means of tactical adaptation to optimize existing anti-submarine equipment while waiting for technical improvements. The tactical doctrine, presented here, has been derived from an extensive analysis of the contemporary tactical manuals and doctrine papers which were written by naval officers with considerable anti-submarine experience during or in the immediate aftermath of the war. They also benefited from the close interaction between the operational, engineering and scientific communities in the Admiralty and Commands. This was a big business operating on a small business ethos. As a result the documents tend to be more pragmatic than theoretical, and therefore do not present the historian with the overly geometric and formulaic vista found in age-of-sail treatise.[16]

Even so, these manuals and papers present analytical challenges. The surviving papers are voluminous and have to be condensed so that their often arcane nature becomes more easily digestible, but without over-simplification. There is no guarantee that men at sea actually followed them to the letter – indeed the opposite is clearly the case.[17] Furthermore, in the confusion, uncertainty and dynamics of battle, the skill and aggression or passivity of leaders, the vagaries of the environment, and so on, mean that individual actions are unique. To see the effect, and to test how tactics were actually put into effect, a number of wartime operations were examined. There is not space here to recount them in detail, so the analysis has been used to provide a more discerning interpretation of the formal tactical manuals. Peacetime exercises provide another challenge because of their 'artificiality'. As the Admiralty frequently noted, exercises gave false impressions of the tactical outcome because of the inhibiting effects of safety rules and because the 'enemy' was unlikely to respond as he would in war – he might even cheat![18] Thus when the time came to set out the post-war doctrine, it was done against a background of little hard evidence. The threat they had to deal with, if not wholly new, presented itself in ambiguous ways and there were no certain signposts.

The task of defining the anti-submarine doctrine for the immediate post-war era fell to a small group of officers in the Admiralty. These men, Captain P.W. Burnett, DSO, DSC, RN, Commander G.A.G. Ormsby, DSO, DSC, RN, and Lieutenant Commander J.P. Mosse, DSC, RN, were all career officers. They were all practised and pragmatic seamen with distinguished wartime records, who had fought against German wolf-packs and had later adapted to the new schnorkel-fitted U-boat tactics. It helped that they were all anti-submarine specialists, who had learned their trade during specialist professional courses and in subsequent appointments during the 1930s.[19] The doctrine they were taught was rooted in the operations in the last years of the First World War, and modified by the subsequent development of 'asdic' (later known as sonar) acoustic echo-location of submarines. This is hardly surprising, for, as has been noted, there are some basic continuities in anti-submarine warfare. Thus the knowledge of the tenets of anti-submarine warfare acquired by Burnett and his team forms the template for this monograph. To track the pull-thought of ideas it must necessarily (if rather briefly) cover the period from 1917–43. This exposed the rationale for the methods employed from 1944–49, by which time Burnett and his immediate successors had laid the foundations of the doctrine which served the Royal Navy well for several decades. There was, of course, subsequent modification, in part because of the formation of NATO – with its greater emphasis on alliance warfare – but also to take account of the improved weapons and sensors that began to appear in volume with the rearmament spurred by the Cold War and the potential of the Russian submarine threat.

The way that the subsequent story turned out could be seen as the script which logic might have predicted for Burnett and his team. While it is true that there was a robust strand of continuity flowing through their work and stretching back to the First World War, it was by no means certain that one particular path would be taken between 1944 and 1949. Rather like the ultimate goal of their deliberations, the safe passage of shipping across the oceans, neither took prescribed, bounded routes. Terms such as shipping 'sea lanes' are figurative constructs. They do not exist, any more than did a preordained line of development exist through the complexities of the late- and post-war anti-submarine debate. The analogy with the sea is neatly captured in the Canadian sea shanty of the Second World War:

'From Halifax to Newfiejohn or 'Derry's clustered towers
By trackless paths where conning towers roll.'[20]

In describing these events, certain assumptions have been made. Firstly, that the tactical and technological interaction can be discussed for the period of 1944–9 with little reference to finance (at least for anti-submarine operations). This is for two reasons. To begin with, the cost of tactical development revolves around the provision of sea and shore-based trials. Whilst these were not lavish, there is little evidence to support the contention that tactical development was seriously curtailed by lack of resources caused by financial restriction. This monograph demonstrates that quite the opposite was the case. Tactical development (even post-war) proceeded at a reasonable pace, because much of it was a cerebral process. As for the provision of new technology, the sheer complexity of some of the developments (especially asdic and acoustic torpedoes) was as much a limiting factor as any lack of material or personnel (which was in some important areas soon rectified).[21] These equipments were deployed, as expected in the early 1950s. Of course, post-war financial restrictions did curtail the strategic application of some tactical options, notably by limiting the more offensive force levels and deployment patterns. But it is easy to forget that there were resource limitations in wartime too. To some extent post-war shortcomings were redressed by the rearmament programme of the early 1950s which coincided with the availability of new anti-submarine equipment. However, the way the ships and equipment were to be used remained as planned despite financial constraints.

The impact of atomic weapons seems to have had little effect on the way the British conceived of their post-war anti-submarine doctrine until the next decade. They maintained a keen interest in the likely effects on sea warfare, and whatever the outcome of arguments over 'broken-backed warfare', if war at sea was protracted, then the defence of trade remained a central concern of the Royal Navy.[22] British concepts of anti-submarine warfare were probably more affected by the demands of the Cold War than by the direct influence of the atomic bomb. There are also other aspects of anti-submarine warfare that will not be covered in detail. Mine warfare was employed extensively during the war and formed a substantial element of post-war anti-submarine planning, both as an offensive weapon in the enemy's own waters, and defensively to protect shipping routes and harbours. Mining is a topic which deserves full treatment in its own right but space here precludes more than brief mention of it. Similarly, submarines were employed in both world wars on anti-submarine operations, however their use this role bears only obliquely on most of the narrative presented here, until between 1947 and 1948 when anti-submarine warfare became their primary mission. Lastly, the case for anti-submarine aircraft is more awkward. Because aircraft, as will be seen, lost their power to destroy submarines by the introduction of the schnorkel, they played a less central role in anti-submarine warfare from 1944 onwards and did not begin to recover their primacy until new acoustic detection and weapon technology became available towards the end of the 1950s. For this reason, there is less emphasis in this monograph on airborne tactics than on those used by surface forces.

The main thematic strands of this monograph are heavily intertwined and treating them separately risks losing the essential complexity of anti-submarine warfare and, for this reason, it is presented as a chronological narrative that is unavoidably nuanced, complex and dense. The central issue for Burnett, Ormsby, Mosse and the other staff officers in the post-war era was how to deal with fast submarines, based on the technological challenge represented by the wartime German Type XXI design, and now potentially operated by the Russian Navy. Their experiences from the war had a large influence on how they conceived the doctrine that was set out in 1946–8. What is striking at this, the dawn of modern anti-submarine warfare, is the speed with which these officers drew together the operational strands in this short span, particularly when their perspicacity is compared with the protracted and indecisive adjustment when the Cold War ended. This is partly explained by, what was in some ways, the skewed chimera of 30 years of Cold War and its stultifying effect on operational thinking, as against the dynamic impact of six years of global war and the fight for national survival.[23] But, while the experience of the Second World War had its effect on how Burnett and his colleagues rationalized the anti-submarine problem it also became apparent during the research for this monograph that their interwar experiences also had a great bearing on their post-war work. They were all regulars, who had completed the long anti-submarine specialist course in the 1930s during which they had acquired an anti-submarine philosophy that owed much to the operations of the last year of the First World War. Thus, in writing this monograph, it became apparent that, in order to understand the rationale for the concepts developed at the dawn of modern anti-submarine warfare in 1944–9, some preliminary inspection of the developments from 1917–43 were necessary. They reveal a remarkable continuity in the story in the face of major technological changes. It is here, then, at the end of the First World War that the monograph begins.

1   Echoes from the past, 1917–40

British anti-submarine warfare, 1917–40

The U-boat of the First World War relied on surface travel for tactical mobility and for searching for its targets, where using their diesel engines they could achieve 18½ knots in good conditions. They would submerge when threatened by anti-submarine (A/S) forces or, sometimes, in rough weather. Once underwater, the U-boats relied on their batteries and electric motors for propulsion, which gave them a top speed of about eight and a half to nine and a half knots but only for an hour. At, say three and a half knots, however, the U-boat's underwater endurance was about 24 hours. Charging the batteries could only be done on the surface when the diesel engines could be run, so these boats were in every sense 'submersibles'.[1] While submerged the U-boat's range of vision through the periscope was restricted. The type and rough course of a victim could be distinguished at about six or seven miles (in reasonable visibility by day) but this required a considerable exposure of the periscope.[2] The periscope was, of course, normally used only intermittently. It is not surprising, therefore, as the Naval Intelligence Division (NID) noted, U-boats preferred to remain on the surface, unless forced to dive by anti-submarine patrols. On the surface their visual horizon was much extended, they could keep their batteries fully charged, and they were able to manoeuvre into an attacking position ahead of a convoy before diving to attack unseen. The search was considerably extended when two U-boats operated in concert, spread at right-angles to the convoy's track. Such tactics had been noted, although there was no positive evidence of greater numbers working together. With the U-boats widely spread, they had to rely on wireless telegraphy (W/T) for passing sighting information, though, even with this advantage, it was not supposed that U-boats could easily deliver simultaneous attacks. The disadvantage of the method was that the British were able to intercept the radio transmissions, and by applying direction-finding (D/F) techniques, warn the convoy of a U-boat in its vicinity. The shore authority (especially when the enemy's signals were decrypted) might also be able to direct an anti-submarine patrol vessel to the U-boat's rough location.

The U-boat made frequent use of her periscope to assess the relative movement of her target during the final dived approach. Inside about two miles she would be wary of over-exposing her periscope, for fear of it being seen by an escort and the U-boat counter-attacked. The ideal submerged torpedo attack was aimed at a specific ship in the convoy at a range of 500–1,000 yards.[3] With her restricted underwater endurance, a U-boat could only get into a firing position from a relatively narrow angle ahead of the convoy. If the initial sighting was made on the beam or quarter of the convoy, the U-boat had to race on the surface around the convoy until she gained a position ahead of the convoy where she could dive to make a covert final approach. The further ahead she was, the further off the convoy's track the U-boat could afford to be. Subject to the restricted underwater speed and endurance of the U-boat, she could therefore start from positions within what were known as 'limiting lines of submerged approach' (LLSuA), which for a seven and a half knot convoy were angled about 40° off each bow of the convoy. Dived attacks could only be made in daylight, or on nights were there was strong moonlight, for on a dark night, when a U-boat was practically blind, she would at risk of being run down by a convoy. However, the Admiralty's Anti-Submarine Division noted by October 1917, that on moonlit nights submarines would probably operate on the surface with very little buoyancy, which would make them very difficult to see, even as close as 400 yards. When night attacks were made, it was thought unlikely that the U-boat captain would get between the lines of the convoy, for fear of being run down. Ideally, he would fire from the flank, aiming at an individual ship in the convoy. More often attacks were made at long-range from outside a strong escort (and known as 'browning' shots fired in the hope of hitting any ship in the convoy).[4] The general concept for convoy escort dispositions was, where possible, a line of escorts, spaced a mile apart, across the front of the convoy at a distance of 600–800 yards. By zig-zagging, these escorts would provide a physical obstruction to U-boats about to fire at close range. Escorts would also be stationed on the flanks and, where sufficient forces were available, one or more were placed astern where they could respond to a torpedoing with a broadcast barrage of depth-charges, as the remainder of the convoy cleared the area. An escort astern was also used to deter a shadowing U-boat by forcing it to submerge as the convoy made an evasive turn just after dusk.[5]

Anti-submarine escorts fitted with hydrophones were able to listen for the hydrophone effect (HE) from the U-boat's propellers, principally caused by the collapse of the cavitation bubbles created by a rapidly spinning propeller, and, to a lesser extent, by the noise made by the flow of water past the hull and from internal machinery.[6] Listening in the vicinity of surface ships was unproductive, since their hydrophone effect was likely to drown any noise from the U-boat. When a convoy was attacked, escorts had no means of detecting submerged submarines other than by sighting their periscopes, the trail of oil often left by U-boats, or the water disturbance from a torpedo's discharge and subsequent track.[7] But given a sighting, retaliation could be instant on the part of the escort, and had to be if they were to stand any chance of getting a kill because the U-boat would inevitably move away from its last reported, or datum, position. Depending on the depth of water, the U-boat would either go deep at slow speed, or rest on the bottom, to avoid anti-submarine forces hunting them with hydrophones.[8] The blind barrage attacks by the escorts would not be improved until the introduction of the technique of transmitting and receiving a beam of 'supersonic' sound pulses from an underwater acoustic projector (known as the transducer or oscillator). This equipment was known in Britain as 'Asdic', and 'Sonar' in America. This seemed the most promising device of several being experimented with. When the pulses struck the hull of a U-boat an echo was returned. By timing the interval between the transmission and reception of the sound, an accurate range could be calculated, and by noting the direction of the oscillator, a rough bearing was achieved. Experiments with this method had been carried out since the middle of 1917, but it was only towards the war's end, that seven RN ships were fitted with this gear. In the meantime, several anti-submarine ships working as a team would lay a blind barrage of depth-charges over the suspected position of the U-boat.[9] Initially, escorts were equipped with only four depth-charges, though this outfit was later increased, with individual vessels carrying 30 depth-charges. Up to 40 depth-charges were expended by hunting groups against individual submarines. Escorts were also used on 'extended patrols' at, say, 11 miles, specifically designed to interfere with U-boats on the surface trying to overhaul the convoy. With their greater range of vision and speed, aircraft often replaced surface escorts in this role.[10] Experiments were made with the fitting of searchlights and parachute flares to aircraft in order to detect U-boats on the surface at night. These searchlights were, however, the primary means of detection (not of final attack, as with the later development of the Leigh Light in WWII). Use of the light, therefore, was more likely to warn the U-boat, which could dive before the aircraft had any chance of making contact. The lethality of aircraft attacks, whether by night or day, left much to be desired.[11] Although attacks on convoys had occurred when aircraft were present, U-boat operations were seriously hampered by the constant fear of being sighted by aircraft, for apart from the U-boat, or its periscope being seen, the tracks of its torpedoes were clearly visible from the air. With their low underwater mobility, the U-boats might not be able to get away from the tell-tale beginning of the track before surface escorts arrived to counter-attack. As a result U-boats refrained from attacking convoys with air escort.

The Admiralty's small Historical Section had only been able to narrate the first six months of the main German First World War unrestricted U-boat campaign by 1939. Nevertheless, they noted that defeat by the U-boat was averted principally by the introduction of convoy. It was expected that delays due to convoy assembly, and sailing at the speed of the slowest ships, would reduce the carrying capacity by 12 to 20 per cent. However, '... if the situation was serious enough to require a convoy system', the Admiralty realized, after the war, 'no reduction in carrying capacity might be involved, compared with other methods of trade protection.'[12] Once the decision to institute convoy had been made, its implementation was delayed by administrative difficulties. By July 1917, 90 per cent of the losses continued amongst independent shipping, although gradually the '... proportion of ships in convoy was increased until practically the whole of the traffic was included.'[13] One advantage of convoy that was immediately obvious was that ships in convoy '... could be kept in touch with the latest intelligence.'[14] Both the Official and Staff Histories wondered whether the efficacy of convoy lay '... rather in its power of evasion and its greater power of control than in its power of actual protection by escort?'[15] The imposition of convoy faced the U-boats with a conundrum. By concentrating the shipping into a small area, convoy made it more difficult for the U-boats to find their targets. This was accentuated in the open ocean, where individual convoy routes could be widely separated, and even if the U-boat made a sighting, getting into position to attack without being sighted himself was difficult. Yet if the enemy moved inshore, where convoys would be easier to find, the U-boats would be faced with heavy air and surface patrols, which forced them to operate while submerged for considerable periods and thereby lose their mobility and search capability. These patrols, especially those by hydrophone-fitted trawlers, would also reinforce convoy escorts as they passed through the patrol areas. At least some officers considered that these operations should be combined with '… bold measures to strike at the U-boats at source.'[16] Although evasion by convoys was the priority, it was still the convoys that brought about more actions between the contending forces than any other cause. Overall, about 250 vessels were employed directly on convoy work, and a further 500 were intermittently on convoy duties, escort or support work. These vessels represented about 15 per cent of the ships in commission in the Royal Navy.

These lessons were emphasized in post-war histories and staff papers. The inter-war years have been portrayed as a period of stagnation in anti-submarine development, both tactically and technically. However, recent research has begun to prove that this was not the case, especially after 1932 when British anti-submarine policy was reviewed. During this period, Germany was not seen as the major threat to British trade. That would come later with her development of ocean raiders and finally U-boats.[17] At the detailed tactical level, attention was paid to increasing the weight of depth-charge attacks to make them more effective. By 1935 it was also recognized that if aircraft were to be effective U-boat killers, they would have to be armed with depth-charges. However the post-war Naval Staff History claimed that, as late as 1937, the Admiralty had had no intention of introducing:

> … A/S bombs larger than 100 lb into the Naval Service, since it is considered that a stick of 100 lb bombs is far more likely to sink or damage a submerged submarine than an equal weight of larger bombs … .[18]

The key here seems to be the emphasis on attacks on submerged submarines. The aircraft of the inter-war period were all slow and were only able to carry relatively small bomb-loads, except for Royal Air Force (RAF) Sunderland flying-boats, itself a slow aircraft. Speed was important to convert a sighting into an effective attack, otherwise an aircraft would not be able to attack before a submarine had submerged for long enough to make the aiming point uncertain. It was thought that there was a greater chance of one bomb bursting close to the submarine if a large stick straddled the aiming point. There seem to have been no rigorous tests of the anti-submarine bombs at sea, which might have exposed the poor effectiveness, either when bursting close to a submerged target or even from a direct hit. Attacks by escorts could, however, be deadly, but these too had to be started as soon as possible after contact was gained, normally without waiting for a consort to complete the hunting unit. This was designed to throw the U-boat onto the defensive, to avoid it being able to complete an accurate torpedo shot. Attacks were then to continue with two ships cooperating until the U-boat was destroyed, if this was considered to be expedient. It was recognized at the time that lessons drawn from exercises had to be treated with some caution. It was difficult to divert merchant ships from trade, so convoy exercises had to use naval and auxiliary vessels acting as a convoy. The Admiralty repeatedly noted that the results were also devalued by artificialities imposed by peacetime safety rules, and the desire to get maximum training benefit, which lead to an unrealistic number of anti-submarine units being involved during actions. The analysis of sea exercises was compared with the results from strategic board games at the War College at Greenwich.

Convoys and striking forces

The central role of convoy was firmly established both theoretically and in exercises, though the threat from U-boats was not the only, nor even the main, threat. Combined attacks by surface raiders and U-boats was seen as the critical threat, and was known to be a tactic being explored by the Germans.[19] If British heavy ships were required to be part of the escort, convoys would be sailed infrequently and may have to be large, varying between 40 and 90 ships. And as the inter-war years passed, the Admiralty also had to consider the increasing threat of air attack on convoys. Here the focus will be on measures adopted to counter the U-boat, though it was not treated in isolation by the Admiralty during the 1930s. Britain's geographic position *vis-à-vis* Germany forced commerce raiders to make long, hazardous passages to their hunting grounds. The Scandinavian convoys of the First World War showed the danger of an enemy able to sortie from the flank of a convoy route (as the German possession of the Biscay ports was to demonstrate again in the Second War). Principal among the anti-submarine measures was that evasion was the best defence for convoys, particularly if the enemy adopted unrestricted U-boat warfare from the outset. Of course, diversion of a convoy had its limits, if both elements of the 'safe and timely arrival' dictum were to be met. From wartime experience, and peacetime exercises, it was '… not envisaged that the escorting vessels will be able to prevent a submarine attacking the convoy, but it is hoped that they will be able to destroy the submarine after it has made its attack.'

Yet, while a successful defence might be the primary consideration, '… in general', it was thought, 'the most certain means of obtaining security from enemy submarines is by carrying out a vigorous offensive against them.' Furthermore:

> The moral effect of early success against enemy submarines is likely to militate heavily against the value of his subsequent operations. It is, therefore, of great importance that organization and training should be such as will allow of the full development of offensive A/S measures immediately on the outbreak of war.[20]

Such protestations were not merely the product of bravado, or an overly optimistic view of the technical progress in asdic development. During the 1930s (when Burnett, Ormsby and Mosse were taking their professional anti-submarine courses) although asdic made significant advances in operational capability, its limitations became evident at the most senior levels of the Royal Navy.[21] A U-boat could be detected out to 6,000 yards, though a more realistic working range was about 2,000–3,000 yards, and once detected its position was known to within 2° in bearing and 25 yards in range. Although once in contact, the chances of continuing to hold the echo were reasonably assured, however, gaining initial detection was by no means certain, especially when water condition were difficult (such as during rough weather, or as a result of unwanted bottom echoes).[22]

Up to the mid-1930s the practice was to station the few anti-submarine ships available for escort on the quarters or astern, where they were best positioned to pounce on a U-boat which had attacked the convoy. Now, with increasing numbers of asdic-fitted escorts it was planned, initially, to fill the stations on the bows of the convoy, where they could hopefully prevent or deter the U-boat from getting into a good firing position. As more escort vessels became available, so the quarter and stern stations were filled. However, with the emphasis now on stationing ships ahead, the Admiralty worried that a U-boat which succeeded in making an attack might then escape destruction. Although the dense asdic screens provided for the Fleet at sea were able to detect over two-thirds of submarines in exercises, it was realized that such performance would not be mirrored by the relatively sparse coverage afforded to wartime convoys.[23] Investigation continued on the use of aircraft on extended patrols around a convoy, both to warn off U-boats concentrating on the surface ahead (which the convoy might then avoid), and those trailing the convoy astern. Defence of a convoy was by no means assured, though the Admiralty were aware of the German judgement in their Official History (translated for the Admiralty by 1937) over the difficulty U-boats had in closing their targets unless they remained on the surface.[24] Thus to prevent the weight of U-boat attack increasing, it was felt that a spirited attrition of U-boats was necessary from the outset. It was planned for some groups of anti-submarine vessels to be stationed round the coast as striking forces, though it was recognized that, even with anti-submarine ships capable of 20 knots, they could not be expected reliably to detect U-boats reported more than 10 miles distant. A later Naval Staff History later put it another way:

> … if A/S vessels take more than two hours to reach the reported position of the submarine, the one thing certain is that by the time they arrive at the spot the U-boat will be somewhere else. It is much the same as looking in a dark room for a black cat that isn't there.[25]

But unlike the monograph being advanced in the Staff History, striking forces were not an alternative to direct convoy protection, for as the Admiralty had already noted, 'A thorough investigation into the best methods of employing patrol vessels and aircraft, both for protection of trade and for independent anti-submarine operations, which to a certain extent are interlinked, is being carried out.'[26]

Instead of the 'defensive' convoy or 'offensive' hunting strategies, traditionally depicted in the historiography as mutually exclusive alternatives, they are here expressed as a hypostatic relationship, and this forms a major thematic strand of this monograph. It was a dual policy, which was criticized by subsequent historians.[27] This, it seems, was the philosophy that formed the basis for teaching on the three-and-a-half month long anti-submarine specialist course at HMS *Osprey* during the 1930s which produced many of the officers who rose to prominence during the Battle of the Atlantic and in staff appointments after the war. The course also taught the specialists how difficult anti-submarine warfare could be and how easy it was to miss a submarine. One of these officers, (then) Lieutenant C.D. Howard-Johnston, an anti-submarine specialist, remembered:

> The ordinary U-boat had a silent speed of about 1½ knots. At this speed there was NO hydrophone effect and no sure means of classification if the U-boat laid low. As an A/S Specialist (1930) I knew only too well that a stationary S/M often was a very bad echo target. But once the S/M revved up there was a roar in the water.[28]

These lessons were to become significant towards the end of the coming war. Furthermore, the Admiralty noted that all U-boats should be considered as potential minelayers. Convoy was to prove to be a weapon against the mine itself, because it allowed minesweeping to be coordinated with shipping movements to best advantage. However, the U-boat culprit would never have to come near the convoy escorts and therefore stood little risk of destruction.

The Naval Staff History later claimed that the Admiralty, when comparing the loss of carrying power in war due to convoy, failed to take account of the '… crippling delays experienced in war-time by the hold up and routeing of independently routed ships.'[29] But, Captain T.S.V. Phillips, Director of Plans (D of P), drawing on a Ministry of Shipping report after the First World War, argued in a Memorandum of early 1938, that:

> … it is open to doubt whether the delays due to convoy will be any greater than those caused by evasive routeing and shipping being afraid to sail on account of real or imagined dangers. … Moreover, if, as seems probable, losses in convoy are considerably less than losses in independent sailings, then the number of ships available to carry cargoes will remain greater under a convoy system.[30]

The point was concurred in at the highest level in the Admiralty, and the memorandum despatched to all the Commanders-in-Chief, and enshrined in the manual on the protection of shipping issued in early 1939.[31] Phillips also noted that not only the shipping industry, but '… the nation as a whole is "convoy minded".' The sinking of SS *Endymion* off the coast of Spain in January 1938 provoked questions in the House of Commons and in the press over the use of convoy. So, looking to the future, Phillips considered that:

Any attempt the Admiralty might make in war to avoid going into convoy, however good the reasons might be, would merely be regarded as short-sighted and pig-headed obstruction, which would increase the public agitation for the institution of convoy and weaken the public faith in the Admiralty.[32]

The assumption was that the Germans would embark on unrestricted U-boat warfare from the outset, and thus it was intended to institute convoy immediately on the outbreak of war. This decision was announced in Parliament in 1938.[33] It was generally accepted, Phillips observed, that convoy could not be started until at least six weeks after the outbreak of a war. In the memorandum, Phillips sought ways in which this period could be shortened, by ensuring that the earmarked naval control of shipping officers and commodores of convoys were in place as soon as possible after the commencement of war. Sufficient numbers of cruisers would be available at the outbreak, and armed merchant cruisers soon thereafter, to cope with attacks by enemy surface raiders, though there were not enough heavy ships to escort all convoys if they were needed. Not all the anti-submarine and anti-aircraft (A/A) convoy escorts would be available until the reserve fleet was mobilized, but the shortfall was counterbalanced, because the first homeward bound ocean convoy would not reach the Western Approaches for about two weeks. The Admiralty later noted that some 25 per cent of the available escorts would be required to protect the passage of the Army and RAF to the Continent in the opening weeks of war.[34] As for trade, during the opening weeks many of the ships already at sea would have to complete their passages independently. The question was how could protection be afforded to these ships?

It has been claimed '… that the Royal Navy was as ready to defend against a U-boat campaign as the German navy was ready to mount one.'[35] It was assumed in January 1939 that the enemy would adopt an unrestricted submarine campaign from the outset and the best counter was convoy with surface and air anti-submarine escorts in waters where submarine attack was likely. Although Germany had only 25 U-boats suitable for ocean operations, a force much below that employed during the peak of 1917–18, the Admiralty warned that:

> … a few highly skilled German U-boat Captains caused a high percentage of our shipping losses and that in 1939 the German submarines will be commanded by peace-time trained and presumably efficient Captains.[36]

Initially, in-bound trade would be ordered to adopt an approximation to the convoy system, with ships rendezvousing in loose groups at selected ocean positions, from where escort groups would accompany them to their destination ports. Ships which were unable to make the rendezvous were to sail independently on wide diversionary routes.[37] The escort groups, when not involved in direct support of trade, would carry out offensive patrols in the shipping areas. This system was needed only until all ships in threatened areas could be brought into convoy and adequate anti-submarine forces became available. Even then, offensive operations were not to be wholly abandoned.

It should not be supposed that the lessons from the First World War, or inter-war exercises, were directly used by those planning future counter-measures, rather the experiences were infused by a process of osmosis.[38] What was well-established was a holistic doctrine of defensive and offensive measures, which formed the basis of the new version of the *Anti-Submarine Warfare Manual*, issued in February 1939. This Manual confirmed the value of convoy by increasing the difficulty of U-boats in finding targets and, where intelligence was available, of diverting shipping clear of U-boat concentrations. If U-boats were to get into position to attack convoys, they had to move on the surface, where they were vulnerable to detection by wide-ranging aircraft. Even if the aircraft were not able to destroy the U-boats, they could home surface escorts to the location and this, for the enemy, was far more dangerous. Aircraft were to be used to support convoys or Fleet units. The Fleet would normally have sufficient aircraft for inner and outer anti-submarine patrols, though convoys would seldom be supported by enough aircraft to carry out both types of patrol simultaneously. The priority was for an outer patrol to be flown some 15–20 miles ahead of a convoy, where it would cover the area in which U-boats would be moving on the surface to get ahead of the convoy. This plan, proposed by the Admiralty after wide consultation was agreed by Coastal Command.[39]

Convoy also forced U-boats to attack merchant ships where they had to accept the risk of counter-attack by the anti-submarine escort. Although asdic-fitted escorts could not provide an impenetrable screen ahead of convoys, they were better able (than previously) to detect escaping U-boats and exact retribution. The Manual exhorted anti-submarine ships to adopt an aggressive posture, for:

> It is evident that the destruction of a submarine reduces the risk to subsequent convoys. Further, enemy submarine morale must be considerably affected by the knowledge that an attack on a convoy is inevitably followed by swift counter-measures.[40]

The formal doctrine was thus heavily centred on defensive measures necessary for the protection of trade and the Fleet, albeit conducted aggressively. Offensive operations were the subject of a draft Memorandum by Captain D.A. Budgen, RN, Director of the Tactical Division (D of TD) in the spring of 1938. The Memorandum made slow progress around the Naval Staff and Commands afloat. There was general agreement with Budgen's proposals that groups of four, or more, asdic-fitted anti-submarine vessels with air support would be disposed to take advantage of intelligence. Ship–air communications and accuracy of reporting were crucial to the success of the cooperation. However, only a few months before the outbreak of war, the Director of the Naval Air Division noted that:

> The training of the RAF in A/S tactics in conjunction with the A/S School at Portland is proceeding better than heretofore, but much remains to be done. It is hoped that it may be possible to arrange later in the year for [Fleet Air Arm] aircraft to cooperate with the A/S School in the investigation of A/S tactics.[41]

These were serious limitations, though largely organizational in nature. Where intelligence was sparse, the chances of the anti-submarine group making contact were slight, but where accurate reports were available, or a sighting was within, say, 10 miles of the hunting force, there was a good prospect of the ships gaining contact and being able to prosecute the U-boat.[42] The tactical concepts were incorporated in the formal anti-submarine tactical manual when it was re-issued in 1940. Meanwhile, the Memorandum was broadly welcomed, though Captain V.H. Danckwerts, now D of P, cautioned that:

> Although it would clearly be desirable to start a vigorous offensive against enemy submarine on the outbreak of war, the extent to which we can do this is strictly limited by the number of A/S craft which we can afford to keep in commission in peace time.

And to hammer home the point, Danckwerts added that:

> Generally speaking, it is considered that the most profitable and effective method for providing this security with limited forces available in the initial stages, is by providing escorts for all movements most likely to be menaced by submarine attack.[43]

Realistically, he considered that with all the commitments for direct escort, there would be no anti-submarine craft to form striking forces for some time. When he reviewed the Staff comments on the employment of striking forces, Budgen wondered whether he might have over-emphasized their tactical importance. But, Budgen added, whether protection was provided by escort of striking forces, it would '… fail unless the personnel have been, firstly, efficiently trained and, secondly, kept efficient by constant practice.'[44]

Wartime experience

'Except for the first two months of the war, before the convoy system had been fully instituted, there have been no destroyers available for A/S Hunting Forces', Captain A.G Talbot, Director of Anti-Submarine Warfare Division (DASW), wrote in February 1940.[45] During these two months, 75 per cent of U-boat attacks had been against independently routed shipping, which had not yet been brought into convoy.[46] Initially, protection for this shipping was provided by Striking Forces, some of them based around aircraft carriers. One of these hunting operations accounted for *U-39*, the first U-boat sunk during the war by three ships of Captain C.S. Daniel's 8th Destroyer Flotilla while escorting *Ark Royal* on an anti-submarine sweep.[47] The carrier had been narrowly missed by the U-boat's torpedoes, having unnecessarily exposed herself while flying off aircraft. One of the other carriers, *Hermes*, had an unexciting time, but a few days later the *Courageous*, also on anti-submarine hunting operations, was attacked in similar circumstances and sunk. The Staff History later concluded that: 'In the light of events there is no doubt that the employment of large aircraft carriers for hunting submarine was a mistake.' However, the History also, rightly noted that:

> At the same time, it is only fair to state that it was no more than a temporary measure intended to cover the period before the full convoy system came into operation. The risk to a hunting carrier was by no means ignored, and the opinions of the Naval staff all emphasized the vital necessity for a full-time, effective A/S screen, especially as a carrier was obliged to maintain a steady course during periods when aircraft were being flown off and on ... .[48]

The loss of *Courageous* on 17 September 1939 has been portrayed as a damning indictment of the Admiralty's offensive policy during the opening months of the war, and the direct reason for its abandonment thereafter, for the other two carriers were recalled on 18 September and took no further part in anti-submarine operations. Yet the draft Naval Staff narrative (which was abandoned) of the Battle of the Atlantic, although criticizing the Royal Navy's offensive policies, notes a significantly different reason for the withdrawal of the carriers. This was that after:

> ... the *Courageous* was sunk ... the Admiralty decided that the *Ark Royal* should no longer be used for hunting submarines as the influx of independent ships had now diminished.[49]

These views were echoed a month after the loss of *Courageous*, as the Naval Staff considered *Hermes*' anti-submarine patrol in the South-West Approaches, during which one U-boat was sighted by aircraft and three contacts gained by the weak force of escorting destroyers, but none led to a kill. The Naval Air and the Anti-Submarine Divisions warned against exaggerating the power of aircraft to locate and destroy U-boats.[50] More significantly, Captain J.H. Edelsten, in D of P, was '... of the opinion that, since the institution of convoy, the results expected from the employment of carriers on A/S hunts do not justify the risks involved.' Crucially, Edelsten added, '... our carriers are now urgently required for hunting surface raiders.'[51] It was these reasons, and not simply the loss of *Courageous*, which motivated the withdrawal of the carriers from these offensive operations: for losses were expected and accepted. Moreover, the Admiralty issued further guidance on the use of aircraft carriers in trade protection, following considerable discussion within the Naval Staff during the month following the loss of *Courageous*. The view was not that the carriers had been misused, but that the tactics of their air and surface striking forces had been inadequate, both in locating and destroying U-boats as well as protecting the carrier.[52]

The Home Waters Staff History also claims that the destroyer hunting groups were equally a waste of time and curiously suggests that their successes were more due to chance than design, and the more detailed Staff History on the anti-submarine war wrongly credits some of the U-boat losses to 'escorts'.[53] A detailed examination of the first two months of the war shows that, of the seven U-boats sunk, three fell victim to mines, one to anti-submarine escorts which were shifting from one convoy to another, and the remaining three U-boats were destroyed by surface anti-submarine hunting groups. Aircraft, both carrier and land-based, although they made plenty of sightings were unable to convert them into lethal attacks, being too slow and still equipped with the ineffective anti-submarine bomb.[54] Attacks, therefore, remained ineffective until the introduction of the airborne depth-charge, a saga which would benefit from further research. However, right from the start, and with increasing emphasis as the war progressed, considerable weight was placed on the provision of support groups of fast escorts, along with land-based aircraft and escort carriers, either to reinforce convoys or to operate on independent offensive operations.[55] When discussing the relative vulnerability of carriers to conventional weapons, Commander G.A. Titterton, Historical Section, later wrote, that:

> ... briefly the position appears to be this. In the last war, between the outbreak of war and VE-day 63 British carriers were commissioned. Of this number, eight were sunk by enemy action; five by U-boat; one by internal explosion, one by warships' gunfire and one (*Hermes*) by aircraft bombs. Several ... were damaged and put out of action for some months by bombs.[56]

Long before the creation of the Operational Research Division, every avenue to improve performance was sought, including the setting up of a committee under Vice Admiral T.H. Binney reporting directly to the First Sea Lord. Binney was distanced from actual operations and his Committee was to investigate war problems and generate ideas which might be of use to the Naval Staff. In his first report Binney considered 'The Submarine Campaign', and was '... struck by the fact that anti-submarine vessels can only be certain of a kill if they are situated within a very short distance of the reported position of a submarine.' It followed, the Committee concluded:

> ... that the best position for anti-submarine vessels is in *company* with a convoy. ... We recommend that for the present every anti-submarine vessel with sufficiently good sea-keeping qualities should be employed with convoy rather than being dispersed in hunting units when the time factor of reaching the submarine will always make success very doubtful.[57]

This, the Naval Staff noted on the report, was '... the principle adopted ...' and no further action was needed to amend operational priorities.[58] Binney's comments were selectively quoted by the Naval Staff and Official Historians.[59] At least Roskill noted the Naval Staff's annotation but he failed to comprehend the need for area operations before the full imposition of convoy was possible. Within a few days, Binney's committee was exploring the use of 'Q' Ships along with supporting anti-submarine vessels, and a month later was expressing the idea of anti-submarine ship patrols to deter U-boat minelaying operations. By the end of the year, Binney, noting the increased numbers of U-boats likely to appear in the immediate future, concluded that '... there is no possibility of being able to relax our present measures for the A/S offensive.'[60]

Churchill, the First Lord, was also unceasing in his search for offensive operations. One of his schemes expressed in a typical minute to the First Sea Lord in November 1939, read:

> Nothing can be more important in the anti-submarine war than to try to obtain an independent flotilla which could work like a cavalry division on the approaches, without worrying about the traffic or U-boat sinkings, but could systematically search large areas over a wide front. In this war these areas would become untenable to U-boats, and many other advantages would flow from the manoeuvre.[61]

Unmoved, Pound passed the note to Captain A.G. Talbot, the new Director of Anti-Submarine Warfare, asking for his comments in view of his experiences while commanding a striking force. Talbot, an evangelist of offensive operations, replied a couple of days later expressing himself to have always been very much in favour of anti-submarine striking forces, though he stressed that their success relied on adequate intelligence of the U-boat positions. Talbot described the tactics he used. If searching for a surfaced U-boat, his four ships could be spread out and able to cover a front of about 35 miles. Even this made the search of large areas (often as much as 50,000 square miles) problematic. However, if the destroyers could close on a merchant ship being attacked they stood a better chance of gaining contact. He found that, with the relative navigational uncertainties inherent in these operations, that it was better to steam along the direction-finding bearing than to attempt to close the reported latitude and longitude. Once the U-boat had submerged the search front would be very much reduced, to six miles at the most, and possible less when the number of non-sub contacts was high. Talbot thought that the:

> ... key to success in killing a U-boat by this means is for the Striking Force to be able to sight it on the surface. Assuming that this is done and that the U-boat dives when the destroyers are 8 miles away, a minimum of three ships is required to locate her.[62]

Over the winter of 1939–40, Captain Edelsten, Deputy D of P, and Captain Talbot, DASW, each considered the progress of the anti-submarine campaign and developed ideas for future policy. Edelsten, in a brief but perceptive examination reiterated that the:

> ... pre-war A/S plan was to attack U-boats with hunting groups until it became necessary to go into convoy, and then to rely mainly on attacking them at the convoys themselves, by allocating most of our A/S craft to escort duties.

'This convoys system, augmented by other subsidiary measures', he observed, 'was sufficient to defeat the U-boat campaign in the last war, and has succeeded in inflicting considerable casualties on the U-boats in this war.' But Edelsten was sure that convoy:

> ... will not in itself defeat the U-boat campaign ... if the U-boats vary the localities and forms of their attacks to such a degree that we are unable to meet them in all places and against all forms simultaneously.

U-boats, he noted, were already using mines in addition to the torpedo. Mines, of course, could be laid on the convoy routes without the U-boats coming anywhere near the escorts. In the future, Edelsten prophesied the enemy might employ other weapons, including:

> ... a wireless controlled torpedo ... which can be brought into contact with our ships without serious risk of counter-attack on the submarine herself by our escorting craft.[63]

In addition the U-boats could also vary their geographic areas of operation, probably as far afield as Halifax, Nova Scotia. The number of anti-submarine vessels required to provide security against all such forms of attack in all possible areas was probably far beyond British resources, so, Edelsten concluded:

> ... the U-boat will only be successfully mastered once and for all by offensive measures designed to destroy them regardless of the mission on which they are engaged.[64]

The offensive measures he envisaged were the planned combination of minefields, seabed indicator loops and shore radar sites, that could cue hunting groups of destroyers onto transiting U-boats. Radar-fitted aircraft, which were due to start coming into service shortly would also be useful. Edelsten, a logical and incisive thinker, was persuaded that any shift towards more offensive operations needed to be undertaken gradually, and only when the direct protection of convoys by anti-submarine escorts was assured. In this he was supported by others on the Naval Staff.[65] Characteristically, Talbot was broadly in favour of the offensive measures, except for the use of indicator loops in the open sea because large numbers of anti-submarine vessels were required to re-locate a loop contact. These vessels, he thought, would be better employed elsewhere.

At the end of February 1940, Captain Talbot completed his own review for the Naval Staff of the methods of dealing with U-boats, which echoed much of Edelsten's earlier minute.[66] He expected the U-boat commissioning rate would soon accelerate and, therefore, unless sinkings by anti-submarine forces could also be increased, the number of operational U-boats would escalate dangerously. For operations in the Western Approaches, U-boats could best be dealt with by:

(a) A continuation of the convoy system coupled with resolute offensive action by the convoy escorts should a ship in convoy be attacked. A U-boat, having

once given away her presence, must be hunted even if this leaves the convoy temporarily unescorted; one ship remaining in the vicinity for 24 hours or until relieved.
(b) The provision of a fast anti-submarine Striking Force cruising in the area, operating on intelligence provided by direction-finding, and air and surface reports of U-boats.[67]

However, as Edelsten had pointed out, the policy of escort of convoy would do little to curb the activities of mine-laying U-boats. Taking a leaf from Edelsten's paper, Talbot thought it prudent to assume:

> ... that the enemy will intensify not only their mine-laying campaign in Home Waters but also unrestricted warfare, using the torpedo and gun, in waters further afield where there is less likelihood of counter-attack by our A/S forces.[68]

The response to the mine-layer was to try to stop these U-boats reaching their operational areas. The measures considered included the blockade of raw materials, the bombing of submarine building yards and factories, and training establishments (though these measures could not be implemented because of the existing restricted air bombardment policy). Talbot also suggested that it would be profitable to repeatedly mine U-boat training areas and base exits, and use British submarines off German harbours to attack U-boats entering and leaving. He also worried that the enemy might change his tactics, by attacking the escorts, which meant they needed to be more conscious of their own self-protection. In part this was so that escort forces would not be whittled down, for Talbot wanted fast Striking Forces as soon as practicable. Their effectiveness would rest on every effort being made:

> ... to improve our supply of information about U-boat sailings. Such information would greatly increase the chances of destroying U-boats before their arrival on their hunting grounds owing to the added incentive to all A/S forces of knowing that a U-boat is on passage.[69]

Air reconnaissance was essential and would be extended at night or in poor visibility by the deployment of radar-fitted aircraft already carrying out trials. Air–sea cooperation in these conditions would be even more difficult and would require considerable practice to perfect. But although exploring these offensive measures, Talbot emphasized several times, the first commitment had to be convoy escort. But, while this might ensure the safe arrival of shipping, it would not defeat the U-boat. The only way to do this, Talbot was sure, was to destroy the U-boats at every opportunity.

Captain C.S. Daniel, now D of P, noted from personal experience that the use of Striking Forces on a stale scent was a waste of time and wore down personnel and equipment unnecessarily. The trick was to get the ships into close proximity of the U-boat, when asdic could come into its own. Still he was not against the concept and distilled the essence of Talbot's paper into the three constituent, and interrelated, methods of countering the U-boat menace, which was broadly agreed by the First Sea Lord, Admiral Sir Dudley Pound:

(a) Dealing with them at source.
(b) Restricting their passage to certain areas where small anti-submarine forces can attack effectively.
(c) Making them face destruction when they reach a position to attack their target.[70]

The Admiralty is sometimes seen as espousing a dogmatic approach to anti-submarine warfare that leans heavily towards unproductive offensive operations. In reality, the Admiralty, and the Commands, had formulated a more subtle and flexible doctrine, which was to prove its efficacy throughout the war and into the post-war years. This does not mean that every avenue was covered. The Royal Navy was presented with night surface attacks by U-boats about one year into the war. It is not evident that this came as a surprise to the Royal Navy. Captain N.A. Prichard, another professional anti-submarine officer and a wartime Director of the Anti-Submarine Division thought that:

> ... it would have been a 'long shot' to have foreseen this method of attack in peace time, though ... a few night exercises against submarines on the surface were carried out which were abandoned owing to the danger to the submarine.[71]

One British submariner had gone so far as to champion the night surface attack as an important, but subsidiary, tactic a few months before war broke out.[72] Although experiments had been conducted with flares during the First World War, in reality little could be done to counter these tactics until the widespread introduction of radar.

Overall, the Admiralty's approach was underpinned by a widespread realization that anti-submarine warfare was difficult. For example, Captain R. Kerr, Captain (D) of the highly efficient Second Destroyer Flotilla, highlighted an issue that was a constant concern to the Admiralty and Commands, that '... peacetime restrictions have to be observed which unless properly considered are liable to give false conclusions to A/S vessels and submarines.' By way of illustration, Kerr noted that submarines were often allowed to remain at periscope depth until they had fired a torpedo during Fleet anti-submarine exercises, which '... gives the A/S personnel a wrong impression of how to counter-attack as they are not allowed to go within 1,200 yards of a periscope ... .' As a result, the submarine's reaction would be unrealistic. Kerr also considered that anti-submarine warfare:

> ... is unlike any other form of attack. It is an attempt to sink an invisible enemy by a sense which is not in every day use. A/S efficiency depends on the appreciation of the quality of a sound. It is very much harder to distinguish between two notes of the same pitch played by different instruments, than to appreciate that a note is being struck.[73]

Kerr had been the senior instructor at the anti-submarine specialist school at HMS *Osprey* and also had the benefit of a flotilla of new ships whose training had been rigorously pursued over the previous three years by a keen staff of anti-submarine specialists, including Lieutenant J.P. Mosse.[74] The essential problem was that of differentiating between submarine and non-submarine asdic echoes. 'The Asdic operator', Kerr wrote, 'has to keep in mind what a submarine echo may sound like under all conditions and so distinguish it from other almost exactly similar sounds.' The difficulty was that '… a sound is very much more difficult to memorize than something that can be seen or felt.' So, to maintain their ephemeral skill, operators required '… frequent practice at sea … in bad conditions as well as in good.'[75] At the same time other members of the team should rehearse the operation of the asdic range recorder used to indicate the time to fire, while the integration of all the tactical information on the asdic plot needed practice. The environment, therefore, made anti-submarine warfare difficult even without the submarine adopting stealthy anti-escort tactics. These problems would be exacerbated by the later development of submarines capable of high underwater speed.

This chapter has examined the developmental threads connecting the Royal Navy's experiences in the First World War and in the opening phases of the Second World War. The relatively low performance of individual anti-submarine methods, the general difficulty of anti-submarine warfare, and the vital need ultimately to defeat the U-boat (and not merely to protect shipping in the short-term), all impelled the Royal Navy to adopt a consistently holistic strategy which combined defensive and offensive tactics. An appreciation of anti-submarine tactics and their technical limitations are recounted in the following chapter. These details are crucial to understanding the problems of how the fast submarine was to be countered.

2 Mastering the submersible, 1939–43

U-boats and their tactics, 1939–43

Anti-submarine tactics were designed to exploit the weaknesses in U-boat operations. For their part, U-boat commanders made every effort to capitalize on the submarine's chief characteristic and strength, which was its invisibility when submerged. They hoped to create surprise and attack from an ambush.[1] Such stealthy methods, however, were not conducive to finding targets, and this conundrum was to exercise the enemy throughout the war. For the attack itself, however, the U-boat gained great advantage by remaining undetected until the moment of striking. The U-boat was not only more likely to make an undisturbed, and therefore more accurate, attack but the target stood practically no chance of taking avoiding action. Amidst the mayhem created, it was then hoped that the U-boat could withdraw unmolested. The U-boat was forced to use such stratagems because advances in technology had made anti-submarine forces deadly. There was, Admiral Max Horton, Flag Officer, Submarines, warned, '… no margin for mistakes in submarines, you are either alive or dead.'[2] The U-boat was not a vehicle well adapted to self-defence and the U-boat's use of stealth was a matter of necessity for self-preservation, which rather muddied the issue of the legality of unrestricted U-boat warfare.[3]

The defensive power of the U-boat was weak. They possessed little reserve of buoyancy (to allow for rapid submergence) and were therefore sensitive to even minor damage during attacks by anti-submarine forces. Initially, their defensive armament was puny, as befitted a vessel whose primary power was in her offensive weapons, principally salvoes of up to four torpedoes, which by the middle of the war included straight- or pattern-running torpedoes.[4] The pattern-runner, or LuT, torpedo carried out a ladder pattern which passed across the target's track, theoretically giving more opportunities for a hit. The greatest chance of the torpedoes striking their target still occurred when firing ranges were short, ideally in the order of 300–800 yards, and fired from a position about 60°–120° off the bow of the target. Long-range attacks posed severe fire control problems for the submarine – even when using LuT – and allowed the target time to take avoiding action.[5] Thus, the U-boat's ideal firing window was relatively small. This limitation was partially removed by the introduction of the German Naval Acoustic Torpedo (Gnat), which, it was assessed, could be fired from 5,000 yards and, being fitted with hydrophones which controlled the rudders, could home onto the target's propeller noise. The Gnat was effective against ships travelling between 12 and 19 knots, that is, travelling fast enough to produce sufficient hydrophone effect on which the Gnat could home from a reasonable range, but slow enough for the 25 knot torpedo to be able to catch its target. Operationally, the weapon was not particularly effective in terms of ships sunk. Of the 640 Gnats fired, only 3 per cent hit (though the Germans claimed 53 per cent as successful).[6] The weapon was first used against convoys ONS18 and ON202 in September 1943, where Commander P.W. Burnett was Senior Officer (SO) of one of the Escort Groups. On this occasion, in the face of heavy U-boat attack, it was the aggressive tactics of Burnett and the other escort Senior Officers, Horton noted, which '… prevented the enemy from gaining the initiative and resulted in comparatively light losses in the convoys.'[7] The Gnat was soon countered by tactical means and the use of a towed noise maker, the Foxer, as predicted by Leon Solomon in the Directorate of Naval Operational Research (DNOR) three months before the torpedoes were first used.[8] Nevertheless, escort tactics would now have to take account of this new weapon.

The design of the 1939–43 U-boat was fundamentally the same as the boats used during the First World War, although their mechanical reliability and operational range had improved. To move at high speed the boat had to be on the surface, when the diesel engines could be used. The most common U-boat, the Type VII, was capable of 17 knots, though in heavy seas the speed might be reduced to five to 10 knots, depending on the relative direction of the sea, especially if the crew was to keep an efficient lookout. Once submerged, the British knew from trials with *U-570* captured in August 1941 that U-boats when propelled by electric motors had a maximum speed of about seven and a half knots, but this could only be maintained for about two hours before the battery was exhausted. The greatest submerged endurance and distance travelled could be achieved at about two to two and a half knots.[9] Ultimately, the U-boat's underwater performance was limited because it could not recharge its battery or recycle the breathing air while the boat was submerged (the latter probably being more of a limitation to the U-boat's underwater endurance than of its battery power). For submerged attacks, the U-boat's limited underwater mobility constrained an approach to a narrow sector ahead of a convoy. However, a U-boat on the surface could use its high surface speed to attack over a much wider angle, theoretically extending all round a convoy, though use of very high speed gave escorts a better chance of sighting the incoming U-boat.

The easiest prey were independent ships or convoy stragglers: attacking convoys was an altogether more dangerous occupation, with the attendant risk of being overrun by the merchant ships, or attacked by the escort. As the proportion of ships in convoy increased, the Germans were faced with little option but to attack convoys. The DASW noted in 1941 that the more daring U-boat Commanders were picking their targets and making individual attacks on each ship, though the less courageous were content to fire spread salvoes from a distance. Although some U-boats had closed inside a convoy, this was normally when the columns were disordered, or where ships in the columns had fallen badly astern. Few U-boats were prepared to penetrate inside a closely formed convoy.[10] British intelligence, echoing German tactical instructions, assessed that U-boats would fire long-range salvoes whenever an opportunity arose, and were likely to attack the escort too.[11] The U-boat had to be submerged and reasonably stable to carry out the cumbersome procedure of manually reloading the torpedo tubes, which made multiple salvo attacks impossible. By the autumn of 1942 as a result of the '… recent rough handling …' by the escorts, the U-boats had adopted more diverse tactical stratagems. Night surface attacks were still preferred and attempts were made to lure escorts away from the convoy to give other U-boats a chance to attack, but submerged, daytime attacks were also being used more often (partly because, as less experienced U-boat captains took command they lacked the skill necessary for night surface attacks). This trend continued into 1943.[12] At the end of 1942 some 11 per cent of U-boat attacks on convoys were by day, but by the early spring of 1943, the Allies noted a substantial change. In March 36 per cent of attacks were by day, and by June this rose to 43 per cent.[13] Also in March 1943, the average torpedo firing range was about 3,000 yards, with about two-thirds of the attacks launched from about 2,000–4,000 yards.[14]

The extension of convoy had a dual effect on U-boat operations. Firstly, as *The U-Boat Commander's Handbook* noted:

> … the concentration of numerous steamers to form convoys, the sea routes lose their characteristic peacetime appearance and become desolate, as it is only at relatively long intervals that a concentration of steamers passes along them.[15]

As British anti-submarine operations improved and were reinforced by the release of anti-submarine ships and Coastal Command aircraft from anti-invasion duties, so the U-boats were forced to operate further from the focal areas. In the open ocean, convoys could be dispersed to a greater extent, so the location of convoys became the most difficult challenge faced by the U-boats.[16] This was the second effect of convoy on U-boat operations: it induced them to disperse to locate their prey, and then to move at speed to concentrate for the attack. Crucially, this could only be achieved if they operated on the surface. The method adopted was an extension of the First War practice of several U-boats working together in what became the 'combined attack' (better known as pack tactics). The primary purpose of the pack system was to maximize the number of contacts per U-boat by enabling all members of the pack to exploit a sighting made by any one of them. The U-boat in contact sent a high-frequency wireless telegraphy (H/F W/T) report in naval enigma to *Befehlshaber der Unterseeboote* (BdU, the U-boat High Command) ashore. The signal was then re-broadcast to the remainder of the patrol line. The ability of the shadower to operate unmolested while other members of the pack converged onto the convoy was vital to the success of the operation. Once a sufficient number of U-boats had concentrated around the convoy, BdU would order the attacks to begin. This control by wireless telegraphy resulted in considerable radio traffic on high frequency, as well as short range homing signals on medium frequency. There was no attempt at close tactical coordination within the U-boat pack, but rather a crude attempt to overwhelm the escorts with a heavy concentration of U-boats.[17]

This system was well understood by the British, who also concluded that a pack of 25–30 U-boats might sink some 15–20 ships in a normal sized convoy of, say, 50 ships. But a pack would not function properly if too many U-boats tried to operate round a single convoy, so a typical pack consisted of 15–20 boats, which was in stark contrasts to the United States Navy (USN) practice of using three, or at most four, submarines in coordinated attacks.[18] As Professor W.H. McCrea, DNOR, noted, because the U-boats had to be spread out in a search line to locate the convoy, it took some two to three days for the whole pack to concentrate round the convoy. The inevitable heavy use of wireless technology by the enemy provided cues for anti-submarine forces. The delay before a strong attack could be mounted also allowed time for the threatened convoy escort usually to be reinforced with additional air cover and a support group of anti-submarine vessels. Only about 70–80 per cent of the pack normally made contact, mainly due to navigational difficulties, and many had difficulty remaining in touch with the convoy. About one in three U-boats that made contact were able to attack, and one in three of these attacks yielded a torpedo hit.[19] By contrast, the American submarines in the Pacific, albeit against a far less expert and determined defence, proved highly effective operating in small packs, with tactical control exercised by a senior officer at sea. Even with these limitations, the German U-boats operating in packs probably achieved three times the number of sinkings up to 1943 than would have been the case if the U-boats had operated individually.[20] The results would have been even greater had the U-boats had the benefit of wide-ranging air reconnaissance, leaving the U-boats to concentrate on sinking shipping. However, poor cooperation between the *Luftwaffe* and the U-boat arm, lack of sufficient numbers of long-range aircraft and ill-trained aircrews, scuppered any chance of the scheme working. In the main, U-boats had to provide their own reconnaissance, for which they were singularly ill-suited.[21]

Methods of detecting and attacking U-boats

On the Allied side, the level of operational cooperation between the air forces and navies was, by and large, excellent and provided one of the main sinews of the Allied success in defeating U-boats dependent on surface scouting and movement. Although the use of radar by aircraft is usually given the pride of place in their ability to detect surfaced U-boats, half of the contacts were made visually. However, binoculars were not routinely used until mid-1943, but thereafter some 20 per cent of U-boat sightings involved their use (though on two-thirds of these occasions the binoculars were used for recognition purposes, rather than initial detection). The low usage was due partly to the focus in training on operation of new aircraft types and their increasingly complex equipment, and partly on the awkward observation positions in many of the aircraft. Although binoculars improved the visual detection range by almost 60 per cent, they were heavy and tiring to use for more than 15 minutes at a time. Nevertheless:

> A good visual lookout is of outstanding importance in ... [anti-U-boat] operations. ... Although luck plays a big part in the sighting of U-boats, there is no doubt that the greatest number of sightings and attacks have gone to those crews with the best lookout. It is also a fact that large numbers of U-boats come within visual range of aircraft and pass unseen.[22]

At the same time, the Operational Research Section (ORS) at Coastal Command, recommended that:

> Crews must not get into the habit of relying mainly on radar when the visibility conditions are such that visual lookouts are likely to pay bigger dividends. The *reverse* is true when visibility is poor.[23]

The value of radar for detection of surfaced U-boats at night or in low visibility had been recognized in early 1939, when experiments were started with radar equipped aircraft.[24] Radar also provided a valuable navigation aid, which for aircraft returning from long-range missions over the Atlantic could be a '... life saver.'[25] Improved detection meant that more U-boats were forced to dive (and even if not attacked) lost their surface mobility for hours at a time. Aircraft were especially valuable in this regard and the operational and psychological effects of constant air surveillance on submarines should not be lightly discounted.[26]

Perhaps the greatest problem for the aircraft of Coastal Command was that:

> ... 'half of the long-range sorties failed to find their designated convoy because of bad homing, while inter-communication left much to be desired'. In late 1942 the RAF set up a special training groups with Western Approaches, and in 1943 'remarkable improvements' were registered, with a 90 per cent contact rate being achieved.[27]

These direct convoy escort operations were supported by aircraft missions over the main transit routes. Thus intensive patrols were flown over the Bay of Biscay, together with searches over ocean transit routes based, whenever possible, on intelligence cuing.[28] Professor Williams in DNOR noted that Coastal Command patrols over the Bay were relatively profitable for purely offensive operations in 1942–43 and had '... worked out in great detail the best methods of conducting such an offensive by a balanced force of day and night aircraft ... .'[29] The Bay, Williams reasoned, presented a small area to search, compared to the total area of U-boat operations in the Atlantic. (Williams does not mention that in the area around threatened convoys there would also be a relatively high density of U-boats.) This made up for the relatively short time the U-boats spent transiting the Bay, compared to the time they spent on operations. The Bay was therefore an area of comparatively high U-boat density, as well as being accessible by large numbers of medium range anti-submarine aircraft.[30] Furthermore, the U-boats could not disengage, for they had to cross the Bay if they were to get to their ocean operational areas. These operations, and those around convoys, provided aircraft with the opportunity to attack U-boats. Now that they were equipped with effective aerial depth-charges, and through the work of ORS and Coastal Command's Development Unit, aircraft became effective U-boat killers. This was starkly illustrated by the proportion of lethal attacks against surfaced U-boats rising from 8 per cent to 28 per cent during 1943, with aircraft attacks accounting for some 70 per cent of U-boat casualties during the last half of the year.[31] Unfortunately, this lethal capability was not to continue, as will be seen.

The Royal Navy (and its Allies) provided surface vessels for the direct protection of convoys and, at times, for independent offensive operations. About half the U-boats found by anti-submarine ships were initially on the surface. Just over 40 per cent of these U-boats were detected visually and the remainder by radar, which, as with aircraft, was of greatest value at night or in poor visibility.[32] However, the earlier, lower frequency, longer wave-length, radars suffered from considerable 'clutter', caused by unwanted echoes from waves, which in rough seas might extend as far as 2,000–3,000 yards from the ship and seriously reduced the chance of detecting a U-boat. Even in calm seas, these sets could not hold contacts inside about 1,000 yards. Closing to visual range was therefore difficult, while at longer ranges the problem was in identifying a contact by radar alone. At 4,000 yards, for example, a surfaced U-boat gave an echo practically indistinguishable from a destroyer. The means of tentatively identifying a contact was by the range of first detection, and if it first appeared in a position not previously occupied by an echo. The eventually introduction of the Plan Position Indicator (PPI) radar display was invaluable because it gave a continuous view of contacts all-round the ship. Even with these limitations, radar allowed escorts to maintain almost unbroken coverage of the perimeter against approaching U-boats. It also relieved them of the constant worry over station keeping on the convoy, for colliding with merchant ships in poor visibility was a constant worry for escorts without radar. It also allowed them to coordinate their movements during U-boat hunts. Distant escorts could maintain touch with the convoy, even in poor weather, and they were themselves less likely to be confused with enemy contacts.[33]

If the U-boat was submerged, the escorts used the asdic to gain detection and almost half of the initial detections of U-boats were by this means.[34] By mid-1942 a new asdic, the Type 144, had been introduced into the Fleet which used the same oscillator as the earlier sets, but the inboard equipment had been completely redesigned to squeeze the last ounce of information out of the underwater sound.[35] Much of this development was carried out under the supervision of J. Anderson, the Superintendent Scientist at HM Anti-Submarine Experimental Establishment, Fairlie (HMA/SEE), who had been involved in asdic development from its earliest days.[36] The Type 144 transmitted and received sound over a narrow 16° conical, 'searchlight' beam which could be rotated in the horizontal plane through 360° but could not be depressed. In the receiving, or listening, mode the set could detect returning echoes as well as U-boat (or torpedo) hydrophone effect. The latter gave a rough bearing but, of course, no range, so the primary mode of the asdic was as an echo-ranging set when a sound pulse was transmitted, followed by a listening period when echoes, hopefully from a U-boat, were received. The asdic could theoretically detect echoes out to 2,500 yards, but this range was affected by a number of factors. The returning echoes were weak because they contained only a fraction of the transmitted power due to spreading and absorption losses as the sound passed both ways through the water. The echoes also had to be detected against the background noise caused by water flowing around the asdic dome, hydrophone effect from the escort's own propellers, and unwanted asdic echoes, known as 'reverberations', produced by discontinuities in the water structure, the surface and the seabed. As a result, 1,500 yards was a more realistic working range, though even then detection was not guaranteed. Such a range was wholly inadequate to provide complete asdic coverage around the perimeter of a convoy, which might be 20 miles or more.

For example, if a U-boat was end-on to the asdic, its reflecting area would be considerably less than if beam-on, so the echo would be weaker, or possibly masked by the U-boat's wake. And, in rough weather severe pitching by the escort would cause highly aerated water to surround the asdic, known as 'quenching', which interrupted the reception of echoes. Furthermore, the vertical temperature structure of the water was not constant, and this had the effect of bending the asdic beam. When this was severe, shadow zones were created where no pulses from the asdic penetrated. If the U-boat was in this zone, it was 'invisible'. Sometimes definite submarine-like echoes, termed 'non-subs', were obtained from wrecks, rocks or shoals of fish. Thus classification of echoes was important and could be assisted by hydrophone effect from the target or, when the U-boat was moving, by using an effect known as 'doppler', which was an apparent frequency increase or decrease in the echo when compared to the reverberations and depended on whether the U-boat was moving relatively towards or away from the escort.[37] Perhaps the most important factor in gaining detection was whether the operators were alert, and this could be heightened by their knowledge that a U-boat was in the vicinity.

Escorts would normally search using the asdic to sweep over the forward arc from 80° off the port bow to 80° off the starboard bow, that is, Red 80° to Green 80°. The arc was covered in 5° steps each consisting of a transmission and listening cycle, starting at Red 80° and through to dead ahead. The oscillator was then rotated aft without transmitting to Green 80° and the sweep restarted, stepping forward again to dead ahead. A U-boat could pass through the arc while the asdic was searching on the other side of the ship, although this was unlikely for escort speeds below 14 knots. At higher speeds, or when asdic conditions were bad, the arc was reduced. Because of the time taken to complete a full sweep and the movement of the escort, the effective width of the lane searched was reduced. So, in round terms, for a working range 1,500 yards, the effective lane searched was only 1,100 yards on either side for an escort at 12 knots, and 950 yards at 18 knots.[38]

Once a contact was gained, its distance from the escort was available from the asdic range recorder but there was no means of directly measuring the bearing of the U-boat. Determining where the target lay in the beam and thus calculating its bearing relied on the cumbersome 'cut-on' procedure. The asdic was trained off to one side of the target until contact was lost and then stepped back in 2½° steps until contact was regained. The bearing of the asdic was noted, and the procedure repeated on the other side of the echo. This gave two 'cut-on' bearings, and midway between them was the supposed target's centre bearing but there were inherent errors due to the target's movement during the time the procedure took. Moreover, neither of these bearings was accurate because the boundaries of the target echo were not sharply defined. For practical purposes the 'cut-ons' could be measured to within ±5°. Experiments were already underway to produce an improved operating procedure, which relied on a 'step-across' method in which, more or less, continuous contact could be maintained.[39]

In the early stages of the war attacks were made with depth-charges, filled with either 290-lb. Amatol or 300-lb. Minol fillings and released from the escort's stern and dropped far enough ahead of the U-boat to allow them to sink to the U-boat's depth before they exploded. Immediately the escort gained contact, she turned to place the asdic echo directly on the ship's head, otherwise it was not possible to resolve how much of the observed bearing movement was due to the ship's or the U-boat's crossing components. Thus, with knowledge of whether the U-boat was moving left or right and with an estimate of her movement towards or away, from the echo's doppler, a rough course of the U-boat was obtained. Ideally an attack was started from a range of 1,000–1,500 yards and at a speed of 12–15 knots. The asdic system could only calculate a collision course that would take the escort directly over the U-boat. So a throw-off, inspired by guesswork and honed by practice, had to be applied to the attack course to take the escort's stern over the aim point ahead of the U-boat. This throw-off might be as much as 45° against a deep U-boat travelling at six knots.[40]

Trials had demonstrated that the asdic was able to locate a U-boat with an average radial error of some 20 yards in the horizontal plane but, at first, there was no means of directly measuring the U-boat's depth. Because the asdic could not be depressed, a shallow U-boat would pass out of the asdic beam at close range, while a deep U-boat would be lost sooner. This effect could be used to provide a rough estimation of the depth, so, if contact were lost at 100 yards the target could be between 50 and 100 feet, whereas if contact were lost at 400 yards the target depth was could be between 200 and 400 feet.[41] However, if contact was lost the estimation of the U-boat's position also degraded to a radial error of some 100 yards. This was well outside the seven to eight yards lethal range of a single depth-charge. At 13–17 yards they could cause enough damage to force the U-boat to surface, while at 27–33 yards range a depth-charge would severely shake the U-boat and was sufficient to cause the U-boat to break off a torpedo attack.[42] To mitigate the aiming errors, the standard attack was made with 10 depth-charges, in two five-charge patterns roughly coincident in plan and, depending on the assessed depth of the U-boat, separated by 90–350 feet in depth. It is no wonder that the probability of a kill with depth-charges was about 6 per cent per attack on a U-boat at medium depth.[43] If the U-boat were to evade by going very deep, in the order of 500–700 feet, the normal depth-charge attack stood little chance of success. For this circumstance the 'Creeping Attack' was promulgated in the autumn of

1943. The attack was controlled by an escort which remained in asdic contact and who controlled up to three other ships to fire a barrage of 62 depth-charges at the U-boat. It took about three minutes to complete, but had a 75 per cent kill rate provided the enemy remained quiescent until the moment of attack.[44] Holding contact at close range was largely solved by the 'Q' Attachment, an additional asdic with a narrow horizontal but 60° vertical beam, slaved to the main set. But accurate depth measurement had to wait the introduction of the short-range Type 147B asdic, fitted in addition to the Type 144 and 'Q'. It was fixed on the ship's head, and had a 60° horizontal and 2½° vertical beam, which could be depressed to a maximum angle of 45°. By noting the angle of depression and the target's range its depth could be calculated.[45] The main error, however, in the attack remained that caused by the inexact measurement of the target's bearing.

Most of the limitations of depth-charge attacks were eliminated by the introduction of ahead throwing weapons (ATWs) fired when the escort was still some 200-300 yards from the U-boat. Contact could normally be held on the main asdic at the moment of firing, provided the U-boat was no deeper than about 260 feet, or on 'Q' down to over 1500 feet depth (which was well over the crush depth of any U-boat). There were two types of ATW – the Hedgehog, which fired 24 contact-fused bombs into a 40-yard diameter circle centred on the U-boat's future position, and the ultimate wartime weapon system, the Squid, which fired three depth-charge like bombs to form a 40-yard sided triangle, timed to explode at the U-boat's depth. A double-Squid fired two of these patterns, arranged to explode 60 feet apart in depth. The ATW projectiles were also designed to have a high sinking rate, so the time taken for the bombs to reach the target's depth was much less than during a depth-charge attack and this gave the U-boat less time to evade when compared to Hedgehog or depth-charges. Moreover, ATW attacks were normally carried out at slower, deliberate speed of seven to 12 knots, because there was practically no danger of the attacking ship being damaged by the exploding pattern, so the U-boat had no cue as to when the attack was launched.

When attacking with ATW, the escort steered for the centre bearing of the asdic contact with alterations made to keep the contact dead ahead. The deflection was then obtained from the bearing recorder or by estimation, which gave the angle the weapon had to be aimed off the centre bearing of the asdic contact in order to allow for the time of flight and sinking time of the projectiles. This was known as the 'Gun Bearing' and as soon as reasonably consistent readings were established during the run-in, the escort altered course to this bearing. In ships with the latest gear, this was done by ordering the helmsman to 'steer by asdic' in which case he followed an indicator controlled by the settings on the bearing recorder. As the range closed, the escort's heading was altered to follow any changes in the Gun Bearing. It took some time for the Bearing Recorder to settle down on new settings, so, especially during the last 30 seconds before firing it was preferable for the escort to remain on the same course. Small discrepancies between the Gun Bearing and the ship's heading could be eliminated by the ATW mounting, however, the prediction of the target's future position was nowhere as sophisticated as contemporary gunnery systems and against an evading U-boat it was advisable to delay the moment of attack until the enemy became quiescent.

Exercises showed that against a shallow U-boat, Hedgehog gave a 60 per cent chance of success, while a 10-charge depth-charge pattern achieved 20 per cent.[46] Operational results, however, gave a more stark comparison. Although Hedgehog initially achieved only a 7½ per cent kill rate, this eventually improved to 28½ per cent, while depth-charge attacks started at 3 per cent and only improved to 6 per cent (largely due to improved explosive content of the charges). Squid was a more complex, integrated system whose operational performance increased from 21½ per cent to 60 per cent by the end of the war. Put another way, the quantity of explosives required by each of these weapons to sink a U-boat was: depth-charges, 23 tons (for the 10-charge pattern); Hedgehog, two tons; and Squid 0.7 tons. These heavy bombardments proved the resilience of U-boats to withstand attack. Squid was the preferred weapon during anti-submarine engagements, for not only was it the most lethal weapon, but like depth-charges and unlike the contact-fused Hedgehog, near misses had a morale effect and the chance of causing cumulative damage to a U-boat, which could force it to the surface where it could be despatched by ramming or gunfire.[47] Because the target was not overrun during ATW attacks, it was often possible for the attacking ship to remain in contact, and therefore mount another attack at short notice. ATWs were thus semi-automated, precision weapons that largely eliminated human error. Especially with Squid, attacks against slow wartime U-boats were comparatively academic affairs. They required a different philosophical approach from the anti-submarine teams by emphasizing attention to detail and accuracy and deliberate stalking of the U-boat up to the moment of firing. Gone was the 'artistry' of the depth-charge attack, as anti-submarine warfare became more remote and mechanical.

These methods of detection and attack were only of use, however, if the escorts could be stationed around fleets and convoys in such a way as to maximize their chance counterattacking a U-boat before it fired, or of locating it after a merchant ship was struck. The disposition of escorts was laid down in anti-submarine screening and escort diagrams. Initially, adequate tactical instructions did not exist to cover the most likely event of having to respond after the U-boat had attacked and individual escort group Senior Officers initiated their own procedures. Gradually, with the formalization of the training and tactical developments organization (especially at the Western Approaches Tactical Unit and at sea centred around HMS *Philante*), the situation improved and led to the issue of voluminous tactical manuals.[48] The emphasis here will be on the protection of convoys which was the more onerous task. Station-keeping in an ocean convoy was easier if the merchant ships were arranged in short columns on a broad front. Thus, with columns spaced 1,000 yards apart, and the individual ships within the columns 400 yards astern of each other, the overall size of a convoy of a typical 60-ship convoy was about one to two miles in depth and six miles in breadth (though later in the war, with the increasingly inexperienced merchant officers, the distance between columns was doubled to give greater safety).[49] U-boats could fire from 5,000 yards, and this range defined the torpedo danger zone (TDZ) around the perimeter of a convoy, the circumference of which was advanced on the convoy's track to allow for the torpedo running time.[50] The limited underwater speed and endurance of a U-boat meant that it could only reach a firing position from a relatively small distance to the left or right of the convoy's front. This distance increased if the U-boat was further ahead of the convoy. The starting points, therefore, for a U-boat to close to a firing position were described by the LLSuA (which were tangents to the TDZ) and angled outwards at about 30° for a nine-knot, fast convoy. The angle would be larger for a slow, seven-knot convoy but much smaller against a fleet steaming at 15 knots.[51] The high speed of U-boats on the surface meant that, in principle, they could approach from much wider angles to an attack position, though the use of high speed could make them more visible by creating a large wake.

The distance across the front of a convoy, from which a U-boat could approach submerged was too large for the available escorts to sweep with asdic, even if they zig-zagged around their stations. Against a surfaced U-boat better radar cover was possible, provided the sea was not too rough.[52] Anti-submarine vessels were disposed on 'Escort Diagrams' optimized to frustrate a U-boat's approach and position the escorts to be able to take offensive action against U-boats that had got into a firing position. Thus escorts were placed one and a half to two miles ahead and on the bows of the convoy to intercept approaching U-boats, and one mile on the quarters from where they could close the position from which the U-boat attacked, or to attack those retreating after a torpedoing. These distances gave the best compromise between keeping the escorts as close as possible to each other (thereby increasing the chance of detecting a U-boat trying to penetrate the defences, and providing mutual support between escorts), and the need to maintain as much 'fighting room' as possible for offensive action against incoming U-boats. It was noted from operations that the great majority of anti-submarine contacts were made after a ship had been torpedoed or the attacking U-boat sighted. However, experience also showed that it proved more difficult to destroy a U-boat after the inevitable dislocation caused by a ship being struck, than if the U-boat was caught before it had fired.[53]

These close escorts were deployed in the 'red area', which extended to six miles from the perimeter of the convoy. Outside this was the 'white area', an annulus from six to 12 miles, and beyond that was the 'blue area'. Support groups, just like the extended patrols of the First World War, were stationed in the white area where they could catch surfaced U-boats attempting to gain bearing on the convoy. Aircraft operated in the blue area where they could disrupt the approach of distant U-boats attempting to get into position ahead of the convoy. Although use of high definition radar, tactical Radio Telephony (R/T) and plotting facilities (and, later, radio navigation aids) in escorts had dramatically improved during WWII, the integration of the systems was still primitive and thus the coordination between ships (and aircraft) was still prone to confusion in poor weather or at night. Thus with these tactical zones, physical separation was enforced which reduced the chance of tactical confusion. Of course, the area boundaries could be breached when units were pursuing a U-boat.[54]

Tactics on gaining contact

Allied operational experience showed that a single anti-submarine vessel was capable of dealing with a U-boat in good asdic conditions. However, in difficult asdic conditions, or when the water was disturbed from attacks a U-boat could easily escape. A second anti-submarine vessel could help by maintaining asdic contact on the U-boat and thus resolve false echoes from ship's wakes or Squid and depth-charge explosions. Since the asdic and attack ranges were relatively short, the whole action took place in a relatively small area; any additional escorts served little purpose and tended to get in the way. They usually stood off at a short distance, patrolling around the action area and covering the U-boat's escape routes.[55] The two close-in ships manoeuvred so that their bearings relative to the U-boat were 90° apart. This helped ships avoid putting their wakes (and thus confusing asdic echoes) between the U-boat and their consort and, if the U-boat tried turn bow or stern on to one escort, it exposed its beam aspect to the other, so at least one escort had a good asdic echo. In a heavy sea, the pair would try to maintain the weather gauge, which lessened the effect of quenching (to say nothing of the fatiguing effect on the crew of the ship's motion), and reduced the danger of the ships inadvertently drifting downwind and out of contact. Asdic performance was usually better too, because transmitting downwind produced less pronounced surface reverberations from the waves. U-boats, for their part, would often try to make ground to windward.

The most modern escorts were fitted with a semi-automatic plotting table on which tactical information was mapped out though it did not allow for tidal movement or ship's drift due to the wind and sea, and the U-boat would therefore appear to 'drift' upwind. Nevertheless, soon after gaining contact, it was possible to calculate an estimate of the U-boat's course to within ±30° and the speed to within a knot or so. Because the plot kept a record of the U-boat's movements, if the ship lost contact during the final stages of an attack it was possible to estimate the time to fire. The plot also gave the Senior Officer of the Escort an overview of the tactical situation, from which he could plan more extensive lost-contact procedures, especially at night or in conditions of poor visibility.[56] Even though the U-boats could only travel underwater at a relatively slow speed, when contact was lost the area to be searched expanded at an exponential rate, being proportional to the square of the U-boat's speed. Given the comparatively slow search rate of the asdic, rapid action was needed if the U-boat was not to slip away. Immediate lost-contact procedures included 'Search Scheme No. 1', which consisted of an all-round asdic sweep by each ship steaming at seven knots on the last known mean course of the U-boat. While this was being done the Senior Officer would signal the action to be taken if contact were not regained.

Depending on the number of anti-submarine ships present, he could order a 'Square Search', commonly known as an 'Observant', where the escorts were equally spaced and followed each other round the square. With more escorts the Senior Officer could order a 'Box Search' where ships steamed in line abreast round the square. The idea of these searches was for the anti-submarine ships to pass each point on the square often enough, so that the U-boat could not cross the perimeter without coming within asdic range of one of the escorts.[57] Alternatively, in 'Search Scheme No. 2' the ships swept through the U-boat probability area twice in line abreast 2,000–3,000 yards apart. It was possible, in average asdic conditions with a working range of, say, 1,500 yards, to search a box about four and a half miles square in 35–45 minutes. To escape the U-boat would have to make a speed of at least three or four knots, at which speed she might betray her presence by producing sufficiently loud hydrophone effect. If contact was still not regained, an expanding 'Box Search' could be ordered, in which the legs of the search were adjusted so that the search would follow a vignot spiral formed from the locus of all the intercept points which could be reached by the target and the searching force for various U-boat escape headings.[58] This was the search concept favoured by the Americans. However, British experience suggested that greater probability of success could be achieved if some limits were placed on the likely escape courses. Searching was therefore focussed on a relatively narrow sector in the form of a 'Gamma Search', consisting of escorts sweeping in line abreast at right-angles across the U-boat's assumed escape course. The Gamma search was started at a point on the U-boat's anticipated track equal to its 'furthest on' predicted position (based on the U-boat's expected maximum transit speed) and continued until the 'furthest back' position (based on a prediction of the slowest U-boat transit speed) passed through the patrol line. The zig-zagging escorts were stationed three miles apart in daylight and five miles apart at night, when the U-boat was more likely to attempt to escape using its high surface speed. Two anti-submarine vessels were required to patrol a lane 10 miles wide, and four for a 30-mile lane, though, in practice, the 'Gamma Search' never succeeded in locating a U-boat.[59] This illustrates the difficulty of locating a submarine if anti-submarine ships could not arrive at the datum very soon after it was created, and the 'Gamma Search' was withdrawn from the tactics books in 1945.

By 1943 with the growing power and numbers of escorts, particularly those in support groups, came the freedom to hunt attacking U-boats to destruction. These hunts usually took some time and required persistent, deliberate attacks by the anti-submarine vessels. However, for actions close in to a convoy, escorts had to rapidly appreciate the level of threat to the ships being escorted. If the U-boat was in a position to carry out a torpedo attack, the escorts would respond with an immediate counter-attack, emphasizing speed rather than accuracy. This was designed to put the U-boat off his aim and to seize the initiative so that more deliberate and deadly attacks could be mounted. Squid or depth-charges were useful in this regard. If the initial contact was more distant, and there was plenty of fighting room, the escort could afford to make the first attack a deliberate one. Any of these attacks by escorts always risked the U-boat deliberately targeting them with a torpedo, a risk unhesitatingly accepted if the ship being screened was a fleet unit or a troopship. Against the conventional straight-running weapons, provided the torpedo was detected, the escort could turn towards the incoming torpedo which substantially reduced the chance of it hitting. When Captain C.D. Howard-Johnston, Director of the Anti-U-Boat Division (DAUD), was asked how far a Captain should hazard his own ship when attacking a U-boat, he remarked that:

> There is no risk yet. The U-boat is out to sink merchantmen … [and the escorts] are a confounded nuisance to its Captain, not a target. When the first

escort vessel is torpedoed deliberately you will know that the Hun is beaten and the war is won. Everything else after that date is just a mopping up operation.[60]

Howard-Johnston accurately foretold (as Captain Edelsten had done earlier) the introduction in the autumn of 1943 of the Gnat homing torpedo. In fact, the British already made a fairly detailed assessment of the way Gnat operated from Special Intelligence aided by an understanding the techniques employed in the similar American Mk XXIV Mine (an air launched homing torpedo).[61] Countermeasures were therefore developed rapidly. Escorts were soon equipped with the towed 'Foxer' made up of two pipe noise makers (PNMs), each consisting of two pipes connected together at their ends but allowed to vibrate against each other as they were towed through the water. The resultant noise was some 10–30 times noisier than the ship's propellers, and would thus seduce the Gnat away from the ship. So, ships closed the U-boat as fast as possible until within asdic range their speed was reduced, the Foxer tripped, and a single depth-charge dropped to 'shake-off' any Gnat close astern. The remainder of the hunt was then carried out at eight knots at which speed a Gnat could only home from very close range. The problem with these tactics was the time taken to close the U-boat. Ships capable of 25 knots, could outrun a Gnat, and could therefore make a direct approach to the U-boat, though at high speed their self-noise would limit the chance of making a detection. The tactical compromise was the use of the 'Step-Aside' approach to a U-boat. When the escort reached a range of just under three miles from the U-boat's estimated position, she altered course 60° to port or starboard, while maintaining her best speed. This new heading was held for three minutes which would laterally separate the escort from the Gnat's track outside the torpedo's detection range. The escort then again altered course to make a direct track towards the U-boat's position.[62] The diversion of the 'Step-Aside' also slowed the escort's approach to the U-boat's datum position and increased the chance of her escape. A contemporary assessment was that of the 24 escorts which became Gnat casualties between September 1943, when the weapon was introduced, and May 1944, only two were hit while taking anti-Gnat counter-measures.[63]

Captain Walker, who was frequently employed on hunter–killer operations, disliked the use of Foxer because its noise interfered with asdic performance. He directed that all ships were immediately to slow to seven knots if a Gnat threat was imminent, and in the spring of 1944 had obtained permission to land his Foxer gear prior to carrying out independent hunting operations. However, Walker saw the merit in using the Foxer while escorting a convoy when the escort would be zig-zagging ahead of the convoy and steaming at above the safe speed of seven to eight knots.[64] Gretton, too, disliked the interference with the Asdic the Foxer caused and did not stream it in his destroyer, though it was occasionally used by the slower ships of his group.[65] Once in contact, escorts in close action could be embarrassed by the trailing Foxers as they manoeuvred to attack the U-boat.[66] The primary aim, Walker stated, was '… to destroy U-boats, particularly those which menace our convoys.' This object was amplified in his standing orders for the Second Escort Group (EG2):

> Our job is to *kill*, and all officers must fully develop the spirit of vicious offensive. No matter how many convoys we may shepherd through safely, we shall have failed unless we can slaughter U-boats. All energies must be bent to this end.[67]

As a result he was willing to take risks with his ships in order maximize the chance of a U-boat kill. He was convinced that defence for support groups against the Gnat:

> ... must lie in tactics and not Foxers, which greatly reduced the chance of killing U-boats, especially in vile Asdic conditions when echoes were poor and faint. He considered that occasional casualties must be accepted, but emphasized that Gnats could not home on sloops at low speed. The Commander-in-Chief agreed – in the case of experienced groups.[68]

Admiral Horton, Commander-in-Chief, Western Approaches, understood the dilemma for Senior Officers and ships' captains. 'It *is* a game, this U-boat struggle', he remarked:

> ... the 'Gnat' is a nasty snag and delays the approach – all ships hit to date have not completely carried out instructions [careful approach to the U-boat], but in the heat of the moment the offensive spirit of the escort vessels takes charge, and it is hard to blame them severely.[69]

The aggressive spirit amongst anti-submarine practitioners is evident from these views.

Beating the submersible

The foregoing account suggests, at face value, a rather banal tactical pattern. Indeed, at a very early stage in the Battle of the Atlantic it was noted that the German '... tactics conform to a stereotyped pattern so that counter-measures may be uniformly applied.'[70] The British counter, however, was the complex interaction of tactics on three main fronts. Firstly, convoy made it more difficult for the U-boats to find their targets, and most convoys escaped detection altogether. Secondly, the enemy relied on the use of the surface, for searching and tactical mobility (which was severely limited when the U-boat submerged). Thus aircraft both on area searches and patrols in the vicinity of convoys could locate U-boats, sometimes destroying them, but at least forcing them to dive. Surface support groups, patrolling at a distance round a convoy, did the same. Thirdly, the extensive use of radio by the U-boats gave the British the ability to locate U-boats in the wide expanse of the ocean. Aircraft on area patrols could be more effectively tasked, threatened convoys could be reinforced with surface and air escorts, and individual U-boats close to convoys could be forced to dive and often attacked. The results were adduced by the Government Code and Cypher School, Bletchley Park, at the end of the war. They wrote that by May 1943:

> The nature of the problem facing the U-boat Command had ... changed. Whereas in the first three of four years of the war the effectiveness of the arm was limited by inadequate numbers, there was now almost an *embarras de riches*. The U-boat Command found itself in control of a fleet of over four hundred boats, which it was unable to deploy fully, as the types of which it was composed were no longer suited to contemporary operational conditions. The expectation of life of a U-boat joining the operational fleet in the third year of war (September 1941 to September 1942) had been about eleven and a half months; in the following year, a 500-ton boat might expect to survive only about eight months ... .[71]

Much of this was achieved by the improved use of technology but success also depended on the development of appropriate tactics. Nor should the latter be seen as the imposition of some dogma in a 'one-size-fits-all' formula. Notwithstanding that the enemy's tactics were largely stereotyped in concept, the vagaries of individual performance, weather and the scale of forces pitted at any one moment, meant that particular anti-submarine actions were each unique events and required considerable skill on behalf of the proponents. That said, the reinforcement of threatened convoys was an idea that had served the Royal Navy well since the eighteenth century in a very different technological era.

It was impossible for every convoy to be given an escort capable of countering the heaviest pack attack. If adequate intelligence were available, it ought to be possible to reinforce threatened convoys. Aircraft were able to be rapidly re-deployed in this manner, but, valuable though they were, they were not the whole answer, for additional surface escorts were needed too. The progressive increase in the size of convoys over the winter of 1942–43 and the lengthening of the convoy cycle helped to relieve the pressure on the direct escort groups, and free vessels to form support groups. These could then be used to reinforce threatened convoys. The direct linkage between these tactical moves is not clear, for the support group requirement had already been established in 1942 on tactical grounds, but it was only in February 1943 that Rear Admiral J.H. Edelsten, now promoted to Assistant Chief of Naval Staff (U-boats and Trade) (ACNS(UT)), was satisfied that there were sufficient escort vessels to form support groups on a permanent basis (aided by the temporary cessation of the Arctic convoys). The escort's strength for each convoy was, in theory, calculated using the formula of three escorts per convoy, plus one extra for every 10 ships in the convoy, provided air escort was also available. It was emphasized by the Naval Staff prior to the Casablanca Conference in early January 1943, that:

Without air escort this provision of escorts is totally inadequate against wolf-pack tactics on the scale that we must now expect. In fact, it may be said that, without air escorts, convoys attacked need at least one escort for every U-boat attacking – and at present 'packs' may well consist of up to 15 U-boats. It is therefore assumed that all convoys will:–

either

(i) be so routed as to be able to receive escort by shore-based aircraft, or,
(ii) be accompanied by an escort carrier.[72]

Initially, the escort carriers, or CVEs, were employed by the British as an integrated part of the convoy escort, where they provided not only anti-submarine air cover but also fighter protection on some routes closer to enemy controlled coasts. Only later were they briefly used on more offensive operations.[73]

The value of the support groups, like air cover, was in harassing and attacking U-boats that were attempting to shadow or gain bearing on the convoys, and their ability to conduct prolonged hunts of U-boats that made attacks. Anti-submarine ships and, especially, aircraft could profitably be used in distant patrols around the convoys where U-boats were most likely to be on the surface. The analysis of support group operations (and air escorts) undertaken in the middle of 1943 illustrate the point. The attacks on U-boats by the close escort and the supports for Convoy SC130 (the last convoy to be seriously threatened by U-boat pack attack in Spring 1943) show that half of the attacks were as a result of surface escorts either joining or sweeping at a distance round the convoy. Overall, during the 10 hunts by close escorts and support group ships the initial detections were, in one instance, the result of a high-frequency direction finding (HF/DF) contact, two were by asdic, two by radar and five were by visual sightings of U-boats. Aircraft contacts were between 10 and 30 miles from the convoy and in every case the contacts were obtained visually.[74] An earlier DNOR study had shown that Groups had spent 31 per cent of their sea time supporting convoys during the period of the last major U-boat campaign on the ocean convoy routes between September 1943 and January 1944. They had spent 21 per cent of their sea-time in U-boat probability areas and 48 per cent in transit, as would be expected in supporting the widely spaced ocean convoys.[75] The other points which emerged from the analysis of these support group operations in May and June 1943, was that the groups spent only about one tenth of their time at sea with shadowed convoys (though convoys received support for about 40 per cent of the time they were being shadowed). Lest these figures seem low, it should also be noted that only about 15 per cent of the close escorts' sea time was with shadowed convoys. What is also significant is that the support groups spent between 50 and 60 per cent of their time on passage.[76] This rather high figure might be viewed alongside the time spent by hunting groups early in the war accused by some historians of 'fruitlessly' scouring the seas for enemies. The operations of the support groups also demonstrated the increasing probability that aggressive U-boats would suffer fatal consequences.

The *Admiralty Convoy Instructions* (ACI's), reiterated that the primary objective of the of convoy escort was: 'The safe and timely arrival of the convoy at its destination … .' This aim was echoed precisely by the USN instructions. Though the British instructions were revised by one of the most aggressive Escort Group Commanders, Commander P. Gretton, many contemporary anti-submarine practitioners took the 'safe and timely arrival' objective as imposing too great an emphasis on the defensive.[77] The criticism seemed compounded by the British instructions which went on to say that '… attempted evasion may attain the primary object … .' However, this edict was then conflated by:

> … the need for reducing the time spent in dangerous waters and desirability of reaching an area of air cover must be considered when planning evasive measures.[78]

Those who, in the spring of 1943, condemned these instructions at the height of the Atlantic Battle, did so with little idea of the true nature of the 'Nelsonial' aggressive spirit. This philosophy of offensive action in the Royal Navy certainly extended back to the days of the Elizabethan Navy. But, as Corbett notes (albeit while discussing Fleet actions):

> … the maxim of 'seeking out' for all its moral exhilaration, for all its value as an expression of high and sound naval spirit, must not be permitted to displace well-reasoned judgement.[79]

The critics also did not see, as many of the more experienced officers did, that the lack of sufficient high-performance anti-submarine vessels in relation to the threat and the size of the escort task, meant that for much of 1941–42, the Royal Navy was obliged to remain on the defensive. Ultimately, the Royal Navy understood that 'defensive' and 'offensive' anti-submarine operations were not alternatives but were combined in a symbiotic relationship. Simply carrying out offensive operations randomly, as noted for an earlier era, was '… almost bound to end in a blow in the air, which not only would fail to gain any offensive result, but would sacrifice the main defensive plank … .' However, the Royal Navy did not follow an 'offensive' trait simply because its apparent opposite, the 'defensive', was a negative form of warfare, or that the offensive was positive and led to glory. Only the offensive would, ultimately, lead to victory, but that offensive, however, had to be based on a sound defence. Convoy had often been seen as a 'defensive' strategy. Corbett modified the idea that the defensive was synonymous with passivity, in fact it was imbued with '… an attitude of alert expectation.'[80] Indeed, convoy was described by Admiral Sims, Commander of the US Naval Forces in Europe during the First World War as 'a purely *offensive* measure'.[81] This is echoed by other writers, but although they and Sims rather overstate the case, the point is clear: convoy provides for a concentration of anti-submarine assets, well placed to destroy attacking submarines, and the aggressive spirit is maintained by offensive action, or at least the thirst for it. Howard-Johnston, as an escort group commander early in the war knew that, when resources were stretched: 'Our business is to bring home the merchantmen. The sinking of the enemy is only a secondary consideration at this stage of the war. Our turn will come later.'[82]

That such criticism should re-emerge in the spring of 1943 is somewhat surprising, given the contemporary shore-side teaching at the Western Approaches Tactical School (WATU), in Liverpool, and the advanced tactical training of formed escort groups at sea based around *Philante*. Captain G.H. Roberts, at WATU found it necessary to issue, under the Commander-in-Chief, Admiral Sir Max Horton's signature, additional guidance on the interpretation of these tactical instructions. In essence, Roberts pointed out, the offensive school saw the issue in terms of:

> Failure to destroy the U-boats will enable their numbers to increase to such an extent that we shall eventually be overwhelmed by sheer weight of numbers. The morale of the crews will remain at a high level unless a reasonable number of casualties are inflicted, and as a result their offensive spirit will be sustained at a high pitch.

This approach, as Horton succinctly expressed it, was to 'keep their tails down'. On the other hand, Roberts noted, the defensive school thought that:

> If trade can be maintained by the continued passage of convoys in comparative safety, the war can be won by other means. Furthermore, the continued failure of U-boats to achieve any great measure of success will sap their morale and weaken their determination.[83]

Both sides of the argument contained valid points. As the war turned out, the defensive approach was largely forced on the Allies (at least in 1941–42) by the lack of escorts for the expanding convoy system. They were simply unable to take the offensive, without seriously jeopardizing the safety of convoys. Coastal Command had been faced with a similar situation as a Cabinet Committee appreciated in 1941:

> ... the great potential value of aircraft, freed from routine patrols on convoys, as a 'harassing force' to take the offensive against U-boats and would welcome the provision of such a force in the Western Approaches. But, with our primary object of the safe and timely arrival of our shipping in mind, it is believed that such a force can only be justifiably instituted when the close protection of our convoys has been made reasonably sure.[84]

On both sides of the Atlantic it was appreciated that the matter was '... largely a question of numbers.'[85] The U-boat was very difficult to locate in the open ocean unless precise and timely intelligence was available. More effective use could be made of anti-submarine forces by deploying them where the enemy also had to concentrate in fairly large numbers, that is, off his bases and around convoys. The crux of the philosophy was to bring anti-submarine forces into contact with the enemy so he could be destroyed. As the Admiralty and Commanders-in-Chief, through ACIs, reminded Escort Commanders:

> ... it must be borne in mind that if enemy forces are reported or encountered, the escort shares with all other fighting units the duty of destroying enemy ships, provided this duty can be undertaken without undue prejudice to the safety of the convoy ... .[86]

But these instructions were not dogma: WATU taught:

> Senior Officers of Escort Groups have complete freedom to exercise their initiative under all circumstances, and it is not desired that they should be rigidly bound to comply with any of the diagrams of operation orders laid down in ACIs.[87]

Not the least reason for adopting such a policy was that, as the British readily appreciated, the enemy was bound to react to improved British tactics with changes of his own. Senior Officers were encouraged to be on the lookout for new methods employed by the enemy and to initiate appropriate countermeasures. As operational experience had amply demonstrated, the best insurance was provided by escort groups well organized, well trained, and well led by their own Senior Officer. It was, ultimately, the Senior Officer who drove the training of his group and created its general efficiency. The formal training organization, from the individual work-up base at Tobermory to the shore training at base ports and at WATU in particular, as well as the sea training with *Philante*, were valuable in providing the foundations of group efficiency. But it was the leadership of the individual Senior Officers who made the difference between effective and inefficient groups.

By the end of 1943 it was recognized by the British that, as a direct result of Allied air anti-submarine countermeasures, U-boats were rarely to be seen on the surface during the day. The enemy thus substantially reduced the chance of being located, but as a consequence also relinquished much of their mobility and search capability, along with the ease of rapid communications. Locating and shadowing convoys immediately became more difficult. In particular, as the Western Approaches Command noted, U-boats were denied the capacity to concentrate because they now lacked the '... mobility which enabled more distant U-boats to intercept a reported convoy.' But, Western Approaches noted, although these U-boat submerged tactics had '... already greatly promoted the safe and timely arrival of the convoys, but they must inevitably give us fewer opportunities to destroy the enemy.' As a result, every fleeting opportunity was now to be taken to destroy U-boats. Support groups, and even portions of the close escort were to be detached after a convoy battle to return to the scene of the engagements '... for mopping up' operations. Unless anti-submarine vessels encountered a U-boat in an immediately threatening position, when an urgent counter-attack was required, engagements were to be deliberate with the object of destroying the U-boat. It was emphasized that standard depth-charge attack approach provided ample warning to the U-boat of the moment of firing (because the attacking ship would pass roughly overhead at high speed). Against a deep U-boat, free to manoeuvre, this made the attack ineffective. Western Approaches pointed out that in the Hedgehog and in the Squid:

> ... are combined the two attributes of precision and surprise which ensure its effectiveness in a deliberate attack. For a U-boat which is too deep for the Hedgehog, the 'Creeping Attack', which has the same attributes, has recently proved on three occasions its deadly day accuracy.[88]

Standard depth-charge attacks on a deep U-boat were no longer seen as justified, other than to drive the U-boat deeper, so that a 'Creeping Attack' could be used. The growing emphasis on the use of ATW would prove devastatingly effective against slow U-boats, and would be valuable in the event of the enemy's high-speed U-boats becoming operational. However, technical modifications to existing U-boats, to allow them to operate continuously submerged, were to start the process of re-defining anti-submarine tactics in the last year of the Second World War and in ways which continued throughout the Cold War and beyond.

3 Elusive victory
Countering the schnorkel, 1944–45

Introduction of the schnorkel and its effect on anti-submarine operations

The German Naval High Command became increasingly aware that despite the growing numbers of the U-boat fleet, individual U-boats were sinking progressively fewer ships. Moreover, the enemy were growing ever more concerned at the delays to U-boat transits caused by Allied air power in the Bay of Biscay and, towards the end of 1942, they began feverishly searching for ways to redress the situation. One solution was to adapt their existing U-boats by fitting an extendable air intake, known as the 'schnorkel' (literally a 'nose'), which allowed them to draw air into the boat while submerged at periscope depth. This made it possible for the U-boat to propel itself on diesel engines without depleting the battery charge, and simultaneously to refresh the boat's air. It was assessed by the Admiralty that this system could be used in sea states up to 3–4 and that the schnorkel head would present only a small target that would be extremely difficult to detect by radar (or by eye) and would make the U-boat practically invulnerable to air attack.[1] Even with the urgency needed by Allied pressure, the Germans had only begun sporadic development of the schnorkel. By late 1942, *U-448*, while working-up in the Baltic, was fitted with an H-shaped, experimental type and, although the equipment achieved moderate success, it was removed and further sea trials temporarily abandoned. Nevertheless, by December 1943 an improved design was being fitted to operational U-boats at St. Nazaire, with the first Baltic boats equipped and an instructional programme started in the following February. The enemy's priority was fitting U-boats in the Biscay ports as a means of safely transiting the Bay *en route* to their Atlantic operational areas. Only later did the Germans realize that schnorkel boats would have an advantage in operations against an invasion of the Continent. The last boats to be fitted were those based in Norway, the first of which only appeared in early September 1944 (though not all Biscay boats had been fitted by that date). British interrogation of prisoners-of-war (PoW) revealed that by mid-August 1944 about one third of the Type VIIs and most of the Type IXs had been fitted.[2]

By February 1944, the Admiralty were anticipating that the enemy could be expected to operate U-boats close inshore, a change of tactics which the escorts had to be prepared to repel. That month, the first U-boat (*U-264*) fitted with schnorkel had been sunk in the Atlantic, though she appears to have been operating conventionally. By the end of February the Admiralty had deduced the true nature of the schnorkel and by May some attacks had been made on schnorkelling boats off the Guernsey coast. The first extensive experience with schnorkel boats was during the operations in support of the invasion of the Continent in June 1944. Those U-boats not fitted with schnorkel that tried to penetrate into the invasion area had been roughly handled and further attempts were abandoned. Within a fortnight, Professor Williams and Dr Solomon of DNOR completed a rough analysis of anti-submarine operations against the schnorkel-fitted U-boats in the Channel. They concluded that aircraft capability against these U-boats was about a fifth of that expected against their non-schnorkel cousins, and therefore the onus of dealing with schnorkel U-boats largely fell on surface anti-submarine vessels. However, at first, they fared no better. Williams and Solomon calculated that escort groups should have made contact with each of the U-boats about four times, assuming the escorts were each able to sweep a path 3,000 yards wide, which was the performance to be expected in the Atlantic. However, actual results suggested that the individual escorts were only achieving a swept width of barely 600 yards. From Special Intelligence the OIC concluded that, when searching for U-boats using 'Gamma' patrols, the support groups had probably passed directly over U-boats on about 10 occasions, but had made only one contact. The enemy, on the other hand, had detected 65 per cent of the escorts which passed within about three miles. The U-boats were using their hydrophones and '... it was the sound of the foxers which was first detected.'[3] At that range the U-boats stood a good chance of slipping through the gaps in the escort groups asdic front, or even passing round the flank of their search.

The low asdic detection performance was due to the prevalence of bottom echoes and high reverberations, which distracted inexperienced asdic operators. Furthermore, it was soon discovered that, when near anti-submarine vessels, the U-boats tended to lie on the bottom. Here their echo merged with all the other unwanted asdic returns and made them very difficult to distinguish, as Professor Rutherford had predicted in 1915.[4] Operators could, however, be more successful when alerted to the presence of a U-boat in their vicinity. Part of the problem was that the escorts failed to follow up aircraft sightings, even though some 30 per cent were less than 30 miles, or two hours steaming from a support group. DNOR noted that the 'bird in the hand' was systematically ignored, and had ships made even '... moderate use of aircraft sightings their total chances of contacting U-boats would have been more than doubled.'[5] Within a month these deficiencies were rectified and the proportion of kills rose to a level equivalent to that previously achieved by support groups in ocean waters. Now, ships made better use of aircraft sightings, and spent more time searching the datum, though DNOR thought that these investigations should last at least 24 hours. Trials were also in hand to explore the cooperation of escorts working with aircraft using air-dropped omni-directional sonobuoys. Although some USN squadrons were using sonobuoys by June 1944, after months of trials only one British squadron had used the equipment on operations.⁶ Thereafter, some, albeit slow, progress was made. By the end of the war, Howard-Johnston was able to note that sonobuoys had:

> ... enabled aircraft to track submerged U-boats in calm weather once they have been located, but this requires good drill and competent listeners and may be rendered much less reliable by the background noises of a breaking sea or tidal stream. As a rough guide an aircraft with eight sonobuoys should be able to hold contact for 60–90 minutes, and one with twelve sonobuoys for three hours.⁷

But, the technology was in its infancy. Initial detection remained problematic and, for the British at least, unsupported classification evidence from sonobuoys was not considered conclusive evidence of the presence of a U-boat.

In August Captain R. Winn in the Operational Intelligence Centre (OIC) came to the judgement that:

> The evolution of the Snort [i.e. schnorkel] U-boat will be found to have affected profoundly the balance of power between hunter and hunted .... The U-boat will be able to remain submerged for up to 10 days without presenting any target detectable by radar or visually except at short range.⁸

At the same time, Williams and Solomon drew together the available information from operations and special intelligence. Their analysis was undoubtedly made easier, for at around this time, the British, too, had been considering the adoption of the schnorkel in the design for the 'A' Class submarine, drawn up in October 1942, to counter the rapid improvement in radar performance. However, it was soon decided that the threat to British submarines did not warrant the adoption of 'submerged dieseling', which brought with it operational limitations.⁹ DNOR reckoned that the weather often precluded schnorkelling in seas greater than force 5, though as experience was gained some boats did better. By assuming that U-boats maintained a speed of two knots while fully submerged, DNOR were able to make a direct comparison between the schnorkel and non-schnorkel boats on passage:

	Schnorkel	*Non-Schnorkel*
Hours charging per day	5 hours at schnorkel depth	2 hours surfaced
Distance made good per day	50 miles	70 miles¹⁰

However, considering the lower battery usage when in an operational area, the average time schnorkelling was thought to be about three hours per day.¹¹ This helps to explain why, amongst Coastal Command crews, there was a '... growing frustration of failing to sight U-boats known to be in specific areas.'¹² Worse, over the months that followed many of the claimed sightings were actually incipient waterspouts, or 'willywaws', misidentified as schnorkels because of the mistaken belief that the schnorkel emitted smoke. This may have been culled from a captured

German document of April 1944, which could have come into NID's possession at this time, and described '... puffs of exhaust gas of Schnorchel ... .' The document suggested that measures were being taken to redesign the schnorkel head and other measures to reduce both this and the wake from the schnorkel.[13] From the number of contacts gained by aircraft, the amount of flying done, and the total time assumed to be spent by the U-boats schnorkelling, the analysts were able to estimate that the swept width achieved by Coastal Command's aircraft was less than 700 yards by day and 100 yards by night. Even taking account of errors in the data the swept width was unlikely to be more than a mile by day and fifth of that by night. This meant that if an aircraft was searching a five-mile wide lane, then its effectiveness would be about 4 per cent. By comparison the swept width for an aircraft searching for a surfaced U-boat was about five miles by day and three to seven miles by night. Williams and Solomon concluded that when U-boats were able to charge their batteries by schnorkelling, they were nearly eight times safer than if they chose to operate on the surface.[14]

Williams continued to assess anti-submarine operations against the schnorkel-fitted U-boats. He deduced that the best opportunities for offensive action against U-boats operating inshore were in the shipping areas (and not just with convoys). Williams reasoned that the shipping areas were small, compared with the U-boats' extensive transit routes, and so it was there that the U-boat density would be highest, and thus the opportunities for action greater. Of course, anti-submarine forces in the shipping area also had a direct deterrent effect on the U-boats' activities. The question then was, whether the escort groups should operate in the close vicinity of the convoys in direct support, or patrol in probability areas? The answer depended on the frequency of attacks by the U-boats. If attacks were infrequent, it was better for the escorts to search in probability areas, since the U-boats would only rarely be encountered around convoys. On the other hand, if attacks became more frequent, then:

> ... the surface groups should be close to a convoy, since this would not only contribute to the direct defence of the convoy, but also offer the surface groups with frequent opportunities for attack.

Williams suggested alternatives for the stationing of the surface escort. He thought that the safety of the convoy:

> ... would be temporarily best assured if the surface groups formed a screen ahead and on the flanks of the convoy, to maximise the chance of forcing the U-boat to bottom or of detecting the U-boat *before* attack. On the other hand opportunities for counter-attack would probably be greater if the surface group kept astern of the convoy and pounced on any attacking U-boat.[15]

When the escort was weak, ships should tow foxers to deter or confuse approaching U-boats, but, Williams reasoned, where the escort was strong the anti-submarine ships should rely on zig-zagging for protection against Gnat attacks. The reduction of noise by not towing foxers would make it more likely that the escorts would gain contact on a U-boat. If this happened, or the U-boat betrayed itself by attacking, then surface forces were to concentrate on the area to produce a flooding effect. The search should then be maintained for at least 24 hours, particularly in shallow water where the U-boat could bottom. Other staff in the Admiralty considered that the search should be continued for at least 48 hours. It was also clear that there was not complete agreement over when escorts should tow foxers. From the discussion over the employment of aircraft, it is evident that the staff were still of the opinion that in rough weather the U-boats might be unable to schnorkel and eventually forced to surface. Williams, in particular, took a rather theoretical stance by suggesting that air resources should be husbanded for just this circumstance, when they might be used to greatest effect. The DASW staff, on the other hand, thought that air cover was best employed attempting to interrupt schnorkelling.[16]

British tactical countermeasures

When, in mid-1944, the schnorkel-fitted U-boats began operating in the Channel against the invasion forces this yielded poor results, and they soon transferred their attention to the North-West Approaches.[17] The British had anticipated such a move and were able to implement pre-formed plans when the move was detected by British intelligence. The plan called for support groups to be deployed in widespread patrols, known as Operation 'CW' and later 'CE', across threatened trade routes where they were at hand to reinforce convoys (just as had been done with the hydrophone trawlers during the First World War). The anti-submarine groups could also carry out offensive sweeps in their areas. This was an extension of the operations of support groups, which since the winter of 1943 had been used in the Atlantic on offensive sweeps 60–120 miles ahead of threatened convoys, as U-boats adopted less aggressive tactics of maximum submergence by day.[18] These tactics continued to be used in the Arctic, where 'hunting' groups were sent out ahead of convoys to keep the U-boats down. In each case the greater reluctance of the U-boats to engage in convoy battles, meant that the anti-submarine forces had to operate further afield if encounters were to be forced and U-boats destroyed. The anti-submarine operations in late 1944 were of a more static nature, matching the U-boat tactics. Perhaps three escort groups, with air support, would be assigned to an area roughly 100 miles square. The groups did not operate as a cohesive unit but patrolled the area as directed by their individual Senior Officers, responding to intelligence cues and aircraft sightings, reinforcing the close escort of convoys passing through the area.[19]

Directly supporting convoys accounted for about 20 per cent of the support groups' time at sea, the remainder being spent patrolling their area. The object was: 'The safe passage of shipping through the focal areas.' But when no convoys were present, the object was '... the destruction of U-boats operating in these areas.'[20] DNOR calculated that the patrolling support groups would have passed within five miles of a U-boat at least once per day, even if the Groups had been disposed at random.[21] Since they were actually deployed on the available intelligence, it was likely that U-boats would have been aware of a support group, perhaps two or three times a day. PoW confirmed that the U-boats had indeed been swept over frequently without contact being made by the anti-submarine ships. Added to which, the U-boats would have been subjected to constant overflights by Coastal Command aircraft. 'Consequently,' McCrea concluded, 'the U-boats lived under a constant threat of detection and it is small wonder that they were slow to take the initiative in attacking.' This assertion was borne out by PoW reports. 'The weakness of the situation from our point of view,' McCrea continued:

> ... was thoroughly appreciated. It required only one or two U-boats a little bolder than the rest to demonstrate to their fellows that, despite the strength of our patrols, they could attack with but little fear of retribution.[22]

The U-boats were inexpert in submerged, inshore operations, especially in the effective use of the schnorkel. To carry out attacks the enemy were expected to operate singly, and to bottom under a shipping lane, waiting for a convoy to approach. The U-boat would then rise and attack using periscope observation by day, or in bright moonlight. The enemy was also experimenting with attacks using hydrophone bearings to fire from deep into the brown of convoy's hydrophone effect. This method could be used at night, but with existing equipment was not successful. Either a single homing torpedo, or a salvo of pattern-running torpedoes were fired at the convoy or the escort, often at long range and sometimes from astern.[23] The operational timidity of the U-boats had long been noted, and in September 1944 they were still not operating in an offensive manner, except for the occasional aggressive U-boat commander. They rarely gave the escort groups the opportunity to destroy them. At first the escorts were also inexperienced in the subtleties of inshore operations and only exacted retribution on about one in eight of the U-boats which attacked. The difficult acoustic conditions and the tendency of the U-boats to bottom when near anti-submarine ships, reduced asdic performance to less than 20 per cent of its normal efficiency.[24]

Classifying contacts on the bottom was especially difficult, as Commander J.D. Prentice, RCN, Senior Officer of EG11, discovered. Echoes from wrecks were often better than those obtained from a U-boat which were often woolly. There was no doppler and no wake echo both of which helped in classification in deep water; and in a strong tidal stream, trying to plot the movement of the target could be deceptive, and it was easy to shift target inadvertently from the initial contact to an adjacent non-submarine, without the use of radar or radio aids (such as QH) to fix the ship's position accurately.[25] Although the numbers of U-boats destroyed was low, they still lost one U-boat for every two ships sunk in the convoys. Thus there was a kind of stalemate, as Captain Howard-Johnston, DAUD, noted. The problem of dealing with the schnorkel-fitted U-boat was very different from the open ocean operations of 1941–43, in particular the U-boat was practically immune from location by aircraft.[26] However, with the imminent loss of the Biscay ports, the U-boats would find it very difficult to renew ocean operations against convoys that could be spread across a greater swathe of water making them more difficult to find. It seemed certain that the U-boats would confine their operations to inshore waters, however, Howard-Johnston thought:

> ... the enemy will [not] gain any further marked advantage from his operations until the advent of the fast U-boat either inshore or in deep waters, when our future asdic successes may be seriously reduced by the enemy's power to evade the individual attack.[27]

Whether on patrol, or when searching for a U-boat that had betrayed its presence, escort groups had to attack laboriously every suspect contact to try to bring up evidence of a U-boat. The problem, as Commodore G.W.G. Simpson, Commodore (D), Western Approaches, himself a renowned submariner, noted, was that '... the disintegration of the hull cannot reasonably be expected however many charges are dropped on it.'[28] During attacks about four out of five brought up only oil or nothing at all – not enough to differentiate between a U-boat and a wreck.[29] Moreover, attacking an indifferent asdic contact posed problems. A series of trials were carried out to determine in which direction the U-boat was lying, and several of the escort groups developed attack methods based on the use of the echo-sounder so that the ship could pass directly overhead of the U-boat and accurately place a small number of depth-charges on the target.[30] Escorts often persevered with these attacks against individual contacts continuously for up to 48 hours. 'It is most strongly emphasised,' Howard-Johnston remarked, 'that *persistence* in the search or hunt is of the greatest importance until clear evidence of destruction is obtained.'[31] Such persistence was equally vital in other operational areas, such as the Indian Ocean, where environmental conditions were very different. For example, Commander G.A.G. Ormsby, Senior Officer of EG60 in company with two CVEs of Force 66, hunted for *U-198* for a week before she was sunk in August 1944.[32] Some months later, Lieutenant Commander J.P. Mosse in command of HMS *Mermaid*, was instrumental in the destruction of two U-boats in the Arctic after long hunts. The convoy escorts were arranged in depth, with *Mermaid* and others forming advanced striking forces. They carried out a '... a vigorous defensive [that] resulted in hard blows being struck at the enemy.'[33]

Maintaining this level of aggressive searching was not easy for tired escort group commanders.[34] It was in any case very time-consuming, and some escort commanders sought for methods to catch an attacking U-boat before she managed to reach the bottom. Commander P.W. Burnett, one of the best U-boat killers and now Senior Officer of the EG10, for example, complained about the difficulty of getting contact on a bottomed U-boat.[35] There were days, he wrote 'when one gets no echoes from a known wreck ... .' He reasoned that '... there must be about 20 minutes when a U-boat attacking a convoy is clear of the bottom and not manoeuvring to avoid detection.' By stationing his support group in a dense screen ahead and astern (and even inside) of the convoy, his idea was '... to have an escort within Asdic range of him when he fires.' This, Burnett thought, was '... much more important than a tidy organized sweep which gets there half an hour later when he is back on the bottom.'[36]

Here, indeed was a conundrum. The key was to get as many as possible of the escorts within asdic range of the U-boat. Speed, as Burnett and others highlighted, was crucial. But so was an organized search, which ensured that as much of the U-boat probability area was covered as possible. When this was not achieved the U-boat would often escape. Burnett commented in early 1945, that:

> In coastal waters if one obtains no contacts it may be concluded that detection conditions are bad, and a bottomed U-boat is likely to be swept over undetected. If conditions are good, on the other hand, thorough investigation of all contacts delays a search so long that a reported U-boat has a good chance of escaping.[37]

The Admiralty promulgated a search plan called Operation 'Scabbard' designed to locate a U-boat which had retreated to the bottom after attacking a convoy. The most probable area where the U-boat was likely to be was within an annulus 2,500 yards to 4,000 yards around the torpedoed vessel. It was assumed that the U-boat would lie on the bottom head to tide. One escort was to close the position of the torpedoed ship to obtain information from survivors and establish the datum. Meantime, all other available escorts were immediately to form up 5,000 yards from wreck and search across the U-boat probability area, sweeping across the tide so that the ships would, hopefully, approach the bottomed U-boat on its beam, where its asdic echo was most pronounced. The search was then repeated in the opposite direction. After that the ships reverted to a square search around the perimeter of the 'Scabbard' area. The plan, though not formally included in the tactical manual until the end of 1945, was soon being practised by escort groups in their continuation training between convoy operations.[38]

Operation 'Artichoke' was another organized plan designed to search for a U-boat which had attacked a convoy in daylight (or bright moonlight) and was either still under the convoy, or had escaped on the quarters or astern of the convoy. The escorts in the van turned onto a reciprocal course to the convoy and search back through the convoy columns until they came abreast of the rear escorts, these, too, would turn and join in the search until the ships were 6,000 yards astern of the convoy. All ships would then about-turn and sweep back towards the rear of the convoy. Only the escort vessel in position 'S' directly astern of the convoy acted differently. She was to close the wreck, taking anti-Gnat precautions, and try to determine on which side that ship had been torpedoed (not easy if the ship had been hit by a Gnat or Lage-Unabhängige torpedo (LuT)), before carrying out an 'Observant' around the position of the torpedoing. If 'Artichoke' failed, the support group could continuously cover the six-mile square centred about the position of the torpedoing for at least 48 hours, depth-charging every likely contact in the area. Even if these tactics failed to find the U-boat, it was assumed they would force the U-boat to continue its anti-asdic tactics until finally forced to move when the air in the boat ran out. The escort's asdic then had a chance of detecting it. If there were escorts which could be spared from this 'inner search', or if reinforcements arrived, they were to be employed on an 'outer search' as directed by the Senior Officer on the spot. This search was to extend from the boundary of the inner search to the U-boat's likely furthest-on position, assuming she was tying to escape at a speed of two and a half knots.[39]

The operating authority would, '... issue tracking appreciations of the most likely movement of the U-boat to assist the Senior Officer present in disposing his patrols on the Outer Search.'[40] In addition, the whole area was to be flooded with aircraft to prevent the U-boat from surfacing and making good its escape outside radar range of the anti-submarine vessels. Any possible Schnorkel sightings by the aircraft were to be followed up immediately. The Senior Officer was able to establish new datums based on these sightings if he considered they warranted it and to detach ships from the outer searching force to carry out investigations along the lines of the original inner search. This inner search, however, was to be maintained until cancelled by the operating authority who would also decide whether a new datum was to replace the initial one. This control by the shore authority, with its better access to intelligence, was a feature of the inshore campaign, but occurred without too often interfering with the Senior Officer's tactical initiative, so assiduously developed during escort group training sessions.[41] And the intensive training had its effect. During the later stages, one in four of the U-boats' attacks resulted in their own destruction. But the big increase in U-boat sinkings was not in those associated with torpedoings. Ships and aircraft on patrol also began to take a heavy toll. This suggested to McCrea, who had no access to special intelligence, that the improved results had more to do with increased experience amongst the anti-submarine forces and not merely to the changes in dispositions. Thus, when the U-boats made their final spurt, their days of comparative immunity had vanished. Nor was the risk to the escorts minimal. McCrea concluded that on average 40 escort vessels had been at sea with the support groups between July 1944 and March 1945. These ships had destroyed 37 U-boats, but the U-boats had, in return, sunk 10 of the anti-submarine escorts.[42] Nevertheless, the tactical use of anti-Gnat material countermeasures, Howard-Johnston realized, 'must be left to the Commanding Officer's discretion.'[43]

These searches were used principally in the vicinity of convoys after an attack had occurred. The detailed convoy instructions for the conduct of the close escort and support groups, were contained in Horton's Operation 'Gooseberry', which was '... designed to cover the probable actions by a U-boat Commander when operating in an area where his evasive measures may include bottoming.' To meet this kind of attack by a U-boat, the success of counter-measures would depend largely:

> ... on escorts reaching the scene without delay. Broadly speaking, the plan allows for close escorts in positions astern of the convoy to search for the U-boat should he bottom in the immediate vicinity; an inner patrol to contain him to the limits of exhaustion, and an outer patrol to catch him should he by chance have evaded the net thrown round him.[44]

The dispositions furthest from the convoy were made up of air patrols, designed to force the U-boat to approach submerged and, if there were enough aircraft available, to have some chance of detecting an unwary U-boat using schnorkel or periscope. The air escort for convoys in the focal areas was normally to consist of four box patrols parallel to the convoy track, and moving to keep pace with the convoy's progress. The path ahead of the convoy that would be swept was to a distance of 28 miles either side of its mean line of advance out to approximately 60 miles ahead of the convoy. A close air escort was sometimes provided in addition to the box patrols, which, in the absence of other instruction from the Senior Officer of the Escort, was to carry out a continuous patrol round the convoy at a distance of five miles, where it might be able to detect a U-boat using its periscope as it worked itself in a firing position on the convoy.[45]

The planned dispositions of the surface escort around, and supporting, a convoy were designed to maximise the chance of locating and destroying an attacking U-boat. Thus, for an ocean convoy formed on a broad front and approaching one of the focal areas, the close escort was to be stationed in accordance with Admiralty Convoy Instructions, if no support group was available. At the time this close escort was expected to consist of between five and eight escorts. These would be disposed roughly equidistant around the convoy with the emphasis on ships stationed on the wings and astern of the convoy.[46] If a support group was present by day the best way of disposing it was, firstly, to augment the close escort so that an anti-submarine screen could be formed, with the support group ships normally occupying the wing positions. This screen, with ships spaced 3,000 yards apart was designed to catch a U-boat which had risen from the bottom on hearing the approaching convoys, and was now manoeuvring into an attack position. With this screen ahead formed, any spare escorts were to be stationed astern and on the quarters of the convoys to act as 'pouncers', able to rapidly react to a torpedoing. By night, except in bright moonlight, it was unlikely that a U-boat would be manoeuvring to make a torpedo attack from periscope depth. The priorities for stationing the support group were therefore reversed. Its ships were, firstly, to fill the 'pouncer' positions, where they might catch a U-boat which had fired a long-range 'browning' shot, possibly from astern of the convoy. Any spare ships of the support group were to augment the close escort on the forward screen, preferably taking the wing positions. Once the convoy entered the cleared channels through the defensive minefields it would reform with a narrow front (thus resembling a long column). The close escort was then to be evenly disposed round the convoy, with the support group disposed on both sides, and nearer the rear than the front of the convoy. Horton emphasized that if a U-boat was detected by the screen or revealed its presence by attacking the greatest chance of killing:

> ... is whilst the scent is fresh. Any delay in closing the datum point reduces the chance of a kill. The situation calls for the utmost rapidity of decision, combined with speed and clarity of communications, as well as the efficiency of weapons, instruments and their operators.[47]

When such an attack took place, anti-submarine forces were to carry out an asdic sweep of the immediate area surrounding suspected position of the U-boat.

Numbers of escorts permitting, this was best achieved if at least two anti-submarine ships were stationed close astern of the convoy to act as pouncers. Of course, these neat 'textbook' tactics were more difficult to carry out in practice. Even in daylight when the ship torpedoed could be seen and the side of the attack ascertained, it was not easy to identify the correct position of the datum. The result, said Lieutenant Commander Raymond Hart, Senior Officer EG21, in early February 1945 was that a hunt commenced '... along the lines of "Gooseberry"'. The many non-submarines in the coastal waters prolonged the search, but supported by EG5, Hart's persistence, probably resulted in the destruction of one U-boat and heavy damage to another.[48]

Tactics refined from experience

By February 1945 the Admiralty had refined its advice of the previous autumn on convoy protection in Inshore waters for the Escort Groups. They once more pointed out that on ocean routes the U-boats normally had had considerable distances to cover if they were to reach favourable attacking positions. Allied air cover and distant screens of anti-submarine ships were able to prevent U-boats moving freely on the surface. However, the introduction of the schnorkel by the Germans required considerable changes in the employment of anti-submarine forces for convoy protection. In coastal waters U-boats were able to operate in areas where shipping was easy to locate on the well established convoy routes. As a consequence the U-boats did not have to move over large distances, and with the adoption of continuous submerged operations (made possible by the use of the schnorkel), Allied air patrols and distant screens of anti-submarine ships were rendered largely incapable of detecting any U-boats lurking in the path of a convoy. By the early spring of 1945 the U-boats were becoming more adept in exploiting the difficult environmental conditions and the anti-submarine forces limitations. They surfaced very rarely in areas of heavy air reconnaissance and normally charged their batteries by schnorkelling at night in quiet areas. Attacks were generally made from periscope depth during the day or by moonlight. McCrea's estimate of the effectiveness of escorts in detecting U-boats in inshore waters was rather pessimistic. The data suggested that the escorts had only about an 8 per cent chance of detecting a U-boat as it approached to attack a convoy.[49] There was little new in this discovery. Anti-submarine practitioners, like Howard-Johnston and Burnett, would have remembered the results of tactical screening exercises in the late 1920s. These had shown that at least 45 per cent of submarines passed through a screen without being detected, and this in exercise conditions, with the operators fully alert to the presence of a submarine.

Accepting the low probability of detection, British tactical countermeasures nevertheless were based on the policy of providing maximum asdic protection and immediate counter-attack after a U-boat had attacked. Protection was afforded by deploying a strong asdic screen two miles ahead when a convoy in ocean waters was formed on a broad front. For coastal convoys the escort was to be maintained both ahead and alongside the flanks when convoy was formed on a narrow front.

This concept was not new. Earlier tactical instructions had suggested the use of a closely spaced, line abreast escort screen ahead of the convoy when it was assessed that submerged U-boats were lying in wait ahead of the convoy. If a support group was available it was deployed to reinforce the close escort by extending the screen ahead of the convoy. Meanwhile, at least one escort was stationed within a mile of the rear of the convoy to act as a 'pouncer', which was well placed to close the wreck and start the search in the likely area where the attacking U-boat could be, while the scent remained strong. When a support group was present at least one ship was to be used to reinforce the 'pouncer'. If a second support group was available, the whole Group was to be deployed astern of the convoy to act as a powerful 'pouncer' force to exact retribution on a U-boat that had attacked. The key was to start the search without delay and before the U-boat could have moved far away, or ensconced itself on the bottom. The anti-submarine tactics recommended were designed, firstly, to concentrate rapidly practically the whole of the escort, including any support groups, in the likely area where the enemy could be, and secondly, to seal off that area while the search continued until destruction of the U-boat was achieved. Minimal protection of the convoy was accepted (because these schnorkel-fitted U-boats were operating singly, rather than in packs, so another U-boat was unlikely to be found close-by).

As soon as a ship in the convoy was torpedoed, one, or ideally two, 'pouncers' were to close the wreck from the rear of convoy and carry out a standard Operation 'Observant', with sides two miles long. Remaining escorts initially stationed in the rear of the convoy were to establish a 'Square' Search outside the 'Observant'. The size of the 'Square' Search was recommended to be a six-mile sides, unless in the prevailing circumstances the Senior Officer present decided on a different size. Meanwhile, the ships in the van were to contribute to the asdic search most effectively by executing an Operation 'Artichoke', during which the escorts would sweep back through the columns of the convoy. Once clear of the rear of the convoy, these ships were to take up positions on the 'Square' Search, with any ship left over after filling the 'Square' Search used outside it to search on the U-boats most probable escape course. Once these immediate countermeasures were in place, at least one ship of the close escort should be detached to rejoin the convoy. When one or more support groups were with the convoy, the whole convoy close escort was to re-establish the forward screen after Operation 'Artichoke'.[50]

The action recommended on completion of the immediate searches appeared in an amendment to the 'Atlantic Convoy Instructions', issued in April 1945.[51] If the 'Observant' and 'Square' searches did not yield a contact, the force was to carry out two sweeps through the area at right angles to the tide and with the ships in line abreast and spaced 3,000 yards apart. Subsequent searches, it was suggested, might be carried out down tide of the original datum.[52] Recent experience of inshore operations indicated that after U-boats had attacked and especially when escorts were close by, they would immediately bottom or drift with the tide. Any movement by the U-boat was likely to be at silent speed of three knots or less, though the enemy might accept the risk of using higher speed if the U-boat could make enough ground to outflank a searching force, or to make a withdrawal up wind. To make it more difficult for the U-boat to get round the flank of an approaching search force, the searching ships should be stationed two miles apart and they should carry out a wide 30°–50° zig-zag to broaden the search front even further, accepting that the speed of progress would be diminished. The U-boat would therefore be faced with a difficult and changing problem.

Professor McCrea's analysis of Operation 'CW' supported this policy. He deduced that to make the search as difficult as possible for the U-boat to evade, the ships should be widely spaced and should carry out a broad zig-zag. The alternative of a narrower front and a less drastic zig-zag would '… invite the U-boat to attempt to evade the group as a whole.' Although wide spacing might tempt the U-boat to try to pick his way between the ships, the broad zig-zag would tend to confuse his assessments of the positions of the 'holes' in the escort line.[53] Where no direction could be decided, the area to be searched would be bounded by an expanding 'furthest-on circle'. The size of this circle would be dictated by the time elapsed since the U-boat attack. The recommended figures were: three miles for the first half hour; 10 miles for the first two hours; and three miles for every subsequent hour.[54] When the new, faster Type XXI U-boats appeared, the Admiralty warned, the enemy might attempt to make more positive attempts to escape at higher speed, but in doing so they would have to accept the risk of exposing their hydrophone effect to detection by the escorts. But the higher speed and longer endurance of these U-boats meant the area to be searched by the escort forces would expand much more rapidly, than in the case of a conventional, schnorkel-fitted U-boat. In February 1945, however, there was no indication that Type XXI U-boats were ready for operations.

Coastal Command's response

Coastal Command had also been devising new search tactics against the schnorkel-fitted U-boats. These were briefed and discussed at the bi-annual Squadron Commanders' Meeting held at Coastal Command Headquarters at the end of November 1944. At the meeting Captain Peyton-Ward, the Senior Naval Staff Officer at Coastal Command, observed that since the last meeting in March of that year the U-boats had completely revised their operational stance. Those which were not fitted with the schnorkel were unable to operate effectively because of the growing power and ubiquity of Allied air patrols. These boats were, therefore, forced to spend the majority of their time submerged where they were unable to re-charge their batteries and could make little progress on passage. Only with the introduction of the schnorkel could U-boats survive under the intense air cover.[55]

Trials had recently been conducted by Coastal Command on aircraft detection capability against the schnorkel. When there was no sea clutter, radar could detect a snort at four to eight miles. However, at night operational experience showed that when aircraft passed within four miles of a snort they had about a one in 50 chance of achieving a detection followed by a sighting with illumination. Sea returns probably played a major part in this poor performance, as did homing failures, and the snort diving on detecting the radar or illumination. Further trials were needed to identify the factors which contributed to success or failure.[56] At the November meeting Air Vice Marshal A.B. Ellwood, CB, DSC, Coastal Command's Senior Air Staff Officer (SASO), explained that the introduction of the schnorkel had made:

> ... the U-boat so difficult to detect that ... [the Command] had partially to abandon the offensive in the Northern Transit Area, and allocate the forces to the protection of our convoys. For the schnorkel enables the U-boats to slip through the transit areas almost undetected, and will similarly enable them to get to their operating areas without too much interference from the air.

Coastal Command's first call, Ellwood went on, was the protection of threatened convoys. This now meant that '... we are not able to be, as we should like, completely offensive in our policy.' The Command had, '... in fact been driven on the defensive to a certain extent.' To overcome this problem it was proposed:

> ... to adopt an offensive method to apply a defensive policy. The future method of looking after convoys will not be by putting on a single aircraft at a time, but will consist in flooding an area ahead of the convoy in the same way and to the same frequency of cover as we flooded areas through which the U-boats had to pass during 'Overlord'.

These patrols were '... designed to sweep out an area along the path of the convoy in force to prevent the ... [U-boats] getting at the convoys.'[57] It was expected that, once the Germans were comfortable with the operation of the schnorkel-fitted U-boats, they would start another major offensive in the near future, making use of the tactical advantage bestowed by the schnorkel. Since the enemy had not yet reached this stage, Ellwood stated that Coastal Command was taking advantage of the lull in U-boat activity to concentrate on squadron training before the battle re-started. The training would be focused on the new tactics of 'flooding' sweeps ahead of the convoys. Group Captain Taylor explained these tactics to the Meeting. He began by referring to SASO's explanation of the factors which had led the Command to adopt an offensive–defensive policy. The tactics to be adopted consisted of 'offensive' patrols concentrated into a relatively small area ahead of each convoy. Each patrol would be designed so that an aircraft would pass over each part of the patrol area every half an hour. This, it was hoped, would ensure the detection of any U-boat which attempted to intercept the convoy. These patrols were in the form of four parallel boxes, each containing two aircraft and flown to keep pace with, and ahead of the convoy. Assuming that the radar detection range on a schnorkel was three and a half miles, this allowed the total area swept each side of the convoy's track to be 28 miles. The total width of the patrol area ahead of the convoy would therefore be 56 miles.

The patrol would normally be flown to a distance of about 60 miles, though the performance of each type of aircraft would dictate the precise range. So that the spacing of the two aircraft assigned to each box was maintained, the intention was that, whatever the aircraft type, each should spend exactly one hour on each circuit of the box. Clearly, the faster types of aircraft would have to fly further ahead of the convoy than the slower. To maintain the accuracy of the patrols, each aircraft was to check its position relative to the convoy by taking a radar bearing and range, before setting out on the next circuit. This was, Group Captain Taylor pointed out, '... a new departure in navigation technique, and no part of the standard drill.' Curiously, Taylor announced that this relative navigation technique would reduce the need for '... the numbers of winds found, drifts, and positions fixed by other means would be tolerated while the aircraft remained with the convoy ....'[58] How accurate aircraft positioning during the rest of the patrol was to be maintained, without accurate wind-finding, was not explained, though there was some concentration on transit navigation.

Results of the anti-schnorkel campaign

According to a DNOR report, less than 20 per cent of the schnorkel-fitted U-boats were destroyed at sea by air attack.[59] However, ubiquitous Allied air patrols compelled the enemy to remain submerged, and rely on their schnorkel, which restricted their tactical mobility. Airpower also put the U-boats under constant fear of detection. The log for *U-247*, for example, contains almost daily reference to sightings of Allied aircraft. There was the possibility that the aircraft would home anti-submarine vessels onto the U-boat's position.[60] An escort group summoned by an aircraft had a good chance of relocating the U-boat, but success relied on speedy communications and accurate navigation. These factors also highlighted one major difference between the ocean and inshore operations. Howard-Johnston noted that:

> In the former, any action by the operational authority is unlikely to be of immediate assistance due to the distances reinforcements must travel. In the latter, air or surface reinforcements can usually be sent in a very short time and intelligence is likely to be more detailed and accurate.[61]

Howard-Johnston's allusion to more detailed and accurate intelligence was, of course, based on the Admiralty and Command's access to high-grade special intelligence. The U-boats rarely transmitted at sea, though when they did it often led to intensive air and sea searches and the destruction of the boat.[62] What was more valuable was the decryption of messages from U-boat Commands to their U-boats, giving approximate details of routes and operational areas. Although more research is needed to understand this aspect, it is clear that the British shore authorities were making great use of this source to deploy escort groups and air patrols in areas where U-boat activity was likely to be greatest. It is also clear that towards the end of 1944 and into 1945, the German substantially increased their communications security for reasons which are not yet clear. This, as the OIC observed, made the U-boats deployments obscure.[63] Support groups could sometimes, therefore, be deployed into relatively small patrol areas, where they could search for U-boats and reinforce transiting convoys most easily. Even though the convoy cycle was altered and the size of convoys substantially reduced in late 1944, it proved possible to form more British support groups from the faster escorts released from ocean groups, and by the retention of escorts originally destined for the Far East. In addition, an appeal was made to Canada for more RCN support groups to be transferred to British Waters. A similar reorganization of shore-based aircraft (both Coastal Command and Fleet Air Arm) was undertaken, though in the sort of operations envisaged CVEs were of less value.[64] Command boundaries were also amended to provide more cohesive direction of the operations centred on Horton's Western Approaches Command.[65] These measures were made more effective by another significant difference between the ocean and inshore campaigns. This was the adoption by the U-boats of static tactics in place of the mobile tactics which had been a feature of ocean operations. This might be temporary, for if new high-speed U-boats under development became operational, the enemy could return to more mobile tactics, albeit operating while submerged.[66]

McCrea's analysis of the employment of the Support Groups showed that about 20 per cent of their time at sea was spent supporting convoys. Since the patrol areas were close to the bases, most of the remaining 80 per cent of the time was spent on anti-submarine patrol. All told there were about 50 escorts in the support groups in November and December 1944. This figure rose to about 60 during 1945. These ships were responsible for sinking most of the 37 U-boats destroyed, which equated to about one U-boat per ship-year spent on operations. McCrea compared this to the results of a Canadian study which concluded that the Royal Canadian Navy (RCN) ships had sunk one U-boat per 19 ship-years. 'This comparison,' McCrea asserted, 'has nothing to do with efficiency.' He quoted it:

> ... merely to contrast two sets of experiences and to indicate that the operations in coastal waters did provide any individual ship with an exceptionally favourable chance of destroying a U-boat.[67]

McCrea's analysis showed that very nearly 50 per cent of the U-boats were sunk by patrolling support groups. Why such a high proportion should have fallen to support groups on apparently 'random' patrols is unexplained, but may be due to searches actually being focused by special intelligence assessments. The support groups (which did most of the killing) spent only 20 per cent of their time with the convoys, but it was during these periods that almost 30 per cent of the U-boats were sunk, just over half of them after a ship in the convoy had been torpedoed. This was, McCrea noted, confirmation of the obvious fact that a ship had the best chance of avenging an attack if it is already present at the scene. The number of U-boats killed before they were able to attack was roughly proportionate to the time spent by the support groups with the convoys. McCrea also noted that the aggressive tactics of the support groups in attacking Gnat-armed U-boats led to one escort being torpedoed in each of the 10 months of the campaign. To minimize the danger it was important that at least two escorts should engage a U-boat. The pair also had a greater chance of holding contact and avoiding the confusion caused by non-submarines, especially if they made use of their anti-submarine plots and accurate fixing aids, like QH.

Amidst the non-sub infested inshore waters two chief lessons Howard-Johnston and Prichard highlighted in relation to searches were:

(a) that it is better to search meticulously a comparatively modest furthest-on area (e.g., speed of U-boat two to three knots) than to dissipate the effort by allowing for an improbably high speed of retirement; and
(b) that a concerted search dependent on accurate station-keeping soon becomes disorganised as each ship in turn attaches herself to a doubtful asdic contact.

They also perceived that:

> When there are insufficient A/S vessels to cover even a modest furthest-on area, it is advisable to endeavour to forecast the U-boat's most probable movements and commit the forces available to the best appreciation that can be made. Such tactics should, however, be limited to cases of necessity, and the temptation to 'plunge on a guess' should be resisted whenever a systematic search is possible.[68]

Strictly, as Professor McCrea earlier pointed out, a 'random' search was just as likely to gain contact as 'systematic' searches, such as 'Gamma', 'Vignot', 'Observant', etc. McCrea also noted that a systematic search might be easier for a U-boat to avoid. Theoretically, this was possible but it relied on the U-boat being able to determine from its sensors where the escorts were and what they were doing. This was far from easy. The great advantage of a systematic search, McCrea acknowledged, and as Howard-Johnston and Prichard realized, was '... that it can quickly and easily be put into operation.'[69] Not all escort groups got it right.[70] Furthermore, even with faultless tactics it seemed that more U-boats had been missed by poor classification than by searching in the wrong place.

The Allies were faced with what seemed to be the dawn of a revolutionary 'new' U-boat war ushered in by the schnorkel-fitted U-boat. However, this threat bore many similarities to those encountered during the First World War and the submarine tactics practised in the inter-war period. That the gloomy forecasts of the outcome of the campaign were not matched by the actual results was, in part, because the enemy's tactics were quickly understood, but was also in large measure due to the British and Canadian crews of anti-submarine aircraft and ships. Their training had imbued them with confidence, initiative and a flexibility capable of coping with the new tactical situation brought about by the new German technology. The British were able rapidly to institute rigorous training for aircrews and escort groups. This was vital, since early on in the campaign:

> The standard of operational efficiency responsible for the defeat of the U-boat in the Atlantic, is now lacking due to absence of training in the last three months [during operations in support of 'Overlord']. This will be particularly applicable to new groups about to be formed. It is therefore essential that a proper group training cycle be instituted at once for all A/S forces operating in the focal areas.[71]

Two of the aspects in which training was shown to be necessary were:

(a) Senior and Commanding Officers needed to practice to realise the differences between asdic and radar screens or searches; the effects on the U-boats movements of the possibility of bottoming and the concentration of traffic; and the difficulties of thorough search in an area where non-submarines are prevalent.
(b) A/S teams required practice to realise the effect of tide on the plotted movements of bottomed contact, and on the problems of holding contact and attacking them. They also required practice in the techniques of classification by echo sounder.[72]

In some ways these were the easier aspects to correct. Professor McCrea, having analysed the anti-submarine operations from the beginning of September up to the end of 1944, thought it was also vital that training be given in the greatest problem of anti-submarine operations in inshore waters which was that of initial detection. Howard-Johnston agreed that this was a weak spot in the training and undertook to discuss it with DASW and then Western Approaches.[73] Yet, even with these shortfalls the British position was unlike the period at the beginning of the war. Now the British commanded an adequate level of combat strength and a training machine able to instil the necessary skills to counter the German onslaught. During the last weeks of the war, the enemy was beginning to find the losses unacceptable and had withdrawn most of his U-boats from British coastal waters, except off the East Coast, and was trying to operate them in the more distant South-West Approaches. In McCrea's opinion, the campaign ended in a victory for British forces. Overall it had been one of a great deal of improvisation on both sides, though the Allies were more adept at responding to German initiatives.[74] But McCrea warned that such an optimistic view needed to be balanced against the future threat of the new, fast U-boats. Of course, much of the focus of the British planning effort was in preparing for a U-boat campaign in which the Type XXI and Walter high-speed U-boats would have played a prominent part. In the event these boats were not ready in time.

Prospects of the U-boat war

There was general agreement with Captain Winn's view that the prospects in the anti-submarine war were heavily dependent on the character and ability of individual U-boat commanders.[75] Horton, for one, saw that his task was:

> ... to destroy as many as possible of the existing U-boats, thus preventing experienced officers and men from manning the new types. He also hoped to damp their enthusiasm by continually hammering at morale.[76]

Principal among these new U-boats was the ocean-going, schnorkel-equipped Type XXI. Their streamlined hulls would make them hard to detect, especially end-on, and with their high underwater speed, thought to be in the order of 13–15 knots, they would be difficult to attack with existing equipment. If they were also commanded by experienced men they could pose a substantially greater threat than the existing schnorkel-fitted U-boats, both in the ocean and in inshore waters. Large numbers of these boats were known to be working up in the Baltic, with some 15 expected to be operational by the end of 1944 and perhaps 95 by April 1945. Trials were being carried out to investigate tactics to counter these fast U-boats, as will be described in the next chapter. Meanwhile, as Horton pointed out, the immediate issue facing the anti-submarine forces was the normal schnorkel-fitted U-boat. The challenge was to devise counter-measures that would combat this threat, and at the same time delay or dilute the forthcoming problem of the Type XXI.

Certain material measures were readily adopted, including the formation of more escort groups. Other, more innovative but more complex, developments were undertaken. For example, it was hoped that a new scheme to reduce the ship's propeller noise and the use of off-board, expendable noise-makers to deflect Gnat attacks, would both lead to improved asdic performance in shallow waters. Asymmetric anti-submarine measures were also taken. These included use of concrete-piercing bombs for attacks on U-boat pens, increased defensive anti-submarine mining off convoy routes and offensive mining of U-boat training areas, the use of US Magnetic Anomaly Detection equipment and better means of marking the position of wrecks were all considered at an early stage.[77] At the end of November 1944, Professor E.J. Williams in DNOR produced a '… tentative and provisional …' paper, which drew on earlier work and the shape of which, he thought, might be useful for the next Cabinet Anti-U-boat Committee. Williams calculated that the schnorkel was probably 20 times more difficult to detect and attack by aircraft than a surfaced U-boat, especially by night, and estimated that '… asdic *search* (as distinct from attack) has only been about 20 per cent of its value in average ocean conditions.' Nevertheless, Williams noted, experience had shown that once found, the chance of killing a U-boat exceeded earlier figures for open ocean hunts. This, Williams thought, was because shallow water reduced the uncertainty in depth estimation and, more importantly, reduced the dead time between firing and explosion of the anti-submarine projectiles.[78]

Having been approved by Professor P.M.S. Blackett, the Director of Naval Operational Research, the bulk of Williams' paper was incorporated into a note by Howard-Johnston which he drafted at the end of November in consultation with Winn and DASW. They concluded that the enemy had sunk one ship for every three U-boat cruises, and had lost a U-boat for every two ships sunk. This dismal performance was, however, expected to be overtaken in a renewed offensive in the New Year, which would include the new U-boat types. Howard-Johnston concluded that as many as 160–200 ships could be sunk during the first three months of 1945, half of them by the Type XXIs. The counter-measures identified reinforced those already being developed, that is, the concentration of more escort groups in inshore waters along with intensive training, the extensive use of anti-submarine mining, and bombing attacks on U-boat construction yards and oil supplies.[79] Howard-Johnston's note was reviewed by ACNS(UT), Rear Admiral Edelsten.

The losses attributed to the Type XXI were reduced by half, perhaps because there was more awareness of the difficulties of operating the Type XXI effectively in submerged pack operations because of communications difficulties and the encouraging results obtained during the recent trials with a fast British submarine, which had confirmed that the problems of detection and attack (at least up to 12 knots) were tractable.[80] The casualties anticipated were therefore some 120 ships during the first three months of 1945, a number which, Edelsten remarked, would be heavily influenced by the degree of offensive spirit exhibited by the U-boats, and which remained the unknown factor.[81] Although the forecast figures were again altered, Edelsten's paper was broadly accepted and formed the basis for subsequent appreciations by the First Sea Lord, Admiral of the Fleet A.B. Cunningham, and in his submissions to the other Chiefs of Staff, and the Cabinet Anti-U-Boat Warfare Committee.[82]

In addition to his discussion with Williams, Winn and Prichard, Howard-Johnston had also asked a former colleague in DAUD, Commander H.W. Fawcett, RN (Ret'd.), to offer his views on the coming U-boat offensive. Fawcett was an anti-submarine specialist, with experience of the First World War and who had served in DASW and then for a year in DAUD, where he had been involved in tactical appreciations, along with Leon Solomon of DNOR, which implies that Fawcett, too, was indoctrinated into Special Intelligence. Fawcett was now attached to Captain Peyton-Ward's staff at Coastal Command and, Howard-Johnston thought, was a man not only of ideas but '... willing [and] able to back them up with statistics.'[83] Unfortunately, Fawcett's ideas arrived too late to affect Howard-Johnston's paper, but echoed the concepts abroad in the Naval Staff. Wider opportunities for destroying U-boats had to be found Fawcett thought, because the schnorkel had reduced the overall killing power of aircraft and escorts to a tenth of their former value. Concentration on purely 'defensive' measures would mean that too many merchant ships would be sunk for every U-boat that was destroyed, and this would not be enough to 'get their tails down'. Offensive action was needed, too, especially against the new fast U-boats. This, he hoped would be possible due to the excellent U-boat tracking from intelligence, even if this was not as accurate as formerly because U-boat traffic was now not so voluminous. In any case his ideas did not depend on precision targeting of U-boats at sea. Instead what he had in mind was an 'obstacle race' consisting of the whole gamut of action ranging from bombing of building yards and factories, bombing and mining of bases (including attacking enemy minesweepers to prevent mine clearance), attacking enemy supply shipping serving the U-boats bases, use of Allied submarines off those bases, continuous anti-submarine air cover over U-boat transit routes and intercept them with anti-submarine vessels and, of course, surface and air escort of Allied convoys. Fawcett analogy was: 'If we put 100 horses over a steeplechase course consisting of six jumps each of which is cleared by 96 per cent of the horses, then only 78 horses finish the course.' This concept, as Fawcett pointed out, had a resonance with the strategy employed in the First World War.[84] The key was that defensive and offensive measures were not seen as alternatives. Instead they were mutually interrelated.

In reviewing the 1944–45 inshore campaign against the schnorkel-fitted U-boats Professor McCrea noted the poor asdic performance of the escorts but concluded that it was '... the high U-boat density which permitted a satisfactory outcome despite this low efficiency.' This was demonstrated by the statistics. Of the 37 U-boats sunk by anti-submarine ships, only two were detected in the first place by radar and two visually. The rest were initially detected by asdic. Only about six of the U-boats were detected at night, which '... probably was connected with the fact that the U-boats wanted to attack by day and so were more likely to be in the patrolled areas then.'[85] Commander P.W. Burnett, Senior Officer of EG10, wrote in early 1945:

> The five confirmed U-boats with which I have been in contact in the last year have all been detected by asdic, without any pervious warning of their immediate presence. Although several others must have been swept over, these five have all been detected by day.[86]

McCrea also realized that to understand how factors such as the weather affected U-boat operations '... as regards schnorkelling, sighting, attacking, etc. would require a big investigation.' It does not appear that this was done, nor did McCrea have time before the war ended to assess whether the disposition of the escorts was the best to take advantage of opportunities to detect U-boats approaching a convoy to attack. Once the Admiralty took possession of the German records, McCrea thought it entirely possible for a detailed analysis to be done, which would identify dispositions around convoys which would ensure that the most probable positions from which the U-boat fired were swept over by as many escorts as possible. Howard-Johnston was of a like mind. He asked '... for three months with my Division to *analyse* every U-boat incident when the U-boat got away. ... But my Division was closed down immediately after VJ-Day and the analysis was never done.'[87] The Admiralty drafted a short paper intended for consumption by the British and Americans in the Pacific preparing for the invasion of Japan. It contained the main lessons from the inshore campaign. Howard-Johnston in conjunction with Captain N.A. Prichard, DASW, emphasized:

> The marked deterrent effect of strong patrols which attack all suspicious contacts without undue regard to conservation of ammunition is apparent from German records now available. In particular the value of aircraft patrols may be out of all proportion to the number of U-boats they sink.

The Directors jointly recommended that:

> ... aircraft should patrol in order to detect U-boats charging, rather than fly close escort duties. If there are any spare after the area in which the U-boats must charge has been saturated (i.e. each point is swept over at least every hour) they are better used as extended escorts by night rather than as close escort trying to detect submerged U-boats by day.

However, direct convoy protection by surface escorts remained their central concern. 'The necessity,' Howard-Johnston and Prichard wrote:

> of guarding against submerged attack by a U-boat which remains bottomed until the last moment, and of investigating innumerable asdic contacts, has resulted in changes in [convoy] Screening Diagrams.

These changes were briefly stated:

> An advanced screen has not time to differentiate between the many non-sub contacts and a U-boat lying 'doggo', though there is a good chance of detection if the U-boat is manoeuvring to attack. A/S vessels should, therefore, be formed into a comparatively dense screen closer ahead than has been usual. When this requirement has been met any remaining vessels may be disposed astern ready to deliver quick counter-attacks after a torpedoing, or be placed in positions on the bow or beam which would be suitable firing positions for a U-boat.[88]

In the event the abrupt end of the war in the Far East forestalled the despatch of the paper. The lessons were not forgotten, for when Burnett was later appointed to the Admiralty, he was to use his wartime experiences and long-term professional education when re-assessing anti-submarine warfare doctrine. However, before covering these events, it is necessary to follow the way in which the Admiralty dealt with the incipient threat of the fast submarine.

4 The dawn of modern anti-submarine warfare, 1944–46

The problem of the fast U-boat

By mid-1942, the ubiquity and increasing effectiveness of Allied anti-submarine counter-measures had impelled Dönitz to press for the technical means to employ submerged U-boat operations for the remainder of the war. Conversion of existing types with the schnorkel was only a short-term palliative because of their low underwater mobility. What was needed was a U-boat with high underwater speed and endurance. This, it seemed, could be achieved by accelerating the development of novel submarine types powered by the Walter turbine, which could be run submerged, powered by the decomposition of oxygen-bearing hydrogen-peroxide fuel. High submerged speed was achieved by sacrificing surface performance and optimizing the streamlined hull for underwater travel. However, as the technical difficulties with the system became more apparent, it was soon realized that they would prevent this type becoming operational in the near-term. Development was therefore started on a hybrid U-boat, combining the Walter-boat's streamlined hull, with a powerful, but conventional, diesel-electric propulsion train and a very large battery, capable of being recharged while submerged by using the schnorkel. This was the Type XXI U-boat.[1]

During the winter of 1943–44 NID suspected that the Germans were developing new U-boat types, although their exact nature remained obscure until Spring 1944, when the Type XXI U-boat was identified.[2] Captain Prichard, DASW, rapidly drew on the existing Admiralty expertise to define the measures necessary to counter this new threat. Prichard quickly concluded that such a U-boat, which was assessed to have an extreme diving depth, long endurance and high underwater speed, would be able to make long submerged approaches to convoys from any direction, making all-round convoy protection necessary at greater distances than previously. The Type XXI could also operate stealthily at slow speed, but be able to use high speed to evade anti-submarine vessels. A single escort was unlikely to be able to hold contact and would need the help of a consort. Even so, attacks would be difficult, given the U-boat's high manoeuvrability. Depth-charge attacks were likely to be ineffective and, although ATWs offered the best chance of success, their short range, combined with high-speed evasion by the U-boat, would make attacks highly dynamic, and accurate aiming difficult because the rate of change in the target's bearing would be close to the maximum turning rate of the attacking ship.

During an approach, anti-submarine ships would have to be wary of counter-attacks by the U-boat with the Gnat. Counter-measures, such as the 'Step Aside' tactics, or reducing speed, would delay the approach and give the Type XXI ample time to avoid the escort. A high speed approach degraded asdic performance and the escort risked overrunning the U-boat.[3]

A brief, provisional appreciation of the Type XXI U-boat was issued to the Fleet in September 1944 by Captain Howard-Johnston, DAUD, in the Monthly Anti-Submarine Report.[4] The article was based on a more detailed analysis by Professor E.J. Williams, of DNOR, who was one of the Special Intelligence confidants. His paper was therefore based on recent Ultra material.[5] This intelligence revealed that the Type XXI U-boat was about 245 feet in length, with a displacement of 1,600 tons, a submerged speed of 17 knots and long endurance from its abnormally large battery. Not only did this information allow the earlier assessment of the Type XXI to be refined, but it undoubtedly provided the impetus for potential counter-measures to be analysed and exercised on the tactical table at the Western Approaches Tactical Unit (WATU) in Liverpool under the guidance of Captain G.H. Roberts and, on occasion, with DNOR scientists.[6] As Captain Howard-Johnston later recalled the convoy system would still have been the most effective means of defeating the Type XXI U-boat, especially as it could have benefited more from independent routing of trade than the ordinary U-boats.[7] Essentially these theoretical and practical investigations suggested that the Type XXI's higher speed meant that the area into which it could escape would increase exponentially and this, in turn, would substantially reduce the effectiveness of the escorts' asdic searches, unless they could arrive at, and cover, the area quickly. However, at high speed, the Type XXI might make enough HE noise to give the escorts a chance of detecting the U-boat. There remained the problem of attacking the Type XXI, for it could use its high submerged speed and rapid acceleration to prevent an escort settling in on the asdic echo. What was needed were new hydrophone effect tracking tactics and greater reliance on ahead throwing weapons.

HM Submarine *Seraph* trials[8]

In October 1943, when the prospect of a German U-boat with high underwater speed was emerging, NID requested Charles Lillicrap, Director of Naval Construction (DNC), to investigate the possibility of providing a British fast underwater target. Lillicrap had concluded that by streamlining the hull and removing all the appendages required for fighting, including the deck gun, a British submarine could achieve a submerged speed of 13 knots for about 20 minutes.[9] So, when Dr Goodeve, the Assistant Controller (Research and Development), convened a meeting on 6 June 1944 to discuss the Type XXI threat, Lillicrap was ready with outline proposals for a fast underwater target that could be used to test existing British anti-submarine equipment and tactics. HM Submarine *Seraph*, awaiting repairs after a diving accident, was the boat selected and thereafter events moved rapidly. At the Deputy Controller's Meeting a week later it was agreed, anticipating formal approval, that conversion work was to start immediately, with completion due at the end of August. The modifications fell into three parts. Firstly, her main electric motors were up-rated and propellers with coarser pitch were fitted, so that *Seraph* could develop greater propulsive power. Secondly, her hull was streamlined by the removal of guns, the fairing off of apertures and a reduction in the size of the hydroplanes and conning tower. These modifications reduced the hydrodynamic drag by 55 per cent, while the propulsion power was increased by 13 per cent. Thirdly, a high capacity battery was installed to extend her underwater endurance. The results were impressive, for when *Seraph* began her high-speed trials towards the end of September the speed and endurance figures showed a significant improvement, especially in her endurance at medium speeds:

Speed	*Seraph's* Endurance	
	Before conversion	After conversion
4 knots	14 hours	35 hours
6 knots	4 hours	8 hours
10 knots	–	2 hours
12 knots	–	¾ hour[10]

Of course, these figures are slightly misleading, since lacking a schnorkel, *Seraph* had no method of replenishing the air inside the boat. It was realized that the crew's concentration would deteriorate after about 12 hours dived, though classic symptoms of carbon dioxide poisoning and oxygen lack would not become evident for another five hours. The greatest problem was that *Seraph* could not recharge her battery at sea, and this limited her value in tactical exercises.

At the end of September 1944 *Seraph* carried out a series of asdic and tactical trials, the first with HMS *Kingfisher* and the latter with the EG19. The trials' teams included Professor W.M. McCrea from DNOR in the Admiralty and J.A. Hakes, a scientist from the nearby HMA/SEE, Fairlie.[11] The tactical trials were organized by Admiral Horton, Commander-in-Chief, Western Approaches' Headquarters in cooperation with representatives of Commander US Forces in Europe, RAF Coastal Command and Naval Aviation, Flag Officer (Submarines), and the Directors of the Anti-U-boat, Anti-Submarine Warfare, Naval Intelligence, and Naval Operational Research Divisions, as well as training and experimental establishments. At sea, the trials were controlled by Lieutenant Commander D.R. Mitchell, DSO, DSC, who was now part of the training staff onboard *Philante*. For the tactical trials Mitchell assumed the title of Training Commander, 'Rockabill', denoting the area of the Irish Sea where the trials took place.[12] It was intended that the tactical settings for the trials reflect the work done at WATU and pre-trial practice was carried out ashore in the HMA/SEE attack teacher. It can be seen, then, that these trials brought together the full weight of the Admiralty, the operational commands (including their training organization), and the scientific community. The modifications to *Seraph* were started on 16 June, just one month after the first Type XXI, *U-2501*, was launched. Subsequent trials with *Seraph* were run some seven months before the first operational cruise by a Type XXI, *U-2511*.[13]

With the asdic trials lasting only a week and in changeable acoustic conditions, it was difficult to correlate the results. They were, at best, only able to give rough indications of echo and hydrophone effect strengths. Nevertheless, the data were adequate to provide more realistic information for the continuing tactical table trials. These trials showed that, while *Seraph*'s beam-on asdic echo was little changed, at fine inclinations it was much smaller and, consequently, asdic ranges on these bearings were reduced by three-quarters or more. It is likely at this stage of scientific understanding that asdic echoes were thought to be returned from the outer surfaces of the submarine. In fact the sound also penetrated to the inner (pressure) hull and reflections could occur from 'internal' structures. These additional reflected highlights probably contributed to the uneven echo pattern observed. At fine inclinations, when *Seraph* was travelling at high speed, the echo's doppler allowed the operators to distinguish even the weak echo against the background noise and other interfering echoes. For example, although *Seraph* at 12 knots had been held on the asdic recorder at only 750 yards stern-on, her echo, picked out by the doppler, was heard out to 2,700 yards. It was also discovered that the streamlined *Seraph*'s hydrophone effect was weaker when compared to her pre-converted state. This was because less power was needed to turn her propellers and they turned at a slower rate, to propel her at any given speed. They were therefore less likely to cavitate and gave her a higher 'silent' speed.[14] Thus when *Seraph* was travelling at six knots, or less, *Kingfisher* could not detect any hydrophone effect from her; even at ranges as short as 500 yards. But, as *Seraph's* speed rose above six knots, her hydrophone effect became easily detectable. The hydrophone effect rapidly increased in intensity, reaching a peak at nine knots and remaining at this level even as *Seraph's* speed increased to 12 knots. At these speeds the submarine's hydrophone effect could be detected by *Kingfisher* at up to 5,000 yards, though because there was no transmission-echo elapse time, range could not be measured, and only a bearing found. Unfortunately, for an escort to keep up with a fast submarine, her own speed would create a great deal of self-noise, so that for speeds above 16 knots the asdic range might be reduced by 45 per cent and hydrophone effect detection range by 50–60 per cent.

There were thus complex interactions between submarine and ship speeds, and relative orientation, and the resultant detection range that could be achieved. Nevertheless, the hydrophone effect ranges seemed remarkably constant and unaffected either by water conditions (which caused wild fluctuations in echo ranges), or the submarine's depth, though McCrea wondered whether this would hold true for the Type XXI, which was assessed to be able to dive to great depths. For it was thought that while hydrophone effect ranges would increase with target speed, as the submarine went deeper the hydrophone effect range was likely to decrease markedly because the greater pressure at depth would inhibit the onset of propeller cavitation. This finding was consistent with the experiments by Directorate of Scientific Research and the Admiralty Research Laboratory, at Teddington. *Seraph* had only operated down to 200 feet (the limitation possibly imposed by structural weakness caused during her accidental dive in May 1944). However, the interaction between speed and depth was by no means linear. Post-war trials with a Type XXI showed hydrophone effect levels at six knots reducing significantly between 50 and 150ft, while at 10 knots they remained unchanged, and at 15 knots the hydrophone effect level increased marginally.[15] Thus, while target hydrophone effect could not be guaranteed, its use was important for two reasons. Firstly, the hydrophone effect was sometimes loud enough to mask the asdic echo, not only on the recorder but aurally too, so that hydrophone effect might be the only means of holding contact. Secondly, with an asdic that transmitted a narrow 'searchlight' beam, there was little margin of error when holding contact on a high-speed submarine. The submarine could rapidly move outside the asdic beam and escorts '... could easily be thrown off the scent', especially if operating singly.[16] However, the asdic could be used to sweep for hydrophone effect about 10 times more rapidly than probing for an echo over a wide angle. Once the target's bearing was established the asdic could transmit once again to obtain an echo.

Subsequent tactics would depend on whether the escort was able to gain asdic contact, or had to rely only on hydrophone effect bearings. The problem here was that the speed at which an escort was likely to hear hydrophone effect would probably be less than the speed at which the U-boat was travelling. So, in order to close, the escort would have to employ bursts of high speed interspersed with periods of slow speed to listen for the hydrophone effect. If the proportion of slow speed was kept to a minimum (typically 25 per cent) it was found possible to close a conventional U-boat. However, especially when deep it was found that the U-boat's wake would mask the hydrophone effect from its propeller if the escort was within 20° of directly astern. Care had to be taken during the periods of high speed not to overrun the U-boat, should it slow down, or to mistake own ship hydrophone effect for that of the submarine. It was recommended, therefore, that the escort's speed should be reduced to carry out a listening sweep at least every five minutes. There was also the danger of the U-boat counter-attacking with a Gnat. In any case it was desirable for asdic contact to be gained as soon as possible.[17]

These features concentrate on the high maximum speed of the new submarines and are emphasized in nearly all the post-war literature on the Type XXI. However, both to conserve battery power, and to reduce the chance of its hydrophone effect being detected, a high-speed U-boat was likely to make use of its long endurance at higher 'silent' speed to avoid contact by escorts.[18] Initial tactical planning of counter-measures had to take account of both the potential of a U-boat making off (at least initially) at high speed, before carrying out its main evasion at silent speed. The key was to get the escorts near to the submarine's datum position as quickly as possible. This was complicated by the need to take anti-Gnat precautions. Most ships could not approach at high enough speed to be safe, and using Foxers made so much noise that the chance of gaining contact was greatly reduced. To this end existing procedures were adapted, with the nearest ship executing an immediate reaction 'Delta' search, bringing her over the datum, while making allowance for the threat of a Gnat counter-attack (by the 'step-aside' manoeuvre). The next ship to join was to start a 'Double Observant' square search, four miles out from the submarine's diving position. She was to be joined by the first ship on completion of the Plan 'Delta'. Thus the Plan 'Delta' would cover the possibility of the U-boat remaining in the vicinity of the datum, while the 'Double Observant' was designed to catch the submarine if it evaded at 12 knots. However, it proved impracticable to play out these tactics at sea because of *Seraph's* limited high speed endurance. Instead tactical investigations continued ashore using a tactical table, while the sea trials concentrated on attack procedures.

The main trials effort by the EG19 was therefore directed towards exploring the problems involved in attacking a fast U-boat. It was assumed that ATWs gave the highest probability of success but it was necessary to establish whether the Type 144 asdic-fitted escorts could apply the necessary deflection at the instant of firing to allow for the submarine's movement during the flight of the projectiles. The ship's anti-submarine teams had practised the procedures ashore in HMA/SEE's attack-teacher and had achieved successful attacks, though there were many practical operating difficulties, as well as random errors, that were likely to reduce the overall accuracy of attacks. Howard-Johnston, quoting Lieutenant Commander Mitchell, warned that:

> ... the difficulty in attacking [was] primarily due, not to the unsuitability of ships or instruments ... but to the very reduced margin or error which [*Seraph's*] high speed permits the hunting ships.[19]

Even so, when *Seraph* took modest avoiding action attacks were possible, provided a recordable echo was received. Up to submarine speeds of 12 knots it seemed that, with adequate training, asdic teams could operate the cumbersome 'cut-on' procedure to determine the target's bearing and generate adequate fire-control solutions for an ATW attack. Professor McCrea sounded a prescient note of caution. The Type XXI U-boat's higher assessed speed of some 15–17 knots might just be enough to tip the dynamic tactical balance in favour of the submarine, and perhaps make countering the Type XXI an insurmountable problem.[20]

Admiral Horton reported to the Cabinet Anti-U-Boat Committee after the trials, that EG19, a '... particularly experienced group had had no success during the first week of such exercises, but had rapidly improved thereafter.'[21] Initially, *Seraph* proved to be elusive and difficult to attack. However, such was the level of training amongst the escorts, that by the end of the period, the ships were able to achieve almost continuous contact on *Seraph* for two hours and execute five attacks, even though *Seraph* was at nine knots for nearly 40 per cent of the time. The tactics, partly developed by the Group, used the hydrophone effect to hold contact whenever *Seraph* went fast, while waiting for her to slow down before delivering an attack.[22] The Group adopted a loose diamond-shaped formation which conformed to the movements of the attacking ship and covered the likely evasion courses of the submarine. The formation tended to gravitate towards the stern arcs of the submarine due to the dynamics of the engagements.[23] When teams were worked up, Mitchell considered that a fast U-boat was unlikely to escape from two hunting ships, unless the asdic conditions were exceptionally poor. This positive note was struck when Captain Prichard, DASW, held the first meeting of the sub-committee of ACNS(UT)'s U-boat Warfare Committee at the end of November 1944. Prichard reported the conclusions reached by Mitchell. He concluded that a U-boat could successfully use high speed to evade ships only in rough weather and, although a U-boat with high submerged speed would be difficult to attack, highly trained ship's teams should have good chances of success. Commander-in-Chief, Western Approaches' representative, added that:

> ... further exercises had proved that training in attacks on a fast submarine was 90 per cent of the battle. It had also been proved that ships fitted with the bearing recorder and helmsman's indicator (Asdic Type 144) had a tremendous advantage over ships not so fitted.[24]

In Mitchell's view, there were no grounds for changing established pair-ship tactics. More ships would simply get in the way and should carry out a containing 'Box' search round the close anti-submarine action. A contemporary American report summarized the issues, by noting that:

> The appearance of the new German XXI submarine does not seem to present any radical new implications, but merely a more difficult presentation of already existing problems.[25]

DASW ended the discussion by saying that the exercises with *Seraph* showed that minor modification to asdic operating procedures were necessary. The principle one being the combining of two successive asdic sweeps from 80° left to 80° right of the ship's head, taking about six minutes, with two all-round hydrophone effect sweeps, lasting about 40 seconds. This combined echo and listening procedure marginally reduced the asdic search efficiency, but gave a better chance of gaining hydrophone effect contact if the U-boat was travelling at speed. In addition, the tactical trials with *Seraph* showed that two escorts, by exchanging simultaneously recorded hydrophone effect bearings, could plot the intersection of the bearings and thereby locate the submarine, as had been suggested by an earlier DNOR theoretical study. The procedure relied heavily upon the efficiency of the plotting organization, and of rapid inter-ship communications. After the trials with *Seraph* a number of improvements to the asdic control were put in hand, designed to restore the efficiency of operation to that experienced with normal U-boats by providing automatic training of the sound beam to compensate for the relative movement of both ship and target, and devices to improve the use of the attack instruments.[26] Only in the longer term did improved detection gear and weapons become available. In the meantime, tactical adaptation could exploit the potential, and mitigate the limitations, of existing technology.

While considering the results of the trials with *Seraph*, McCrea thought that there might be some value in countering fast submarine with sonobuoys. These expendable radio sonobuoys consisted of a hydrophone suspended below a buoyant cylindrical case about three feet five inches long by four and a half inches in diameter. The sonobuoy was dropped near a suspected U-boat contact and any sounds picked up on the hydrophone were transmitted by a radio set to the aircraft.

The sonobuoys had a nominal life of about four hours, after which they self-scuttled. However, because of the acoustic frequencies at which these sonobuoys listened, their performance was likely to rapidly deteriorate as the target's depth increased.[27] It had originally been intended to follow the EG19's exercises with Coastal Command and the Fleet Air Arm trials but these were delayed and eventually flown spasmodically between November 1944 and April 1945 by Coastal Command's Air Sea Warfare Development Unit (ASWDU).[28] The sonobuoys used were American AN/CRT-1A types. The ASWDU concluded that the average detection range showed a tendency to increase as *Seraph*'s speed rose above five knots, with ranges in the order of 7,000–8,000 yards at speeds in the order of 12 knots. The results, however, were very dependent on the weather, so that when the sea state was greater than 4 the equipment ceased to be of much operational value. Although these results were encouraging, the trial contained no tactical element. *Seraph* was constrained to run in a straight line between pairs of sonobuoys at the prescribed speed and depth for the serial and the sonobuoys had to be launched by a range vessel, to avoid at least one third of the buoys failing if they were launched from an aircraft. Even then, their performance deteriorated as the battery ran down. The sonobuoy technology, introduced '… prematurely, in 1943 after inadequate trials and with over-optimistic ideas of its performance' was not sufficiently mature until the 1950s for open ocean searches.[29]

Further assessment of the type XXI

The details of the *Seraph* trials had been passed to the Americans and during the spring of 1945 the USN repeated the *Seraph* trials with USS *R-1*, which had also been streamlined (though with no other structural or propulsive changes). *R-1*, like *Seraph* for the British, was then used for training at the USN Fleet Sonar School, Key West, Florida. In Britain, too, further studies were initiated, training programmes started at WATU and a programme of sea training with *Seraph* begun for British and Canadian escort groups.[30] Some of the groups found the problem a difficult one, even when carrying out searches with five escorts on the tactical table, or attacking during sea practices.[31] The Type XXI would not always use high speed. The British thought that it would be used by the enemy to evade an aircraft or a ship (which the U-boat suspected had reported her position), to avoid an imminent attack during an anti-submarine action, or to reach a favourable attacking position when approaching a convoy.[32]

For the time being, the British had to make the best of the equipment they had to hand and to optimize its performance by adapting existing tactics and procedures. Considerable work was done at the research establishments on the effects of the new U-boats' speed and manoeuvrability on anti-submarine weapon performance, even though based on inadequate information. The trials with HMS *Seraph* had provided only a partial answer to the problem, because of the very limited time available to test equipment and tactics in all environmental conditions and against varying submarine tactics. The latter would, of course, be circumscribed by safety rules (though not to the same extent as in peacetime exercises).[33] Nevertheless, the trial results were seen by Captain R.J.R. Dendy, the Captain of HMA/SEE, to have been '... on the whole reassuring.'[34] Indeed the subsequent experience of high speed exercises with *Seraph*, and other converted S-class boats, suggested that certain factors weighted an engagement with a fast U-boat in favour of the hunting forces. While it was true that anti-submarine attacks had occasionally to be broken off, the prominent hydrophone effect had proved to be '... an aid to contact keeping, the prolongation of hunts and the provision of further opportunities for attack.' Also, due to the U-boat's relatively limited endurance at high speed the escorts could afford to wait until the U-boat slowed down before attempting an attack. Dendy was also comforted by the greater size of Type XXI, as against *Seraph*, or the captured Type VII, HMS *Graph*, so that the new U-boats would give stronger asdic returns and make them an easier target. The Mine Warfare Department produced a somewhat more cautious assessment that aligned more accurately with existing intelligence. They observed that the plan area of the Type XXI was only 20 per cent greater than *Graph*, which was not crucial to success with either Squid or Hedgehog. This was more dependent on the U-boat's speed, depth and subsequent manoeuvres.[35]

As the European war drew to a close McCrea produced a somewhat bleak but perceptive analysis of the effects of high submerged speed and endurance on submarine tactics and their consequences for anti-submarine forces. Up to the middle of 1943, U-boats had operated in packs and, by remaining largely on the surface, had maximized the chance of one member of the pack sighting a convoy. The mobility conferred by surface operations meant that some 70–80 per cent of the pack would intercept the convoy though, largely because of navigational difficulties, this would normally take two or three days. Without radar, the U-boats also had difficulty in remaining in contact, especially if forced to dive while the convoy executed an evasive turn. But it was the growing ubiquity of Allied air cover, which by 1944 forced the U-boats to spend two-thirds of their time submerged, that finally defeated the ability of the U-boat packs to locate and concentrate against convoys.[36] When aircraft were absent, the U-boats had normally been able to make an average transit speed of about 12 knots. Since most of the U-boat pack was able to make contact with the convoy within the first two days, the furthest U-boats would have converged from a range of some 500 miles. Assuming that navigation was no more difficult and that communications difficulties could be overcome, McCrea thought that a submarine operating entirely submerged, capable of an equivalent speed and endurance, that is, 12 knots for 48 hours, would achieve similar results. While beyond the capability of the Type XXI U-boat, McCrea thought that such performance could be developed within the next 10 years.

The Germans had also tried to use pack tactics to overwhelm a convoy's defences by concentrating a large number of U-boats around a convoy and attacking simultaneously. This objective proved elusive. Indeed so great were:

> ... his difficulties in bringing the majority of members of a pack into contact with the convoy sometime within the two or three days following an initial sighting, that the attainment of this primary objective represented about the limit of his capabilities. Once any particular U-boat gained contact it had to

make the best of its individual opportunity and no attempt could be made to concert its action with that of another member of the pack.[37]

McCrea pointed out that during the period of surface operations by U-boats, roughly one third of contacts led to an attack, and about a third of these attacks resulted in a torpedo hit. Most of the failed approaches were due to interceptions by the convoy escorts. Some of the failures were due to the navigational problem of achieving a firing position, given the relatively limited engagement envelope of the torpedoes then in use. For the future, the situation would be different because a fast deep U-boat would be very difficult to intercept, unless there were revolutionary developments in escorts. Moreover, with pattern-running and homing torpedoes there was '... practically no problem of reaching a firing position other than merely getting within range.' In addition these torpedoes could be fired without use of the periscope and each salvo fired was expected to claim a greater number of casualties. In the future torpedoes were likely, McCrea thought, to have a much longer range, so that, together with improved underwater performance, future U-boats were not expected to have much difficulty in converting contacts into attacks.

McCrea noted that US submarines, '... admittedly against a moderately ineffective defence', had been able to use their high surface speed to regain attacking positions, so that they could deliver an average of two (and sometimes as many as six) attacks during a single convoy engagement. The Type XXI, with its rapid re-loading torpedo system, ought to be able to achieve as much. Indeed, he gloomily predicted, if these boats could attack in packs, they might be able to create such confusion that there seemed little reason why, with a total load of 400 torpedoes, their attack might not annihilate a 100-ship convoy. McCrea thought this offered a challenge, for:

> ... the U-boat pack of the future (say about 10 years hence) could be more dangerous than the typical pack of the present war by a factor that might be of the order 100. This is not to say that its achievements would be measured by such a factor, but the figure is some index of the very big advances required in A/S measure[s].

But, he went on to say, the:

> ... primary objective of the pack would be rendered unnecessary if the U-boats could be informed of the position and movements of shipping from other sources than their own reconnaissance. If the enemy could maintain adequate air reconnaissance (or some system of radar relays) combined with adequate navigational aids, he might choose to dispense with the pack system. In certain circumstances he might thereby achieve a dispersal of our A/S forces and more immunity for his U-boats.[38]

At first sight McCrea's paper seems to offer a rather gloomy prognosis for the future, and was quite out of character with his numerous other analyses. But his paper, with remarkable insight, captures the nature of the problems and neatly encapsulates the challenge to be faced by anti-submarine forces for the future.

There is no doubt that the wartime Admiralty was confronting the issue with determination, if some apprehension too. They had focused the necessary resources of manpower and technical development on seeking solutions at sea, though these were likely to yield sparse results, given the evasive power of the new U-boats and the limitations of existing anti-submarine gear. The nascent problem drew attention to alternative methods, as Fawcett had pointed out. These were to include the intensification of bombing, in what became known as a strategy of 'attack-at-source', whose targets were U-boat production sites, the transport infrastructure needed to bring the prefabricated parts to the assembly yards, direct attacks on the assembly slips, an escalation of the mining of U-boat work-up areas, and so on. Although the enemy disparaged the operational capability of Allied anti-submarine forces to locate and attack the new U-boats, they were very alive to the severe threat posed by an Allied attack-at-source strategy, as was known by the Admiralty.[39]

Captain Roberts' interrogation of German U-boat officers

However, just as the threat became a reality, the war in Europe ended, and with it the resources rapidly began to diminish with the demobilization of many of the wartime experts. McCrea, for one, soon left the Admiralty. Nevertheless, it was clear to everyone that the Type XXI technology would set the future standard of submarine capability. It is not surprising, therefore, that the British (and the Americans) put a great deal of effort into extracting as much information as possible from their former enemies once the war was over. Thus, barely a fortnight after the European war ended, Captain G.H. Roberts of WATU led an Allied team of experts on a week-long visit to the Continent to interrogate German U-boat officers. He was accompanied by Commander P.W. Gretton, an experienced Escort Group commander, Group Captain Gates and representatives from Director, Naval Intelligence (DNI), DNOR and the USN.[40] There were no surprises from the interrogations. Roberts' visit largely confirmed British assessments of German tactics and also revealed the enormous gulf between the two navies in their ability to coordinate all the operational, technical and training aspects of the campaign. The agenda for the visit, however, illuminates the main British concerns over future anti-submarine warfare. Roberts clearly wished to interrogate as many German officers as possible but was limited in his subjects by the poor state of communications, the general dispersal of personnel (many of them were PoW in Russian hands) and the chaos following Germany's defeat. Nevertheless he was able to interview a number of key personnel, including Rear Admiral Godt, who had taken operational control of the U-boat arm after Dönitz became C-in-C of the German Navy. Other key witnesses were Commanders Hessler, Cremer and Schnee. The former, a successful U-boat commander before becoming Staff Officer Operations at the U-boat headquarters, had helped plan for the first Type XXI operations and clearly had a detailed, if somewhat uncritical, knowledge of their capability. Cremer and Schnee were also experienced U-boat commanders and had commanded the first two Type XXI U-boats, *U-2519* and *U-2511*. (A third veteran U-boat commander, Erich Topp, was appointed to *U-2513*.) Cremer's boat was, however, heavily damaged in an Allied air raid but Schnee, after a faltering start (due to serious technical defects), made one short operational sortie.[41]

Roberts concluded that the German plan was to continue the inshore campaign with the coastal Type XXIII, gradually replacing the Type VII schnorkel-fitted U-boats in this role, which had been a stop-gap solution. The Type XXI, itself a stop-gap until the Walter Type XXVI was available, was to re-establish ocean anti-convoy warfare.[42] Both Godt and Hessler affirmed that it was planned to resume U-boat pack operations in deep water with the Type XXI, although they admitted that '… the projected methods of attack in Packs by Type XXI had not yet been worked out …' in detail. Hessler, however, later mentioned that the:

> … final 'Battle Instructions for Type XXI and Type XXIII U-boats' were compiled from the evaluation of extensive sea trials carried out in one boat of each type, commanded by two well-trained officers, *Korvettenkapitän* Topp and *Kapitänleutnant* Emmermann.[43]

Consequently, the Germans had planned to operate Type XXIs individually in ocean operations until their capabilities were fully understood. They might then be used in shallow waters, though this large U-boat presented a strong asdic target and would be difficult to bottom safely. Furthermore, being a more complicated boat, it would be less resistant to depth-charge attack. Overall, the Germans thought, Type XXI was better adapted to open ocean operations. It became clear during the interrogations that the Germans had not developed a coherent concept of operations for the Type XXI and this impression was reinforced by subsequent questioning of U-boat personnel which became available to DAUD and DASW by the end of June 1945.[44] There was much faith that the 'new' technology would overcome operational problems, though for these to achieve their full operational capability would not be possible until their crews had gained experience. This would have taken time, which would have given the British the breathing space to hone their tactical counter-measures.

The Germans were pressed on their concepts for using these U-boats in ocean attacks. Ultimately, they wanted to use pack tactics after the crews had gained experience during solo operations. The intention was for pack tactics to be carried out submerged, which raised the tricky problem of communications, essential for coordinating the concentration of the pack and avoiding mutual interference during attacks. The Germans thought that the difficulties would have been overcome, perhaps by use of the new 'burst' radio transmitter system.[45] Cremer was of the opinion that submerged pack attacks could be made by using the good hydrophones and *Niebelung* (asdic) of the Type XXI, combined with the use of periscope observations either by day, or at night with a good moon. The great advantage conferred on the Type XXI by its high submerged speed was that it could close convoys from much wider angles than earlier boats, as Schnee remarked to Group Captain Gates. Closing at a speed of 10–11 knots was economical in battery usage, and left sufficient capacity for subsequent evasion. Once contact was made the

Germans would soon have the option of firing from outside the screen using long-range torpedoes. The balance of opinion was that the final screen penetration would be made at silent speed, about five knots, with the submarine bow-on to the convoy, so that she would present the smallest asdic echo. Even at eight or nine knots the Type XXI was no noisier than a Type VII at three or four knots. Once through the screen, the Type XXI's speed and endurance would allow her to get under the convoy where, in relative safety, she could fire torpedoes from deep. The most difficult problem, once under the convoy, was to maintain station there. It was easy, Roberts deduced, for the U-boat to fail to appreciate an alteration of course by the convoy, though he did not press the questioning for fear of revealing that this was in the current British inventory of counter-measures against a U-boat sheltering under a convoy. The Type XXI's high speed and great manoeuvrability was best reserved for avoiding attacks by anti-submarine vessels. However, Gates, drawing together the opinions of the other interrogators considered:

> ... that, generally speaking, we had given ... [the Germans] more credit than was their due. We were about 3 months ahead in anticipating the effects of the Type XXI U-boats and that we were inclined to give more credit than their tactical ability would really warrant.[46]

The potential threat posed by the Walter-boats, however, seemed altogether more formidable, and was at the forefront of Admiralty and Roberts' thinking. Roberts spent a fifth of his time in Germany specifically locating the positions where the Germans had scuttled the prototype Type XVII Walter-boats. He also questioned the German officers on the tactical use of the Type XXVI Walter-boats. These boats, Admiral Godt stated, were to have been large, ocean-going submarines, similar in size to the Type XXI, though construction had not yet started. The Type XXVI was planned to be capable of sustaining 23 knots for six hours, using its Walter-turbine propulsion system, after which it would have expended all of its hydrogen-peroxide fuel. The high, but limited endurance, sprint speed of the Type XXVI could be used to gain bearing to get into a good firing position and to avoid being attacked. These U-boats were also equipped with a conventional diesel-battery system, though of much lower capacity than that fitted in the Type XXI and little better than that of the Type VII. During the interrogation Admiral Godt exposed his technical ignorance of the Type XVII's capabilities, which he confused with those of the much more ambitious Type XXVI design.

Horton succinctly summarized the situation. 'We must be prepared,' he observed:

> ... for a definite increase in underwater speed with a new type of self-contained submerged propulsion ... and the U-boat virtually need never surface. But hand in hand with high underwater speed goes an increase in underwater noise. Hence, if the future U-boat decides to use its speed at an inopportune moment, it may well give away her presence at a considerable distance. It may, therefore, be deduced that if such high speed is to be available, it will be used mainly for withdrawal from being attacked by an escort vessel or

withdrawal to safety after firing torpedoes. I believe that the actual method of attack in the future will still be slow, stealthy, and silent.

This new propulsion may also affect torpedo design, and we may find long-range fast torpedoes fired at convoys from outside the screen. Yet I believe that the skilled torpedoman will prefer to get to short range in order to obtain maximum hits. This again implies close range and stealthy infiltration of the screen by the U-boat.

New tactics for attacking the fast U-boat must be devised, new types of faster escort vessels, and new types of weapons are very early and pressing requirements.[47]

The thrall of the Walter-Boat

At the end of February 1945 DNI reported on the German development of the small Type XVIIB and the large Type XXVI U-boats, both incorporating the Walter gas turbine propulsion unit for very high speed submerged. DNI's report confirmed that the Germans had completed at least three Type XVIIB and were building five more. DNI also thought that the Germans would start producing the Type XXVI shortly.[48] These boats potentially posed a dangerous threat and one that concerned the Admiralty. Perhaps the mesmerizing quality of high underwater speeds and technological novelty overwhelmed the objective review of their serious operational limitations, particularly their poor endurance. Nevertheless, Roberts paid a great deal of attention to these boats during his visit to Germany. When his report arrived in the Admiralty it was undoubtedly noted amongst the senior members of the Staff dealing with anti-submarine matters. Roberts' assessment emphasized the lack of any coherent German doctrine for the use of the Walter boats, but this did little to ameliorate the Admiralty's concern over the ability of existing weapons to deal with this 25-knot submarine.[49] Prichard immediately wrote to the Captains of HMS *Osprey* and HMA/SEE, enclosing a paper on the 'Use of Squid against the 25 Knot U-boat' and asking for comments as well as trials on the attack teachers. The problem, Prichard suggested, was a complex one, because the analysis would have to consider the '... efficiency of the asdic set and the manoeuvring qualities of the ship ...' in order to arrive at an estimate of the effectiveness of the weapon. It was also necessary to consider the modifications already planned to the weapon and asdic gear, which would be forthcoming in about five years' time.

In his paper, Prichard proposed to deal with the problem, firstly, over the next five years and, then, for the longer term. Squid, he noted, had been designed to destroy '... a slow-moving U-boat whose maximum diving depth was about 800 ft.' Because of the high sink rate of the Squid bombs, it was unlikely that a U-boat, even at great depth, would be able to avoid the pattern by an alteration of course, unless he used speeds in excess of three knots, or had ample warning of the moment of firing by the anti-submarine ship. Wartime experience suggested that conventional U-boats achieved neither of these criteria. Consequently, during the last months of the war, Squid-fitted ships were achieving a 60 per cent kill rate, double that of Hedgehog and 12 times higher than depth-charges. However, against a submarine capable of up to 25 knots the probability of success would be '... wholly different ... .'[50] Prichard cited several reasons for this. In any deliberate hunt against a fast submarine, attacks tended to delivered from the stern of the submarine, as the trials with *Seraph* had shown. At this aspect, accurate asdic ranging on the target would be made more difficult by the interference caused by the submarine's wake. Errors would, therefore, be introduced in the calculation of the moment to fire, and this, in turn, would degrade the accuracy of the attack. It was also possible that the hydrophone effect from the target would be so loud as to obliterate the echoes in the operator's headphones and on the asdic recorder, making it impossible to fire at all. Even if contact could be maintained, the submarine could make much greater use of the weapon's dead time, that is the time between the moment of firing and the arrival of the bombs at the preset target depth, to avoid damage from the pattern. The situation was equivalent to attacks with depth-charges against slow submersibles.

It might not be possible to set sufficient deflection on the Squid mounting to hit a submarine on a crossing course when it was taking avoiding action. The firing bearing would, therefore, have to be estimated by the ship's team. Similarly, in a counter-attack, when the submarine might be closing the anti-submarine ship at high speed the accuracy of the attack could be compromised by the high dynamics. 'In fact,' Prichard concluded:

> the difficulties of attack with present asdic and Squid gear are so numerous that nothing other than a 'snap' attack could reasonably be attempted against a U-boat travelling at 25 knots.[51]

At 25 knots, however, the hydrophone effect from a submarine, Prichard thought, would be very loud, making it possible for the anti-submarine ships to hold contact fairly easily, as least for a time. However, this presupposed that the asdic would function as a hydrophone at the high speeds necessary for the escorts to remain close to the target. This might be a particular problem if the submarine chose to evade at high speed and up sea. Anti-submarine ships might not be able to keep up and '... loss of contact might well be the rule ... .' Prichard observed that a new dome to house the asdic was being produced at the highest priority, which, he hoped, would allow asdics to be operated at 25–30 knots, by reducing effects of flow noise round the dome. In all this he was ignoring the possibility that, if the submarine were able to evade at great depth, then the hydrophone effect from its propellers might be much reduced, as DNOR and ASWORG had noted in earlier analyses.[52] Beyond the next five years, Prichard hoped that certain modifications would improve the situation. Squid, as had been foreseen a year earlier, needed to be '... adapted ... for use as an A/S gun.' In such a form the weapon would be used to fire salvoes of bombs '... with a fair degree of accuracy ...', either in a counter-attack or in a series of firings to achieve a kill. But this could only be attained '... in conjunction with improvements to the asdic gear ... .' These improvements were the adoption of the asdic split-beam technique (which eliminated the need for the 'cut-on' procedure) and PPI displays, which would allow a high speed contact to be held accurately. To hold contact, the asdic domes would have to be modified to allow operation '... in any seaway in which high speed is possible.' The asdic amplifiers, too, had to be modified '... to overcome the heavy masking of the echo by the hydrophone effect of the target, thus enabling a succession of attacks to be delivered on a fast moving target.'[53]

In this paper, Prichard had not quite defined the ultimate requirement for this type of weapon: the capability to fire on any bearing and at a variable range. He did, however, think that a weapon of the anti-submarine gun type held one major advantage over a homing torpedo, which could only hit or miss, and, therefore, was of little use in a counter-attack. Prichard hoped, too, that a submarine approaching a convoy at very high speed would produce so much noise that ample warning would be achieved, allowing the convoy to manoeuvre out of the U-boat's path. This tactic might be successful, he thought, since the U-boat itself would be deaf at these high speeds and would not appreciate the convoy's evasive turn until it slowed down to fire, when it might be too late. Prichard, however, was not taking into account the possibility mentioned elsewhere, that future submarines would be able to fire long-range torpedoes from well outside the detection range of escorts. At the time of writing the paper Prichard still anticipated that a partial answer to this problem would be deduced from the forthcoming trials with the captured Type XXI U-boats.

Over the next month both *Osprey* and the HMA/SEE wrote appreciations and carried out trials on the asdic attack tables to determine whether Squid would be able to cope with a submarine travelling at 20–25 knots. Their conclusion was that it would not. HMA/SEE considered the problem further in August but returned to the same conclusion. He also considered the relative merits of rocket-propelled and Squid-type weapons in dealing with these very fast submarines and concluded that the Squid-type seemed the more promising of the two. A few months later, in October and November 1945, Commander J. Grant, Commander (D) at Londonderry (another specialist anti-submarine officer), and HMA/SEE used the Londonderry Flotilla for trials against a high speed motor torpedo craft, simulating Walter-boats, to investigate the requirements for a future Squid-type weapon. These trials concluded that the current Squid and anti-submarine gear were inadequate and what was needed was a weapon capable of firing at a variable range and over an increased arc of training. This idea would eventually be the basis for the 'Limbo' anti-submarine mortar Staff Requirement issued in the following year. Meanwhile, *Osprey* and HMA/SEE investigated the ability of a '... striking force of five 35-knot escorts with air cooperation' to chase a 25-knot submarine. Their reports concluded that:

> A/S vessels could maintain contact provided surface weather conditions allowed them their full speed, but [the escorts] would have difficulty in attacking. Aircraft cooperation with sono-buoys would help but [it was HMA/SEE's] view that sono-buoys would have to be super-sonic and directional.[54]

Osprey and Londonderry undertook only one investigation into attacks on a convoy by a single Type XXI U-boat, which had to be cleared out from under the convoy. The emphasis in the first few months after the German war ended was clearly on investigations to counter the potential threat of the Walter-boat. At the end of the war:

> ... our Assault Teams entered Germany, and the secret of the German accomplishment was revealed. The importance of this discovery was appreciated at once and steps taken ... to control the establishment where this research was being carried out and to hold the German personnel employed there.[55]

These activities were a closely guarded Anglo-American secret.[56] This interest was reflected in the extraordinary measures taken by both Britain and the US to secure specimens of the existing Walter-boats, the Type XVIIs *U-1406* and *U-1407*, whose locations were confirmed and reported by Captain Roberts in May 1945. These boats had been scuttled, contrary to the surrender terms at the end of the war. The British were so irritated by this action that the German officer responsible was tried and imprisoned. So important was this acquisition that the British delegation negotiating the division of the German fleet with the Russians in August 1945 were told that the hydrogen peroxide fuel (known as high test peroxide, or HTP) facilities, needed to support these boats, should not be discussed with the Russians. The British had raised *U-1407* in June, and at first intended to re-fit her in Kiel. But in mid-July, the Controller called a meeting to discuss the Admiralty's policy on the future of submarine design, taking into account the information then being discovered in Germany. Considering the high potential of the Walter propulsion system, the meeting decided that *U-1407* should be brought over to Britain along with the higher powered Type 18X Walter-turbine (after it had been bench tested in Germany), with the project to be supported by Professor Walter's technical team. So, in August, *U-1407* was hurriedly sealed up and taken under tow to Barrow-in-Furness, followed shortly by much of the German personnel and test plant from the *Walterwerke* in Kiel. (By this time the USN had transported *U-1406* to America.)[57] As HMS *Meteorite*, *U-1407* became the only running Walter-powered submarine in 1949.[58]

Planning U-boats trials

In the autumn of 1944, while the trials with *Seraph* were still underway, Rear Admiral G.E. Creasy, Flag Officer (Submarines), proposed that some U-boats should be taken over at the German surrender for technical investigation and sea trials. Thus, naval trials were planned with Type VIIs *U-1105* (covered with rubber anti-asdic coating, 'Albrecht') and *U-1171*, as well as Gnat and LuT torpedo firings. Radar trials of schnorkel detection were also planned for Coastal Command.[59] Most of these trials were completed by the end of 1945.[60] Both Creasy and DNI thought that trials with the Type XXI were of '... the greatest importance.'[61] At first sight the captured Type XXIs appeared impressive. They were large submarines with a sleek hull form, as had been noted by Captain Gilbert Roberts during his inspection of two Type XXIs during his visit to Germany in late May 1945. Captain

Ashbourne, the Captain (S/M), Third Submarine Flotilla, conceded, that the Germans were '... streets ahead of [the British] ... in hull forms both as regards surface and dived speeds and deep diving depths.' But on closer inspection the '... general impression is one of admiral [sic] conception, but poor execution.' Overall, he added:

> ... these German submarines [were] ... a queer mixture of very good and very bad points. The acute shortage of non-ferrous metals is evident everywhere. Wiring and switch gear copper is cut to the barest minimum, and there is continual trouble with seizure of steel valve spindles and similar gear. There is lavish use of synthetic rubber for silent and anti-shock mountings and even deck mats.[62]

In a post-war lecture A.J. Sims of DNC's department, doubted the claim that German submarines were structurally any better than the British types. Sims thought '... that there have been many exaggerated statements concerning the actual achievements of the Germans. The type XXI class is a very good example ... .' The Germans hoped to achieve a collapse depth of 300 metres (975 feet) – slightly deeper than the British 'A' class. In fact due to design weaknesses the boat could only go to 180 metres – and even at this depth '... local structural weaknesses were observed.' There was, he claimed, '... no evidence of abnormal structural strength of German hulls compared with our latest standards.' They had achieved greater diving depths not by improvements to the hull designs but by reducing the safety factor applied to the operating depths permitted.[63]

In July 1945, as America, Russia and Britain were haggling over the fate of the surrendered German fleet, and especially the remaining U-boats, Creasy was preparing to start the trials with a Type XXI, in advance of any formal allocation of U-boats to Britain. British planning was already well advanced and by mid-July 1945, Admiral Creasy wanted to start with a Type XXIII, *U-2326*, followed by the Type XXI, *U-2502*, after completion of her essential docking. Consideration was also being given to experiments with the more radical design Type XVII Walter-boats. The Admiralty approved the proposed trials programme at the end of August, even though manpower to crew captured U-boats was scarce. It is easy to see why the British were so keen to undertake trials with a Type XXI U-boat, since it was the only existing submarine capable of 15 knots submerged, as well as with the even faster Walter-boats. But it is more problematic to understand why they continued with the trials with the Type XXIII. Probably sheer habit and curiosity played their part and the organizations simply wanted to know whether their assessments during the autumn of 1944 had been accurate. Furthermore, it should be remembered that the British knew at the time that Type XXIII U-boats had made at least three cruises in British waters, and that none had been sunk.[64]

With the defeat of Germany, there was no immediate threat to counter, for the Japanese were thought unlikely to make use of such technology in the short-term. Furthermore, at least notionally, Russia was still an ally, though in the longer term, it was realized that she now had access to the German operational methods and technology, and in particular the details of the Type XXI and Type XXVI boats. This would pose a serious post-war threat, and one which required urgent attention. However, for the immediate future, the Admiralty may have been hedging their bets in case the war against Japan was protracted, in which case a serious inshore threat might be met when British forces were faced with the prospect of invading the Japanese homeland. There was a wealth of tactical knowledge amassed by the British in inshore anti-submarine warfare over the previous year, and there seemed clear benefits to this wisdom being passed on to British and American commands in the Far East in an easily digestible form.

Interrogation of German PoW had established that details had been passed to the Japanese on U-boat designs, including the schnorkel, as well as new torpedoes, communications, radar, and German Search Receiver (GSR) equipment.[65] The British did not rate the Japanese submarine force as highly as the defeated German U-boats, but it seemed logical that British developments should be measured against the technical capability of the Germans, even though it was assessed that the Japanese were unlikely to adopt all the German technology.[66] The HMS *Osprey* Captain, Dunoon, had been kept informed and had formed a new tactical unit at Christmas 1944 to deal with training for Far East operations.[67] Notwithstanding the effort being devoted to forecasting countermeasures to fast U-boats, the main operational focus remained on dealing with existing U-boat types. Prichard, for example, made it clear that fast U-boats were to be expected in any future wars, and investigation of the tactics involved was to be prominent in the instruction of anti-submarine specialist officers. But, for officers earmarked for operations against the Japanese the emphasis should be on inshore operations against conventional U-boats, and Prichard:

> ... considered that to give undue prominence to fast U-boats would not only be a waste of time but might lead to the employment of wrong tactics against the U-boats more likely to be encountered.[68]

In mid-June 1945, Captain Howard-Johnston, DAUD, instructed his staff to prepare a paper encapsulating the experience of inshore operations against German U-boats, which might have application to the Allied operations in coastal waters during the planned landings on the Japanese mainland.[69] Over the next few weeks, the British inshore anti-submarine experience was drawn together during a series of weekly meetings, in cooperation with Captain Prichard. A joint draft paper was issued to other interested staff divisions on 5 August with comment requested within 10 days. They clearly had no knowledge of the imminence of the atomic bomb attacks, although the uncertainty over the effects these weapons would have may have not deterred Howard-Johnston and Prichard. The paper was then to be sent to the Commander-in-Chief, East Indies, and to Admiral Nimitz. In the event, the Japanese surrendered after the dropping of the two atom bombs on 6 and 9 August 1945 and the joint paper was withdrawn.[70]

Prichard emphasized that the Admiralty's assessment of the future threat in Japanese waters was more focussed on an inshore campaign, rather than the start of ocean pack tactics. As a result information was being collated from PoW and captured German papers.[71] Against this background, trials against the coastal Type XXIII could prove an invaluable addition and the Admiralty were keen to pursue them using the captured *U-2326*. In any case the British hand was forced by the series of defects with the Type XXIs which meant, DASW pointed out, that '… only the Type XXIII coastal U-boat, *U-2326*, was now available as a target.'[72] But *U-2326* also had her share of engine and schnorkel defects and it was not until July that she successfully completed her first dive, followed by First of Class trials at the end of August 1945 during which *U-2326* only achieved 9.7 knots submerged. This, Admiral Creasy pointed out, was below her '… reputed speed of 13 to 13½ knots …,' though her endurance was just under two hours.[73] A higher speed of just over 11 knots was eventually attained, but only at the expense of overloading (and damaging) the main motor.[74] Then under the control of Commander J. Grant, Commander (D) of the Londonderry Flotilla, in HMS *Fame*, she was used for a repeat of the earlier *Seraph* tactical serials. One key element of these trials was to determine which was the best weapon and attack procedure against the U-boat. The anti-submarine ships were to stream Unifoxer continuously, which would allow any tactical disadvantage during high speed avoiding action by the submarine to be noted. During the trials the escorts were using the now routine combined 80°–80° echo and hydrophone effect sweep. It had also been planned to investigate sonobuoy tracking of the Type XXIII but Grant reported that Coastal Command had cancelled these trials, which were, instead, to be completed against a British S-Class fast submarine.

In the opinion of Captain Lord Ashbourne, Captain, Third Submarine Flotilla, there was '… little to commend this cheap submarine.'[75] Nor, during the tactical trials, was naval opinion greatly improved. Grant reported that '… the Type XXIII U-boat does not appear to be of particularly robust construction nor can it dive to great depths or proceed at very high speed.'[76] Although, Captain W.J.W. Woods, who had relieved Ashbourne in September 1944, later admitted that *U-2326* had proved to be '… a small and handy submarine' that had advantages in both attack and evasion, it was difficult, he thought, for a Type XXIII to remain under a convoy as an evasive tactic. He also emphasized that, given her small size, *U-2326* offered a surprisingly good asdic target, which made it unwise to bottom to evade modern anti-submarine vessels. However, the trials did not go as well as these comments might suggest. *U-2326* operated at various speeds between three and seven and a half knots, and occasionally bottomed, but as a result of peacetime safety rules, anti-submarine ships were not to counter-attack during the tactical serials until five minutes after a ship in the convoy was 'torpedoed', by which time *U-2326* would have cleared the immediate area unhindered.[77] Of course, as her Captain noted, the U-boat was not put under realistic pressure by the anti-submarine ships, because they could not actually drop depth-charges, and consequently, neither the submarine nor the escorts behaved as they would in war. Although Grant conformed to tactical doctrine by ordering 'Artichoke', 'Square' and 'Scabbard' searches, he failed to find *U-2326* because, as was normal for shallow water operations, interfering echoes and non-subs delayed the full implementation of each plan.

The subsequent analysis of the serial also showed how untidy tactics could be in practice, when compared to the geometrical neatness of the tactical manual.[78] This was well understood by experienced practitioners and helps to explain the emphasis placed on initiative by the wartime training organization. As the exercise played out, Grant was faced with an impossible dilemma: whether to try to cover the furthest extent of the U-boat's possible evasion, or to assume that she had bottomed near the position of original torpedo attack. He did not have the assets to cover both possibilities, and in any case did not have the strength to cast the wider search. And this against a U-boat capable of only 11 knots!

Type XXI trials and tribulations

As the summer of 1945 wore on, the Type XXIII trials, although reasonably successful in their own right, highlighted the shortfall in these submarines' speed when compared to their design performance. Doubts, too, were soon entertained over the performance to be expected from the Type XXIs in British hands, when these boats experienced a series of major defects (some of them dangerous to submarine safety), and inspections revealed their poor build quality. At the time it seemed, therefore, a reasonable supposition that the Type XXI would be little faster than the British modified S-class submarines. The prime purpose of using the Type XXI boats was to establish the capability of existing anti-submarine gear in dealing with a 15-knot target, but, if this speed could not be obtained, there was little advantage in persevering with the German boats and having to cope with the endless defects. The British S-class would do. Furthermore, towards the end of the year the problems surrounding the Walter types became apparent. A meeting was held by DNC at Bath on 27 November 1945 where future submarine design was discussed.

It quickly became apparent that a fast submarine target for anti-submarine detection and weapon development would not be available for some years and *U-1407* would not be available until late 1948 at the earliest. Other possibilities, such as new construction, were even more remote. The meeting concluded that a more extensively modified S-class submarine would be able to achieve speeds of up to 16 knots and, given the urgency of providing a fast target, plans for such a conversion should be pressed forward as soon as possible.[79] The problems with the Walter-boats were largely technical in nature. *U-1407*, considering her dilapidated state when she arrived in Britain, needed a substantial amount of work before she would be ready for sea trials. The Walter-turbines also needed further development, and there was the major task of supplying and storing adequate quantities of the hydrogen peroxide fuel (as well as specialized diesel fuel). All this entailed major expense.[80] This lack of a high-speed target was becoming critical if adequate testing was to be carried out of the new, improved anti-submarine gear and weapons which would be ready at the beginning of the 1950s.

Once the trials with *U-2326* were completed, Admiral Creasy, Flag Officer (Submarines), reduced her to care and maintenance at Lisahally and, after a long delay, the Admiralty approved her loan to the French Navy in early 1946.[81] While the trials with *U-2326* were underway, it had been hoped to run the Type XXI, *U-2502*, but she proved to be an even bigger headache. She suffered a depressing series of defects, which required the U-boat to be docked, but while on passage to the shipyard at Cammell Lairds she suffered a main motor breakdown '... in a big way ... .' The repairs to *U-2502* would be a complicated and expensive operation and there was no guarantee that she would not break down again. All in all, she was becoming a project the British could ill afford. 'It has therefore been decided,' Ashbourne wryly commented, 'to return this model to Lisahally and draw another one.'[82] This boat, *U-3017*, was in little better state, but it was still a heavy blow when she suffered a battery explosion in August 1945 that caused extensive damage and put her out of commission.[83]

The explosion damaged *U-3017* and injured one officer and seven ratings. The Board of Inquiry found that the accident was due to the abandonment of British procedures in favour of those used by the Germans. The Board suggested the German practices had caused a number of battery explosions in other Type XXIs, and had possibly led to their loss.[84] These rumours were supported by the interrogation of an experienced German Engineer Officer who recalled four battery explosions in Type XXIs. He stated that the main electrical cables ran in the bilges under the battery compartment, and that low insulation and the presence of bilge water caused arcing. With poor ventilation when the battery was freely exuding hydrogen (during charging), the likelihood of an explosion was high. This was a problem that also exercised the designers of the 'Guppy' conversions of US Navy fleet submarines to achieve high underwater speed. At least one, USS *Cochino*, suffered a battery explosion and sank.[85] This dangerous design fault, along with other defects, meant, in Creasy's opinion, that:

> ... before *U-3017* or any other Type XXI U-boat could be considered suitable for trials of a prolonged nature ..., a complete and extensive refit and survey would be necessary.[86]

A despondent Ashbourne realized that they were virtually back where they started and it looked as though the working-up of this type would be a protracted business. These engineering problems with the Type XXIs in British hands showed that if any of them were to be made fit for trials they would need substantial dockyard work. This would strain the existing British submarine refit facilities desperately needed for work on war-worn British submarines. These boats if they were to be more than 75 per cent effective also needed to be fitted with the latest periscope radar equipment.[87] Moreover, as Creasy observed, the Germans had not succeeded in getting these submarines into an operational state. He also had in mind the preliminary results of the speed trials with the Type XXIII, *U-2326*, which had failed to achieve its design speed by over two knots, when he pessimistically questioned whether the Type XXIs would achieve a submerged speed much in excess of the converted S-Class.[88] This proved to be a crucial though, in hindsight, wrong assessment.[89] Still, at the time, Creasy's judgement made sense and he therefore recommended that the trials of a type XXI U-boat should be cancelled. He consoled himself, and the

Admiralty with the knowledge that the US were intending to carry out trials with two Type XXIs, the results of which, it was hoped, would be shared with the British. In the meantime, a complete report of the type XXIII trials was forwarded to the USN.[90] On 14 October 1945, the same day as the tactical convoy exercise with *U-2326*, the Admiralty accepted Admiral Creasy's recommendation and cancelled the trials with the Type XXIs, *U-3017* and *U-2518*, remaining in British hands. These two U-boats were to receive 'Care and Maintenance', though the Admiralty accepted, they would both require a substantial amount of work before they could be made ready for any future trials. There was, however, little prospect that they would ever be brought forward. It was against this background that the decision was taken to loan the Type XXI, *U-2518* (along with a Type XXIII, *U-2326*), to France. Thus, until a British 15-knot underwater target was available, the British remained reliant on the results of the US Type XXI trials, further trials with the 12-knot *Seraph*-types, and on theoretical assessments.

The decision, sound though it seemed at the time, provoked considerable concern amongst many departments. The wide interest in the planned trials the Type XXI highlighted the importance attached to investigations with a submarine capable of speeds in the order of 15 knots, both to test existing anti-submarine equipment and tactics, and also to provide data from which new weapons and tactics could be developed. The cancellation of the trials with the Type XXI was, therefore, a serious blow to these development programmes. Leon Solomon of DNOR suggested that the Americans should be asked to confirm their intention to continue with the trials, for if they too were to cancel it would leave both nations with a lack of information on fast submarines, until data was available from the captured Walter-boat, *U-1407*.[91] The Director of the Operations Division replied that he had ascertained, unofficially, from a submarine officer on the US Navy staff in London that the Type XXIs in America were being refitted, after which it appeared that the Americans planned to continue with sea trials.[92] The British decision to abandon the Type XXI trials was made just as the anti-submarine warfare divisions were undergoing a major reorganization. In particular, the streamlining of the anti-submarine divisions under Captain Lord Ashbourne was to help focus attention on the review of anti-submarine doctrine as will be recounted shortly, but in the meantime Ashbourne knew nothing of the decisions to abandon the trials.

Ashbourne had not been party to the discussions over the cancellation of the Type XXI trials until November, when Solomon, who had worked closely with the anti-submarine divisions during the war, included Ashbourne on the distribution of the relevant files. Coordination at this time was not helped by considerable turmoil in the Naval and Scientific Staffs as the organization was streamlined.[93] Ashbourne caustically complained that he was acutely interested in the prospect of tactical trials with the Type XXI. 'The absence of a 15 knot target for A/S Trials,' he pointed out, 'will greatly handicap long-term development work on a weapon to counter 20 knot or faster U-boats.'[94] Ashbourne, partly from first hand experience of these boats, reluctantly accepted the situation and, in turn, added other departments to the file's distribution. DNC noted that a great deal of technical data was available on the Type XXI from German sources and this would be distributed in due course. He added that investigations were underway into a further increase to the underwater speed of the converted S-Class, so that the control of submarines at these high speeds could be explored. Such plans were also supported by the Director of Scientific Research (DSR), and the Director of Torpedoes and Mining (DTM), who was pursuing weapons to counter the fast submarine, and who was firmly of the opinion that essential trials should be carried out with a British fast target.[95]

New organization and old timers at the Admiralty

First, some myths have to be disposed of. The Admiralty has often been characterized as an organization where there was:

> ... discomfort with new ideas, a preference for 'wait and see', gradual acceptance of initiative if and when established by senior or political decision, much referral to committees, much consultation, much anxiety to involve every one with an interest.[96]

There is some truth in these assertions, and may reflect what the Admiralty eventually became, but during the period under consideration here, the Admiralty proved to be a very different animal. When Admiral of the Fleet A.B. Cunningham joined the Admiralty as First Sea Lord in October 1943, he was shocked by the number of departments and people who had to be consulted before decisions were possible. Cunningham had been used to a small operational staff in the Mediterranean, but he soon realized that the Admiralty was actually a well lubricated organization. By 1944 it had developed into a supple and creative agency, well able to meet the challenges of tactical and technical changes by the enemy, though to outsiders, like Cunningham, who were unused to the changes of pace brought about by the war, it treated most complex problems as matters of daily routine.[97] It was, unlike the War Office and Air Ministry, staffed by relatively few service officers, so delegation was commonplace.[98] Nevertheless, by the end of the war it had become a massive bureaucracy with parts of the organization spread across the country. The Naval Staff alone consisted of 17 Divisions, compared to six in April 1939.[99] Work had been in hand for some time to rationalize this structure, and in particular to bring together many of the aspects of underwater warfare. As a result of the conclusions of the Phillips and, later, Middleton Committees, it had been decided to amalgamate the Torpedo and the Anti-Submarine Branches and this decision resulted in the formation of a single division of the Naval Staff whose '... prime concern ... was the more effective integration of A/S training and weapon development.'[100] This new Division, responsible to Assistant Chief of Naval Staff (Warfare), subsumed the wartime DASW and DAUD, and elements of four other divisions. It was known as the Torpedo, Anti-Submarine and Mine Warfare Division (DTASW), and formed in September 1945. DTASW included a submarine qualified staff officer, though Flag Officer, Submarines, continued to provide detailed advice in his sphere of expertise.

The first Director of the TASW Division was Captain Lord Ashbourne, who had specialized in submarines in 1925 and had served as Chief Staff Officer to Flag Officer, Submarines, between 1940 and 1942. He had also been the Captain of the Third Submarine Squadron during the planning of the trials with the captured German Type XXIII, *U-2326* in the autumn of 1945. The section of DTASW which is most important to the events being described here was the anti-submarine section under Captain P.W. Burnett, DSO, DSC, and included Commander G.A.G Ormsby, DSO, DSC, and Lieutenant Commander J.P. Mosse, DSC. It took some six months for the vast Admiralty machine to slow down, and during that time the Staff Divisions still worked seven days a week.[101] Initially there was much to do and DTASW's responsibilities were legion. Those which pertain to anti-submarine warfare included policy, planning, tactics (of ships and aircraft), dispositions, staff requirements for new sensors and weapons, and training, but he was also responsible for publications dealing with these topics, documenting their history, and attending various committees.[102]

It was Burnett, as Assistant Director (A/S), with his team, who shouldered most of this burden. All of them were anti-submarine specialists. Burnett had completed the long anti-submarine course in 1933, when Howard-Johnston was a course officer, and at the time when anti-submarine warfare was undergoing a major review which emphasized the problems of direct convoy defence (even though asdic was at last becoming effective), and the need for vigorous offensive measures.[103] The other two, Ormsby and Mosse had completed their courses in 1935 and 1936. In DTASW Burnett and Ormsby appear to have worked closely together on the staff papers. The former was noted as a man with 'a fresh analytical approach to AS warfare.'[104] Both men had passed out of Dartmouth in the top half dozen of their course. Mosse had been indoctrinated into Ultra during the war, while in a staff appointment. All three had had considerable experience in command at sea, where both Burnett and Ormsby had been Senior Officers of Escort Groups in the Atlantic, Arctic and Indian Oceans, and all three had been instrumental in the destruction of several U-boats.[105] Most of the early high-scoring U-boat killers had been non-anti-submarine specialists or 'salt horse' officers. Captain F.J. Walker had been something of the exception, though many of the regular anti-submarine specialists had, perforce, been employed in the early stages in training and staff appointments, for at the beginning of the war there were only 60 anti-submarine specialists available for appointment.[106] Burnett was one of the anti-submarine specialists who was very successful when he went back to sea in 1943.[107] It was these men, under Ashbourne, all of whom had risen through merit and not through peacetime patronage, who set to work to produce a comprehensive review of how anti-submarine warfare should be conducted in the face of the new threat from Russia.

5   Short-term problems, long-term solutions, 1946–47

Assessments of the Russian threat

Anti-submarine warfare during the interwar period '... was initially driven by a general awareness of the potential threat posed by submarines.'[1] This generic view had only become more focussed in the late 1930s, as the strength of the nascent German U-boat arm became apparent. Thereafter doctrine had developed rapidly to counter the immediate and dangerous threat as the U-boat campaign escalated through the Second World War. In the immediate aftermath of the Second World War the anti-submarine measures necessary to deal with the wartime submersible and schnorkel-fitted U-boats were well understood, but there had been no practical experience against submarines capable of high underwater speed. It was assumed that there would be no resurgence of the submarine threat from Germany (and much had been done to ensure that this was the case). Russia was, therefore, the only possible future enemy. Indeed, many in the British establishment had come to that conclusion several years earlier. By 1943–44 some elements, at least, of the British intelligence organization were convinced that states outside the Axis powers would pose a post-war threat, and Russia was singled out as an especially important case. The intelligence agencies began (and in some cases, continued) covert operations against her.[2]

As the war came to a close, Intelligence Assault Units, such as 30 AU, were moving into Germany with the forward combat elements '... looking for all kinds of German documents, experimental weapons and atomic plant.'[3] This was as much to exploit the sources for Allied benefit, as to deny them to the Russians. In the immediate aftermath of the war, however, there seems to have been little direct penetration of Russian encrypted communications as had been of inestimable importance in the war against the Axis powers, even though the Russians used captured Enigma machines at the end of the war.[4] They changed the settings and were more careful in the use of the machines, a factor which boded ill for the post-war cryptanalysts. There was, however, continued penetration against some Middle-East nations in the post-war era. It is possible that some Russian activity was revealed by these sources.[5] Thus, although some of the sources may have been of a sensitive kind, most intelligence of Russian capabilities and intentions was '... compiled largely from general background information ... .'[6] At least, the wartime cooperation between Britain and America in communications intelligence matters was set to continue with little interruption, albeit with some organizational changes.⁷ The extent of the intercept organization was, however, much reduced when compared to the scale of effort employed against Germany. And, as the British Chiefs of Staff (CoS) noted in May 1947, another problem was '... the high standard of security achieved [by the Russians] renders our collection of intelligence difficult ... .'⁸ It was not until the 1950s, too late for many of the deliberations covered in this monograph, that, so it seems, some, if limited, progress may have been achieved in communications intelligence against the Russians. As Admiral F.S. Low, USN, reported:

> The most important source of intelligence on Russian Undersea Warfare is Communications Intelligence (Comint). This now supplies a large measure of the authentic information obtained, and is potentially the most valuable component of operational intelligence in wartime. ...
>
> The present Comint facilities can obtain and analyze only a fraction of the traffic estimated to be on the air. Moreover, the presently available personnel cannot fully exploit the traffic which is now acquired.⁹

In the late 1940s, however, detailed calculations of Russian intentions and capabilities could not be based on much direct empirical evidence. The Admiralty was thus driven by default towards a generic threat assessment. This might seem an unsatisfactory, even worrying, state of affairs, but the conclusions drawn proved to be remarkably prescient. The deliberations owed much of their success to the six stressful years of practice during the war against Germany. The secret lay in the cooperation between the various departments of the Royal Navy which meant, for example, that widespread home-grown technical expertise could be brought to bear on accurately interpreting an often piecemeal and partial intelligence picture. Nowhere was this more evident than in the assessments of the German fast U-boat development. The Admiralty had become adept at gauging enemy capability, if not always intentions, and this expertise could be turned against the Russian threat during the first months of peace. What little knowledge that was available on Russian submarine capabilities tended to discount any immediate threat to Western trade or military operations.¹⁰ After some deliberation, the Joint Intelligence Committee (JIC) concluded in the spring of 1946, that Russia took '... a great interest in submarine warfare and in this particular arm of the Naval Service she has shown herself to be more proficient than in any other,' but that, 'She is, however, still inexperienced in attack tactics.'¹¹ A few months later, NID reinforced this assessment. 'The Russians,' they thought:

> ... are far from being a nation of seamen, and this weakness is reflected in the operation of their submarines, however technically good these boats may be. Their attack technique is amateurish to a degree ... . The submarines themselves are probably capable of carrying heavy armament a long way with reliability, but are by no means certain of hitting the target when they get there. Unless their evasive tactics have been much improved in the last year

or so, they would stand little chance against our escort groups, and we have no information that attack-training has been carried out by them to any degree. This particularly applies to the large Russian submarines.[12]

The apparent strength of the threat came from the large numbers of submarines in the Red Navy. They had already successfully carried out one large building programme, and now possessed about 210 submarines, which included 10 ex-German types. However, many of these Russian boats currently in service were obsolete submersibles and, although most of their ocean-going submarines were similar to the wartime German Type VII, none were fitted with a schnorkel. As for the future, it was assumed that Russia would, with:

> ... German assistance and methods, particularly in connection with pre-fabricated submarines [Type XXIs and the like], would enable her to construct a formidable Submarine Force in a comparatively short time.[13]

NID later assessed that '... 40 sections of Type XXI submarines were brought to Leningrad between October 1946 and June 1947 from Danzig.'[14] Apart from the four Type XXIs sent to Russia as part of the Tripartite Agreement, NID soon formed the opinion that they had about an additional eight of that type, along with a number of ex-German schnorkel-fitted Type VIIs and IXs and, perhaps a few Type XXIIIs.[15] Furthermore, it was known that the Russians had captured plans of the Type XXI and the Type XXVI Walter-boats, though NID thought it unlikely that they could produce a home-grown version of this latter type until 1949 at the earliest. (In fact, a Russian-built version of the Type XXVI was used for trials between 1955 and 1959 but, following an explosion during a submerged run, she was decommissioned. By then the British were successfully running HM Submarines *Explorer* and *Excalibur* both with improved HTP turbine designs. In 1945–46, it was widely assumed that the Russians would make use of the Type XXI U-boats allocated to them after the Allied negotiations over the disposal of the German Navy, as well as other partially completed examples captured during the Russian's advance into Germany. It now seemed, however, that the Russians gained little benefit from their trials. All the captured Type XXIs were scrapped or scuttled by early 1948, though the Russians ran their allocated Type XXI boats until 1958.)[16]

The intelligence assessments between 1945 and 1948, notwithstanding the lack of direct current Soviet sources, could benefit from wartime experience of Russian operations. For example, a great deal of operational intelligence on the Russian air forces was obtained during the war from Ultra decrypts of *Luftwaffe* intelligence reports from 1943 onwards.[17] To this was added a substantial corpus of information derived from German officers who were either interrogated, or employed to write studies of German operational and technical matters. In addition, the vast haul of captured enemy documents was exploited by NID, and others, to derive lessons from German technology and operational techniques.[18] This latter source included items such as interrogation summaries and translations of Soviet press articles relating to internal conditions of the Soviet Union. At the tactical level, the 'Operation of U-boat Type XXI', issued by the German Naval Headquarters, was thoroughly examined by DAUD, just before it was absorbed into DTASW, and a précis reproduced in the last wartime issue of the *Monthly Anti-Submarine Report*.[19] The Admiralty also produced detailed assessments of lessons which could be drawn from German errors, because it was assumed that the Russians might arrive at similar conclusions. An example was the German failure effectively and consistently to integrate aircraft reconnaissance with U-boat operations, which reinforced the Admiralty's interest in the Soviet air forces. It later transpired that the Russians had indeed realized the significance of the German failure.[20]

The German documents were ruthlessly mined by NID until 1948, by which time much of the initial post-war anti-submarine doctrine was established by the Naval and Air Staffs. The files were then transferred to the Historical Section where they continued to be used for historical analysis.[21] These sources were compared with the direct experiences of British and American liaison officers to the Soviet services during the war. Together they confirmed no very great opinion of the Russian submarine operational capability, as Commander H.S. Mackenzie, for example, noted after at least one war patrol in a Soviet submarine. He recalled that since '… their A/S training is so backward is it not likely that their submarine tactics, particularly in attacks may be backward also?' His belief was that Russian submarine Commanding Officers' attacks were, at best, amateurish.[22] These views, the Historical Section later pointed out, had to be considered in the context of the difficult environmental conditions in which many Russian submarines had operated.[23] NID noted, however, that the Russians appeared to be taking a great interest in the use of hydrophones and, in this connection, were exploiting the German scientists and technicians they held.[24] Mackenzie himself went on to become 'Teacher' at the Royal Navy's Submarine Commanding Officers' Qualifying Course, before representing Flag Officer, Submarines (FOSM) at the Sea/Air Warfare Committee meetings.[25]

When all this work was integrated with the detailed studies completed on both sides of the Atlantic by the wartime Operational Research and technical staffs, the whole represented a comprehensive evaluation of the potential to be expected from the new submarine types. This picture of the threat was all available to Burnett and his team, and could be used in two ways. When the limitations of current Soviet technology and operational art were stripped out, a 'worst case' scenario was generated and this allowed the Admiralty to gauge the ultimate counter-measures needed. This was complicated because anti-submarine equipment development programmes had to be formulated on assumptions of the enemy capabilities some 15 years hence. But when the threat assessment was taken as a whole, it allowed the Admiralty, with some confidence, to accept the risk of deferring immediate, extensive modifications to ships, equipment and weapons, for it assumed that Russia's poor submarine operational competence ameliorated the severity of the threat, at least in the short term. For example, by late 1948, the JIC believed that even by 1957 the Russians would still not '… think themselves capable of coordinated pack attacks on escorted convoys.' The JIC further considered:

... that their methods are far more likely to be comparable to those used by the Germans in World War I; but they may hope that such devices as homing torpedoes will at least partially offset their tactical shortcomings.[26]

When DNI circulated its 'Russian Naval Tactics' paper in October 1946 to the Naval Staff, Deputy Chief of Naval Staff (DCNS) '... directed that an argument was to be developed as to the number of escort vessels we would require to meet this threat ... .'[27] This task would fall heavily upon D of P and others, but within DTASW there seems to have been no direct pressure from an impending threat to drive anti-submarine development, because the Russian danger was not yet well developed and would not be so until, it was assessed, 1955–60.[28] There was, of course, as the Chiefs of Staff noted in May 1947, a need for a state of preparedness.[29] Over the next two years the Admiralty repeatedly asked the JIC to assess:

> ... the capabilities and intention of the Russians and to forecast the probable scale and nature of attack in various possible theatres of war both in the near future and in some years ahead.

The appreciations were, generally, accurate in terms of actual strength of the Russian forces, but, the Admiralty were concerned that the JIC '... tended to exaggerate Russian potentialities.' This was serious, because, the Admiralty pointed out:

> ... not only our present plans but also the future disposition of forces and the build up of military strength depends so greatly on what we estimate to be the Russian plans ... .[30]

Financial considerations would heavily influence the outcome of these deliberations, at least in terms of the quantity of equipment that could be provided. But at least a start was being made on the development of the doctrine for how these forces were to be operated. These implicitly assumed the ultimate state of British strength which could be achieved some years into another World War. These were the conditions which officers, like Ashbourne and Burnett had been accustomed to for much of their seagoing wartime experience. Compromises would have to be made at the beginning of a future war, as had been the case at the start of the Second World War. However, apart from issues over the numbers of ships, aircraft and submarines available to counter the predicted threat, there remained the question of how the anti-submarine units, and their equipment should be best used to counter the enemy's high-speed submarines. The wise counsel of staff officers, like Ashbourne and Burnett, was that unless work was done now and the issue kept at the top of the naval agenda, it would be too late to improvise technical counters within the likely warning time available, after the Russians realized their potential.

E.M. Gollin, the new Director of Operational Research (DOR), was also involved in the process. Gollin had been seconded to DNI as the Senior Scientific Officer during the war and was closely involved in the assessment of the fast submarine threat from 1944 onwards, and was undoubtedly indoctrinated into Special

Intelligence matters.[31] The Admiralty and Air Ministry were to form the Sea/Air Warfare Committee (SAWC) to coordinate anti-submarine developments, as will be described shortly. The SAWC, and its sub-committees, all regularly attended by DTASW, considered '… special papers of a particularly secret nature …', which doubtless contained, or were based on, intelligence assessments. On occasion papers considered were directly provided by DNI. American attendance at these committee meetings was commonplace, and the papers – especially those relating to anti-submarine matters, were passed on to the USN via the British Admiralty Delegation (BAD) in Washington.[32] It seems, then, that in the early days of peace, DNI was mainly concerned with the exploitation of German documents. This is little different to the practice adopted during the war when the fast submarine threat was first identified.[33] Intelligence and operational divisions had been highly integrated during the Second World War, and there is no reason to suppose that this close relationship entirely evaporated in the early days of peace. It is certain, with the increasing focus on the developing Cold War, that by the end of the decade that the Naval Staff divisions – including DTASW – were working in close coordination with DNI.[34]

Policy review of methods for attacking submerged submarines

As soon as they were in post, Ashbourne's Anti-Submarine Section under Burnett began work on the policy and doctrine papers to guide anti-submarine tactical and technical development during the immediate post-war years. They first surveyed the methods of attacking submerged submarines by surface vessels and aircraft. The paper, which was ready for Admiralty Board approval in March 1946, divided the future into two periods, separated by the year 1950.[35] For the near-term, up to 1950, anti-submarine forces would be pitted against submarines of the capability of the German Type XXI and Type XXIII U-boats, which probably represented the best submerged performance currently available in an operational-type submarine. The anticipated performance of the various types was tabulated by Ashbourne. The trials carried out by the Londonderry Flotilla with the Type XXIII, *U-2326*, in the autumn of 1945 had confirmed that against a submarine capable of submerged speeds up to 11–12 knots, the existing Squid and asdic gear were able '… to ensure a reasonable chance of success in an attack.'[36] The urgent requirement, then, was to establish whether existing ship anti-submarine gear was capable of competing with submarines with a submerged speed of 15–18 knots. However, with no fast targets available, and the prospect of one a distant hope, Ashbourne had to settle for comprehensive sea trials with *Sceptre*, one of the modified 12-knot S-Class submarines. He hoped it would be possible to extrapolate the results to be expected against a 15-knots submarine. *Sceptre*, which only seemed to be capable of 11 knots, exercised for two days with HM Ships *Fame* and *Hotspur* of the Londonderry Flotilla and the results merely confirmed those discovered with *Seraph* two years before that, '… the factor which limits a ship's success with a fast submarine [was] the skill of the attack team rather than the capabilities of the instruments.'[37] Nevertheless, training was seen as crucial to success and further trials were planned with the Portland Flotilla. The trial area was roughly uniform in depth at about 200 feet and free of wrecks – hardly operationally representative, but chosen for safety reasons.[38]

Lacking practical sea-based data, the DTASW paper concluded that Squid was the only in-service weapon adequate for attacking the modern submarine. The intention was to fit a Squid double mounting in specialized anti-submarine types and a single weapon in other escorts, which, in the case of fleet destroyers, would entail mounting the weapon on the quarterdeck, so that the ships' normal anti-surface, and anti-aircraft armament would not have to be reduced. As for Hedgehog, it was, by now, considered to be an obsolescent weapon. The alternative had, for some time, been seen as the development of a ship-launched target seeking weapon, such as the passive acoustic homing torpedo 'Bidder'.[39] However, these weapons were limited by their own self-noise (and hence the speed of homing) as well as their reliance on the submarine making sufficient noise (and therefore travelling at speed). Against the latest fast submarines, 'Bidder', in its present form, was too slow and too limited in its applications to be worth putting into production, but might prove to be the stepping-stone to a more effective weapon.[40] But in the face of these technical difficulties, there seemed to be some optimism, for the tactical investigations already carried out by *Osprey* in the early part of 1946 suggested that the basic plan of defending a slow convoy with a limited number of surface escorts remained '… unaltered and largely unalterable.'[41] The Anti-Submarine School at Londonderry, however, found that it was possible to dispose a limited number of escorts in depth to give reasonable protection, at least against a 'single' submarine. More work had to be done to see if sea–air cooperation could be improved. Further work was to be included in the investigation programmes at the *Osprey* and Londonderry Anti-Submarine Schools and the Greenwich Tactical School.

Turning to the period beyond 1950, Ashbourne thought it likely that in the more distant future, the Royal Navy would have to be reckoned with a 'true submarine' capable of a submerged speed of 25 knots and of diving to 1,500 feet. To improve the search rate of asdic an 'all-round scanning' set was being developed. Initial detection would be made easier if a ship's self-noise, particularly from its propellers, could be reduced. Searching would then be possible at higher speeds, and the anti-submarine ship would be less vulnerable to anti-escort homing torpedoes. To increase the accuracy of weapon aiming against fast submarines, a new attack asdic, the Type 170, was well advanced. This was based on the 'split-beam' principle, which had been under development since 1941.[42] It allowed both azimuth and depth data to be measured instantaneously, thus avoiding the laborious 'cut-on' procedure of the searchlight asdics. The resultant fire control solution could be applied to a relatively short-range 'Anti-Submarine Gun', the three-barrelled 'Limbo' mortar, firing Squid-type projectiles all-round and at infinitely variable ranges from 300–1,000 yards which was also under development.[43] To extend the firing range further, it would be necessary to use a rocket projectile (as was being explored in America), due to weight considerations of the mounting.[44] However, it was difficult to find an accurate method controlling the propellant (and therefore the range), and it seemed that the 'gun' method was likely to be the more promising of the two. Simultaneously, investigation was underway into a proximity doppler fuse for the weapon. Research was also in hand into a homing weapon, called 'Zeta', which would benefit from data from the trials on the interim 'Bidder' and 'Dealer' weapons, which could be fired on the longer range data from the new asdics.[45] The testing and refining of these weapons was hampered by the lack of a 15-knot target.

The DTASW paper also considered the operation of anti-submarine aircraft. In the near term, aircraft possessed four means of detecting submarines. Firstly, visual means were practically useless against fully submerged submarines, but in favourable weather conditions it was possible to spot periscopes, schnorkels and oil slicks, albeit at very short range. Secondly, radar could only detect a periscope or schnorkel at short range, and then only in calm weather. Thirdly, sonobuoys were able to detect fully submerged submarines, but ranges were highly dependent on submarine speed, while rough weather would render the equipment useless. Moreover, the size and weight of these sonobuoys meant that relatively few could be carried by an aircraft and when dropped they suffered poor serviceability. Current stocks were American types and were limited in numbers, until a British version was available. Fourthly, the Magnetic Anomaly Detector (MAD), was an American device able to detect a submarine at very short range but, although a version of this equipment had originally been developed in Britain in 1940, it was not used operationally by British aircraft.[46]

None of these methods offered a reliable method of detecting submerged submarines, so that aircraft remained constrained by chance detections, and operated on the optimistic hope that submarines might make occasional use of the surface. The primary aircraft anti-submarine weapons were the wartime shallow-exploding depth-charge and the rocket projectile (RP), but these were useless against dived submarines. Although a new, variable-depth bomb was nearing the completion of its development, it was only effective if the position and depth of the target were accurately known at the moment of attack. 'Dealer', a 15-knot passive homing torpedo, was in experimental production, but it was only effective against a submarine travelling at between two to 12 knots. Nor, in the longer term, was the outlook optimistic. It was hoped that directional passive sonobuoy types would help to mitigate the interfering noise from nearby convoys or cooperating anti-submarine vessels, but they would still be critically dependent on the noise levels from the submarine and this could be reduced by technical advances, or by the submarines operating at slow speed. Active sonobuoys were also being considered, but these would be expensive, heavy and of short endurance. There were no immediate plans to adopt a MAD and until some novel means of detecting submerged submarines from aircraft appeared the most promising developments were in the use of helicopters with a towed asdic. Although high priority was accorded to '... an air-launched anti-submarine target seeking weapon capable of carriage by Naval aircraft ...' (known as 'Zeta'), there remained many difficulties before an operational system was likely to appear.[47]

Following on from Ashbourne's review his anti-submarine team embarked on a wider analysis of developments in anti-submarine warfare in early spring 1946 which restated the problems but also looked forward to methods for their solution. The paper was passed round the Naval and Air Staff divisions in May before being sent to RN and RAF C-in-Cs in September 1946. It was clear, the paper observed, that since June 1944 anti-submarine warfare had undergone considerable changes, first with the deployment of schnorkel-fitted U-boats, followed by the imminent introduction of fast submarines, such as the battery-powered Type XXI and the more exotic Walter-powered, very fast Type XXVI. The submersible was successfully countered and stalemate had been reached against their schnorkel-fitted cousins as the war ended. Anti-submarine warfare was now presented with a threat that was rapidly progressing towards the 'true submarine', which would not rely on any surface exposure. Ashbourne and his team formalized these developments in two phases: the 'Short-Term Problem' up to 1950; and the 'Long-Term Problem' after 1950.[48]

The short-term counter-measures had to be developed against the 15-knot, schnorkel-fitted submarine, equivalent to the German Type XXIs. It was Ashbourne's hope was that it would be possible, in line with current Admiralty policy, to rely on existing gear with no major modifications, until completely new and much improved equipment became available after 1950, when the long-term problem of the Walter-boats would have to be countered. The outlook for aircraft, as has been noted, was less optimistic. The focus in the short-term was on tactical development and training of escort forces. Beyond 1950, the threat was more challenging and the emphasis would be on basic research to support the formulation of new ship and aircraft equipment requirements. The strength of these future submarine types, based on the German design for the Type XXVI, was their very high underwater speed, which might allow them to penetrate the anti-submarine screen and get into a firing position, even if detected. They would also be able to outpace surface escorts under most circumstances, but their endurance at high speed was ultimately limited by the quantity of HTP fuel carried and the submarines left an observable trail at depths less than 60 feet. Their maximum operating depth on Walter propulsion was also limited. Future British designs for HTP submarines were intended to overcome the worst of these shortcomings. In the more distant future, Ashbourne conceived of a 'true' submarine powered by atomic energy and at this point:

> The submarine of the future, then, can be expected to remain submerged continuously, using Schnorkel for short periods. It is probable, however, that they will sacrifice their surface performance entirely. It will be capable of high speed and endurance submerged and of detecting any transmissions made by the enemy. These submarines will attack with greatly improved weapons in close tactical packs assisted by accurate instruments. Finally they will be difficult to detect by echo, noise or magnetic field and they will be difficult to destroy due to their high submerged speed.[49]

Overall tactical development would have to take note of surface vessel and aircraft (both RN and RAF) requirements and was to progress through three stages, starting with theoretical studies, followed by simulations (using shore-side training equipment) to better understand the dynamics of proposed tactics. However, conclusions derived from these investigations would still be tentative and unreliable, until they were confirmed by sea trials against a fast target. Creating the opportunities for 'realistic' sea trials, as always in peacetime, was to prove problematic. Firstly, there were no major exercises planned for 1946. Secondly, there would be no high-speed submarines available until late 1947, when the extensively modified HMS *Scotsman* (designed to achieve 16 knots) and the captured *U-1407*, would be ready for trials as HMS *Meteorite* (and capable of 17–19½ knots). It would not be until the early 1950s that British designed 25-knot HTP submarines and new 21-knot conventional diesel-electric submarines would be available. In the meantime the British would have to rely on exercises with the existing 12-knot S-Class conversions, though these remained ill-suited for tactical work.[50] Peacetime safety rules, too, would limit realism so precluding the recreation of wartime 'blood and guts' testing. Tactical solutions would never become fixed, for they were bound to be in a constant state of flux because of the interrelated advances in, on the one hand, submarine technology and operational methods, and on the other hand, developments in anti-submarine countermeasures and tactics. Ashbourne emphasized that the conclusions from these investigations would '… be guesswork based on the tentative results of other investigations … .' It was vital, he thought, that all the departments involved in these investigations should pool their information.[51]

As a fall-back, it was hoped that data would be gained from the US trials with two captured Type XXIs, *U-2513* and *U-3008*. These were in the hands of a combination of naval and civilian organizations that started sea tests only after a substantial period of docking for repairs (for which the Americans had greater capacity). Even then, the US trials proceeded at a pedestrian pace, with little tactical data emerging for nearly two years. Initially *U-2513* appears to have been used for sea trials, which showed that she was capable of maintaining 17 knots submerged for one hour. During the following year the U-boats only achieved a maximum speed of 15–15½ knots, and also revealed a number of defects in the Type XXI design.[52] These results, however, did not begin to filter through to the British until the spring of 1947 in a summary produced by Commander R.G.C. Haines, the Staff Anti-Submarine Officer on the British Admiralty Delegation in Washington. It was hoped that a complete report might be available at a later date. The letter from Haines summarized a report from the American Woods Hole Oceanographic Institution, which had carried out technical performance tests with two Type XXIs. It was the lower maximum speed of 15–15½ knots that were passed to the Admiralty. The British staff in Washington hoped to send the full US report at a later date.[53] The Americans were hardly better informed, for as late as spring 1948, one American submarine squadron commander complained that there was insufficient data on the Type XXI '… upon which to base even a preliminary analysis of its full potentialities or weaknesses.'[54]

No documentary evidence was discovered which described the German plans for operation of the Type XXVI Walter-boat, so the Admiralty constructed its own tactical concept based on their own earlier operational and technical analysis, and the results of interrogations of German U-boat officers. Ashbourne was, however, in possession of a captured German document which described their plans for operation of the Type XXI. It is not entirely clear why Ashbourne chose to use a précis of this paper as a template, given the more balanced analyses produced by DNOR, and others, during the war. Perhaps, because it came from an enemy who had kept anti-submarine forces engaged for the whole of the war and required considerable effort to defeat, the threat of the Type XXI (which would now be in Russian hands) was given greater *gravitas* by citing the paper. The German paper contains many contradictions. It is also vague on many of the important issues, such as how convoys were to be located and how they could be attacked using Type XXIs in packs. Much was made of the greater underwater performance of these U-boats, especially in their ability to close targets by underwater travel from considerable distances, even though this might consume 80 per cent of the battery power. This seems rather profligate, compared with the views of one ex-Type XXI captain, Erich Topp, who compiled the 'Battle Instructions for the Type XXI and Type XXIII U-boats', and thought that battery capacity ought to be maintained at a minimum level of 60–70 per cent, unless in an emergency.[55] Such problems would be overcome if the submarine operated in focal areas, where shipping targets would be more plentiful, but where anti-submarine forces would also be stronger.

The Germans considered that the overall defensive fighting power of the Type XXI was still weak, for the paper – echoing Dönitz' long-held philosophy – emphasized that the key to success was to remain unobserved before an attack so that the enemy would not take evasive action. Although the Type XXI had a much improved acoustic suite, greater emphasis was placed on the use of the periscope, which would inevitably restrict attacks largely to daylight hours. The Germans realized that attacking in packs was the most effective method of achieving substantial numbers of sinkings. However, it was apparent that the Type XXI was not well-suited to working tactically in close company with other boats. (This seemed to contradict some of the views expressed in Roberts' interrogations.) To compensate, the Type XXI could fire a larger salvo size of six LuT torpedoes and, with its rapid reloading system, could fire a second salvo five minutes later, and a third salvo after another 20 minutes. The recommended tactics for the attack were for a submerged approach to a convoy from forward of the beam. The screen would be penetrated at slow speed, either deep or at periscope depth, and then to fire salvoes of LuT torpedoes in rapid succession. The Germans calculated that there was a '… theoretical possibility of 95 to 99 per cent hits in an average convoy … .'[56] After firing the Type XXI would dive under the convoy to reload, where the 'Nibelung' asdic set and 'Balkon' hydrophones were used to detect any alterations in the course of the convoy and, via a specially designed plotting-table, to allow further torpedoes to be fired from deep. After the third salvo the U-boat was supposed to remain deep under the convoy for a couple of hours and then escape at slow speed. This was not as easy as it seemed.[57]

Had the enemy been able to employ these submarines in the manner proposed, Ashbourne concluded, they would have been able to defeat the most effective British counter-measures and, since the Type XXI did not need to use the surface, except to schnorkel for short periods, aircraft would be virtually powerless to sink them while in transit, except on rare occasions. The Type XXI's weakness was reconnaissance, so support by aircraft would be especially valuable in locating targets. An advantage was the use of the 'Squash' or 'Kurier', pulsed radio system, which allowed short, formatted messages to be cleared in less than one half of a second. Existing ship-borne direction finding equipment could not exploit these signals, though this might be possible from shore stations within the next few years. It had been assessed that had the Germans possessed this system during 1943 that convoy losses might have increased by 30–50 per cent.[58] In summary, Ashbourne wrote:

> The Type XXI has therefore neutralised air, shore and shipborne radar and D/F, but this type can still, with patience, be destroyed after detection by asdics. However, the power of asdics to prevent an attack is probably diminished. The larger salvo, rapid reloading gear and ability to keep station under the convoy, enormously increases the damage that can be done by any U-boat that penetrates the screen. The price of these advantages is the inability to concentrate and intercept convoys or to carry out effective pack tactics.[59]

There were chinks in the Type XXI's armour, but it would have posed a serious threat, and one that was in Russian hands if they were capable of converting the potential of this German technology into an effective weapon, which, at least in the short term, it seemed that they would not be able to achieve.

The first tranche of doctrine papers

The post-war continuation of formed escort groups, the restructuring of the anti-submarine Branch, and the maintenance of a large reserve of trained men for future wartime anti-submarine operations were all seen as vital if the lessons of the war were not to be squandered. Ashbourne was determined that advanced operational training would be enhanced by the temporary continuation of a Joint Anti-Submarine School at Londonderry.[60] This organization was, eventually, formalized by the creation of the permanent Joint Anti-Submarine School (JASS). When the general issue of post-war training was being discussed in the Admiralty, the Director of Naval Air Warfare voiced a common concern that:

> … in spite of all that has been done and is being said to the contrary, there remains a very grave danger of our sliding back once more in the coming 'peace' into errors in Naval training similar to those of the last one. The temptation to concentrate on the more amusing and spectacular attack on the Fleet rather than the dull and difficult (but much more important) defence of trade is desperately strong.[61]

Captain G. French, RN, Deputy Director of Plans, went further when he observed that:

> ... the root of this matter is a question of outlook and of the importance ... attached to the adequacy of our A/S training and of trade protection exercises. ... It is improbable that these will be given full weight unless there is a sufficiently powerful body of thought in the Admiralty organization to insist upon it.[62]

Ashbourne agreed and proposed the establishment of a Joint Sea/Air Warfare Committee (SAWC) with both Royal Navy and RAF membership and chaired at the Vice Chief of the Naval and Air Staff level. The Committee, and eventually its sub-committees, would hammer out joint policy on all matters connected with anti-submarine warfare and make policy recommendations to the Board of Admiralty and Air Council. This was to be done via the normal working of the relevant staffs of the Admiralty and Air Ministry. At their first meeting in May 1946 the committee discussed Ashbourne's paper on the implications of the schnorkel-fitted, fast U-boat. Thereafter a steady stream of papers was presented to the SAWC for approval. Furthermore, the Admiralty set up a series of 'TAS Liaison Meetings' at which often 250 officers of the anti-submarine community were present, and including representatives from the Commonwealth and the US.[63]

The first meeting of the SAWC's Tactical and Training Sub-Committee on 7 May 1946 was chaired by Rear Admiral R.D. Oliver. The committee spent some time discussing the problems laid out in DTASW's paper on 'The Development of A/S Warfare'. It was agreed that solutions should be developed, in the first place, by the directorates responsible in the relevant areas, incorporating advice from the operational research departments where appropriate. Thus surface search and escort, air search and patrol related to trade defence were to be jointly examined by DTASW for the Admiralty and the Director of Operations (D of Ops) for the Air Ministry. Once these directorates had drafted the joint paper it would then be considered by the Sub-Committee. So, during the later part of the spring of 1946 DTASW and D of Ops worked together to produce a 'Joint Paper on Sea and Air Aspects of Search and Convoy Defence'.[64] This was followed by a complementary 'Joint Paper on Sea and Air Aspects of Fleet Defence against Submarines', which was drafted under the leadership of Captain G. Willoughby, the Admiralty's Director of Air Warfare (DAW), though he, too, consulted with other Admiralty and Air Ministry directorates.[65] Deputy Director of Operations (Maritime) (DDOps(M)), Group Captain V.C. Darling, mirrored Burnett post as AD(A/S) in DTASW and seems to have had a hand in the drafting, though there is no doubt that Burnett provided the lead for both papers.[66]

There was, of course, no specific and immediate threat from a maritime power possessing submarines, similar to the German fast Type XXI U-boat. The only potential enemy, Russia, did not yet possess such a submarine fleet. Thus the counter-measures proposed were pitted against an amalgam of the threat that had been developed by the Germans towards the end of the Second World War, together with improvements that might be assumed from German mistakes.[67] The two papers were, therefore, based on countering a generic threat. Thus it is not surprising that the solutions proposed in the two papers were essentially similar. Indeed, many of the paragraphs are directly transposed from one paper to the other. However, the papers differ in two important aspects. Firstly, the 'Fleet Defence' paper assumes that a naval force would proceed at 15 knots or more.[68] If the naval force were steaming at a lower speed, then the principles established in the paper on convoy defence were to apply. Secondly, the paper on 'Search and Convoy Defence' also covers the use of anti-submarine forces for offensive search operations. These forces are not mentioned in the paper on 'Fleet Defence'. The significance of this exclusion will become apparent shortly.

The drafting of the papers went on throughout the summer of 1946, and by July Burnett had a draft paper ready on the sea and air aspects of anti-submarine search and convoy defence, which was soon followed by a complementary paper on aspects of fleet defence. Each paper started with a detailed historical description of the anti-submarine situation at the end of the war, based heavily on Burnett's own experiences (as well as those of Ormsby and Mosse in his team). The papers then explained the effect of the submarine's improved performance on post-war anti-submarine warfare.[69] They were intended as statements of how, over the next five years, anti-submarine forces equipped with existing weapons and sensors, could deal with submarines whose performance equated to the 15-knot wartime German Type XXI. The papers were therefore to be the basis for training and exercise planning for the immediate future. This was the most pressing issue. The longer term problem of the 25-knot submarine was to be explored in detail once the urgent tactical problems against the 15-knot submarine were worked out. There was some pressure to consider this long-term problem sooner, for '... the escort vessels, anti-submarine aircraft and carriers being designed now which will have to be used initially against the long-term (25 knot) submarine.'[70] These longer term investigations would also have to take into account other equipment, not currently in use in British forces, such as MAD and the Airborne Search (radio) Receiver.

The 'Search and Convoy Defence' paper, unlike that on 'Fleet Defence', began by surveying offensive anti-submarine search in ocean waters before considering the problems of convoy defence. This ordering reflected the inherent desire for offensive operations (as likely to lead to decisive results), but did not mark a shift in the policy which remained firmly rooted in the idea that convoy was the bedrock of anti-submarine operations. Indeed, when the draft paper was discussed at the fourth meeting of the Tactical and Training Sub-Committee of the Sea/Air Warfare Committee it was decided that, should a conflict arise between investigations of offensive and defensive operations, the latter was to take priority.[71] The pre-war analysis of the limitations of striking forces had been confirmed by wartime experience. Even when the U-boats' submerged speed was relatively limited, there might not be sufficient ships to search the whole of the area in which an evading submarine could be, especially when the ships arrived at the datum after some considerable delay. It was usually necessary to limit the search to an area covering the submarines most likely escape course. A U-boat evading at only five knots required at least two ships to achieve a 50 per cent chance of detection, and then only if the escorts were able to close an accurate datum position from no more than five miles away.⁷² The increased submerged speed and endurance of modern submarines forced Senior Officers to assess even narrower limits than before on the submarine's probable action in order to achieve any reasonably prospect of detection. The keys to the problem were, firstly, to improve the accuracy of datum position reporting relative to the anti-submarine ships and, secondly, to ensure that the ships arrived at the datum as quickly as possible, so that the area to be searched would be a small as possible. The means of fixing the datum relative to the ships depended on the source of the locating information. An aircraft, for example, might be able to report the datum accurately if, simultaneously, it held the approaching ships on radar.

Alternatively, if the datum was reported geographically (assuming this report was accurate), then the ships needed a means of establishing their own position exactly, say by the use of a radio navigation aid. Of course, the ships themselves might provide the datum position, perhaps from a number of ship-borne direction finding bearings, though this would be limited if the submarines used 'Squash'. There was also the idea that the datum could be marked by a radio beacon, perhaps fitted to a ship that had been torpedoed. The ships, of course, could home onto the radio transmissions made by an aircraft circling the datum. But the anti-submarine ships not only needed to know accurately where they were going, but also had to arrive as expeditiously as possible. Poor communications was a major contributor to errors in establishing accurate and timely datum positions, as well as delays in getting ships moving in the right direction. Given that speed was of the essence, the captains of anti-submarine ships needed to use their initiative in following up contact reports, and this could be stifled by an inflexible command organization. Unavoidably, ships unfavourably positioned in the first place would take longer to arrive at the datum.⁷³

Preliminary investigations using tactical tables had been going on at Osprey and Londonderry for some time.⁷⁴ Doubtless these confirmed that a submarine capable of high underwater speed would be able to evade '… the normal unit of 4 to 6 ships provided she can estimate its line of advance accurately and in time to use her high submerged speed without fear of Hydrophone detection.'⁷⁵ Anti-submarine ships approaching a datum, therefore, had to try to camouflage their mean course by apparently random zig-zags. For a single ship within 10 miles of a datum, the indirect approach used in the wartime 'Beta' search could be adapted.⁷⁶ If more ships were involved, they should approach the datum using independent zig zags while trying to maintain a coherent search front. But even such artifice would not guarantee that the submarine would be detected on the first pass through the datum. Nor would it then be possible to search the whole area into which the submarine could have evaded. Some guess of the likely evasion course had to be made and the search concentrated around this assumption. The paper recommended that for longer range searches an 'Observant' search should be used to contain the target, while for shorter range searches, where the anti-submarine ships arrived at the datum quicker, a search based on the 'Vignot' principle could be used so that the search spiralled (normally) outwards keeping pace with the submarine's furthest-on position. In US parlance these were known as 'Retiring Search' plans, which approximated to an outward spiral track starting at the datum and designed to intercept the expanding furthest-on position of the U-boat.[77]

The ability of aircraft to locate and destroy submarines had not improved since the end of the war and it was expected that they would not regain the effectiveness enjoyed in 1943 until new or improved initial detecting equipment was in use. It was the long detection ranges achieved against surfaced U-boats, combined with the aircraft's high speed which gave the anti-submarine aircraft a high search rate and its greatest potency against U-boats by denying them security on the surface and hence the mobility needed to close their targets. Even before aircraft had developed a high lethality in attacks, U-boats had preferred to submerge on sighting an aircraft to avoid the chance of even minor damage. But from 1944 onwards this had changed for the worse, from Coastal Command's point of view. It had been the introduction of the schnorkel, and the consequent continuous submerged operations by the U-boats that had denied Coastal Command aircraft of their wide area search capability. The advent of this device had reduced the aircraft's detection range against submarines from some 16 miles to three quarters of a mile, or less in poor weather conditions.[78] Without a visible point of aim aircraft attacks with depth-charges or RPs would have very little chance of success.

During the war Coastal Command aircraft had been equipped with sonobuoys which could be dropped in the vicinity of a U-boat that had already been detected by some other means. Contact could be maintained on a submerged submarine, provided it was travelling at a speed and depth conducive to propeller cavitation. These sonobuoys, however, were not suited to wide area search because of their low performance which would require very large numbers to be used. Nor could these sonobuoys be used in the vicinity of a convoy because the noise of the convoy at a range, say, of five miles, would drown the hydrophone effect signature of a submarine only one mile from a buoy. It was thought that directional sonobuoys would enjoy greater effectiveness in this situation. No British specimens of these types existed in 1946, though a few US buoys were due to arrive in Britain for evaluation. British directional sonobuoys were unlikely to be well advanced until 1948.[79] Also during the war the Americans had used MAD equipment with some success. Its detection range, however, was extremely short, so that the use of this equipment was limited to small area searches. An early version had been developed by the British but had never been adopted by the RAF.[80] The prospects for aircraft were not good, for aircraft had little chance of detecting submarines that were in transit or on patrol. However, they could at least keep the submarines submerged and, if there was the possibility of submarines being badly handled, give the anti-submarine aircraft an opportunity for attack. Overall, however, is seemed that aircraft would '... probably not again prove as effective as they did in 1943 until a new initial detecting device is in use.'[81]

It seemed likely, therefore, that the main burden of searching would fall principally on the anti-submarine ships. However, it was hoped that aircraft would provide positive assistance by accurately fixing a datum and homing the hunting ships onto its location. It would be especially helpful if the aircraft was able to report the position relative to the ships, say by using radar, and thereby eliminating the navigational errors inherent in geographic reporting. The anti-submarine aircraft would also be able to confirm that the U-boat had not attempted to escape on the surface and if a suitable pattern of sonobuoys were used, it would also be able to assess whether the submarine had used high underwater speed to evade. The presence of the aircraft would also deter the submarine from using its periscope to ascertain the approach of the hunting ships. These measures would assist the ships in their search by refining the area to be searched, either by confirming the U-boat had not used high speed, or providing some idea of the direction of escape if it had. At the same time, if the enemy submarine was not able to use its periscope freely, it would have less knowledge with which to assess the best course for evasion. For such sea/air cooperative tactics to work effectively, good communications and mutual understanding would be even more important than they had been in the past. This would be assured by the induction and continuation training courses being set up by the Joint Anti-Submarine School at Londonderry.

Having dealt with offensive operations, Burnett and his team moved on to consider the problems of trade protection and later Fleet defence against submarines with high underwater speed and endurance. The counter-measures in both cases show a congruence, though the high speed expected of the Fleet on passage and the higher degree of protection made significant differences in the mode of anti-submarine operation. In both cases, the Limiting Lines of Submerged Approach would now describe a much larger sector from which a modern high-speed, schnorkel-fitted submarine could approach. The distance between the Lines would be longer and would require more anti-submarine ships to cover it. In addition, if escorts were to have a chance of destroying an attacking U-boat, they would need more 'fighting room' than had been needed against the older, slower U-boat during the war, when it had been practice for escorts to be stationed at ranges of one and a half to two miles from the convoy during the day, and two and a half miles by night (when surface, and hence higher speed, attack by U-boats was more likely).[82] Now some of the escorts would have to be stationed further out from a convoy, perhaps as far as three to four miles.

The same principle was established for the screen ahead of Fleet units, which was advanced to some three miles, instead of the wartime two miles. So that a least two escorts could concentrate against an approaching U-boat, their overall dispositions would need to be arranged to provide 'defence in depth'. This was especially important in Fleet defence, for the detecting ship might not have time to turn to counter-attack, given the high relative closing speed of the submarine and the main body of the Fleet. Of course, there was still no idea that a convoy's escort could provide an interlocking asdic front, as was expected for Fleet protection. In both cases, however, if escorts were to be disposed further out, then larger numbers of anti-submarine ships would be needed to provide the same degree of cover as given to wartime convoys or the Fleet. It was felt that the submarines would still favour firing torpedoes at close range from a position broad on the bow of their target. However, improvements in torpedo firing ranges and the use of homing or pattern-running programmes would give submarines the option of firing, not only from longer ranges, but from all compass bearings. Such shots had been practised during the late war, though not with great success, for long range attacks posed severe fire control problems for the submarine.[83] Escorts would, therefore, have to provide cover on bearings abaft the beam of a convoy or Fleet. In the latter case, account would also have to be taken of the requirement for aircraft carriers to turn into wind for extended periods to launch and recover aircraft. Since this heading was unlikely to be the same as the mean line of advance, it was likely that anti-submarine escorts would have to form a 'circular' screen around the Fleet. This was reminiscent of the screens formed to cover convoys and Fleet units in the Arctic and Mediterranean during the war.

Support groups had been formed early on in the war and had been used to reinforce threatened convoys, though not Fleet units. During the later phase of the U-boat campaign in inshore waters, relatively weak close escorts had been provided, while support groups were stationed in geographic areas where U-boat activity was expected either from attacks or intelligence. For a future anti-submarine campaign, Burnett thought, the majority of escorts would, once more, be more effectively deployed in support groups, provided there was sufficient intelligence of the enemy's patrol areas. Burnett considered it more likely that these support groups would be used directly to augment the convoy's close escort, just as they had done in the latter stages of the war. Earlier in the war it appears that the support groups tended to patrol at a distance around the convoys to deter surfaced U-boats from using their high speed to gain ground so that they could make an attack. Now, with submarines likely to remain submerged distant patrols would have less effect, and anti-submarine escorts would be better placed close to the convoy from where they could either detect submarines as they manoeuvred into a firing position, or counter-attack them if they had penetrated the escort line. Of course, if the total escort force was sufficiently powerful, it might still be possible to detach some anti-submarine ships to patrol further afield where they might be able to harass submarines concentrating against the convoy. These ships could also be used to follow up contacts made, say by aircraft, at a distance from the convoy. This could also apply to Fleet screens, though here the problem was that the detached vessels would have to steam at very high speed to catch up the main body, which would cause a heavy expenditure of fuel.

As for air support, the paper reiterated that the chance of aircraft detecting submarines travelling deep or at slow speed was small. The best that aircraft could achieve was, by the use of sonobuoys, radar and visual search, to deter submarines from using the surface to snort or use their periscopes and radar aerials with impunity. If a submarine were detected and its position known within reasonable limits, it was possible for an aircraft to track it with sonobuoys for a limited period of time, provided the submarine was travelling at speed. Burnett, who had experience of this type of ship–air cooperation, thought that the absence of contact should lead to the assumption that the submarine was evading at low speed. The anti-submarine vessels would then have to search a smaller area. Even relatively sparse air patrols would make it extremely hazardous for submarines to travel on the surface to close a convoy or gain bearing once in contact. During the war U-boats attacking while submerged had to get into a relatively small sector ahead of the convoy or Fleet. Aircraft had not paid a great deal of attention to this sector because of their ineffectiveness in detecting submerged U-boats. Now, however, with their greatly increased submerged speed and endurance, submarines were able to close to a firing position from a much broader sector. The aircrafts' ability to detect the submarine were little better than during the war, so it was now felt that they could be most useful when patrolling this sector immediately ahead of the convoy's or Fleet's escort. Here, in what became known as the 'look zone', a submarine might wish to make last minute, high speed adjustments to get into a firing position, or to use their periscope or radar mast to confirm the point at which to penetrate the anti-submarine escort, or to refine the submarine's fire control solution. A submarine with the characteristics of the Type XXI would be able to intercept a convoy from great distance off track, if it were ahead of the convoy, but would be unable to close from far astern without surfacing. If air patrols were therefore extended to cover the aft sectors they would provide a considerable degree of protection. This would, in turn, allow the surface escorts to concentrate on the most dangerous sectors forward of the convoy's beam.

This system of air and surface escort, the papers emphasized, would benefit from close cooperation between all the forces involved. There was a need to resolve the division of responsibilities when both carrier-borne and land-based aircraft were operating in support of an individual convoy. But this apart, the cooperation of the air force and naval forces was already being fostered by the work of the Admiralty and Air Ministry Joint Sea/Air Warfare Committee, the Area Combined Headquarters (ACHQs), and the teaching of the Joint Anti-Submarine School at Londonderry. As far as the latter was concerned, a crucial function would be the development of anti-submarine tactics, especially '… to specify more definitely than has been done in the past the immediate action which should be taken if a submarine gets in its attack undetected.' This was, marginally, already better covered for convoy defence from wartime experience, though not against fast submarines. In any case, the tactical instruction now needed to combine surface and air actions, and which would be applicable world-wide.[84]

The joint papers made a number of recommendations. So that the Admiralty's and Air Ministry's '… present trend of thought in these matters …' was understood, the papers were to be forwarded to the British Naval and Air Commanders-in-Chief, and the relevant training and experimental establishments, as well as the Dominion Naval and Air Headquarters. As for future progress the key was to establish the best methods of search in open ocean operations and for trade defence using combined air and sea anti-submarine forces. Of these, trade protection was seen as the first priority. The Joint Anti-Submarine School at Londonderry, which was already investigating the convoy problems, was, in consultation with Headquarters Coastal Command, to propose tactical schemes, given current equipment. These schemes were to:

> … then be considered by the operational and research departments on purely mathematical lines and then returned to the Command and the School so that investigations could be started, first on the tactical table and subsequently in practical sea trials.[85]

Similar requests were made to Cs-in-C, Home Fleet and Coastal Command on the air and surface screening requirements for the Fleet. Initially all these investigations were to concentrate on the 'short-term' problem of submarines with performance comparable to the German Type XXI and employing current anti-submarine equipment. Thereafter thought would be needed on how to counter the future 'long-term' problem of the 25-knot, Walter-type submarine.[86]

The ability of future submarines to make contact

DTASW was concerned with developing a realistic basis for a review of the anti-submarine doctrine to deal with the modern schnorkel-fitted, high-speed submarine. These submarines would, of course, operate underwater, which gave them a certain degree of immunity, particularly from air attack but these tactics also inhibited the submarine's ability to find its targets, without the help of air reconnaissance or accurate intelligence. This issue had been discussed at a Tactical Staff Meeting in the Admiralty, presided over by DCNS, in December 1946 and resulted in Admiral G.N. Oliver, ACNS, calling for a joint appreciation on the matter from DTASW and DAW.[87] Ashbourne opened the process by considering each of the methods a submarine could use to detect its prey. The periscope was the primary method and in good weather the following table shows the ranges to be expected, compared with those from the bridge of a surfaced submarine:

	Large warships	*Merchant ships*	*Escorts*
By periscope	14 miles	12 miles	10 miles
On bridge on the surface	18 miles	15 miles	13 miles

However, periscope observation was, by its nature, intermittent, so that the maximum ranges would not always be achieved. Poor visibility and rough weather would also substantially reduce these ranges. In a 15-foot sea, for instance, the visual distance through the periscope would be practically zero, while at night, with the existing technology, ranges were extremely limited in any sea state. At high speed no periscope observation could be made. Ashbourne estimated, taking all these factors into account, that average ranges would be roughly:

	Large warships	*Merchant ships*	*Escorts*
By periscope	10 miles	9 miles	7 miles

The Germans had made great use of hydrophone detections, and it was assumed that the Russians would learn these techniques. Acoustic ranges vary significantly, depending, amongst other things, on the depth of water and the speed and size of the target. The noisiest targets (high speed Fleet units or convoys) might be detected at 20 miles, provided the submarine itself was travelling at slow speed. The British and Americans were making use of radar in submarines, though detections from periscope depth were unlikely to be at a range greater than that obtained by visual means unless the visibility was poor. As with normal periscope observation the submarine would be unable to use radar when travelling at high speed. In addition, use of radar by the submarine exposed it to counter-detection by escorts fitted with suitable search receivers. The reverse of this was also true, that is, submarines could make use of detections of radar (or wireless telegraphy) transmissions from escorts. Lastly, the enemy submarine might be fed intelligence information from its operational headquarters ashore.

Ashbourne concluded that the submarine of the future, limited to its own resources, would have less opportunity of detecting its targets than had the submersible of the late war. 'It will be practically blind when proceeding at high speed', Ashbourne noted, and harking back to the debilitating problem faced by the Germans throughout the war, he deduced '... that if the submarine of the future is to make use of its strategic mobility, it will require reconnaissance of its targets and accurate direction onto them.' From this Ashbourne concluded that if the modern submarine could be denied air reconnaissance, then a proportion of the operational submarine force would have to be used passively in the reconnaissance role.[88]

The convoy strategy continued to influence the enemy's approach. In February 1943, when Dönitz had just become C-in-C of the German Navy, a memorandum from the German Naval Staff to the Air Force Command Staff contained these words:

> Our submarines are operating in steadily increasing numbers without positive results ... . All efforts of the Naval Staff to maintain contact with enemy convoys by assigning more submarines or by repeatedly changing the operational areas, are limited by the vast distances of the Atlantic and by the resulting difficulty of establishing contacts with convoys far away from their point of assembly or port of destination. We must continue to gain a maximum of information about the course of the enemy convoys if the Battle of the Atlantic is to remain successful. This can be done only by means of air reconnaissance. Aircraft must penetrate to mid-Atlantic; aircraft must locate the convoys; aircraft must keep contact with these convoys; and aircraft must lead the submarines to the targets.

A Naval Staff comment some months later said:

> The new submarines, even more so that the earlier types, depend on aircraft for observation at sea.[89]

At the end of January 1947, having received Ashbourne's input, Captain E.H. Shattock, the Director of Air Warfare, produced his appreciation to answer the question: 'Can we prevent this air reconnaissance, or make it too expensive for the enemy to keep up?'[90] There were, in fact, two problems to solve, Shattock realized: preventing the enemy's searching and, separately, denying him the ability to shadow located targets. He thought that searching, particularly for slow-moving convoys, would require only a few fixes per day in the Western Approaches for the enemy to have a good idea of the shipping movements. There were three broad possible types of search the enemy could adopt. He could sweep the area with fast, high-flying aircraft fitted with Air-to-Surface Vessel (ASV) capable of detecting a convoy at a range of about 80 miles. This would employ, perhaps 20 aircraft per day and these flights would rely on their height and speed to avoid interception by fighters. It ought to be possible, Shattock thought, to detect these aircraft at long range. This meant that high-performance fighters could operate from deck-alert, thus obviating the need for standing air patrols, which were expensive in aircraft numbers. Deck-alert would probably require only six high-performance fighters to protect each convoy, but these could only be operated from modernized carriers. It seemed, he conjectured, unlikely that there would be sufficient numbers of modernized carriers to undertake the task, making the chances of stopping this type of reconnaissance remote.

The Russians could use slower aircraft carrying high-powered Airborne Early Warning (AEW) radar that could detect convoys at about 200 miles. Clearly, far fewer aircraft would be needed for this method, but their lower performance would make them vulnerable to fighters. However, even if ship's radars could be improved to allow direction of the interception at these long ranges, the fighters may not have enough endurance, added to which, if the AEW aircraft were handled intelligently, the fighter director's task might be impossible. The last method, Shattock considered, was the use of low-flying aircraft, which relied on remaining below radar coverage of the convoy for their own safety. This flight altitude, however, would reduce their performance (especially if jet-powered) and limit their individual search capability. Although their performance was relatively limited, the warning given of their approach would mean that fighters would have to be kept on airborne patrol to stand a chance of intercepting. This would mean that there would have to be about six aircraft on the carrier for every one aloft on patrol, and this would, in turn, exclude the carrying of any anti-submarine aircraft. Only by such measures would it be possible to shoot down these low-flying reconnaissance aircraft. On the other hand, the enemy would have to use large numbers of aircraft to complete his task.

For the Russians, the shadowing task was more difficult. Aircraft would have to remain in contact, while the submarines were concentrating on the target. AEW aircraft might be able to achieve this, relying on their long range from the convoy for safety. However, these types were more open to radar deception and their reports might not be sufficiently accurate for the submarines due to the technical limitations of the AEW sets. For the other types of enemy aircraft, the close shadowing which they would have to contemplate could be made expensive, Shattock thought, since there were likely to be repeated opportunities for the defence to intercept them. Efficient shadowing was probably preventable, Shattock concluded, provided threatened convoys could be given carrier-borne fighter protection. He did consider the use of RAF shore-based long-range fighters, but the obstacles seemed to be overwhelming, given the problems of fighter endurance versus performance and the need for long-range control of the interceptions. As a result of this appreciation, Shattock considered that it was unlikely that the enemy could be denied reconnaissance of the convoy routes without a huge deployment of modernized aircraft carriers and this seemed '... a most unlikely proviso ... .'[91] It seemed reasonable to suppose that fighter cover could be provided to threatened convoys, and therefore, there appeared to be a good prospect of preventing, or at least discouraging, the enemy's efficient shadowing of convoys. Shattock felt that the whole problem needed to be explored further in a series of tactical table games and large scale exercises at sea.

In the spring of 1947 the NID circulated a US Office of Naval Intelligence report based on German Naval Staff documents which reinforced the issue of air reconnaissance support for U-boat operations. 'The lesson for us is clear', ACNS minuted:

> The interception and destruction of enemy long distance over-sea reconnaissance aircraft must go hand-in-hand with the attack and destruction of the U-boats themselves.[92]

He proposed that the Sea/Air Warfare Committee should review the problem to encourage work in this area. In June DAW forwarded the final version of the appreciation on the prevention of enemy air reconnaissance cooperating with enemy submarines, which took account of staff comments within the Admiralty and Air Ministry, and by Flag Officer, Submarines, as well as incorporating the historical perspective from the German experience.[93]

In the spring of 1947, E.M. Gollin, the young and brilliant new Director of Operational Research (DOR) at the Admiralty, minuted some thoughts on a future anti-submarine campaign.[94] He had worked in NID and now began by noting that:

> From the purely economic viewpoint, shipping should sail in convoy rather than independently if more imports would thus be obtained over the total period of a war at sea, i.e., if the gain in imports arising from the reduction of casualties exceeded the loss in imports arising from the delays of the convoy system. Very roughly, it is estimated that against an enemy effort represented by about 15 (or more) U-boats continuously on patrol ... convoys should be instituted in a war at sea lasting 6 month or longer.[95]

But, Gollin explained, just sailing of ships in convoy, instead of independently, would not appreciably reduce the submarines' ability to make contact in focal areas. Each convoy in the focal areas would have to be given a full escort capable of preventing the attack by most of the U-boats making contact or, at least, inflicting a severe loss-rate upon them. At least eight escorts per convoy would be required. The primary aim of future anti-submarine operations was, therefore, initially to drive enemy submarines out of the focal areas and into the open ocean, where they would have to rely on intelligence for knowledge of shipping movements. Outside the focal areas shipping sailed in convoys, even with a token escort this would, Gollin reasoned, probably greatly reduce submarines' ability to locate convoys, unless Russian Intelligence was extremely good. Even then, the Russians would need the tactical and technical skill to conduct pack operations. The complementary tactics of reconnaissance and pack operations were necessary if the scale of attack against individual convoys was to be increased. It followed, Gollin deduced, that:

> ... the escort force required to keep losses at an acceptable level depends primarily on the scale of attack which can be mounted against an individual convoy, rather than on the total size of the U-boat fleet; the nature of this dependence is complex, and the present knowledge of tactics, weapons and efficiency of a future enemy is insufficient to define it.[96]

He also noted that the effect of an increased enemy attack could also be mitigated by alterations to the convoy system itself. Perhaps drawing on the wartime work on convoy size, Gollin thought:

> if the number of U-boats at sea increased, the total imports over a period might well be maintained by sailing few but larger convoys; the slower turn-round being offset by the greater safety of an individual ship in a larger convoy, by the greater number of escorts per convoy made possible by the new cycle, and – outside focal areas – by a smaller number of convoy attacked. This last factor would arise if U-boats were denied good intelligence.[97]

Of course, if the scale of attack (and therefore losses in convoy) were contained, then the convoy cycle could be adjusted to run greater numbers of smaller convoys, which would improve the overall delivery rate.

In Gollin's view the ability of the Russians to gather the necessary intelligence of shipping movements from use of AEW aircraft was overrated. Even the British, he thought, with their superior radar research capability could not produce an aircraft of this type within the next five years and it seemed very unlikely that the Russians could better this timescale. Nevertheless, in terms of counter-measures to submarine attack on convoys, Gollin noted that hitherto the prime function of the escort had been to prevent U-boats from carrying out a torpedo attack. Now, however, directly countering submarines which fired at long range would require a prohibitively large escort force. Might it not be more realistic, he wondered, to plan for future escorts avenging attacks rather than trying to prevent them – a tactic frequently used in the difficult circumstances of the interwar years and during the inshore campaign of 1944–45. Gollin thought that escort might be armed with long-range anti-submarine torpedoes which could be counter-fired against attacking submarines whose position would be estimated from the detection of their torpedoes. The escorts would also have to be able to cope with submarines which attempted to hide beneath the convoy. In either case, two escorts might be detached to hunt the submarine in cooperation with aircraft or helicopters. Sonobuoys would be used to detect the submarine if it tried to escape at high speed, thus giving the escorts the chance to gain asdic contact. Otherwise, if the submarine used slow speed, the area to be searched by the escorts would be relatively small, giving them a better chance of success.[98]

Captain P.G. Cazalet, in D of P, made some comments on Gollin's minute. He expressed the common view when he pointed out that, in a future war, most of the Atlantic coast-line would probably fall into Russian hands at an early stage. Clearly, this would repeat the strategic problems posed in 1940 by the German occupation of the Biscay ports. He also thought that, because of '... the lowly place occupied by the Russian Navy *vis-à-vis* the other Services, its inexperience, and its difficult training conditions ... they will [amongst other things] exploit maritime Air Forces.'[99] The requirement to provide anti-aircraft support for convoys would place an additional heavy strain on British escort forces. Cazalet also observed that Gollin had not taken into account the use of fast, high-flying ASV-fitted aircraft in the reconnaissance role, which had been considered by DAW. This was a theme developed further by Captain H.P. Currey in the Tactical and Staff Duties Division (DTSD), who pointed out that Exercise 'Spearhead', a combined exercise involving all three services, that had been held at Camberley in late 1946, had shown up the enormous numbers that would be required in the future, not only of anti-submarine escorts, but anti-aircraft and aircraft direction (A/D) types as well to cope with the anticipated Russian air threat against shipping. A second exercise followed in early May 1947 which again emphasized the problems of defending seaborne military and trade shipping against modern combined air and submarine attack.[100] Currey observed that, with a Russian occupation of the Atlantic coast, '... the striking range of enemy submarine and aircraft will be greatly extended and our defences stretched to a point which we have never known in the past.' His assessment from this exercise, as well as other staff comments, was that the British had probably reached the point where the number of escorts required for the protection of vital shipping in war was prohibitive and beyond both manpower and building capacity. It seemed to Currey that:

> ... the time has now come when we must face the fact that the purely defensive policy of endeavouring to surround each of our many convoys with an effective A/S and A/A screen is no longer practicable and that we must turn our attention and efforts more towards offensive measures rather than defensive measures.[101]

He thought the most obvious methods were the direct attack-at-source on the enemy's submarine bases and airfields, his communications and industrial capacity. Currey did not contemplate the use of atomic weapons, but did note that the effort with conventional bombing would require substantial resources, and that in the early stages of a war these assets were unlikely to be available. He considered, therefore, that other means would be needed, including the use of mines, small battle units directly against submarine bases, and a blockade by submarines in the anti-submarine role. Even so, he pointed out that defensive measures around convoys would still be needed. Finally, to reduce the onerous nature of this task, Currey suggested that means should be explored of shifting a proportion of the extensive British coastal seaborne trade to inland routes. The ACNS, Oliver agreed with the staff comments and passed the docket on to Vice Admiral Sir Rhoderick McGrigor, Vice Chief of Naval Staff (VCNS), for information.[102] McGrigor considered the large numbers of escorts forecast to deal with the Russian threat was wildly optimistic. 'We need,' he thought:

> ... a lot of clear thinking on the subject of the future escort, and when considering staff requirements, the need for speed, killing power, specialized duty, and so on, the over-riding problems of numbers must be kept clearly in mind, which means mass production, simplicity, and sacrifices of many desirable qualities.[103]

Although the Naval Staff recognized the importance of enhancing methods of attack-at-source, there remained a clear commitment to 'defensive' convoy operations. It was also established during this period, after a protracted and, at times, obscure debate, that the risk of major war was to be taken as low over the five years from 1947, though the risk would progressively increase over the subsequent five years.[104] In the meantime McGrigor directed that '... a lot of clear thinking' was required. Burnett was already drafting a major paper on the technical and tactical problems which had to be resolved over the next few years. The process was one in which the Americans also took a close interest, as the extended visit of the US Assistant Chief of Naval Operations (Operations), Rear Admiral C.W. Styer, USN, was to show.

6 New problems, old recipes, 1947–48

Anti-submarine problems of the future and attack-at-source

Admiral Styer's visit was timely. During 1946 the Americans were concerned, as they put it, to provide '… a more sharply headed up organization …' to deal with the anti-submarine aspects of Operational Readiness and Fleet Operations. As a result, Styer was assigned additional duty as the 'Coordinator of Under-sea Warfare' throughout the USN.[1] Early in the following year, Styer, a submariner by profession, and a team of USN officers visited every British anti-submarine establishment, as well as all the command headquarters and staff divisions. The visit impressed Styer and he left with the firm conviction that the British anti-submarine warfare planning system '… is excellent, well organized, and is worth consideration for our adoption either in toto or a suitable modified form.'[2] He was given a series of briefings, including one by Ashbourne which reviewed the Admiralty's and Air Ministry's perception of the problems of future anti-submarine warfare. This only dealt with the 'Short-Term Problem', and Ashbourne outlined the naval and air force technical and tactical issues that influenced the choice of defensive dispositions round convoys and Fleets, which, in turn, were driven by two major factors:

(a) Submarines are less likely to be on the surface when concentrating or shadowing, so that the presence of our forces in the deep field is less likely to provide warning of the submarine's approach, and will be less hindrance to the submarines.
(b) Submarines will probably fire their torpedoes from longer ranges and the screening vessels will find them more slippery customers to detect and attack.

From these propositions, Ashbourne concluded that:

> … all available surface escorts will be used in the screen and that this screen will be more a deep zone of escorts two to five miles round the convoy or Fleet [rather] than the wartime single line.[3]

He also suggested to Styer that in the future the navies should be prepared for a fundamental change in enemy submarine tactics. During the early part of the war it was rare for U-boats to target escorts deliberately, unless they posed a direct and immediate threat. That changed in late 1943 with more escorts in support groups able to persist in protracted anti-submarine action. Thus, during the last months of the war, one escort was lost for every two U-boats destroyed. In a future war, further improvements in acoustic homing torpedoes might persuade the enemy to intentionally denude convoys and naval forces of their escort by sinking anti-submarine ships from the outset. At a time when escorts would be scarce, and production capacity not fully developed, such a strategy could soon create a critical situation.

Apart from convoy, Ashbourne only mentioned one other anti-submarine strategic measure to Styer: that of deep minefields under the most important coastal routes. Doubtless this focus was due to Ashbourne's own wartime experience in minelaying operations. It was realized that these minefields, being sparsely laid, would not cause many casualties but would produce a constant worry for U-boat crews while on operations, especially if they intended to mimic the German tactics of bottoming under convoy routes. Regarding anti-submarine aircraft operations, the briefing given to Styer centred around the direct air escort of convoys. There was some discussion over the long-held British vision of use of helicopters, which might now be fitted with a towed or dunking sonar. But the main issue was the lack of progress in re-establishing the fixed-wing aircraft's ability to carry out effective anti-submarine searches over large areas (which had been so important with radar-fitted aircraft against surfaced U-boats during the war). Although high priority was also attached to developing an airborne anti-submarine homing torpedo, deploying an operational version of these weapons was a long way off. Aircraft were relegated, therefore, to the unappetising defensive, 'scarecrow' role to deny enemy submarines the use of the surface, thus limiting their strategic and tactical mobility, and their ability to locate targets. Fighter aircraft would, it was thought, also be needed to shoot down enemy reconnaissance aircraft working with submarines to locate convoys (though this, too, was to prove a difficult operational problem to solve before the advent of high performance jet fighters).[4] Much of this was a regurgitation of the ideas outlined in Burnett's doctrine papers, which is hardly surprising since he would have had a central part in drafting Ashbourne's notes for Styer's briefing. Clearly, though, the British were already considering alternatives, for when Styer visited Air Chief Marshal L.H. Slatter, AOC-in-C, Coastal Command at Northwood, the conversation turned to the coordinated use of air and surface craft in offensive anti-submarine operations in ocean waters. These ideas were to become a major theme of subsequent doctrine papers drafted by DTASW.

In late April 1947 Captain R.S. Warne, CBE, another submariner, relieved Ashbourne as DTASW. For the time being Burnett remained as AD(A/S) and, along with Ormsby and Mosse, expanded on the assessment of anti-submarine problems presented to Styer. The draft they produced was also used as a briefing paper to support Sir Henry Tizard's scientific liaison visit to America in August 1947. In the paper Burnett wrote that:

> ... the submarine and anti-submarine war at sea has depended on the ability of the submarine to remain invisible while improving its striking power, and the ability of the anti-submarine forces to locate the submarine, and neutralize its attack. At the moment the submarine is in the ascendent [sic] in the absence of any major improvement in the range of detection by existing apparatus, or in the absence of any new counter to its present 'invisibility'.[5]

When comparing own and enemy capabilities, Burnett thought it advisable to pitch existing British anti-submarine capability against an assessment of an enemy's submarine potential of, say, 15 years hence. For the foreseeable future, there was no anti-submarine detection system which offered a higher search rate to cope with the elusiveness of modern high-speed, long-endurance submarines. Furthermore, on being detected, these submarines could prove difficult to attack because of their great powers of evasion. It was hoped that by 1955 the new Limbo anti-submarine mortar and Type 170 Asdic would largely overcome this disability, though it would take time for the equipment to be fitted fleet-wide and for the development of tactics as well as training in its use to be achieved.

On the air side the picture was far gloomier. The development of effective sensors and weapons for aircraft would take much longer, and there remained many technical problems for which no solution was in sight. A more difficult dilemma, though outside the scope of Burnett's paper, was the provision of adequate numbers of surface escorts. It had been provisionally estimated that 500, or more, anti-submarine vessels would be required, yet by the mid-1950s barely half this number would be available. These difficulties had already persuaded Captain H.P. Currey, DTSD, that:

> ... the time has now come when we must face the fact that the purely defensive policy of endeavouring to surround each of our convoys with an effective A/S and A/A screen is no longer practical and that we must turn our attention and efforts more towards offensive measures ... .[6]

Burnett agreed and pointed out that the history of British anti-submarine warfare clearly showed that solely defensive measures had never been relied upon. During the First World War convoy escorts and hunting patrols had no means of accurately locating U-boats unless they were on the surface. Opportunities for catching U-boats on the surface were fairly common, because these First World War U-boats had to spend about a quarter of each day on the surface, simply to charge their batteries. As a result, between July 1917 (when ocean convoy was introduced) and October 1918, offensive patrols destroyed 16 U-boats, 10 were sunk by submarines and 35 were lost in minefields. Nevertheless, convoy escorts (which were most likely to come into contact with U-boats attempting to attack their charges) accounted for 24 U-boats, and where thus the single most effective means of destroying the enemy.[7] The work being carried out in the Historical Section on the Second World War was showing that while convoy escorts were, once again, the highest single means of killing U-boats, it was also true that roughly half of all the U-boats sunk were destroyed by the broad range of 'offensive' anti-submarine measures.[8]

Burnett recalled that, at the beginning of the Second World War, the British had not had enough patrols to prevent U-boats surfacing to charge their batteries. However, with growing numbers, tactical efficiency and the fitting of radar, the escorts and, especially, air patrols eventually made it too dangerous for the U-boats to operate in these strategically important focal shipping areas. The Germans were then forced into the wide ocean areas to gain respite from the attention of anti-submarine patrols and where, to find convoys, they had to rely even more on the high surface speed of their U-boats now operating in packs and controlled by wireless from the shore headquarters (HQ). Air escorts made it difficult for U-boats to concentrate around convoys, usually enabling the surface escorts to drive off the limited numbers of U-boats that made contact. Initially, U-boats avoided asdic-fitted escorts by attacking at night on the surface but the widespread fitting of high-definition radar in escorts soon defeated this tactic. The intercept and direction finding of enemy radio traffic – aided occasionally by the timely decryption of messages – also allowed support groups to reinforce threatened convoys. Tactically, HF/DF permitted anti-submarine escorts to disrupt individual U-boat attacks and often to destroy them.

By 1944 the U-boats had been fitted with the schnorkel, which allowed them to operate continuously submerged and, thereby, to remain largely immune to detection and attack by aircraft. At the same time, the adoption of the schnorkel reduced the U-boat's tactical mobility and search capacity, in part because they were obliged to operate independently. However, their immunity from air attack allowed the U-boats, once more, to return to the focal areas in UK waters where shipping (even in convoy) was more dense, which made it easier for them to find targets. These more autonomous operations greatly reduced the U-boats' need to transmit radio messages, and thus the Allied opportunities for exploiting these transmissions became extremely limited. Nevertheless considerable tactical intelligence was still obtained from the interception and decoding of instructions transmitted by BdU, especially with the gradual disintegration of the German command structure as the Allied armies advance forced the enemy into greater use of radio for shore-side coordination. This tactical information allowed the Admiralty and Coastal Command to deploy anti-submarine forces more effectively. At sea, U-boats approaching and attacking while submerged put greater emphasis on the surface anti-submarine escorts' use of asdic. Initially, their asdic teams were inexperienced at operating in the shallow, inshore water operations replete in confusing non-submarine contacts. However, their efficiency soon improved, and by May 1945 the escorts were sinking a very high proportion of the U-boats which tried to attack convoys.[9] As for offensive patrols, Burnett, drawing on personal experience, realized that these were protracted affairs, even when carried out in limited areas defined by tactical intelligence. Even so, the searches were often crowned with success.[10] All of this, as Burnett note, heralded '… a new era of A/S warfare … .'[11]

The Germans had realized that the conventional submersible U-boats would lack the mobility necessary for operations in the open ocean if operated predominately submerged. The installation of the schnorkel would barely improve their mobility. They had therefore put high priority on developing new U-boats with a high submerged speed and endurance. These new types were epitomised by the 15-knot battery-driven Type XXI and the 25-knot hydrogen-peroxide, or HTP, driven Walter Type XXVI. Thinking to the future, Burnett cautioned that the results of this German research were known to the Russians and it was therefore reasonable to assume that in another war the Royal Navy would be faced with submarines built along these lines.[12] Further developments in submarine technology over the next five to 10 years presaged an increase in the maximum underwater speed and diving depth. The actual endurance available to a particular battery-driven submarine was difficult for anti-submarine forces to predict, for it would depend on unknown quantities, such as the charge remaining in the battery and its recent discharge and charging profiles. All that could be said, Burnett noted, was that the new submarines' endurance at the higher speeds would be limited, and it was therefore doubtful that they had the mobility to overtake and concentrate round convoys, especially if denied supporting air reconnaissance. However, with improved homing or pattern-running torpedoes, Burnett expected them to fire from wider angles and at ranges of five or six miles, without their hitting power being diminished. These potential firing points bounded an area that was considerably larger than for wartime U-boats, and was outside the immediate reach of normal escort stations. Thus, if a submarine did not betray its presence, other than by the impact of its torpedoes, the area that anti-submarine forces would have to search would be greater that in the past, and the escort would not arrive in the area for some time. Anti-submarine vessels which did approach these submarines would face the threat of counter-attack by anti-escort weapons, from either improved homing torpedoes, or short-range rockets based on the German wartime 'Ursel' project.[13] Overall, it seemed that:

> The rate at which ... A/S vessels will be sunk may well be several times that at which they sink submarines. It is unlikely to be less than one escort vessel per submarine sunk ... .[14]

If anti-escort counter-attacks were to be diluted and contact maintained on a fast, evading submarine in the future, engagements would have to involve at least two anti-submarine vessels. This put additional pressure on the overall numbers of escorts. Thus to avoid prohibitive costs and to expand numbers quickly in time of war, the ideal escort would have to be simple and economical to build and man, and this implied a small anti-submarine ship. But such a vessel would have problems in maintaining speeds of 25 knots, or more, in moderate weather, which would be needed if they were to catch and attack modern fast submarines – or at least hold contact until its battery was exhausted. Ships capable of this performance would have to be larger. In any case, higher displacements were needed to meet the growing demands of weight and space for more sophisticated asdic, radar and radio equipment, and anti-submarine weapons. The asdic system envisaged comprised a search set capable of detecting at longer range and with a higher rate of angular coverage, with another set capable of providing instantaneous range, bearing and depth information to the weapon system. This combination, it was hoped, would allow the ships to search at a higher rate (provided the classification and self-noise problems could also be solved), and to hold contact despite the dynamics of high-speed manoeuvres of the fast submarine and anti-submarine ship. Sinking a submarine with an aimed weapon, would mean replacing the existing ATW with the 'Limbo' mortar capable of engaging the target on any bearing and at variable range, thus leaving the ship free to manoeuvre as required to keep contact. Fine resolution radar and a good Action Information Organization (AIO) system would be essential for ships to coordinate tactical plans, and to manoeuvre in close company without mutual acoustic interference or collisions. The AIO would also be used to combine direction finding information from a submarine's radio, radar or acoustic transmissions, with the resultant fix being used to direct long-range anti-submarine homing torpedoes firings from the new escorts. Four Weapon class destroyers, of the Sixth Destroyer Flotilla (6DF), were being converted into specialized anti-submarine destroyers to be used for trials to establish the detailed future requirements. The more extensive conversion of some older destroyers, integrating the improved AIO, new asdic and anti-submarine weapons, was being considered for inclusion in the next year's programme. If the modifications proved to be successful, there were 35 other wartime destroyers which were suitable for the more extensive 'Type 15 Frigate' modernization.

The high speed and long endurance of aircraft gave them an inherent advantage in patrolling large sea areas. Their high speed also made aircraft ideal for patrolling round convoys or quickly following up fleeting submarine contacts. This had been very valuable when U-boats relied on the surface for search and mobility. However, with modern submarines operating perpetually submerged, aircraft needed a reliable system to detect submarines when snorting or, ideally, when fully submerged. During the war, sonobuoys had been used to detect U-boats, these omni-directional types were still the only ones in service with the British. The remaining stock, it was calculated would all be expended by 1949 during training exercises. The British were developing a new sonobuoy, based on the American design, but incorporating some improvements into the design to improve their performance and make them compatible with the RAF and RN aircraft currently in service. Against a large modern submerged submarine at 10 knots at periscope depth, or 15 knots at 200 feet, it was calculated that the new British buoy would achieve a detection range of eight miles in sea state 1. This was the maximum performance. If the submarine travelled slower, or the sea state increased, the detection range deteriorated rapidly. For example, against the submarine at 10 knots at 200 feet in sea states 4–5, the range was only one and a half miles. To overcome these limitations it was theoretically possible for aircraft to carry expendable active sonobuoys, or an asdic in a body towed below the aircraft at a maximum speed of, perhaps, 40 knots. No research was being undertaken in Britain, but the Americans were thought to be experimenting with helicopters which would hover while deploying the asdic body, though Burnett thought that airships offered more promise in the short term than the low-performance helicopters available in 1946–47.

MAD had not been used in British aircraft, and its limited detection range meant that the swath swept during each leg of a search was very narrow, especially against a deep target. It was, therefore, only moderately effective against relatively shallow submarines and the British, therefore, considered its operational value confined to patrolling narrow channels, or in tactical searches where the submarine's position was known with some certainty. MAD was unsuitable for large area searches. As for airborne radar for long range detection of snorts, the British were not carrying out any technical development, though they were closely following the results being obtained by the Americans, and were studying the operational potential of the method.[15] Another area of enquiry was in the tactical benefit of the detection of submarine radar or 'Squash' radio transmissions. It was not yet known what equipment would be needed for an aircraft to make detections, though it was thought a possible for aircraft to home onto a submarine radar transmission, provided it was of long enough duration. However, Burnett was doubtful of the operational value of such equipment to aircraft, as comparable with its essential worth to ships.

During the war aircraft were equipped with only one weapon, the US Mk 24 homing torpedo, which could be used against a fully submerged submarine. Colloquially known as 'Fido' or 'Wandering Annie', the weapon homed on its target's hydrophone effect, like a three-dimensional version of the Gnat (which it preceded operationally by several months). The weapon had a speed of only 12 knots and an endurance of 10 minutes. Its small, 92 lb. contact-fused warhead was designed to achieve at least 'mission kill', that is, to cause enough damage to a U-boat to force it to return to base.[16] It had to be aimed accurately, ideally on the swirl created by a U-boat which had just dived, though the weapon could also be dropped on the U-boat's position derived from a sonobuoy pattern. Passive homing was technically the simplest system, but relied on low self-noise from the torpedo and (like sonobuoys) on adequate noise from the target. So, if the submarine was travelling at slow speed (less than six to nine knots), or the torpedo travelled too fast (above 20–25 knots), the homing range would be severely compromised. Passive homing torpedoes were also vulnerable to fairly simple submarine-launched acoustic counter-measures.

An active torpedo, on the other hand, was unaffected by a submarine's noise output and less distracted by its own noise. Consequently, this form of torpedo was able to home at a higher speed and, while less susceptible to submarine-launched countermeasures, the target was also more likely to be aware of its presence. The active torpedo's performance, however, could be drastically reduced if the enemy were able to coat their submarines with a suitable anti-asdic covering, such as the German 'Alberich' rubber coating. The British, unlike the Americans, were convinced that '… the homing of torpedoes will not be effective in shallow water with which they are deeply concerned.'[17] 'Owing to its comparatively narrow transducer [beam] pattern, which is necessary to achieve a reasonable homing range,' the paper continued:

the initial location of the submarine by the torpedo presents a serious problem and this will be even more marked in the case of aircraft launched torpedoes where accurate aiming is difficult to attain. The chief difficulty likely to be experienced with active acoustic homing, especially in shallow water, is the likelihood of the weapon homing on 'non-sub' echoes ... .[18]

Forecasts of the likely performance of homing torpedoes were uncertain. At best it was concluded that, for torpedo speeds greater than 35–40 knots, homing ranges of between 1,000 and 1,500 yards would be possible, though not '... for some years yet.' Under less favourable operational conditions, these ranges might easily be less than half these values. One solution suggested was the use of a human operator to guide the torpedo via a trailing wire connection. This system could be applied to aircraft if the weapon trailed the wire from a floating buoy fitted with a radio link to the aircraft. 'The main advantage of this arrangement,' the paper suggested, was:

> ... that the discriminatory power of the human ear [was] retained until the last possible moment, which may permit decoys and spurious signals to be distinguished and disregarded. This method may also render possible some small increase in homing range and/or speed.[19]

Burnett then briefly examined of the use of submarines as anti-submarine vessels. If these submarines were to be used in waters where other anti-submarine forces also operated, the provision of effective recognition equipment was essential if anti-submarine submarines were not to be attacked by friendly forces. Nevertheless, the development of an anti-submarine 'fighter' submarine for use in cooperation with surface forces was under consideration, as was the more likely use of patrol submarines for anti-submarine operations in enemy controlled water. If the necessary performance could be provided, anti-submarine submarines might be able to keep up with fast, evading enemy submarines because they would unaffected by rough weather. Also, working in the same environment as the enemy, Burnett thought that the anti-submarine submarines' asdic would be less affected than were surface anti-submarine ships, though the short range of existing asdics would limit the usefulness of submarines as anti-submarine vessels.[20] Burnett did not envisage any substantial increase in the detection range of ship or submarine anti-submarine sensors in the foreseeable future. Some additional performance might be squeezed out of existing asdics by silencing the ship's propellers through better designs and masking techniques, thus causing less interfering noise at the asdic. The main limiting factor was fundamental physics of sound propagation, including the effects of temperature gradients, background noise and reverberations, which were all extremely difficult to ameliorate with existing technology.

Substantial improvement in asdic performance was only possible if lower acoustic frequencies were used, because the attenuation of the transmitted energy was less as it passed through the water. However, lower frequencies demanded a larger transducer if the transmitted sound was not to be dissipated over too wide an acoustic beam and thus dissipate the original source level. Moreover, larger asdic arrays would required larger hull openings and asdic domes which were difficult to install in existing, small escort hulls. Many of these issues had been investigated in the 1920s and the 1930s, when Burnett was doing his specialist anti-submarine training. But, even if these advances bore fruit, design features of modern submarines would adversely affect asdic performance. For example, hull streamlining to achieve high speed had the effect of reducing the asdic echo, especially on ahead and astern aspects. Submarines could also be covered in asdic-absorbing anechoic rubber coating. Such material, known as 'Alberich', had been applied to a few U-boats during the war, and one captured specimen, *U-1105*, had, in the immediate post-war period, been the subject of British trials to compare its asdic echo with that obtained from an uncoated, bare U-boat. These trials showed that 'Alberich' could reduce the reflected energy by about 15 per cent.[21] As for asdic listening either by anti-submarine vessels or with sonobuoys, this method was critically reliant on the noise output of the submarine. It seemed that, with existing technology, operationally useful ranges could only be achieved provided the submarine was travelling at relatively shallow depths and at about one third, or more, of its maximum speed. Burnett does not seem to have countenanced the use of low frequency acoustic detection methods, though to be fair, this technology was only just being applied to seabed mounted equipment. The project was still highly secret and could not have been directly revealed at the security classification of Burnett's analysis. Burnett did, however, consider other, more novel, methods, such as wake, magnetic and electrical detection, though these were seen as likely to produce operational results only in the distant future.[22]

To achieve all these technical solutions the scientific effort required would be considerably in excess of that normally provided in peacetime. This was especially so, for the available stock of fundamental research had been plundered during the war and now needed to be replenished. The research resources thereby diverted would diminish Britain's direct capacity to develop weapons and sensors, but it chimed well with Government and CoS policy.[23] The Admiralty also had to face the limitations of scientific manpower. Many scientists had been released to resume civilian projects, while many departments were affording insufficient priority to military work, and a proportion of the remaining scientific community were to be transferred to atomic work.[24] Moreover, even if new equipment became available, its efficient tactical use rested on adequate training, which would inevitably impose a further time-lag. In addition, the effective use of the new equipment would rely on the establishment of appropriate authorities '... to direct A/S operations, to analyse recent operations and intelligence and to organize and supervise A/S training.'[25] There was, and is, a common perception was that equipment would also be introduced into service at a slower rate in peacetime, due to '... financial stringency', though delays were probably more to do with the sheer complexity of the new technology and a shortage of electronic engineers. The latter was as much an educational as a financial problem.[26] Financial stringency at least had the benefit of forcing departments to focus on projects which were most likely to meet operational requirements. The trick, of course, was to establish these goals firmly which, during this early post-war period, was done with considerable effectiveness.

Burnett's basic strategic assumptions were that an enemy would use his submarines to attack British trade, though some units might be used for operations against the Fleet, or for firing V-1 type ballistic rockets against British territory, including ports.[27] The attack on trade would be most dangerous, especially if the enemy operated in the inshore focal areas where shipping was most concentrated. This might be supported by a relatively small number of submarines deployed on more distant operations to force the British to disperse their anti-submarine effort and to adopt a comprehensive convoy system, which, in turn, would reduce the effective volume of British shipping. If anti-submarine measures could be concentrated in these inshore areas and achieve a sufficiently high attrition rate of enemy submarines, they might adopt a policy of directly attacking escorts (if they had not done so from the outset). As a last resort the enemy were likely to re-deploy into open ocean areas, where, still operating while submerged, it would be much more difficult for them to find their targets without strong air reconnaissance – a lesson that had been graphically demonstrated by the German failure in this regard.[28] On the brighter side, Burnett thought that the reconnaissance aircraft might prove to be vulnerable targets themselves. The enemy might then be forced to develop methods of coordinating submarine searches to locate targets and attacks so as to oppose a convoy's escort with a tactical concentration of their own. In any case, once in contact, the new submarine types, whether in packs or alone, would pose a much more serious menace than had been faced at the height of the Battle of the Atlantic.[29]

In proposing these anti-submarine measures in 1946–47, Burnett and his team drew heavily on their wartime experience of the tactical ideas conceived in the operational commands and the Admiralty during the war. The fundamental strategic and tactical countermeasure remained the institution of convoy, which made it harder for the enemy to find their targets and forced submarines to move if they were to close to an attacking position, which exposed them to counter-detection. The enemy's task would be made more difficult if their airborne reconnaissance could be curtailed and if convoys sailed at high speed (and ideally on dispersed tracks based on intelligence assessments). As to the numbers of submarines likely to be encountered, it was assumed, taking into account transit times, that about 15 per cent of the total could be maintained on patrol in UK waters. To dilute this number, it was planned to carry out attacks on the enemy's submarine building capacity (through direct attack-at-source and indirectly through economic warfare). And, since at least half the operational Russian submarine force was expected to be in harbour at any one time for maintenance and to rest personnel, they would be vulnerable to attack there. Thus attacks on their bases and training areas were envisaged, either by direct bombing, or with mines.[30] Submarines on passage or in their operational areas would also be subjected to offensive operations by anti-submarine forces and the constant worry of defensively laid mines. Ultimately, escorts were needed to counter those submarines approaching a firing position, but this was tactically difficult owing to the high short-term tactical manoeuvrability of modern submarines.

With the draft of his paper completed, Burnett was relieved in August 1947 by Captain C.E.E. Paterson, another wartime escort group commander, who had completed the long anti-submarine course alongside Howard-Johnston in 1931.[31] Paterson steered the 'Anti-Submarine Problems of the Future' draft though the Joint Sea/Air Warfare Committee where it was approved in spring 1948 as an accurate statement of the state of anti-submarine warfare. Paterson also broadened the discussion in the original paper, for Burnett's object had been to consider the present anti-submarine measures and the avenues for research and development needed to counter the likely threat from potential enemy submarines. His paper had covered measures such as mining, but only skirted the wider issues of attack-at-source. So, when Burnett's draft was discussed by the sub-committees of the SAWC, the RAF complained that it did not take sufficient account of '… what would probably be the RAF's major contribution to this form of warfare: strategic attack on factories, building yards, and bases.'[32] Paterson, took action to remedy the situation. A memorandum was issued, under ACNS's signature, in early December 1947 in which the question of 'Attack-at-Source' was discussed. It recognized the contribution which could be made by bombing of the enemy's submarine support infrastructure, but concentrated on the naval contribution, which needed further detailed study. 'It is evident,' Admiral G.N. Oliver, ACNS, concluded:

> that, so long as we are unable (for lack of some novel method) to detect submerged Submarines at considerably greater ranges than are at present possible, the mere squeezing of the last ounce of usefulness out of our existing means of acoustic detection will not by itself provide a sufficient antidote to the fast Submarine of the near future. In fact, the present tendency is for the Submarine Attack to outstrip the A/S Defence. It therefore becomes necessary to cast around and to consider whether there may not be other ways, as yet not fully exploited, of contributing to the defeat of the U-boat.[33]

Although the enemy's submarine industry and building yards were more susceptible to attacks by air, there was also a contribution that could be made by the Royal Navy by attacks on harbours in 'Special Operations' using 'sneak' craft (i.e. midget submarines), saboteurs and Naval cutting-out operations, just has had been done on numerous occasions during the war. In addition, investigation into these methods would enhance British countermeasures against their use by the enemy. The key was that these operations were seen '… as components of the whole A/S problem.'[34]

Submarine tactical and technical development

By the end of 1947, Paterson had produced two further papers: one reviewed past enemy submarine tactics and assessing their future progression, and the other examined submarine technical developments. Both papers went over wartime submersible operations some detail, since this type was still in use by the Russian Navy. Schnorkel-fitted submersibles and the Type XXI, the latter now being designated 'Intermediate (B)', were also described, as was the Walter Type XXVI boats, now styled 'Intermediate' submarines. The Intermediate (B) emphasized submerged mobility, and these submarines, it was assumed, could sustain speeds of 16 knots for an hour, or 20 knots in short bursts. At 15 knots, the battery was only half discharged after an hour, leaving plenty of power for manoeuvring at slower speeds. This was a slight improvement over the performance of the Type XXI.[35] At medium speeds the Intermediate (B)'s endurance was impressive compared to earlier types. It could maintain 12 knots for four hours, eight knots for 10 hours, or four knots for four days. The snorting speed was about 10 knots and, under ideal conditions, could be as much as 15 knots, though vibration (and thus periscope vision) was likely to be a problem.[36] This data was compiled from a compendium of sources. Direct evidence of Russian developments was sparse, in part, as is now known, because they had made little progress. However, data was obtained from German documents and, at this stage, from the limited results which were just emerging from trials carried out by the Americans on two captured Type XXIs. This information could be interlaced with the results of operational research and technical investigations carried out by British departments during and immediately after the war. There was, in the event, a surprisingly accurate depiction of the Russian order of battle available to Paterson and other staff officers.[37]

In principle, the Intermediate (B) could avoid searching anti-submarine vessels by using high speed, though this might betray its presence at long range, or confirm a doubtful contact for an approaching escort. With its long endurance at medium speeds the Intermediate (B) could close a high proportion of shipping targets (if they could be located in the first place), and greatly reduced reloading times meant that a series of salvoes could then be fired in rapid succession. What was more, the increased performance of modern torpedoes meant that firing distances might be increased by as much as three-fold over wartime ranges. Added to this, the chances of hitting would be maintained by improved fire-control with the use of periscope radar and the use of homing or pattern-running technology. This made the Intermediate (B) dangerous enough, but if they could also operate in packs, both to improve their chances of locating convoys and to make concentrated, albeit unsynchronised, attacks, the situation would become very difficult for anti-submarine forces. Worse still, the Intermediate (B) would be able to avoid anti-submarine attacks, provided it was already at high speed. Its weakness was that if travelling at slow speed, the Intermediate (B) did not have the acceleration to escape the first attack pattern, and its overall manoeuvring power was ultimately limited by its finite battery capacity.[38] These vulnerabilities emphasized the need for escorts to be able to attack early and, if that failed, to be able to hang on to the contact until the submarine was forced to slow down.

The Walter-powered Intermediate submarine, in some ways, posed a more severe threat, for it promised underwater speeds of 25 knots for up to five hours. However, these submarines were expensive to run and their overall performance was unremarkable, except during the bursts of high speed. Moreover, because of the time taken to accelerate and slow down from its high speed (at which it would be practically visually blind and acoustically deaf), the Intermediate submarine would have little advantage over the Intermediate (B), although it might close from much greater distances on specific intelligence reports. Its great advantage was the ability to outrun anti-submarine escorts after an attack, especially if the sea was rough. As for the 'True Submarine', its characteristics were difficult to forecast, other than it was likely to be a large, nuclear-powered vessel. Its high speed endurance was likely to be about 30 knots for six months, enough, the Admiralty lamented, to circumnavigate the world six times! The Naval Staff also resigned themselves to the fact that '… no startling advances …' in anti-submarine detection equipment were foreseen in the immediate future.[39] The Admiralty had come to the view, therefore, that although there had been advances in anti-submarine measures and weapons, these tended to lag behind the parallel increase in the offensive power of future submarines. It appeared possible that Russia could produce Intermediate (B) submarines similar in performance to the German Type XXI U-boats within the next five years, and before new anti-submarine equipment was available. There was therefore:

> … an urgent requirement to establish the best tactics to employ against these submarines with existing equipment, and whether any modifications to the latest A/S Vessels' equipment … are essential.[40]

The joint anti-submarine school's view of anti-submarine tactics

The Joint Anti-Submarine School (JASS) at Londonderry was the direct successor to the wartime WATU at Liverpool and sea/air Anti-Submarine School in Northern Ireland, albeit now in a more streamlined and concentrated form. There were even discussions over the possibility of setting up a US/UK Joint Anti-Submarine School, though these came to nothing – largely, it seems, for lack of funds in the US.[41] The sea exercises and trials at JASS were carried out by both locally based and visiting escort groups and maritime aircraft. At least two of the modified S-Class fast submarines were based at Londonderry to act as training targets and for trials purposes. Additional support came from short visits by the French-run, *Roland Morillot*, the ex-Type XXI, *U-2518*.[42] JASS was therefore the prime national teaching establishment for joint sea/air anti-submarine tactics and technical matters, by providing training for anti-submarine specialist officers, commanding and other senior officers of the RN and RAF, as well as Commonwealth, USN and other Allied officers.[43] Through these courses, JASS wielded a formative influence on the anti-submarine education of many middle and senior ranking naval and air force officers. Simultaneously, though sea exercises, studies and tactical gaming JASS, along with other anti-submarine establishments, continued to have a dynamic impact on the Admiralty's central development of tactics and thus helped to shape much of the post-war tactical anti-submarine thinking.

132 *New problems, old recipes, 1947–48*

During the spring of 1947, under the Joint Directors, Captain R.G. Onslow and Group Captain W.E. Oulton, the JASS staff were teaching tactics firmly rooted in the methods developed at the end of the last war to cope with the 15-knot submarine. During the war it had been impossible to defend convoys against concentrated U-boat pack attacks solely with a surface escort of a realistic size.[44] If every convoy was to be equally protected, there were never enough anti-submarine ships to provide numerically strong escort groups which could form local concentrations against incoming individual U-boats, and be able to detach striking forces for long enough to destroy the enemy, while simultaneously maintaining a guard against approaches by other submarines. Thus supporting forces, both sea and air, were developed which could reinforce convoys which were threatened with U-boat attack. Ultimately, as had been the case in both world wars, the torpedoing of a ship indicated the presence and likely position of an enemy submarine, but defence in depth was more effective. Aircraft were deployed in the deep field, with surface support groups at 15–20 miles and finally the close escort in the immediate vicinity of the convoy. Even if the outer forces were not able to sink U-boats, they could interrupt their concentrations and provide warning of the likely direction of the enemy's approach. This combined with intelligence gained from HF/DF bearings of enemy transmissions and tactical estimates of likely approach directions based on the prevailing weather conditions and operational experience, allowed the close escort and support groups time to form a local concentration against impending attacks and often to kill the enemy before another U-boat attack could be initiated.[45]

Now, however, with the development of the Intermediate (B) submarine the problem for anti-submarine forces had been both complicated and amplified, for, under tactically favourable conditions, the enemy could make an approach continuously submerged. Firstly, aircraft and surface support forces were unlikely to detect these submarines closing their targets, even if they periodically schnorkelled. Intercept of submarine communications – like the wartime HF/DF – might now be impossible because the 'Squash', or burst transmission, radio technology could not be detected with existing ship-borne equipment. Thus, warning of the presence of a shadowing submarine or indications of an impending attack might not be forthcoming. Development work was underway to produce equipment capable of intercepting submarine radar transmissions, and JASS suggested the use of smoke or foxers to make it more difficult for submarines to calculate an accurate fire-control solution and force them to use radar to pinpoint their targets. But, even if these ideas were to mature, the Intermediate (B), armed with long-range torpedoes, which could be quickly reloaded, could still fire a rapid series of salvoes from outside existing escort screens. Catching the Intermediate (B) was going to be more difficult, and even if caught, whether close to, or distant from a convoy, she presented a very difficult target to kill by anti-submarine ships still armed with wartime anti-submarine equipment.

To the staff at JASS who pondered these issues, the problems represented not some revolutionary break with past experience, but a natural extension of the difficulties that had beset surface and air anti-submarine forces during the last year of the war. Ultimately, it was assumed that the wartime operations of individual schnorkel-fitted U-boats would be enhanced by the addition of high underwater speed and endurance, and greater hitting power to revive the capability of submarines to hunt and attack in packs. It would then be especially important to shake off a shadowing submarine before it could home other enemies onto the convoy. Escort dispositions would have to be amended so as to cover the long torpedo firing ranges and to be able to concentrate at least two anti-submarine vessels against an attacking submarine. Moreover, the extended evasive power of the modern submarine meant that more 'fighting room' was needed if escorts were to successfully engage submarines caught while approaching a convoy. Submerged, elusive submarines with the power to avoid escorts, meant that anti-submarine contacts were likely to be fleeting, and this emphasized the need for close coordination between all escort forces if the momentary opportunities to destroy attacking submarines were to be exploited. Thus, the principles of defence in depth now had to be applied to the close screen itself.[46]

All agreed that the technical capability of submarines had, for the time being at least, outstripped those of the anti-submarine forces. Technological counter-measures would not materialize for some time, but wartime experience had taught the anti-submarine specialists that tactical palliatives could be found, once the crucial weakness of the submarine foe were exposed. The limitations of both schnorkel and high-speed U-boats had been analysed in detail during the war by Professors Williams and McCrea in DNOR, amongst others. The considerable corpus of knowledge was thus built up, documented and taught at the wartime anti-submarine schools. This experience provided the groundwork for the JASS teaching and analysis in the immediate post-war era, though the absence of operational experience or trials data against fully capable modern submarines would, for some time to come, hamper the creation of definitive tactical solutions. Nevertheless, the key to developing tactical counter-measures was the identification of the enemy's weaknesses and vulnerabilities. In essence, JASS concluded that these were:

> Submarine limitations are such that the majority of submarines taking part in an attack cannot be placed well ahead on the convoy's track. A certain amount of submarine movement is therefore necessary. Owing to limitations of snorting speed, some of this movement may take place on the surface.[47]

These were crucial restrictions and ones which provided anti-submarine forces with tactical opportunities. The high transit speed normally available to fleets, or evasive manoeuvres by convoys (if the intelligence on submarine dispositions was timely), would force enemy submarines to move if they were to close their targets. Unless they were luckily placed, the transit distance and speed needed could well be above what they could achieve while submerged, even if they used an alternate sprint and schnorkel cycle. High schnorkelling speeds would create a large, highly visible feather and render the submarine's periscope observation non-existent against aircraft due to vibration. Thus if high transit speeds were required the submarine might have to resort to surface travel. Submarines, as wartime operations proved, were extremely vulnerable to air attack with depth-charges or rocket projectile strikes while they were still on the surface, or if attacked within about 30 seconds of crash diving. While on the surface, a submarine using radar would normally detect an approaching aircraft and dive before the aircraft could attack. This had been amply demonstrated by intensive trials with HM Submarine *Viking* during the war. However, the trials also proved that, if the air patrols were sufficiently dense, the submarine would find it difficult to make progress or to keep its battery charged because of the frequent crash dives when threatened.[48] From JASS tactical gaming, the best use of aircraft was patrolling at some distance on the bows of a convoy, where they might be able to catch submarines attempting to close on the surface. There does not seem, however, to have been much consideration given to the chances of detecting the schnorkelling submarine. This is possibly due to the lack of success in the recent wartime operations, when visual lookouts could easily mistake breaking waves or willywaws for the schnorkel feather, and radar search with existing airborne radars proved to be capable of detecting the small schnorkel head only at very short ranges.

Since MAD was not fitted in any British aircraft, once a submarine submerged the only means aircraft had of detecting it was by using sonobuoys, but these only worked effectively when the submarine's acoustic output was high enough to be recognized against the background noise. Thus the sea had to be relatively calm, the submarine travelling at high speed and not too deep. Training continued in the use of sonobuoys into the immediate post-war period, but JASS reminded its students that the buoys were not suitable for searching large areas, in part because relatively few buoys could be monitored by an aircraft, but also because the detection range of individual buoys was short, and only limited stocks of these heavy buoys could be carried in each aircraft (especially in naval types). Although there had been experiments during the war with sonobuoys laid in barriers across the supposed path of U-boats, they had normally been dropped in small patterns, centred on the swirl of a disappearing submarine or the sighting of a schnorkel.[49] These were the tactics employed by aircraft on independent 'High Tea' operations during the war or, as Burnett had attempted, in conjunction with anti-submarine ships (provided their engines were stopped).[50] Now JASS contemplated more integrated tactical uses of sonobuoys, with the buoys laid in 'sono-barriers' on a convoy's bows or stern, designed to pick up those submarines trying to get into a firing position from the flank or shadowing from astern. In either case the submarine would be moving at high submerged speed or needing to snort frequently, and thereby giving opportunities for acoustic detection by aircraft. Against an approaching submarine the first buoys were placed about six miles ahead of the convoy and 10 miles outside the wing columns. Subsequent buoys were laid to create a barrier that stretched some 30 miles ahead of the convoy and parallel to the convoy's mean line of advance (MLA). Against the shadowing submarine, the sonobuoys were laid at right angles to the MLA in a line extending to 10 miles beyond the wing columns. Due to equipment shortages, most of this work was theoretical on the JASS tactical tables, though one live sonobuoy barrier was laid during an anti-submarine exercise in 1947 which detected the submarine and led to a simulated attack.[51]

Meanwhile carrier-based aircraft could be employed on patrols ahead of the convoy.[52] These patrols were aimed at deterring submarines that were lying in wait on the convoy's MLA from freely using their periscopes or radar to gain fire-control solutions. Of course, slow-moving, submerged submarines which knew that they were directly ahead of the convoy would use their periscopes only intermittently, so frequent aircraft patrols would be needed if there was to be a reasonable chance of detecting the submarine. Location of these submarines could be achieved by the asdic-fitted surface escort, though their coverage was thin. Thus against the stealthy submarine lying in ambush ahead of a convoy, the dice were weighed against the anti-submarine forces, who might have to rely on retribution after a submarine fired (a conclusion somewhat akin to that reached in the First World War and the interwar period). However, this option was unpalatable, for to rely upon a torpedoing as a warning of an attack, given the heavy salvo sizes of modern submarines, meant that too many ships could be hit before anti-submarine countermeasures were be started. Any anti-submarine counter-attack action would rely on an intensive air and sea hunt, where close cooperation would be vital to mitigate the weaknesses of individual air and sea anti-submarine units.[53] There was little new in this from the earliest days of anti-submarine warfare, but the modern submarine posed an additional problem, that of getting under a convoy to fire several salvoes. This was somewhat analogous to the wartime night-time surface U-boat tactic of penetrating the escort screen and firing at the convoy from within its ranks, and which had proved to be so problematic for hastily trained anti-submarine escorts. Thankfully, this German tactic had only been used early in the war and then rarely, for it relied on a combination of factors. These included the poor night-time detection capability by escorts against surfaced U-boats, the ill-disciplined stationing of ships within the convoys which created gaps that the U-boats could exploit and the prodigious nerve and tactical skill honed in peacetime training of U-boat captains. The idea of operating 'sub-convoy' with fast submarines had occurred to the enemy and British alike. Admiral Horton notes the German plan to use 'sub-convoy' tactics was revealed during the immediate post-war interrogations of U-boat officers:

> It is of great interest that the German Command intended the [Type XXI] fast submarine to be used to penetrate the convoy defences and to remain under the convoy while firing torpedoes. This advance in tactics had been expected, and instruction and sea exercises in countering the move were already being carried out in Western Approaches Command.[54]

It seemed natural that the Intermediate (B) would be used in this way to fire a series of salvoes unmolested by counter-attack. The most strenuous effort would be needed by anti-submarine forces to winkle out a 'sub-convoy' submarine, for asdic conditions were bound to be difficult in the midst of 60, or more, merchant ships. Some trials were attempted in 1947 with fast S-class submarines, though little conclusive evidence was gained, largely due to the impossibility of providing a realistic convoy and the lack of suitable acoustic instruments in the submarines with which to maintain station under their targets.[55] The anti-submarine counter-measures ran the risk of collision, especially at night, unless the submarine could be induced to leave the cover of the convoy. One method that was tried, called Plan 'Parsnip' in which the 'convoy' made an emergency 90° turn that, it was hoped, would expose the submarine and allow the escorts opportunities to attack in clear water.

Taking these factors together, JASS concluded that the difficulties they posed, strongly suggested that the submarine ought to be destroyed if at all possible before it fired at the convoy. JASS thought, therefore, that advantage should be '... taken of any opportunities to take offensive action against the enemy.'[56] Even so, such opportunities were likely to be few and far between, unless the enemy was either careless or under pressure to achieve high speed transits to reach his operational area. Taking the argument on, JASS concluded that, as a first line of defence, a strategic offensive would have to be undertaken against submarine construction facilities, training areas, and bases to reduce the overall number of operational submarines. The Naval Staff had long held the idea that such offensive operations were important anti-submarine measures.[57] The problem was that a bombing campaign against submarine building facilities took some six months to have an impact on front line forces, unless the submarine training pipeline could also be interrupted, as DNOR had pointed out during the war when faced with the same question. Nevertheless, as has been discussed, the Admiralty were considering the whole question of attack-at-source. Indeed, JASS thought this was '... probably the best means of defence.' 'This', it was hoped, 'will have the effect of reducing concentrations in operational areas and the weight of attack on individual convoys.' However, with limited resources, this countermeasure was '... rarely possible in the early stages of a war.' In the wider context, however, this issue had to be balanced against the possibility that the next war, perhaps fought with nuclear weapons, might be too short for the attack-at-source strategy to have any effect.

Other 'offensive', or hunting, tactics absorbed about a third of the JASS lectures on joint anti-submarine warfare. The joint JASS Directors Captain R.G. Onslow and Group Captain W.E. Oulton both had extensive wartime anti-submarine experience and their philosophy permeated the School's approach to anti-submarine warfare. 'The principle of the offensive,' the Staff asserted, 'applies to anti-submarine warfare as it does to other forms of warfare.'[58] However, just as with the direct defence of convoys, the improved performance of the Intermediate (B) submarines made offensive operations more difficult (unless accurate and timely intelligence was available). As might be expected, the JASS Staff emphasized the need for sea and air forces to be highly trained, if they were to take advantage of any opportunities, either forced by the anti-submarine operations, or occurring as a result of mistakes by the enemy. The forces available for these operations were shore-based, long-range aircraft, fast anti-submarine destroyers and frigates, and escort carrier hunting groups. Though, it should be noted, no CVEs were included in the existing naval force planning, JASS could speculate on how they might be used. The carrier hunting groups, ideally, ought to consist of two CVEs (one of which, depending on the area of operations, might carry a complement of fighter aircraft), operating some 10–15 miles distant from the convoy. The carrier group would have a close screen of four escorts and a 'striking force' of five or six additional anti-submarine ships, a somewhat more generous force than later proposed by the more pragmatic Paterson in DTASW. The greatest danger in using carriers in this role was the risk that they would be sunk, as the USN had discovered in recent exercises with aggressive, fast submarines that had regularly penetrated the anti-submarine screens and torpedoed the carriers![59]

The disposition of the sea and air striking forces was a reflection of the operations undertaken successfully during the Second World War.[60] If the position of the enemy was known, the striking force would operate at 10–30 miles ahead of the carrier and her close escort, depending on whether radio silence was in force or not. Aircraft would fly intensive patrols on either flank of the force, or a search down HF/DF bearings. When no enemy was thought to be close, the close escort and the striking force would all be stationed in a ring about the carrier, with the anti-submarine ships operating in pairs for mutual support. To locate more distant snorting submarines, the carrier's aircraft would search all round the force, using radial 'step-aside diverging' searches, supplemented by shore-based aircraft flying box patrols in ahead of the force. The depth of all these air searches was dependent on the ability of an aircraft to hold a submarine contact for long enough to allow the striking force to arrive with a reasonable chance of regaining the contact. Shore-based aircraft, with larger crews and greater stocks of sonobuoys could hold contact for perhaps two to two and a half hours. Thus, assuming the anti-submarine striking force could steam at about 25 knots and to allow for the relative navigational inaccuracies between aircraft and ships, the air patrols should be, at most, 50–60 miles distant.[61] Even so, the success of the escorts gaining asdic contact was heavily reliant on the aircraft maintaining contact as they approached. If all went well, as the JASS staff pointed out, the striking force would have a 'warm scent'. However, if the submarine eluded the sonobuoy pattern early in the search, the area which the escorts would have to search something like 1,800 square miles, a prohibitively large area using existing ship-borne asdics. However, loss of contact by the aircraft's sonobuoys might simply mean that the submarine was evading at slow speed, and the area to be searched by the anti-submarine ships would be smaller.[62]

Clearly, large numbers of aircraft and anti-submarine ships would be needed to fulfil such a concept of operations based on the use of close escort forces, carrier support groups and distant, independent search groups. As had been the case during the war, it would not be possible for all convoys to be given this high level of protection, and, once more, it was decided that each convoy would have continuous protection by some eight escorts, which could be reinforced by a support group of at least four more anti-submarine ships during the passage of danger areas. The surface escorts would have to be stationed to maximize the chances of asdic detection of incoming submarines. They had, therefore, to be able to cover the wide relative bearings off the convoy's track over which fast submarines could approach, and to be deployed in depth of give sea room in which to counter-attack before submarines could fire at the convoy. Most anti-submarine aircraft would be used on independent area patrols over focal areas or areas of assumed submarine concentrations, but they, too, would be available to reinforce threatened convoys. Once cooperating with the convoy's escort, all aircraft should be under the tactical control of the escort's Senior Officer, who would have the best understanding of the tactical picture.[63] This tactical control, the JASS staff taught, might best be conducted through a carrier if one was present with the escort. The policy was not finally determined, however, for at the Third A/S Tactical Liaison Meeting in May 1947 the JASS representative, while stating the clear need for an undivided command of anti-submarine assets round a convoy, thought that '… no firm opinion had been formed as to whether this should be the Senior Officer of the Escort or the Aircraft Carrier providing the air cover.'[64] This conundrum had been largely solved during wartime operations by adopting a cooperative policy between the senior officer of the close escort and the commander of the support group. The former had the best knowledge of the tactical situation, but the latter was often the more senior. Normally, the support group was deployed in a way to best achieve the close escort senior officer's intentions, without formally coming under his command and thus leaving the support group to act independently to prosecute prolonged hunts for U-boats that were detected. During ocean operations, the support groups had normally been deployed some distance from the convoy, though when anti-submarine operations moved inshore during the last phase of the battle, they directly reinforced the normally weak close escort. Their stations were, however, deliberately chosen to give them the best chance of destroying those U-boats which were rash enough to attack the convoy.

When considering the operations of modern submarines, JASS thought that the failure of the Germans to develop effective submarine–air cooperation would not be lost on the Russians (and, indeed, it was not). If the enemy did develop an air reconnaissance capability, it would be:

> … of particular tactical importance if heavy A/S countermeasures had succeeded in driving the submarine patrols away from the focal points into areas of less shipping density.[65]

Although considerable investigation of reconnaissance problems remained to be done at JASS, it seemed that enemy aircraft could provide a reasonable picture of shipping movements, allowing enemy submarines to home onto their targets and dramatically lessen the value of evasive routeing of convoys. The obvious solution was to provide fighter cover for convoys to shoot down the reconnaissance aircraft. Although, the margin of speed of the fighters over the shadowing aircraft was likely to be small until the sonic barrier was passed with the advent of jet interceptors, JASS assessed that shadowing aircraft might have some difficulty, at least by day, if existing fighters were controlled using radar direction, as had been amply demonstrated during battles around wartime UK-Gibraltar, Mediterranean and Arctic convoy routes, even using fighters, like the Fulmar, with mediocre performance.[66]

To make best use reconnaissance aircraft reports, it seemed that enemy submarines ought to be disposed in depth along the shipping route, consistent with adequate breadth across a convoy's track to allow for mutual navigational errors between aircraft and submarines. With this pattern, it was calculated that individual submarines would have the shortest distances to travel to intercept a reported convoy, and would thus be under less pressure to make a fast approach that would make them more vulnerable to detection by anti-submarine aircraft. Once in the patrol area, the submarines would avoid making radio transmission which would alert anti-submarine forces to their presence. However, as soon as one of the submarines made contact, it would report using the 'Squash' burst-transmission system. The message would then be re-broadcast from ashore for the benefit for all other submarines, which would automatically close and attack independently as they found the convoy. JASS assessed that coordinated attacks by the pack would not be possible until the advent of the higher performance Walter-powered submarines, which were expected to have improved sensors and equipment for inter-submarine communication. A proportion of the initial submarine attacks were expected to be deliberately aimed at sinking escorts, thereby improving the chances of subsequent attacks on the convoy. Individual submarines could fire their first salvo, probably using pattern-running torpedoes, from outside the escort screen, or from closer range having used normal anti-asdic tactics to penetrate the escort screen at slow speed. In either case, a second salvo was likely to be fired in quick succession at close range, after which the submarine might manoeuvre beneath the convoy to reload and fire a third salvo. The submarine's high speed capability would probably be reserved for use when closing from an unfavourable position, or to evade counter-attacks by the escort.

After 18 months of intensive study during sea exercises and tactical table investigations the joint JASS Directors, Captain Onslow and Group Captain Oulton, felt able to set out their findings in a series of papers. The direction of their exploration had been guided by DTASW and D of Ops' concept paper of July 1946 on the sea and air aspects of anti-submarine search and convoy defence, as well as by subsequent discussion at meetings of the Tactical and Training Sub-Committee of the Sea/Air Warfare Committee and from direct contact with Headquarters, Coastal Command.[67] By October 1947, the first of these papers on trade protection was submitted to DTASW, and like the Admiralty's and Air Ministry's paper, it dealt only with the 'short-term' problem.[68] Nor, in this paper, did JASS cover offensive search operations, but they assumed that:

> ... the broad principle will be adopted for having a heavy scale of independent air patrols reinforced by the surface forces in the focal areas, their objective being to drive the submarines into areas of less shipping density or, at least, to prevent the enemy using pack tactics in the focal areas.[69]

The emphasis on aircraft tactics in JASS teaching reflected both the strong RAF presence at the School and the recognition that aircraft played an important part in anti-submarine operations, even if for the present they were limited to the scarecrow role by equipment limitations. The major weakness in air operations was the lack of an effective homing torpedo to attack submerged submarines, for British progress in developing such a weapon had been painfully slow. As HM Underwater Detection Establishment (HMUDE), Portland reported, a considerable amount of preliminary investigation and experiment was still to be done.[70] This was not aided by the difficulty of defining detailed requirements for these weapons because of the British focus on operations in the complex inshore waters around Britain. This led them to suppose – correctly as it turned out – that obtaining effective and consistent performance with an anti-submarine torpedo would be difficult. In the meantime anti-submarine aircraft were armed with a 250 lb anti-submarine depth-charge which could not be used against submarines deeper than schnorkel depth.[71] Once the submarine went deeper, aircraft only had sonobuoys to detect them. As for the future, even with improved sonobuoy performance, if aircraft still lacked an effective weapon, they would rely on close cooperation with surface ships to destroy the submarine. More radically, the idea of using helicopters in anti-submarine was resurrected from limited wartime experiments. The Admiralty were already considering their use when fitted with towed asdic, though a disappointed Ormsby noted that this technique had been omitted in Department of Physical Research's review of airborne acoustic detection. There was, of course, no suitable helicopter available in mid-1947 that could carry the necessary payload, but it had been decided that some investigation should be continued in tactical games at *Osprey* and JASS. It was soon concluded that the use:

> ... of helicopters or blimps with towed asdic would be of greatest value in providing fast escorts with the advantages [of] aircraft to combat the fast submarine.[72]

JASS also made passing reference to the possibility of using submarines in the anti-submarine role for offensive operations, but the urgent need to improve the capability of surface ships in countering the fast submarine was not forgotten. JASS hoped, somewhat optimistically, that the new 'Four Square' (Type 170) asdic which had been under development for some time, might solve the problem, because it would be capable of the simultaneous measurement of the range, bearing and depth of a submarine target.[73] At the same time surface escorts would have to be constantly alert to the possibility of counter-attack by submarines using anti-escort weapons. The, hopefully, temporary incapacity of aircraft served to emphasize the need for close teamwork and efficient use of ships AIOs, though these demands in no way detracted from the need for individual ships to act aggressively and on their own initiative. This recipe would have seemed very familiar to wartime escort and support group Senior Officers, many of whom were now, of course, intimately involved in the definition of these tactics. More importantly, it was clear that the main anti-submarine school and the Admiralty were thinking along the same lines.

Anti-submarine trials at sea

The advent of the fast submarine had made it ever more difficult to locate and destroy the enemy at sea with any certainty, and much of the impetus in developing a broad range of anti-submarine measures was due to the inefficiency predicted for individual methods. These views, well-founded though they proved to be, were largely theoretical in the immediate aftermath of the war, because the British lacked high-speed targets against which to assess the actual performance of their existing anti-submarine equipment and tactics. During the spring of 1946 there were a short series of anti-submarine exercises involving the Home Fleet and, although no fast submarines were yet available, some elements of the anti-submarine problems could be explored. A large number of submarines were employed and they had support from aircraft in locating their target, though communications difficulties limited their value. Even so, many attacks were made on the Fleet, simulating long-range torpedo fire at about 6,500 yards from outside the normal anti-submarine screen. The analysis of the exercise noted that if fast submarines were to approach at high speed from the bow or beam and fire at these long ranges, then the traditional anti-submarine screen would have to be extended, to cover a wider arc and at a greater distance from the main force. This meant that the escorts would be stationed further apart and, with the high relative closing speed, the asdic coverage of the screen would be at an absolute minimum. This could only be solved if more anti-submarine vessels were made available.[74] This was a conundrum which would beset the Admiralty for some time. What to do when one of the escorts gained contact was, however, a more tractable problem.

The potential for high speed evasion by a modern submarine meant that accurate and up-to-date tactical information was vital if the submarine's manoeuvres were to be quickly appreciated. Thus an effective hunt relied on cooperation between the ships, and especially on a close understanding between the ships' Commanding Officers. This implied a good AIO and faultless inter-ship communications, so that both ships kept abreast of a fast-moving engagement against a 15-knot submarine. The plot was helpful for identifying the best disposition of the hunting team and planning lost contact procedures, but it could not accurately track a fast, evading submarine, because the asdic data rate was slow. Conducting attack still had to rely on assessments of the submarine's course alterations deduced from the 'old fashioned' aural detection of changes in doppler or hydrophone effect. This meant that the asdic operators had to be constantly alert, though their task was not made any easier by the interference from the escort's self-noise from hull flow, propeller and unifoxer noise, to say nothing of the possibility of a consort inadvertently crossing the target bearing during these high speed engagements.

After the trials with the 12-knot *Seraph* in the autumn of 1944 DASW had concluded that the existing pair-ship tactics remained effective against a fast U-boat.[75] A single ship ran a high risk of losing contact, while the addition of a third or more ships could be embarrassing during highly dynamic engagements at relatively short ranges. These extra ships were usually consigned to an 'Observant' square search around the scene of the action, where they acted as a long-stop in case the attacking ships both lost contact. Even against slow-moving U-boats a succession of attacks were often needed to ensure destruction, and these were best conducted by a pair of escorts, one to attack and the other to concentrate on maintaining contact. The ships were stationed 90° apart on either quarter of the submarine, which meant that they were less likely to obstruct each other physically or cause acoustic interference. Also the submarine was normally beam-on to one of the ships (thus giving the strongest echo), and they were ideally placed to make use of hydrophone effect bearings to fix the submarine. These tactics seemed fairly robust against 12-knot target, but there was doubt whether they could cope with a faster submarine.[76] These tactics survived into the beginning of 1947, by when it was concluded that '… the additional ships are not employed to the best advantage …' because they were held clear of the submarine and could not contribute to maintaining asdic contact.[77] Against the higher speeds of the Intermediate (B) this was going to be crucial, and it seemed logical that if the submarine could be surrounded by escorts, it would be more likely that at least one of them could maintain contact. It was with this idea in mind that the concept of a 'Ring' formation around a submarine was developed by the Fourth Escort Flotilla (4EF) in early 1947. It was designed as a '… coordinated scheme of A/S action by four or more ships, against the fast U-boat.'[78] During the latter part of 1947 the Third Escort Flotilla (3EF), based at Portland and responsible for tactical investigations, developed the idea further. Such development work was made problematic, because the 3EF ships' operations rooms were equipped with inferior AIO facilities, making the control of dynamic tactical evolutions more difficult.[79] The idea of the 'Ring' was to place all available anti-submarine vessels within asdic range of the submarine. What the escort flotillas were about to discover was that it would not be the ships that would run rings around their victim!

Post-war thinking recognized that the most difficult part of an anti-submarine hunt was gaining initial contact and its classification. Once in firm contact, the problem was to maintain that contact. Thereafter, in theory at least, the first ship to gain contact would be designated the 'Attacking Ship' and attacked immediately. As other ships arrived, they were disposed '… equidistantly apart on the perimeter of an imaginary circle, the centre of which is the submarine,' and whose diameter was between one and two miles, depending on the prevailing asdic conditions. The ships were then manoeuvred by the Senior Officer roughly to conform to the course and speed of the submarine, so that the submarine was always in the centre of the ring. Individual ships would make minor adjustments to maintain themselves in their correct station from the Senior Officer. The Attacking Ship would continue to attack until the submarine was destroyed or she lost contact, when she would take a station on the ring and one of the supporting ships already in asdic contact would take over the duties of the Attacking Ship. It was thus theoretically possible to ensure that continuous attacks were maintained. The apparent advantage of this tactic was that, by surrounding the target, at least one of the anti-submarine ships was well placed to take over the attack if the submarine took violent evasive action. The key was for all the ships to keep an accurate tactical plot of the other ships in the action and the position of the submarine, which would be continuously reported by the nominated 'Asdic Plot Control Ship'. Manoeuvring the ring also relied on strict R/T discipline amongst the ships to avoid confusion, although the level of positive direction could be relaxed if individual ships were able to hold the 'Ring' formation by each maintaining formation on the submarine's reported position.

Early experience, however, showed that close control was '… more suitable for ships with little experience and those who have not worked together as a group.'[80]

3EF's trials reached only tentative conclusions because their preliminary sea trials had been limited by other commitments. They had barely touched on the fringe of the problem, and there were a number of outstanding questions which, it was hoped would be tackled by further trials at sea with Fleet units or those attached to the training schools. Nevertheless, it seemed that the most efficient number of anti-submarine vessels was four or five disposed on a circle of 1,500-yard radius. Any more ships and the formation became unwieldy. Overall, it was considered '… that this type of A/S action is perfectly feasible provided ships have reasonable AIO facilities,' and 'given reasonably good operating conditions it is not difficult to keep the submarine inside the ring.' Indeed, contact keeping was easier when the submarine was going fast, because the hydrophone effect and pronounced doppler were a great aid. If contact was lost, the ships in the ring by carrying out all-round hydrophone effect sweeps, followed by an all-round asdic search, could, it was hoped, regain contact. The Ring tactic had, however, only been tried against the 12-knot S-Class boats, since no Intermediate (B) submarines were yet available. The Admiralty concluded that these preliminary trials:

> … indicate that this method of A/S action has distinct possibilities in competing successfully with the Intermediate (B) submarine. It is considered too that this method possesses certain advantages over the more conventional two ship action – the chief of these being the reduced likelihood of contact being lost once the submarine has been detected. It can be assumed that, providing contact is held sufficiently long, the ultimate destruction of a submarine is assured.[81]

The pitfalls of this tactic were shortly to be graphically revealed when the Fourth Escort Flotilla started exercising with an American fast submarine, closely followed by a year-long series of exercises with the Sixth Destroyer Flotilla. These exercises were to confirm that defensive operations to protect a force or a convoy and offensive hunting missions both had low probabilities of destroying enemy submarines. They therefore reinforced the accepted notion that a much wider cocktail of anti-submarine measures were needed the modern submarine threat was to be effectively countered.

In the late spring of 1948 USS *Trumpetfish* visited Britain at the invitation of the Admiralty.[82] She was one of the early 'Guppy' conversions which, by streamlining and the addition of 'Greater Underwater Propulsive Power', was able to achieve submerged speeds of about 17 knots for an hour.[83] *Trumpetfish* was thus equivalent to the Type XXI and the Intermediate (B). In the waters off Londonderry, she carried out a series of exercises with the 4EF under its Senior Officer, Captain E.A. Gibbs, DSO***. Gibbs had sunk three slow U-boats (and a Vichy French submarine) during the war but was now faced with a wholly different problem when attack, offensive sea–air hunting and convoy exercises began with *Trumpetfish* at the end of May. Gibbs' offensive sea-air hunting serials opened with a Coastal

Command Lancaster gaining sonobuoy contact. The sonobuoys used at this time operated on one of twelve different radio frequencies, split into two groups denoted by a white or black band. Within each group the six frequencies were indicated by the colours purple, orange, blue, red, yellow and green. The standard 'POBRY' sonobuoy pattern derived its name from the colour (and hence frequency) sequence in which the sonobuoys were laid. Thus the purple buoy was dropped on top of the datum, followed by orange, blue, red and yellow buoys normally on the cardinal points at 2,500 yards from the purple buoy. This method of deploying the pattern took about five minutes for naval aircraft and up to 10 minutes for shore-based aircraft. Speed was essential, for an Intermediate (B) at 15 knots could be on the edge of the pattern by the time the aircraft completed laying it, so attempts were made to speed up the deployment speed by laying the red buoy first in an estimated position en route to the datum, and the aircraft then flying a 'Clover Leaf' pattern.[84] If necessary, the aircraft would then lay an extension pattern along the submarine's track to maintain contact until the surface anti-submarine force arrived. Extension patterns were made up of two or three additional buoys (depending on whether one buoy of the original pattern could be used in the extension) laid in equilateral triangles of 2,000 yard sides with the apex close to the submarine's estimated position.[85] These sonobuoy tactics were employed with limited success during the exercises with *Trumpetfish* while 4EF attempted to homed from up to 30 miles away. The tactic relied, however, on the submarine maintaining high speed so that her hydrophone effect could be tracked on the sonobuoys. Submarines quickly learned that while high speed was useful to clear the immediate datum, thereafter moderate speed allowed them to put further distance between themselves and their hunters, while not making enough noise to be detected. Such tactics worked equally well against anti-submarine vessels, and speeds of about eight to nine knots, Gibbs remarked, most often baffled the ships. The submarine was usually inaudible to the ships, while she could often detect the ships approaching noisily at high speed and thus take early avoiding action. By the time the ships arrived, the submarine would be outside the ships' asdic search sweep.

It had been Gibbs intention to use the 'Ring' tactic to contain and attack *Trumpetfish*. But even in the more stereotyped serials he found that manoeuvring his ships in strict formation was something of a strain on personnel during a long hunt. As a result the direct tactical coordination of the 'Ring' was relaxed. The first ship to gain a firm detection of the submarine was designated as the 'Contact Ship', and was given total freedom of manoeuvre as necessary to maintain contact. The rest of the flotilla would then:

> … conform by eye and plot to the contact ship's movements, except in rare conditions when the SO found it was necessary to initiate a drastic alteration of course or speed by signal. Attacking ships were detailed by the SO, the choice falling upon the most suitably placed ship. The hunt was in the main conducted from the Bridge, which has the great advantage of immediate realisation of one's consort's angle of inclination. The flow of information from the Plot to the Bridge was satisfactory and this coupled with the view of

plots necessitated only infrequent visits to the AIC [or Action Information Centre]. The handling of the consorts presented no difficulty and this form of loose 'Ring' has the great advantage of being not in the least tiring, and the hunt could, ... [Gibbs thought], be continued almost indefinitely without undue fatigue.[86]

This optimistic view was not to survive the encounters with *Trumpetfish* when she had a full battery and was travelling at over 14 knots. The frigates found that they had insufficient speed to overhaul the submarine and form the 'Ring', unless she made a tactical mistake. The serials therefore degenerated into stern chases – not dissimilar to those experienced during the *Seraph* trials four years earlier – with the frigates clinging onto the submarine's hydrophone effect bearings. Unable to fix the position of *Trumpetfish*, Gibb's ships became scattered and vulnerable to counter-attack by the aggressive submarine, which was not distracted by trying to attack a convoy. In one serial, assisted by very poor asdic conditions, *Trumpetfish* probably succeeded in '... sinking all the hunting vessels in turn.'[87] The anti-submarine ships achieved little recompense and Gibbs found the entire experience '... disastrous and profoundly depressing.' Nevertheless, he was able to salvage a modification to the 'Ring' tactic. He called the revised tactic Operation 'Umbrella', which was designed to accommodate the inevitable erosion of anti-submarine actions into a general chase. Thus, the ship in contact represented:

> ... the handle of an opened 'Umbrella', and the consorts spread evenly in loose formation around the perifory [sic] of the 'umbrella' astern of the contact ship, the shaft of the 'umbrella' pointing through the contact ship towards the submarine. Once formed there is no need to signal a new shaft and escorts conform to the movements of the contact ship. Wing escorts are well placed to intercept if the submarine breaks out to a flank; rear escorts are well place if the submarine doubles back under the contact ship and contact is lost; and all rear escorts are well placed to form a line abreast search for echo contact if the submarine slows down and HE contact is lost.[88]

However, 4EF did not have the monopoly on problems. *Trumpetfish*, too, found great difficulty in finding and approaching its target during the convoy serials. She had, realistically, to cover long distances to close the convoy. If she was to arrive with a reasonable charge in the battery, she had to snort *en route*. She was also constrained by barriers of sonobuoys laid by Lancasters which forced her to slow down if she was to avoid detection. This reduced her overall mobility and she was often unable to close the convoy. However, it was noted that when the submarine lurked ahead of the convoy, the closure problem was greatly eased and she could sometimes able to penetrate the screen by going deep at high speed, or by first attacking the escorts. *Trumpetfish* also used high speed in an attempt to get under the convoy but was frustrated because, in the poor asdic conditions, she could not determine when she was in station. Nevertheless, the Admiralty concluded that although existing '... methods of defence of a convoy against a fast submarine appear sound, ... [they] constitute little effective defence against long range torpedo attack.'[89]

In reviewing the experiences of these exercises, often in difficult asdic conditions and against an aggressive, well-handled submarine, Gibbs remarked on the value of an early attack by the first escort gaining contact. Immediate attacks he thought would gain the initiative for the escort and possibly inflict some damage on the enemy, both of which would limit the submarine's powers of evasion and offence. Moreover, contacts were often fleeting, so every opportunity for attack had to be taken, for '... the escort Captain who does not take the chance which is given him neither deserves nor gets the chance again.' He also realized that in war the norm would be for single- or pair-ship hunts of a fast submarine, and training of these tactics was just as important as exercising the 'Ring' formation. By contrast, in more favourable conditions, Captain (D), Third Escort Flotilla:

> ... found that the ring of ships, and contact with the submarine, was maintained very easily and on one occasion it was possible to follow *Trumpetfish* with confidence until the submarine was forced to reduce speed for lack of amps.[90]

Comparing these positive results with the pessimistic outcome of the 4EF's exercises raised a conundrum, but, as the Admiralty pointed out, the comparison emphasized '... the caution that must be exercised when assessing results from trials carried out under controlled conditions.'[91] There were many artificialities, the most important being that none of the participants was operating under actual wartime conditions. Even so, these results showed that surface ships (and indeed aircraft) were going to have great difficulties in destroying submarines capable of speeds up to 17 knots, or at times even maintaining contact long enough to exhaust the enemy's battery. The warnings from Professor McCrea, and others, towards the end of the war were justified. During the war, the single most effective place to kill U-boats was around convoys, though towards the end, even this was changing. This was understood by anti-submarine staffs, and propelled them into complementary offensive operations to ensure that, along with defensive measures, enough U-boats were sunk to 'keep their tails down'. The difficulties experienced by Gibbs and his ships served to emphasize the point for the future. Whether the scale of the anti-submarine threat was, as yet, sufficient to warrant treasure being spent on countering it, and whether the Royal Navy – within its current planning assumptions – could undertake such a wide-ranging offensive and defensive anti-submarine doctrine were other questions, to which we must now turn.

7 Future uncertainties, 1948–49

The 'Iron Curtain' and policy deliberations

Much of the British tactical development was conducted against a background of an intensifying political and military threat from the Soviet Union. The political acceptance of the aggressive nature of this threat had been hesitant, and the Americans, in particular, greeted Churchill's 'Iron Curtain' speech in March 1946 with little enthusiasm.[1] The British, too, wanted to work in harmony with both America and Soviet Russia in the immediate post-war era, but problems soon developed. 'The work of the quadripartite administration in Germany', Clement Attlee later wrote, 'was frustrated constantly by Russian intransigence, while at [the United Nations Organization] the Russian representative soon showed his intention of abusing the Veto.'[2] The Americans soon became disillusioned with their prickly wartime ally, and this had the effect of drawing them closer to the British. It was the issue of Marshall Aid in 1947, proposed by the US and instantly supported by Britain, but rejected by the Russians, that dashed hopes for the integration of Europe. The Russian rejection was one stage in the gradual hardening of the political division of Europe over this period and marked another hesitant step into the 'Cold War'.[3] Attlee soon realized that military strength was the only factor which impressed the Russians. Even so, war-weariness amongst all the wartime allies, including the Soviet Union, as well as the American monopoly of the atomic bomb, made all-out war unlikely in the near future.[4] The JIC concluded that while the Soviet Union ultimately sought World domination, she would, at least in the near term, rely on a 'Cold War' strategy, short of all-out war.[5] There was not, however, a sudden schism between the wartime German threat and the new Cold War Russian menace, at least at the political level, and this helps to explain why the Royal Navy was developing its future anti-submarine doctrine against a 'generic' threat. By 1948, as Sir Percy Cradock, a one-time chairman of the JIC, noted:

> The Berlin blockade is in place. The two superpowers confront one another, each with its attendant states and its military and economic groupings. This is the Cold War as popularly understood. But, as the records show, it was preceded by a more fluid and uncertain period, which saw the transformation of Russia from heroic wartime ally to principal enemy … .[6]

Indeed the fledgling Ministry of Defence developed the '5+5 Rule' which assumed that the risk of war over the next five years was negligible, that is, up to about 1952, but would increase thereafter.[7] The Anglo-American political relationship was by no means assured, though at the working level of the Naval Staff cooperation with the Americans was close, as had been shown by the constant liaison visits by DTASW staff officers and the major visit by Admiral Styer in early 1947.[8] VCNS had also recently had a visit from the USN Deputy Chief of Naval Operations:

> ... who had told him that the USN were now giving highest priority to anti-submarine problems, and were anxious that there should be complete interchange of information with the Royal Navy in such matters.[9]

The experience of the Second World War highlighted that the primary striking power in modern navies was provided by aircraft carrier air groups.[10] During the summer of 1948 Captain G. Barnard, the Director of the Royal Naval Tactical School, asked for guidance on the roles envisaged for naval aircraft if war broke out during the next five years. The Tactical School was endeavouring '... to swing thought away from massed "carrier slogging matches" of the Pacific War ... .'[11] He wanted the bias to be on anti-submarine work by carrier support groups, which was to take up a third of the course. Time would also be spent on the defence of convoys in a high air threat environment, along the lines of Operation 'Pedestal', as well as limited attacks at source.[12] Captain E.H. Shattock, Director of Air Warfare (DAW), broadly agreed with these proposed roles. However, Captain H.G. Dickinson, the Deputy D of P, suggested a modification to the list which, he felt, would give a clearer picture of the intentions and limitations of naval aviation policy. The primary mission, Dickinson suggested, was the protection of naval task forces and convoys in open waters. Here the carriers would provide air support either as part of the task force or convoy, or when acting as an independent patrol group, to counter enemy submarines and their supporting reconnaissance aircraft. In enclosed waters, such as the Mediterranean, carriers as part of a task force would provide protection primarily from shore-based air attack. Dickinson supposed that after a future war had been in progress for, say, 18 months, the main aviation strength would have been built up to allow offensive missions, including attack-at-source, to be mounted.[13]

Whether the Royal Navy should, *de facto*, abdicate all offensive roles, at least for the first 18 months of the next war, was already being debated within the Naval Staff. 'At the risk of over-simplification', Captain R. Dick, DTSD, noted in mid-July 1948, D of P's policy implied '... yielding to the Americans all responsibility for offensive maritime operations while accepting for the British Navy the defensive role of convoy escort.'[14] Yet, Dick pointed out, both inside the Admiralty and in the Fleet, tactical investigations were being based on the assumption that the Navy would be used offensively. He thought that this dichotomy with the policy espoused by D of P might be a suitable topic to be included in the forthcoming 'Trident' conference, whose Directing Officer was Vice Admiral Sir Philip Vian, Fifth Sea Lord and Deputy Chief of Naval Staff (Air). When Vian weighed in to the argument, he suggested that DTSD was raising a fundamental issue. Echoing the castigation by several senior officers of what was seen as the 'defensive' emphasis before the Second World War, Vian wondered if it was right to depart from the Royal Navy's traditional offensive strategy (as he saw it) and revert to a defensive policy, simply because the available forces were so small.

These comments, probably unintentionally, tended to accentuate the idea that 'offensive' and 'defensive' measures were alternatives. In the sort of language that, as will be seen, worried the Historical Section, Vian caustically asked if '… a policy under which you are always waiting for the enemy to slog you, and never have him guessing about the safety of his own guts, succeed?' Surely, he thought, '… however slight our forces, should not some proportion be set aside for offensive action?' Vian was personally convinced that:

> … the very foundations of the Navy and all for which it stands will be undermined if we find ourselves at the outbreak of war, and for some years thereafter, having surrendered all striking power to other Services and other Navies.[15]

Somewhat less heatedly, he also pointed out that the draft setting for 'Trident', did depict the Navy defending by attacking. When the new First Sea Lord, Admiral of the Fleet Lord Fraser of North Cape, replied to Vian he firmly pointed out that: 'Planning can only proceed on something we know we must do; escort safely our convoys.'[16] Without detailed intelligence data, Fraser was not convinced that it was possible, at this stage, to identify suitable Russian targets for offensive air strikes, other than obvious submarine bases. Typically, this did not satisfy Vian and he took another swing at the issue. Doubtless, recalling his experiences in the Mediterranean Fleet and, later, as Commander of the British Carrier Task Force in the Pacific, he was sure that there was a definite need for offensive operations against enemy airfields on the flanks of convoy routes. 'Before this dog is laid …' he asked if it was possible for more emphasis could be put into these operations, even if other Allies then had to shoulder more of the 'defensive' burden? Perhaps, too, the British experience in the Mediterranean and, especially, the Arctic would pay dividends, for it was in these theatres that strikes would be most likely against the Russians.[17]

When Captain T.M. Brownrigg, D of P, entered the debate he made it clear that his Division were not believers in defensive warfare, and that they did not agree to all offensive operations being undertaken by the Americans.[18] However, his approach was one of pragmatism. Possible offensive operations were to be considered against their value in furthering immediate objectives, as well as ultimate British war aims. But, account also had to be taken of the weakness of British air striking forces and whether such attacks could both succeed and not prejudice subsequent operations. Even if air strikes would prove difficult, Brownrigg had already obtained Board approval for other offensive operations, including minelaying and an aggressive anti-submarine policy. Plans were also being submitted for offensive operations (mainly with surface ships) in the Black Sea and off the Norwegian Coast if the enemy were to launch a sea-borne assault on Norway. Thus the difference in opinion was reduced to the question of whether an offensive air strike policy should be adopted in the opening phases of a future war. The previous First Sea Lord, Admiral J. Cunningham, had stated that fighter protection and anti-submarine operations were the top priority, thereby leaving negligible forces for the strike role. Brownrigg, like Dickinson before him, followed this line and suggested that the main roles to be undertaken with this small force ought to be fighter defence of fleets and convoys, anti-submarine operations and, where possible, limited strikes might be made on enemy shipping and shore installations.

For the time being, the question was rather academic, because the total first line strength of the Fleet Air Arm was barely 170 aircraft. It was planned to expand these numbers to 300 by 1957. By contrast, the USN had concentrated on naval aviation and in 1948 could deploy about 1,100 carrier borne first-line aircraft, over six times the force available to the Royal Navy! Moreover, the Americans thought that a strike by less than 200 aircraft would be ineffective – an idea with which Brownrigg and others on the Naval Staff agreed. He pointed out that if the existing small British strike force was used it was likely to be decimated, as had happened over Norway in 1940. He considered that, should war come, the Royal Navy ought to employ the fighter and anti-submarine aircraft that were available (which would fulfil the minimum requirements), while conserving the small nucleus of attack aircraft upon which to build an effective striking force of about 200 aircraft as the war progressed. Ultimately, the total front line strength would be expanded to some 600 aircraft over the first year and a half of a future war, distributed in 15 squadrons each of anti-submarine, strike and day fighter aircraft, and five squadrons of night fighters.[19] Fraser agreed to this policy and authorized Brownrigg to discuss it with the Americans in the forthcoming staff talks.[20] This policy appears to run contrary to the later historical perception of future wars being nuclear and short. If must be remembered that, at this stage, although America held a monopoly (which was fast disappearing) of these weapons, the certainty that nuclear weapons would affect the outcome of a future war was open to question, given both the small stock of these weapons and the limited ranges over which they could be delivered. These factors had to be balanced against the vast land mass of the Soviet Union and the proven ability of its economy to survive massed devastation, as during the Second World War.

British and allied tactical doctrine

The tactical use of anti-submarine units was enshrined in national and, increasingly, Allied, tactical publications. It is difficult to establish how far British doctrine specifically influenced the production of the Allied tactical manuals, but at a cursory glance, they conform closely to British philosophy, particularly with respect to the need for wide-ranging anti-submarine methods to counter the modern submarine. The basic concept remains the use of convoy, but the Allied manuals also provide for offensive operations. However, many of the detailed tactical search plans show a strong American influence. That said, in the British national publications that appeared in the early 1950s there is the same influence. Much of this was driven by the increasingly scientific approach forced on anti-submarine practitioners by the retreat of the submarine from surface operations.[21] The success of these Allied manuals would rest on the level of initiative allowed at sea in their interpretation, and the avoidance of dogma in the teaching at the anti-submarine schools.

At the strategic level, a series of Allied planning meetings were held in Washington during October 1949 which produced the revised plan 'Galloper' outlining Allied strategy in the event of war with Russia up to mid-1951. By this stage it was assumed that the Russians would have a limited number of atomic bombs (as well as limited stocks of chemical and biological weapons). The planners realized that Allied strategic alternatives were bounded by their military capacities which, initially, were extremely limited.[22] In broad terms this reduced Allied options to the launching an immediate strategic air offensive (in part using atomic bombs) from land and sea. Vital base areas would also have to be defended, as well as the sea and air communications used to support these attacks and to maintain the flow of supplies while the Allied strength was being mobilized. The British had already made it plain that simply defending sea communications was in itself inadequate and the planning had to encompass offensive operations and attack-at-source in the North Atlantic area.[23] The enemy was expected to make his main assault on Allied sea communications with a submarine campaign, sabotage, air attacks on shipping, and by bombing ports and mining their approaches. As for the submarine threat, this was expected to be strongest in the inshore waters of the western approaches to the United Kingdom. The primary means of protecting shipping at sea remained the imposition of convoy to deal with both the submarine and air threats, though the value of convoy against the mine threat was ignored. This was the plan which, the Chiefs of Staff believed, showed how the Allies would have fought if general war had broken out as a result of the conflict in Korea.[24]

During a visit to America at the end of 1948, Admiral Rhoderick McGrigor, Commander-in-Chief, Home Fleet, discussed anti-submarine strategy with Admiral McCormick, US Commander-in-Chief, Atlantic. They came to the mutually settled position:

> ... that the safe and timely arrival of the convoy must still be the Escort Commander's objective and not the hunting to death of the attacking U-Boat at the expense of the convoy ... .

Indeed, the two Admirals also agreed:

> ... that provision of escorts for convoys should take precedence of formation of hunter/killer groups. When it is possible to form these they may initially have to be confined to dangerous areas where they can be used in close support of convoys.[25]

This initially defensive philosophy was agreed against an expectation that an inadequate number of escorts would be available in the opening phase of a future war. Only later, as in the Second World War would the resources become available for the Allies to assume the offensive. McGrigor's ultimate goal became clear during the Home Fleet exercise, 'Sunrise', which followed in the early spring of 1949, amidst appalling weather more characteristic of North Atlantic winter conditions. McGrigor put into practice the latest anti-submarine doctrine and, notwithstanding the exercise limitations imposed on all the players, the C-in-C observed that: 'In spite of the difficulties of locating and destroying the modern fast submarines, ... the policy of employing hunting groups [was] ... based on firm foundations.' However, he added, that:

> Until ... a more efficient form of detection is developed for carriage in aircraft, it is probable that the majority of submarine 'kills' will take place in the vicinity of the convoy or main body with which the hunting groups are working.[26]

McGrigor's observations resonated with the widespread understanding of the interdependence of the 'defensive' and 'offensive' in anti-submarine warfare. The 'Patrol' or 'Hunting' Group was intended to work with, and not independently of, the main body of the Fleet, though at some distance ahead. The idea chimed well with Admiralty views and the proposals for the employment of Patrol Groups propounded by DTASW at this time. These, of course, owed their ancestry to the wartime use of support groups, which sometimes included escort carriers. In spite of the anticipated shortage of anti-submarine vessels and aircraft at the beginning of a war, McGrigor believed that exercises should be carried out to perfect the techniques for anti-submarine hunting groups. The practical problem of carrying out these 'offensive' tactics was the lack of resources and not any lack of aggressive thinking, nor a lack of understanding of the interrelationship between defensive and offensive tactics. 'Sunrise' was also intended to simulate operations against the threat of atomic attack, and illustrated the difficulties this would pose. While atomic attack was not a serious threat to the Fleet at sea, it did require ships to be stationed further apart than hitherto, which complicated inter-ship communications and diluted the anti-submarine defence, already stretched by the problem of countering long-range torpedo fire from enemy submarines. The Patrol Group was stationing some 20–25 miles ahead and on either bow of the Fleet, because this was where enemy submarines might be exposing their radar mast while trying to locate the Fleet. Exercise 'Verity', carried out later in that year, included convoy serials, which illustrated the pressure for as many ships and aircraft to be involved in anti-submarine actions, so that they could benefit from the training. But this imposed unrealistic force levels during tactical engagements, and a consequent lack of realism. Amongst the 'enemy' submarines in the exercise was the French ex-Type XXI, *Roland Morillot*. She, and the other participating submarines, whilst operating singly discovered that their level of success was heavily dependent on the local environmental conditions.[27]

A much more detailed examination of anti-submarine strategy was undertaken during Exercise 'Trident', in April 1949. 'Trident' was really a conference held ashore at the Royal Naval College, Greenwich and was designed to apply the lessons of the Second World War to a possible war in 1956–57, taking into account scientific and technical developments. In his foreword to the conference pack, the First Sea Lord, Lord Fraser, noted that they were in a period of transition and that new weapons were the order of the day. When war might occur, and what would be the state of weapon development no one could say. 'In such circumstances,' Fraser went on:

> ... the task of the Admiralties is not a simple one and it is hoped through this Exercise to inform the Fleets fully of the lines on which the Naval Staff in London is working and thereby establish principles which will assist in the solution of some of the problems confronting us.[28]

It was as much a staged propaganda event, for by this time the shape of future anti-submarine strategy had been sketched out by DTASW and other staff divisions. Even so, some uncertainties remained, and 'Trident' set out to provoke discussion. But more importantly the conference was to inform UK and Allied maritime staffs of the latest Admiralty thinking, and to focus their minds on the detailed planning for future deployments and development of tactical procedures. The Exercise was therefore designed to illustrate how maritime forces might be operated in 1957, the date by which the Russian threat was expected to become credible. The likely problems in supporting the Army and the Air Force were to be covered, but particular attention was to be paid to the defence of shipping and to the importance of offensive action, within a defensive maritime strategy. All the exercise scenarios were compressed, somewhat artificially, within a single strategic setting six months into a war with Russia in which the British found themselves '... in the throes of the Third Battle of the Atlantic.' Once more a major national effort was focused on a conflict that was expected to be as deadly as its two predecessors. This was mainly because the Russians, it was assumed, would be equipped with the latest refinements of submarine and mine warfare, which meant that the threat had '... temporarily out-run the counter-measures necessary to combat it ... .'[29]

Commanders Barley and Titterton, and Lieutenant Commander Waters in the Historical Section of the Naval Staff, had been almost entirely occupied during the first three months of 1949 in research work for Exercise 'Trident'. They had produced narrative and statistical appreciations of the various phases of the war, much of which was used in the planning of the Exercise.[30] During the first sessions of the Exercise, Vice Admiral G.N. Oliver, the President of the RN College, lectured on the defence of ocean shipping. Although a Gunnery officer with no experience of the Battle of the Atlantic, he had recently relinquished his appointment as ACNS, a post he held while the Naval Staff were considering many of the anti-submarine concept papers drafted by DTASW, including those on future anti-submarine problems and attack-at-source. Nevertheless, before he addressed the conference, Oliver had obtained a briefing from the Historical Section, and in his presentation, he argued at some length on '... the absolute value of convoy.' Oliver also felt it necessary to remind the audience that: 'In our very natural zeal for direct action, let it not be forgotten that the escorting of shipping in convoy is not merely a defensive and negative process.' With guidance from the Historical Section, he also noted that wartime Hunter-Killer group operations had achieved comparatively little, though air patrols over the U-boats transit routes had had considerable success. Nevertheless, Oliver pointed out, it was the convoy escorts, both surface and air, which destroyed more German U-boats than any other single means of attack, according to figures supplied by the Historical Section.[31]

The 'Trident' Directing Staff (reflecting Naval Staff opinion) agreed that both World Wars had proved that '… the most fruitful areas for sinking enemy submarines were in the vicinity of convoys,' but added the proviso that the escorts had to be '… sufficient in numbers to allow detachments for killings.' They also interpreted the Historical Section's data in a different way. The Staff concluded that roughly equal numbers of U-boats were sunk by 'offensive' as 'defensive' measures. This conclusion was accurate and did not contradict the assertion over the primacy of convoy as a U-boat killer, for there were many, individually inefficient offensive measures. For reasons which are not entirely clear, the Historical Section laboured under the impression that the Naval Staff was led by the 'convoy is defensive' school, and were bent on shifting to an all-out 'offensive' anti-submarine strategy.[32] However, while the Staff had already noted that '… defensive measures for protection of our shipping must be maintained and if possible increased,' but, the Staff concluded, these '… will not themselves suffice … .' Nevertheless, the British capacity for offensive operations was limited because the:

> … economic position before the war has not admitted the building up of our maritime Escort Forces to the desired strength, nor has the technical and scientific advance in our equipment run parallel with the progress made in the evolution of the submarine.[33]

It was the latter of these problems, the technological issue, which the Directing Staff considered to be most significant. By 1957, they pointed out, submarines would still be difficult to locate, especially from the air. Consequently, the attack-at-source concept came into greater prominence. It was '… a familiar and self explanatory term …' which referred to attacks on enemy ports, naval bases, and the like, by carrier-borne or shore-based aircraft, by 'sneak' craft, commando raids and other clandestine operations. These attacks were complemented by 'Offensive Control' consisting of offensive minelaying, offensive anti-submarine air patrols, the interception of submarines on their transit routes by Hunter-Killer groups, attacks by our submarines in enemy controlled waters, and attacks on enemy surface forces, particularly minesweepers, supporting the enemy's submarine force. There remained a requirement for 'Defensive Control' involving the close escort of convoys by surface forces (with aircraft carriers), shore-based fighters and anti-submarine aircraft, as well as defensive minefields.[34] All these methods were explored further during the Exercise, though the 'defensive' convoy escort task received more than twice the attention as did the 'offensive' and 'attack-at-source' tasks together.[35]

The Historians staunch advocacy of convoy re-surfaced in a Research Memorandum in 1952, when Captain V.D'A. Donaldson was the new DTASW (having been an Assistant Director for Mine Warfare when the Division was set up).³⁶ While he readily accepted the Research Memorandum, Donaldson thought that it concentrated too heavily on convoy, failed to take account of other measures and worse, summarily dismissed the period of the inshore campaign in 1944–45.³⁷ It was, of course, operations against the schnorkel-fitted U-boats and the incipient threat of the fast U-boats which most influenced the post-war Naval Staff, and not the campaign against the wolf packs in 1942–43. When the period of these great convoy battles is compared with the last inshore campaign, the proportion of U-boats destroyed by surface escorts fell from 43 per cent to 17 per cent, and by air escorts from 22 per cent to 9 per cent. Between the same periods, the effectiveness of sea patrols increased from 4 per cent to 12 per cent, and casualties from bombing rose from 0 per cent to over 12 per cent.³⁸ The historians failed to discern this change between the mid-war and late-war anti-submarine campaigns, and the Naval Staff's continued adherence to convoy. However, the Naval Staff concluded – as Fawcett had prophesied in late 1944 – that precision killing around convoys would no longer be (if it ever had been) an adequate method of destroying sufficient submarines to force them to operate so circumspectly, that the safety of shipping could be reasonably assured. To achieve this aim, other methods, however inefficient, had to be tried. These were basically offensive measures, and the Admiralty's faith in them can, in part, be explained by their early knowledge of the highly secret British 'Corsair' and American 'Lofar' Very Low Frequency acoustic systems, which by 1949 could locate submarines at tens, perhaps hundreds of miles.³⁹ From these seabed arrays fixes could be formed rather like the wartime HF/DF system, and used to vector anti-submarine forces onto enemy submarines.⁴⁰ Similarly, the greater emphasis on attack-at-source only made sense if it was predicated on the acquisition of lightweight atomic bombs and the aircraft to carry them. Ultimately, anti-submarine measures had to extend from the defensive boundary of convoys to the heartland of the enemy.

A second tranche of doctrine papers

During the summer and autumn of 1948, in parallel with these wider debates, Captain Paterson in DTASW was busy drafting a more detailed set of doctrine papers. These extended the foundation work done by Burnett and his team in 1946–47, and took account of the results of sea exercises and tactical table games at JASS. Paterson's papers still contained many echoes of the doctrine developed during the interwar period, especially in the overall function of escorts, and supporting forces, but gone was the explicit historical background included in Burnett's more philosophical work. These new doctrine papers read more like doctrine manuals which, with further expansion over the next three years, is precisely what they became. Emphasis was still placed on convoy and fleet protection by surface and air escorts and two of the major papers dealt with these aspects.⁴¹ However, the more offensive doctrine concepts were now examined in a separate paper which covered the tactical employment of patrol groups, operating either independently or in direct support of convoys.⁴² The papers were originally intended to be applicable to the 'short-term' problem against the submarine threat up to 1950, though this timescale was later extended to mid-

1951 by the Sea/Air Warfare Committee.[43] Copies of these documents were issued widely within British forces, and also sent to Canada and America where they were studied by a Joint RN, USN and RCN Committee meeting in Washington with the object of standardizing anti-submarine tactical doctrine.[44]

It was expected that the enemy would avoid compromising the position and composition of his submarine patrols by enforcing strict radio silence, except for enemy reports, an increasing number of which would be sent using 'Squash' transmissions. It was a moot point, therefore, whether adequate intelligence would be available for evasive routeing units at sea. (As has already been discussed, little hard evidence has since emerged that the British, or the Americans, had broken into Russian codes, though perhaps, more was achieved, at least by the Americans, at the end of the decade. It seems likely that there was little or no special intelligence to assist in an anti-submarine campaign of the late 1940s or early 1950s.)[45] In the meantime, location of submarine operating areas would have to rely on HF/DF and traffic analysis techniques, though this would be made difficult by the reduction in the coverage of the intercept stations since the war and the Russian use of Squash.[46] Nevertheless, it was hoped that the combination of remaining shore station direction finding output, with sightings by aircraft and surface craft, would provide sufficient intelligence to gauge the location of the enemy's submarine operating areas, and thus allow a measure of evasive routeing and the cueing of support forced onto threatened convoys or Fleet units.

However, to obtain accurate fire-control solutions and to coordinate attacks by several submarines, the enemy might have to transmit on radar, V- or UFH radio, each of which could be intercepted with the necessary equipment fitted in escorts. In the past, it had been best to avoid adjacent ships having the same asdic frequencies (so as to avoid mutual interference), and also ideal to separate HF/DF fitted ships as widely as possible to provide a long baseline for triangulation. These constraints remained but, now, consideration would have to given to stationing ships that would shortly start to be fitted with VHF, UHF and centimetric radar direction finding equipment. Paterson was more sanguine over the chances of these capabilities being available in the near term, than were JASS in their tactical analyses.[47] If contact was gained by direction finding, the first reaction was to send an aircraft to investigate. It was inadvisable to send a surface force if the contact was more than 10 miles distant because of '… the great distance that a submarine may cover submerged before surface escorts arrive … .'[48] However, it might be possible to send a striking force further afield if an aircraft were able to maintain contact on the submarine by use of sonobuoys at least until the surface force approached to within about 10 miles. Every detachment would consist of at least two ships for mutual support, which would be diluted for some time while the hunt proceeded and until anti-submarine ships regained station.

Not only did Paterson have little to add to the JASS paper produced towards the end of 1947, but he adopted it as the basis for his own examination of convoy and fleet defence, as well as offensive operations. He went even further with JASS's assessment of the problems confronting enemy submarines by reproducing it practically verbatim.[49] The consensus was that in the near-term, the use of submerged tactics by modern submarines meant that that there would probably be little warning of an attack. It followed that surface escort had to be disposed in such a fashion that it could exploit those initial asdic contacts they did get quickly and also to be able to respond effectively after an unannounced attack. The higher submerged speed of modern submarines meant that to counter approaching submarines, some of the anti-submarine vessels needed to be further out to give them more fighting room, but with others disposed in depth as 'pouncers' able to concentrate on the detecting ship to counter-attack the submarine. The higher submerged speed available to the Intermediate (B) also meant that Limiting Lines of Submerged Approach would be much wider. It was even possible for these submarines to close submerged from a short distance astern of a convoy, though they would probably make a great deal of noise and could therefore be detected from much greater distances. Moreover, it was thought that submarines would still prefer to fire from a position broad on the bow of a convoy or Fleet unit. Paterson agreed with JASS that once a submarine had manoeuvred under a convoy it would be very difficult to counter, but in Paterson's opinion JASS's proposed Plan 'Parsnip', consisting of an emergency 90° turn by the convoy to uncover the submarine long enough for the escorts to locate and destroy it, was of '… limited use.'[50] What was certain was that the escorts would have to cover a greater area, than had been the case against the wartime submersible. Thus, when all these factors were modelled on the tactical table at JASS, it was concluded that the minimum escort strength for a 60-ship convoy was eight escorts (about 125 per cent of the wartime provision), rising to 12 escorts in submarine high threat areas. This would be a heavy – perhaps prohibitive – bill for shipping defence.

The Fleet, of course, would retain one major advantage over convoys, that of high passage speed which, even with a zig-zag superimposed on the mean-line-of-advance, would still limit the enemy's approach to narrower limits on the force's bows. These fast passage speeds, however, would consume fuel at a high rate, especially amongst the screening anti-submarine destroyers and place a heavy demand on frequent replenishment at sea. As in the past, the Fleet and, now, its supporting replenishment units, would be screened by a force sufficient to provide a reasonably 'watertight' anti-submarine barrier, capable of detecting an approaching submarine and counter-attacking it. Defence of the Fleet, when accompanied by aircraft carriers, posed additional problems, for, all-round 'circular' screen would have to be provided to allow the carrier to manoeuvre into wind during flying operations. There would never be enough escorts to provide such luxury for convoys. But, so long as there was an adequate level of intelligence to identify submarine concentrations, the intention, as JASS had suggested, was to reinforce each threatened convoy's relatively weak 'through' escort with a surface 'Patrol Group' (which might include an aircraft carrier), as had been the practice during the war. It was even hoped that the intelligence would be accurate enough to allow some fast ships to sail independently through areas where the danger was slight, and thereby speed up the delivery rate, as well reduce escort requirements.

As for shore-based air support, convoys were, in general, to be given a light escort from aircraft even in a danger area. It was envisaged that most aircraft would be flown on independent patrols over submarine danger areas, from whence they could be diverted to reinforce imminently threatened convoys. These tactics were preferred to providing 'through' air escort because they would ensure that the parts of the danger areas were covered frequently, thus hindering submarines attempting to move at speed. Even if the submarines did not risk surface travel, they would certainly have to snort for a considerable proportion of the approach and would thereby give anti-submarine aircraft detection opportunities. Some consideration was given – and practised on the JASS tactical table – to the use of sonobuoy barriers across the likely approach path of submarines trying to intercept convoys. This was an extension of operations carried out during the war on U-boat transit routes, but to become effective developments in sonobuoy technology were needed, though these would not appear until the 1950s. In the interim, therefore, the best chance of an aircraft detecting a submarine was still when it was on the surface, which they might have to risk if needing to move a considerable distance at high speed to intercept a convoy, given the relatively low snort transit speed of the Intermediate (B). It should be remembered that at this time, the actual Russian submarine threat still consisted, in the main, of non-schnorkel-fitted boats that still relied heavily on use of the surface. As always, in any convoy action the priority was for air escorts to locate and, if possible, destroy the enemy's contact-keeper and then to prevent the other submarines from concentrating against the convoy.

For the protection of the Fleet, on the other hand, continuous anti-submarine air escort was to be provided covering the outer area ahead and on the beam, about 20 miles from the Fleet, just on the limit of a submarine's hydrophone detection range on the Main Body. Here submarines might be found on the surface, trying to get into position ahead of the Fleet from where they could get contact on their own sensors. Once these patrols were covered, other aircraft were to maintain a continuous patrol some three to five miles on the beam and ahead of the Fleet where they could harass submarines using their periscope or radar to gain a final fire-control solution. Any additional aircraft (most likely to be shore-based) could be used for independent searches at a distance from the Fleet. Not only would all these aircraft have a chance of detecting submarines, but would also force others, which might have reported the Fleet's movements, to submerge.[51] The main source of enemy reports of Fleet (and convoy) movements was expected to come from enemy air reconnaissance. This was not lost on the Russians. Admiral of the Fleet of the Soviet Union S.G. Gorshkov wrote in the 1970s that the Germans made '... no small error ... [by] waging the struggle virtually only with submarines, without backing them up with other kinds of forces, especially aircraft.'[52]

Mahan would have understood the point that success is best achieved by the application of multiple and complementary capabilities. This was equally obvious to the British during and after the war.[53] This aspect was not, however, as simple as it seemed. The Joint Intelligence Sub-Committee noted in late 1946 that while the Germans had had many opportunities to modify their strategy early on in the war, the increasing power of the Allies soon circumscribed their flexibility. In their assessment, the Sub-Committee also noted that Dönitz displayed little aptitude for strategic thinking and that the Germans suffered throughout from the poor cooperation between the *Luftwaffe* and the U-boats in the Atlantic, though the system had worked somewhat better in the Arctic.[54] The limited reconnaissance capability of submarines when submerged meant that they would have to rely heavily on reports from shadowing aircraft. If, as expected, the Russians quickly recognized this, their reconnaissance aircraft would be prime targets for Allied carrier-borne fighters (which therefore made Russian air operations an important intelligence objective). But, even if the shadowing aircraft were destroyed, submarine attacks were still likely to develop. The most difficult decision a Senior Officer would have to make was whether the attack was made from outside or inside the screen or, in the case of a convoy, from beneath the convoy itself. In both the defence of convoy and of the Fleet papers Paterson emphasized – no doubt drawing from wartime experience – that, in the event of a surprise attack, there was a need for pre-arranged search schemes, capable of being put into instant operation. There was little that air escorts could do to help anti-submarine vessels if the submarines were already at close quarters with the convoy or Fleet. However, aircraft should be used to search the place where the attack took place as the convoy cleared the area astern, and hopefully detect submarines withdrawing or continuing to shadow. If the surface escorts could thereby be accurately directed, it was possible that they might inflict serious casualties on enemy submarines.[55]

By September 1948, Paterson had completed a paper examining the tactical employment of Patrol Groups which, after comment by the Naval Staff, was put before the Sea/Air Warfare Committee in mid-October. There, after minor amendments, the paper was approved for issue to Naval and Air Commanders-in-Chief, and authorities responsible for training and research in anti-submarine problems. Capitalizing on earlier doctrine from the interwar and wartime periods, this paper advanced a detailed exposition of how offensive anti-submarine operations were to be undertaken. Their primary purpose was to destroy submarines, with the term 'Patrol Group' embracing two methods: either used '… offensively as "Hunter-Killer" groups … or as a reinforcement to the close escort of convoys passing through submarine probability areas.'[56] To achieve this, Patrol Groups were to operate on the enemy's transit routes and in his operational areas, using their aircraft, possibly in cooperation with Coastal Command assets, to search large areas. When a submarine was detected by the air searches or pinpointed by intelligence, a proportion of the carrier's anti-submarine surface escort would be released as a striking force to hunt submarine to destruction. Paterson thought, therefore, that a Patrol Group should consist of a minimum of a carrier capable of day and night operations and at least four anti-submarine vessels able to provide both a screen for the carrier and an offensive striking force. It was realized that early on in a war, it was unlikely that sufficient numbers of carriers and escorts would be available to meet even these modest numbers for Patrol Groups, let along the more generous forces suggested by JASS. Shore-based aircraft of Coastal Command could partly fill the gap, though their poor killing power meant that they would be unable to execute the primary aim of the Patrol Groups, that of destroying enemy submarines.

These offensive operations were divided into two phases: first the gathering of intelligence, and then the hunting and destruction of the submarine. Intelligence would be gathered from aircraft sightings, reports of attacks on shipping, and from interception of electromagnetic transmissions from submarines. The only way that such intelligence would be forthcoming was if the Patrol Group operations were linked – even if at remote range – to convoy or Fleet movements, for these would prompt submarines to move and possibly transmit. Another, though less efficient method, was to deploy a Patrol Group in a relatively narrow submarine transit area, through which numbers of submarines had to pass, such as had been the case on the Northern Transit routes and, more especially, in the Bay of Biscay during the war. These areas were small when compared to the ocean wastes and, therefore, contained a higher average density of U-boats. The naval search effort would be supported by the use of shore-based aircraft flying 'box' patrols within suspected submarine areas or over transit routes. The coordination between the Patrol Group and Coastal Command aircraft would be through the Area Combined Headquarters (ACHQ), and, for specific hunts, shore-based aircraft could be put under the direct command of the Patrol Group Senior Officer. His own carrier-borne aircraft were to be flown on searches, which reflected the practice at the end of the war. The depth of these searches should be no more than 40–60 miles, and was regulated by the distance that surface escorts could steam in about two and a half hours, which was about as long as an aircraft was likely to hold contact with sonobuoys on a submerged submarine. If the escorts arrived later than this, or the aircraft had lost contact, the ships would have little chance of regaining the scent. In this case Paterson recommended that a containing circle of sonobuoys be dropped, unless a rough direction of escape was known, when a sonobuoy barrier could be laid across and ahead of the suspected track of the submarine. A maximum air effort was then to be mounted to fly patrols spaced around the datum, hoping to pick up the submarine snorting, or to follow up with sonobuoys any surface ship hydrophone effect detections. However, attempts to replicate the 'hunt to exhaustion' practised during the war was unlikely to be successful against an Intermediate (B), snort-fitted submarine with its much greater underwater endurance.

The striking force of ships from the Patrol Group were to close the aircraft's contact at high speed, until they reached the submarine's furthest-on-circle (FoC). Here they were to reduce to search speed and carry out a wide zig-zag, mindful of the danger of a counter-attack by the submarine with an anti-escort homing torpedo. The search would concentrate on the most probable escape course in the light of available intelligence, because searching all possible escape courses was likely to be unproductive, for the submarine's probability area would grow exponentially in proportion to the submarine's speed and the time since the last contact. (This problem had been noted during the war even when dealing with the slow, snort-fitted U-boats in coastal waters.) Paterson also examined the problem of a Patrol Group which was operating without a carrier and with no shore-based air support. Mathematical modelling (presumably by DNOR) suggested that the anti-submarine ships should zig-zag in a widely spaced formation to cover as much of the suspected area as possible. Consideration was also given to Patrol Groups working in Inshore Waters, when it was assumed that no carrier would be present. If in any of these scenarios the two-ship striking force were able to gain contact, their chances of gaining a kill were low for, as Paterson noted, a coordinated anti-submarine action required '… up to five ships … to provide the best chance of a kill.'[57] Paterson was, of course, reflecting the results of the sea trials by Gibbs Fourth Escort Flotilla, and others, as well as the work done at JASS on the tactical tables. In this connection DTASW had also made a number of liaison visits to the USN, where considerable effort was being expended on the Hunter-Killer concept. The Americans recognized that at least two escort carriers, with their attendant escorts, were needed to have any chance of holding down a single Intermediate (B).

When Captain Richard Onslow, the RN Director at JASS, spoke to the Naval Air Conference in May 1948 he made it clear that convoy remained the central pillar of British shipping defence philosophy. He also reiterated the problems of surface and air escorts in locating and destroying submarines, as well as the enemy's greater power of attack, especially if supported by reconnaissance aircraft. Onslow reminded his audience of the success of the Biscay and Northern Transit route offensives and suggested that similar results could again be achieved, provided their severely limited sensor and weapon technology against submerged submarines could be improved. For the time being, aircraft would therefore have to work in conjunction with surface forces that would do the killing. Onslow emphasized that the success of the Patrol Group concept rested heavily on intelligence of enemy submarine operations to narrow possible search areas, and this might be achieved by linking Patrol Group operations to convoy movements (as Paterson had concluded).[58] The Americans had come to similar conclusions.[59] One of their reports subsequently noted that:

> Because of the small chance of hunting down and killing a Type XXI or equivalent submarine with present Hunter-Killer groups, emphasis should be placed on convoy escort coverage by Hunter-Killer groups.[60]

Such ideas ran contrary to what are often seen as cherished USN views. In fact, the Americans (like the British) had always been persuaded that the safety of shipping was ultimately assured by the imposition of convoy. But they (like the British) also realized that to defeat the submarine, more was needed. It is true that the post-war USN Atlantic forces were more attuned to offensive operations *per se*, probably as a result of the experiences of their comrades in the Pacific war (many of whom, like Styer, were now in positions of influence in the Atlantic theatre). This was echoed in 1946 when Vice Admiral Sherman, the Deputy Chief of Naval Operations, observed that '… the strategic counter to this sort of thing is high emphasis on attack at the sources of the trouble.'[61] These views also highlight the enduring tension between, on the one hand, 'offensive' search operations, that are always sensitive to technological superiority and (especially) intelligence cueing, and, on the other hand, 'defensive' convoy operations which are more robust to technical deficiencies but cannot, alone, achieve the ultimate defeat of the submarine.

A year of exercises with fast submarines

While the 4EF was exercising with *Trumpetfish* during spring 1948, a year-long series of trials were beginning with ships of Captain Sir Charles E. Madden's Sixth Destroyer Flotilla (6DF), designed to investigate the ability of existing anti-submarine equipment to 'kill' an 18-knot submerged submarine. Two of Madden's ships, *Battleaxe* and *Crossbow*, began in the shore attack-teachers at Portland and operating against a slow T-Class submarine, followed by a four-week work-up with the 11-knot *Selene* in April 1948 to prepare them for exercises with the Guppy, USS *Amberjack*, off Key West during the following July and August.[62] Madden's team, now including *Scorpion* and *Broadsword*, would then return to the waters off Northern Ireland to complete their trials against the 17-knot HMS *Scotsman* and a second Guppy, USS *Dogfish*, from November 1948 to March 1949.[63] Without the pressure of wartime operations, the trials were extensive enough to reach some statistical validity, though interpretation of the results would have to take account of the effect of peacetime safety restrictions on tactical realism in the trials.[64]

The initial work-up soon confirmed the expected deterioration in attack effectiveness due to the submarine's speed. Just over 25 per cent of attacks were successful, that is, achieved a 'kill' or 'surfacing damage', and it took, on average, one and a half times longer and one or two additional attacks to 'kill' *Selene* as compared to the slow T-Class and *Selene* also escaped from the hunting ships more often.[65] The exercises which followed against *Amberjack* were even more challenging. Although the American submarine was much larger and therefore gave a better asdic echo, the water conditions were difficult and, unless *Amberjack* operated at shallow depth, asdic ranges were short. She was capable of 19 knots – considerably faster than anything the British had operated against before and, as a consequence, attack results were worse than against *Selene*, with about 15 per cent of attacks being counted as successful. This low success rate was, in part, due to *Amberjack*'s evasion manoeuvres which were prescribed in the exercise orders, and calculated to give the attacking ships the most difficult target. As the Admiralty later pointed out, 'In unrestricted A/S actions it is more a matter of chance if the target takes avoiding action at the worst moment for the attacking ship.'[66] Nevertheless, many of the failures were due to inability of the asdic to cope with the high target bearing rates experienced during these dynamic engagements, which led to the submarine slipping outside the asdic beam. This problem was already being addressed with a modification to the Type 144 Asdic, known as the 'Ships Component Mechanism', designed to remove the effect of own ship's motion from the equation during an attack. Although trials with a 'lash-up' of this gear were satisfactorily completed in 1947, the bearing recorder would have had to be redesigned if the gear was to be brought into service. Reflecting the modification policy set out earlier by Ashbourne in DTASW, the design was to remain a 'sealed', and was not introduced until the modified Type 164 Asdic entered service in 1950, and was not, therefore, available to Madden's ships.[67]

During the winter of 1948–49, the British ships started working with HMS *Scotsman*. Recently modified, she could maintain submerged speeds of 15–17 knots for about 45 minutes, though at 12 knots she could manoeuvre continuously for up to four hours.[68] Her design had undergone extensive trials in experimental water tanks and at sea to explore her complex handling characteristics at high underwater speed. She still to complete her 'First of Class' trials when she was urgently needed for the exercises with 6DF.[69] *Scotsman* soon proved to be a difficult target, because asdic conditions in the North Channel were poor and the submarine's echo could just be distinguished from the reverberation by its doppler, and then only by operators with good pitch discrimination.[70] Most close actions developed into stern chases, with attack successes running at 13 per cent, and then only when *Scotsman* was travelling no faster than 12 knots.[71] Nevertheless, Madden's ships were growing in experience, and they proved capable of holding contact with *Scotsman* for about an hour, which was longer than in previous trials. There were, however, still too many occasions when contact was lost altogether, though when this happened, at least the ships were allowed to try to relocate the submarine (not always with success) without her artificially signalling her position.[72] The lost contact schemes tried included an immediate all-round asdic search by the ships, which would sometimes pick up *Scotsman* from the high doppler of her echo or by hydrophone effect. If this did not work, a more organized search was needed.

For this purpose, Madden developed an experimental search later known as Plan 'Delta'. This was a reduced version of the elaborate USN 'Barndance' search, and should not be confused with the Plan 'Delta' used in the trials with *Seraph* – that version had been deleted from the tactics books by the end of 1945.[73] The new Plan 'Delta' replaced the simpler 'Box' Search. Instead of a static square barrier, the idea now was that the ships started an outward spiral within five minutes of the loss of contact and searched along the submarine's FoC expanding at 15 knots. Towards the end of the search, the ships turned inwards to search the area nearer the datum, to cover the possibility that the submarine was either evading at low speed or by constant turns was still close to the datum. When three ships were available the more elaborate 'Lambda' Search was used, still based on the same concept. As more ships became available to join the search, so the schemes became more complex but could also cover more water and so, theoretically at least, stood more chance of regaining contact.[74] These search schemes were somewhat more 'mathematical' in concept and showed strong American influences. They stood in apparent contrast to the pragmatic plans described by Burnett and evolved during the war when success was thought more likely if the search was concentrated a selected sector of the submarine's probability area. However, many anti-submarine practitioners, including, for example, Ormsby, adapted the more 'scientific' search plans, when resources and time allowed.[75] Although, in wartime it would rarely be possible for as many ships to be spared to concentrate on a single submarine, tactics for two-, three- and four-ship formations were eventually incorporated into the anti-submarine tactical manual.[76]

During February and March 1949 Madden's last set of trials were conducted against the Guppy USS *Dogfish* in the North Channel during. *Dogfish* was much larger than *Scotsman* and proved to be a better asdic target, but she was quieter and two knots slower than the British boat. Once more attacks were confined very largely to periods when *Dogfish* was travelling at 12 knots or less, though then Madden's four ships achieved a success rate of about 32 per cent. The 6DF ships also confirmed that when close actions were confined to two-ship teams, their effectiveness was roughly 50 per cent greater than when more ships were involved. However, with more ships in the close action, there was a lower tendency to attack non-submarines or to lose contact altogether.[77] The exercises as a whole proved that teamwork and practice were essential to success. The findings also seemed to suggest that the best tactic, as had been the case against slow wartime U-boats, was for the close action to be restricted to two ships, with spare escorts disposed on a containing patrol around the close anti-submarine action, from where they might regain contact if the submarine evaded its immediate attackers. The post-war version of this tactic was the 'Ring' that had been attempted by Gibbs' 4EF and others in earlier exercises. However, Madden rediscovered that the tactic could not be put into practice:

> ... because each A/S action very soon became a stern chase with the submarine doing 18 knots having had a few minutes start, and the two surface ships pursuing at 21 knots.[78]

Against *Seraph*, five years before, a loose diamond pattern of anti-submarine ships trailing the submarine had worked, while Gibbs had formulated the 'Umbrella' formation. These tactics had been passed on to Madden, who adapted the idea further. Madden deployed his ships with the attacking ship following roughly astern of the submarine, supported by wing ships at about 1,200 yards on either beam. When asdic conditions were poor, the wing ships were kept well up on the attacking ship's beam, where they were better able to maintain contact. In good asdic conditions the wing ships could afford to drop back a little, where it was easier for them to conform to the movements of the attacking ship. The dynamic tactical situation could change from moment to moment and this formation allowed the duties of the attacking ship to be shifted to the best placed anti-submarine vessel, and this might happen, Madden discovered, '... a number of times before a particular attack was consummated.'[79] When a fourth ship was available it was stationed about 2,000 yards astern of the leading ships, where it was well placed to cover against the submarine suddenly reversing course and breaking back through the lead ships, which *Trumpetfish* had used against 3EF. Once the submarine began to run out of battery 'amps' and was forced to slow down, a loose 'Ring' formation developed automatically. By the end, the highly practised 6DF were even able to execute these tactics even at night.

When they considered the results of all the exercises in 1948-9, the Admiralty noted that, in favourable tactical and environmental conditions, existing British asdic equipment and weapons in the hands of a worked-up escort group could achieve a killing rate of about 30 per cent, provided the target's speed was less than 12 knots.[80] At higher submarine speeds the killing rate fell off to practically zero, as had been long anticipated, and may have been exacerbated by the reputedly poor handling qualities of Madden's ships.[81] Of course, the anti-submarine gear of Madden's ships had been designed to deal with the pedestrian wartime U-boats, and when a check exercise was conducted by *Battleaxe* and *Crossbow* against the slow, unmodified HMS *Amphion*, the two ships achieved a 100 per cent kill rate. This result should, however, be compared with the wartime attacks with Squid, which ultimately achieved a 60 per cent success rate – the difference between this figure and that achieved against *Amphion* being explained by the effects of wartime operations compared to peacetime exercise artificialities and safety rules. It is likely that, had Madden been operating in wartime conditions, the results would have been reduced by a factor of at least one third. Moreover, in wartime the submarine could have counterattacked with homing torpedoes, and some of his ships would have been sunk (as Gibbs' experiences against *Amberjack* suggested). On the other hand, the peacetime submarine could afford to behave more liberally, when, as one post-war submarine commander recalled, '… the penalty for being detected was one hand grenade as opposed to a full pattern of depth-charges [or Squid projectiles]. The thought', he added, 'doth make the submariner prudent!'[82] Furthermore, *Amberjack*'s battery had been in the fully charged state at the beginning of each anti-submarine action during the trials off Key West. This was, the Admiralty pointed out, '… a state most unlikely to be met with in war.'[83] The trials, they concluded:

> … have shown that whilst the Coordinated ['Ring'] Action is sound in theory, there are many practical difficulties in poor asdic operating conditions, and when wakes left by the submarine and A/S vessels are liable to persist. A submarine which uses high speed under these conditions is liable to elude the A/S ships forming the 'ring'.[84]

Overall, when trying to extrapolate the trials results to a future war setting, it was impossible to deduce an exact outcome of operational engagements. But what was now certain was that the theoretical calculations (heavily based on wartime experience and military judgement) had been right, and anti-submarine close action would yield poor results. The track being taken by the Admiralty firmly to encompass wider anti-submarine offensive measures was correct. The trials also showed that the Intermediate (B), like earlier submarines, was more vulnerable to detection when forced to move at speed and the defensive convoy helped to create this situation. However, the fact that Madden had operated wartime equipment against the modern submarine threat left the question as to whether the solutions to the anti-submarine problems were to be found in a technological remedy.

Technological answers?

The exercises in 1948–49 with Madden's 6DF had confirmed that anti-submarine ships had, as anticipated, a limited capability against a fast submarine. Tactical procedures were needed, therefore, to take advantage of every fleeting detection. As for the ships' systems, while the existing Type 144 Asdic and Squid combination was reasonably efficient against submarines whose speed was less than 12 knots, against faster submarines it would only achieve a kill in very favourable circumstances.[85] The main limitations of the system were, firstly, the speed at which ships could operate the asdic effectively was too low, secondly (and directly related to the slow ship's speed), the rate of asdic search was too slow and, finally, the accuracy of the fire-control solution was constrained by the limitations of the asdic and the existing ahead-throwing weapons. The ship's asdic operating speed was critically dependent on the level of underwater self-noise, which in turn, was dominated by the interference from the ship's propellers, the design of the asdic dome, and the ship's motion in a heavy seaway. Research was underway into improved propeller designs as well as ways of silencing existing propellers by surrounding them with an artificial shield of bubbles. A new experimental asdic dome had already been fitted to HMS *Scorpion* during 1946, which allowed asdic operation at speeds of 25–28 knots, that is, seven to 10 knots higher than was previously possible.[86] Improving the asdic search rate was partly dependent on the ship's speed and partly on the scanning rate of the asdic itself. This had been appreciated for some time and work was in hand to develop an all-round scanning asdic, but this would not become available for many years due to the technical complexity of the equipment, though a set capable of scanning sector-by-sector was expected to be available by 1953.[87]

During the highly dynamic engagements against a fast submarine, inaccuracies were generated in the fire-control solution by the effects of the ship's tactical manoeuvring, which induced unwanted bearing movements of the target echo that could not be easily resolved from true bearing changed due to the target's movement. It was difficult, therefore, to estimate accurately the target's true course and speed which was vital if a precise forecast of weapon aiming was to be made. This error was eliminated by the introduction of the Ship's Component Mechanism to existing asdic installations, which compensated for the anti-submarine ship's movement across the target's bearing.[88] However, errors were still induced by the slow rate of calculating the target's bearing with the wartime searchlight asdic sets using the 'cut-on' procedure and the necessity of roughly pointing the ship at the target in order to fire an ATW, which was made more difficult by the need to fire at a short, fixed range. Research had been underway since the early 1940s into the application of radar 'Split-Beam' technology to asdic to produce instantaneous bearing and depth measurement. This technique was originally intended to improve the fire-control solution against slow, deep U-boats. When the fast submarine threat emerged, it soon became apparent that an effective solution consisted of the integrated use of up-to-date asdic bearing and depth accuracy with an improved anti-submarine mortar (suggested by Prichard in DASW during 1944), capable of all-round training and firing at a variable range. These developments became the Type 170 (or 'Four-Square') Asdic and the Limbo mortar, capable of firing Squid-like projectiles at variable ranges from 400–1,000 yards, and were experimentally fitted together in *Scorpion* in 1950. The probability of success with Limbo was high, although at the longer ranges against a manoeuvring submarine, its fire-control prediction induced errors because it was based on the assumption that the submarine was moving on a straight course.[89]

A programme was also underway to develop a ship-launched anti-submarine torpedo, capable of homing onto a submarine at long range, though the British remained sceptical that the problems of homing in shallow waters could be successfully overcome and this torpedo took lower priority than development of these weapons for aircraft use.[90] The timings for these technical improvements neatly matched the forecast in the Short-Term and Long-Term policy set out by Ashbourne in 1946. The major step forward was the integration of this equipment, initially in frigate conversions, and later into new ship designs.[91] The detailed requirements for the conversions were worked on by Burnett and Ormsby and eventually evolved into the first Type 15 Frigates, *Rocket* and *Relentless* allocated to Third Training Flotilla under Captain Le Fanu.[92] Even with improved asdics, action information centres, the limbo mortar and high ship's speed, exercises with fast submarines were beset with difficulty. The number of practices, Le Fanu noted, had '… not been plentiful but we have had some duels with *Turpin* …' but he added ruefully, '*Turpin* won on a technical knockout.'[93]

The outlook for aircraft still remained gloomy, though the use of MAD and equipment to detect the intra-red or ionized properties of schnorkel gases were at various stages of development.[94] However, the principal methods of locating submarines remained visual or radar detection of the schnorkel head and sonobuoy detection of the acoustic signature. Little could be done to improve visual detection, other than by providing better sighting positions for the crews in aircraft. British research towards the end of the war had concentrated on attempts to use high-frequency radars to reduce the effects of sea clutter.[95] In the post-war era, varying interest was shown in the US development of high-powered Airborne Early Warning (AEW) radar to detect schnorkels. USN aircraft on tour of Britain in mid-1948 had been able to detect a schnorkel at ranges of 17–23 miles in sea states 2–3. However, when the sea state rose to 4–5, which was commonplace in British waters, the number of detections was considerably reduced by the interfering effects of sea clutter. For the smaller carrier-borne aircraft, such as the Avenger, carriage of the heavy AEW radar meant that a separate aircraft had to localize and attack any contacts achieved.[96] The sonobuoys in use were of wartime design and remained limited in range. Their capability would not be improved substantially until Very Low Frequency (VLF) acoustic techniques could be applied to them, and the technological advances needed would not provide results for many years.[97] The provision of homing torpedoes for aircraft attacks on submerged submarines struggled against great technical difficulty.[98] Even so, work continued optimistically to analyse the potential of aircraft used in offensive operations over submarine transit routes. It was clear that if any appreciable level of performance was to be achieved a wide selection of the sensors and weapons under development would have to become operational in the new aircraft, such as the land-based Shackleton and carrier-borne Gannet.[99] The first tentative steps with the use of helicopters for anti-submarine operations had been made by a joint Anglo-US team in 1943, but had foundered on the poor operational performance of the machines. Nevertheless, attention continued to be directed (mainly in America) to the development of an anti-submarine helicopter capable of carrying a 'dunking' asdic. This appeared to show considerable operational benefits, though these, too, would not be realized for some considerable time.[100]

British submarines had sunk 17 and 40 U-boats in the First and the Second World Wars respectively, but this had not been their primary role. All bar one of these successes had been against U-boats operating on the surface. The one exception was HMS *Venturer* in early 1945, which sank *U-864* in an engagement during which both submarines were submerged throughout.[101] The idea of making anti-submarine warfare the primary role of British submarines was initiated in early 1946 by [then] Commander A.R. Hezlet, DSO*, DSC, the submariner on DTASW's staff.[102] Burnett followed up the idea in his paper on future anti-submarine problems during the following year. British submarines, working in the same medium as their prey might be operated to advantage, however, they would have:

> ... to be fitted with a means of detecting and locating submerged submarines. Although submarines may prove to be more efficient vehicles for the asdic than surface ships, the comparatively short ranges of asdic will limit their usefulness on patrols. Also some form of recognition equipment have to be developed before they can be operated effectively in waters used by other A/S forces.[103]

These ideas were developed by the end of 1947 into papers on the use of submarines as anti-submarine vessels. The idea of using submarines as convoy escorts proved to be stillborn, largely due to the problem of mutual recognition between friendly forces.[104] However, the more promising idea of their use as part of the forward attack-at-source strategy in enemy controlled waters had a strong pedigree and considerable potential for the future, not only for laying mines off their ports but in direct attacks on their submarines. Sufficient optimism in the potential of submarines encouraged the Admiralty to announce in early 1948 that:

> In war, the primary operational function of our submarines will be the interception and destruction of enemy submarines in enemy controlled waters.[105]

The technical and tactical problems were the submarine's ability to locate its target at long range (using VLF acoustic techniques), to close to an attack without alerting its prey (requiring long endurance at a high silent speed) and, finally, to be able to attack the enemy with homing torpedoes, thus overcoming the problems of target depth and evasive manoeuvre. Streamlined, snort-fitted submarines were limited by underwater endurance and, for a while, it was hoped that better performance could be achieved by adapting the HTP submarine developments already in train.[106] The mobility and endurance problems were, of course, solved with the introduction of the nuclear submarine, but this brought in its train additional problems of self-noise. These technical solutions were pursued with vigour, but standing at the end of the 1940s, the solutions were often a long way away. At this time, with the experience of the wartime asdic and ATW developments behind them, many officers realized that no sooner were future solutions brought to fruition, than the enemy would have instituted new – perhaps revolutionary – technologies of his own. Thus the technological catch-up cycle would take another turn. The essential element, the naval officers realized, was that a solidly grounded doctrine provided the signposts for the anti-submarine technical developments. This doctrine had to be founded on a clear understanding of the dynamic tension between submarine and anti-submarine forces that showed remarkable continuity even in the face of major technological advances.

Conclusion
Joining up the dots, 1944–49

The nature of anti-submarine warfare

Captain P.W. Burnett, DSO, DSC, arrived at the Admiralty in September 1945, and was followed a month later by Commander G.A.G Ormsby, DSO, DSC, and Lieutenant Commander J.P. Mosse, DSC. These men were all regulars, and from the time they completed their anti-submarine specialist training, during which they were taught principles deduced from the First World War experience in 1917–18, and throughout the Second World War, they had studied and grown to understand anti-submarine warfare. This intellectual pull-through stood them in good stead in the Admiralty in 1946–48 as they wrote the first set of doctrine papers. They knew that the submarine had inherently weak defensive qualities, and therefore relied on remaining undetected. Stealth was also crucial to its chance of making a successful attack with the relatively short-range torpedoes that were initially available. Denying the submarine the benefit of stealth was critical in order to prevent the submarine from attacking, and piercing the submarine's stealthy shroud was a prerequisite to destroying it. Fundamentally, as one experienced anti-submarine practitioner had put it, anti-submarine warfare revolved around '… an attempt to sink an invisible enemy by a sense which is not in every day use.'[1] By this sense he meant the interpretation of complex signals produced by electronic equipment.

There were two ways of doing this. In one the asdic was used to listen for the sounds produced by a submarine. Given the technology of the 1930s and 1940s, this meant that the main source came from the submarine's propeller noise, and was critically dependent, therefore, on the submarine's speed being sufficiently high. The most often used alternative was to rely on detecting the echo returning from an active transmission by the asdic set. These echoes were weak owing to the losses in transmission of the sound and the smallness of the submarine's echoing area. Their detection was made even more difficult by the reception not only of unwanted echoes from the seabed, wrecks and rocks, the sea surface, the body of the water (i.e. reverberations), but also extraneous sounds from the anti-submarine ship's own movement through the water (i.e. self-noise). Classification of asdic contacts into 'submarine' and 'non-submarine' categories was therefore often difficult and time-consuming.

Conclusion: joining up the dots, 1944–49   171

Although the early submarine's underwater speed was low (generally less than five knots) the dynamics of an anti-submarine action could nevertheless be high for two interrelated reasons. The range of initial detection was usually very short, in the order of half a mile, which gave the ship very little time before it overran the contact or the ship passed outside the detection range. Even at the short range-scales at which the asdic was transmitting, the speed of sound (very much lower than radar waves) meant that target data arrived in the ship at best at intervals of several seconds. Added to this was the intermittency of the received echoes due to the vagaries of the sea's structure and interference from reverberations and self-noise. Even when asdic contact was firmly established the problems did not abate. Measuring the range to the target was relatively straightforward, but establishing its bearing involved a time-consuming 'cut-on' procedure. Estimating the target's depth was wholly guesswork until the introduction of a specialized depth-finding asdic (Type 147B), and even then depth measurement was inherently prone to errors because the sound beam was usually bent by the ocean's complex temperature structure.

Attacking the submarine with depth-charges was also fraught with difficulty. Initially, attacks required the anti-submarine ship to pass directly over the aiming point, which was itself some way ahead of the submarine to allow for the time taken by the depth-charges to sink to the target's depth. During the last stages of the attack either contact was lost (if the submarine was deep), or the bearing rate accelerated as the ship passed ahead of the submarine. In either case, the estimation of the submarine's position, course, speed and depth became less certain and resulted in the need for a barrage attack with multiple depth-charges in an attempt to overcome the three-dimensional aiming errors. The introduction of ATW, together with an integrated semi-automated aiming and firing system, removed many of these limitations. The advantages of ATW were, however, severely curtailed by the advances in submarine speed from 1944 onwards.

Before the operational appearance of the fast submarine, the enemy had already adopted schnorkel technology which allowed U-boats to operate continuously submerged throughout their war patrols. Large area searches by aircraft (for which they were uniquely suited) and which relied on detecting U-boats travelling on the surface, were instantly nullified. At the same time anti-submarine ships had to revert to asdic as their main means of detecting the U-boats, and this forced them rapidly to review their tactical countermeasures. The U-boats, too, suffered from considerable limitations as a result of their new operating techniques, not the least being their ability to find and close targets. Fortunately, the schnorkel-fitted submarine problem bore strong resemblances to the threat posed by submarines at the end of the First World War, the interwar period and the opening phases of the Second World War. It was possible, therefore, to adapt existing tactical practice (albeit with the much improved equipment available) to counter this 'new' threat. Against the conventional schnorkel-fitted U-boat at the end of the Second World War, a 'blood-and-guts' confirmation (by way of wreckage) of success in the 'new' procedures was possible, but against the fast submarine the British had to rely on trials and exercises whose realism was compromised by safety restrictions, even in wartime. Conclusions over the ultimate efficacy of tactical measures proposed for defeating fast submarines was therefore problematic. The overall difficulty of anti-submarine warfare underpins much of the rationale for decisions over anti-submarine developments that were undertaken not only, but especially, between 1944 and 1949.

The nature of the threat

By 1944, the submarine threat was immediate and (potentially at least) critical. This had not always been the case. For much of the interwar period, the threat from the German U-boat was meagre and only as war approached did the problem become urgent. The Royal Navy therefore adopted a stance of preparedness. This was, in many respects, repeated in the immediate post-war era when the potential threat now came from the Soviet Union. She had been ravaged by the Second World War and, in any case, had no real capacity to mount a submarine campaign against British trade or military operations. This threat, which was forecast (fairly accurately) to become serious by the late 1950s, would resemble that posed by the nascent threat of the German schnorkel-fitted, high-speed U-boats which had been preparing for operations as the Second World War came to a close. The way in which post-war anti-submarine warfare was conceived, therefore, owes more to the operations of the late war inshore campaign, than to the great convoy battles of 1942–43 against U-boats operating in packs and relying on surface travel for search and concentration around convoys. Because the Russian danger, in terms of actual operational capability (if not of political aspiration) was only just emerging in 1945–49, the threat against which the Royal Navy prepared was a generic one formed by an amalgam of the physical potential of the ex-German Type XXI fast U-boats, together with assumptions regarding corrections of German wartime operational mistakes (such as their failure to provide adequate supporting air reconnaissance). Nor did the reality of the atomic bomb create much impact, partly because the enemy had none, and partly because when they acquired some weapons, the numbers and power of the bombs were not initially thought to ensure the destruction of the will to fight. On the Allied side, the possession of the bomb gave additional impetus to considerations of the efficacy of attacking enemy submarines at source. The resultant doctrine flowing from all these reflections seems to have served its purpose, since it remained broadly in use for the next two decades.

Tactics and technology

Technological measures to counter either specific submarine developments or to overcome difficulties with existing equipment took many years to come to fruition. Thus there was no ready technical answer to the fast submarine and the Royal Navy had to adapt tactical procedures to maximize the potential of existing equipment in dealing with the new threat. Indeed, Burnett concluded that the metric for measuring the Royal Navy's and the enemy's operational facility was to match existing British anti-submarine capability with that expected of the enemy's submarines 15 years hence. The long development cycle for new technologies meant that they cannot be seen merely as emanating from some particular operational requirement. For example, the asdic development (Type 170), which did much to overcome the problem of accurately locating a fast submarine during an attack, began as a means of substantially improving the attack accuracy of depth-charge attacks against a slow, deep submarine. In the meantime, tactical adaptation led to procedures to overcome the original problem (the Creeping Attack), while the combination of existing asdic (Type 144) along with ATWs gave some capability against the emerging fast submarine problem. Tactical adaptation, rather than wholly new tactics, made sense because existing tactics were familiar (thus reducing the re-training load) and, in any case, were interrelated with the equipment which was still to be used. Moreover, the full impact of an enemy's change in operations with new equipment did not have an immediate impact at maximum effectiveness. If anti-submarine forces stumbled to find solutions (and the British generally did better than that), the enemy took time to fully develop their new offensive techniques, which gave the British a breathing space to put countermeasures in place. To some extent, looking back on the problem, it depends on whether Vice Admiral J.M. Mansfield, Flag Officer, Submarines, was right in spring 1947 that: 'We stand ... on the threshold of a complete revolution in submarine design and technique, and consequently in all types of anti-submarine measures.'[2] The alternative view of an experienced anti-submarine practitioner, Captain E.A. Gibbs, RN, Captain (D), Fourth Escort Flotilla, was that: 'Generally speaking the fast Submarine is not so much a new problem as a serious development of the old problem.'[3] The way in which tactical doctrine was developed in the Royal Navy over the period 1944–49 suggests that it was Gibbs' view which prevailed. Pragmatically, until new equipment became available, the Royal Navy could hardly choose another course.

The 'defensive' and 'offensive'

Many historians have followed the line that the primary goal of anti-submarine warfare can best be articulated in the mantra of the 'safe and timely arrival' of trade and that the best means of achieving this is to impose convoy. Furthermore, the convoy 'defensive' escorts are best placed to destroy attacking submarines, whilst the alternative use of these anti-submarine forces on 'offensive' operations is inefficient. Thus convoy, by this logic, is transformed into an 'offensive' measure. There is, of course, some measure of legitimacy in this view, but it is a caricature and will not do. For a start, it confuses the issues and, secondly, it is not how anti-submarine warfare was seen by those who really understood it in 1944–49 (or even 1917–49). Anti-submarine practitioners realized that the 'safe and timely arrival' of convoys was only part of the equation. If, at the same time anti-submarine forces were not able to destroy sufficient numbers of submarines, their numbers would increase and (perhaps more crucially) the expertise and morale of their crews would improve. It was not necessary to sink more submarines than the enemy could build (a mistaken calculus adopted by the Germans as the principal aim of their anti-shipping campaign). It was only necessary to sink enough submarines to 'keep their tails down', though it was not possible then, or now, to exactly quantify this number. As anti-submarine specialists (and others) realized the fundamental difficulties associated with anti-submarine warfare meant that destroying submarines was an inherently inexact and inefficient business, the need, therefore, was to capitalize on every opportunity to attack the enemy. The question was how best was this to be done?

Theoretically, engaging submarines in the vicinity of a convoy put anti-submarine forces at an advantage by concentrating escorts around the submarine's prey. The Germans had attempted to overturn this logic by massing a counter-concentration through their U-boat pack-tactic system. However, against a coordinated and aggressive defence even these enemy tactics failed. It was only when the enemy came up against an escort that was weak in numbers, capability and training, that they scored substantial success. This was, to simplify the complex argument of this monograph, because the convoy system created a number of tactical advantages for anti-submarine forces. Firstly, as had just been noted, a convoy's escort formed a concentration of anti-submarine forces. But the imposition of convoy, by congregating the ships into a small area, also effectively left wide expanses of the ocean bare of targets. This presented the submarine with two problems: locating the convoys, which drove the submarines to disperse to search, and then making them move (at relatively high speed) to close the convoy in order to attack, or to overtake the convoy so as to attack repeatedly. Submarines moving at speed are no longer stealthy, and present anti-submarine forces with opportunities to locate and attack them. Up to 1944 this weakness of the U-boat was ruthlessly exploited by anti-submarine forces in direct and distant support of convoys. These operations were augmented by (albeit often inefficient) operations over U-boat transit routes and attacks at source by submarines, direct aircraft attack and mining. Overall, about half the U-boats sunk were by the, so called 'defensive' forces, and the other half by 'offensive' operations.

The combination of 'defensive' and 'offensive' anti-submarine operations was a well developed doctrine that had originated in the First World War and had survived unabated during the interwar years. The Royal Navy entered the Second World War fully confident that convoy provided the basic building-block of their anti-submarine strategy. This had to be combined with aggressive action close to the convoys, and wider offensive operations designed to sink U-boats and, at least, to harass their every moment at sea and (ideally) in harbour. Force levels relative to the magnitude of the expanding convoy system and the growing power of the U-boats (magnified after the Fall of France) meant that a balanced 'defensive' and 'offensive' strategy had to be held in abeyance for a time, for simply finding sufficient resources for the direct defence of convoys stretched Allied resources to the limit. At moments of extreme peril this defence was largely passive. But as anti-submarine forces grew in numbers and capability, the Royal Navy soon resurrected its long-held doctrine as 'defensive' escorts became more active and aggressive. Sea and air support groups were assigned to threatened convoys, where

Conclusion: joining up the dots, 1944–49   175

they took the offensive, for they had the time to hunt U-boats to destruction. Gradually, too, the means of attack-at-source became more sophisticated with improved bombing techniques. Thus when the enemy abandoned the conventional submersible mode of operation and reverted to submerged patrols with schnorkel-fitted U-boats, the fundamental doctrine for dealing with them was already in use. This doctrine was expanded as the basis for countering the incipient threat of the fast U-boats at the end of the Second World War. The 'offensive' and 'defensive' were not entirely equal strategic or tactical partners, for if the 'offensive' was to be successful, it had to rest on a sound 'defensive' posture. It could not exist alone, whereas, the 'defensive' could at least for a time. The fast submarine formed the benchmark of the post-war threat, against which the Royal Navy took forward the now well-established anti-submarine warfare doctrine based on the holistic, symbiotic relationship between the 'defence' and 'offence'.

Synthesis

This monograph has focused on the period 1944–49, at the end of the Second World War and the opening of the Cold War. It has established a new interpretation of the Royal Navy's anti-submarine doctrine against the threat of the fast submarine and, by extension, against the wartime U-boat. Instead of treating 'defensive' and 'offensive' operations as alternative options, the Royal Navy took a holistic approach to the problem in which the 'defensive' and 'offensive' were seen as interrelated, symbiotic partners. This, seemingly obvious, point provides a significantly different point of departure when assessing the performance of the Royal Navy (and the Admiralty in particular) in pursuing doctrinal development and strategic choices. The failure of the literature to grapple with the complexity of this issue has led to a widespread misunderstanding of application of anti-submarine doctrine by the Royal Navy from the First World War to the end of the Second World War, and into the Cold War. This has been exacerbated by a failure to encompass adequate swathes of the primary record, and a lack of comprehension of the technical and tactical difficulties of anti-submarine warfare. The opening chapters of this monograph have corrected many of these errors, and the remaining chapters have extended the research from the mid-years of the Second World War to the beginning of the Cold War.

This era has not been covered before in the depth presented here, and the analysis presents an image of the Admiralty and of the Royal Navy at variance with much popular myth. Far from being conservative and ponderous, the Admiralty proved to be a flexible and responsive organization, which learned lessons from past operations, and was then capable of making accurate and prescient decisions over tactical policy, even though the intelligence at hand was sparse and the performance of existing operational equipment was marginal. This was achieved through deep professionalism, honed by six years of war, and the osmotic transfer of information between a multitude of departments. The Admiralty was, in the words of the First Sea Lord, 'a well-oiled machine'.[4] More importantly, it solved big business problems with a small business approach. Thus anti-submarine staff in the

Admiralty at the end of the Second World War and in the immediate post-war years was manned by long-service, professional anti-submarine specialist officers. These intelligent, pragmatic experts brought their interwar and wartime experience and knowledge to bear on the new anti-submarine problem of the fast submarine, but who also consulted widely with experts in the staffs and operational commands, in the search for practical solutions. They did not allow practical doctrine to be swamped by theory, and did it in a remarkably short time. The solutions they derived between 1944 and 1949 were characterized by adaptation of current tactical practices to optimise existing equipment against a more difficult technological threat, which offered robust solutions well into the Cold War, even when the new equipment, procured against a different requirement, came into service. In hindsight, the story appears predetermined but, in reality, it was beset by many strategic, tactical and technological uncertainties, through which the Naval Staff had to find their way by many trackless paths.

Notes

Introduction

1 Karl Doenitz, *Memoirs: Ten Years and Twenty Days*, tr. R.H. Stevens, intro. Jürgen Rohwer (London: Greenhill Books, 1990): 429; Kenneth Wynn, *U-Boat Operations of the Second World War*, Vol. 2: *Career Histories, U511–UIT25* (London: Chatham Publishing, 1998): 256–7; Jordan Vause, *Wolf: U-boat Commanders in World War II* (Shrewsbury: Airlife, 1997): 202–3; F.H. Hinsley, E.E. Thomas, C.A.G. Simkins and C.F.G. Ransom, *British Intelligence in the Second World War: Its Influence on Strategy and Operations*, Vol. III, Part 2 (London: HMSO, 1988): 631.
2 Richard Compton-Hall, emails 20 June 2000, 11:27:31 and 16:07:15.
3 'Bergen', in 'Report on Interrogation of German Naval Staff Officers of the U-Boat Arm at Flensburg and Bergen', Group Captain Gates, CC/s.17384 A/U Ops., 6 June 1945, Gretton Papers, MSS/93/008, NMM(G).
4 Marc Milner, *The U-boat Hunters: The Royal Canadian Navy and the Offensive against Germany's Submarines* (Annapolis, Maryland: Naval Institute Press, 1994): 254.
5 Correlli Barnett, *Engage the Enemy More Closely: The Royal Navy in the Second World War* (London: W. W. Norton & Co., 1991): 854.
6 Stephen Roskill, *The War at Sea 1939–1945*, Vol. III, Part II: *The Offensive 1st June 1944–14th August 1945* (London: HMSO, 1961): 290; John Terraine, *Business in Great Waters: The U-Boat Wars 1916–1945* (London: Leo Cooper, 1989): 662; [Günther Hessler], *The U-boat War in the Atlantic, 1939–1945*, Vol. III: *June 1943–May 1945* (London: HMSO, 1989); Eberhard Rössler, *The U-boat: The Evolution and Technical History of German Submarines*, tr. Harold Erenberg (London: Arms and Armour Press, 1981).
7 Jürgen Rohwer, *The Critical Convoy Battles of March 1943: The Battle for HX.229/ SC.122* (London: Ian Allan, 1977); David Syrett, *The Defeat of the German U-Boats: The Battle of the Atlantic* (Columbia: South Carolina University Press, 1994); Michael Gannon, *Black May: The Epic Story of the Allies' Defeat of the German U-Boats in May 1943* (London: Aurum Press, 1998); W.A.B. Douglas, *The Creation of a National Air Force: The Official History of the Royal Canadian Air Force*, Vol. II (Toronto: University of Toronto Press, 1986); Marc Milner, *The U-boat Hunters: The Royal Canadian Navy and the Offensive against Germany's Submarines* (Annapolis, Maryland: Naval Institute Press, 1994); W.A.B. Douglas, Roger Sarty, Michael Whitby, *No Higher Purpose: The Official Operational History of the Royal Canadian Navy in the Second World War, 1943–1945*, Vol. II, Part 2 (forthcoming). See also: Marc Milner, 'The Dawn of Modern Anti-Submarine Warfare: Allied responses to the U-boats, 1944–45', RUSI Journal (Spring 1989): 61–8; Douglas M. McLean, 'Confronting Technological and Tactical Change: Allied Antisubmarine Warfare in the Last Year of the Battle of the Atlantic', *Naval War College Review*, Vol. 47, No. 1

(1994): 87–104, and 'The Last Cruel Winter: The RCN Support Groups and the U-Boat Schnorkel Offensive' (MA, Royal Military College of Canada, March 1992); also M. Llewellyn-Jones, 'Trials with HM Submarine *Seraph* and British Preparations to Defeat the Type XXI U-Boat, September–October, 1944', *The Mariner's Mirror*, Vol. 86, No. 4 (November 2000): 434–51, and 'The Pursuit of Realism: British Anti-Submarine Tactics and Training to Counter the Fast Submarine', in John Reeve and David Stevens (eds.), *The Face of Naval Battle: The Human Experience of Modern War at Sea* (Crows Nest, NSW, Australia: Allen & Unwin, 2003): 219–39.
8 David Zimmerman, 'Tactics and Technology', in Stephen Howarth and Derek Law (eds.), *The Battle of the Atlantic 1939–1945: The 50th Anniversary International Naval Conference* (London: Greenhill Books, 1994): 476 [emphasis supplied].
9 'A "New Look" at "Offence" and "Defence": The Anti-U-Boat Campaign, 1939–1945, A Brief Statement of Facts', F. Barley and D.W. Waters, Historical Section, 15 October 1955, DWW24, Box PT134, NHB [emphasis supplied].
10 'A "New Look" at "Offence" and "Defence"', NHB.
11 Eric J. Grove (ed.), *The Defeat of the Enemy Attack on Shipping, 1939–1945*, revised edn. (Aldershot: Ashgate for The Navy Records Society, 1997): 47–9.
12 Stephen Roskill, *The War at Sea 1939–1945*, Vol. I: *The Defensive* (London: HMSO, 1954): 134.
13 P. Gretton, 'Why Don't We Learn From History', *The Naval Review* (January 1958). Gretton drew much of his inspiration from the Historical Section. Recent scholarship has begun to unpick these ideas, see: Joseph A. Maiolo, *The Royal Navy and Nazi Germany, 1933–39: A Study in Appeasement and the Origins of the Second World War* (London: Macmillan Press, 1998), and George Franklin, *Britain's Anti-Submarine Capability, 1919–1939* (London: Frank Cass, 2003). The latter, however, still contains a number of myth-ridden conclusions.
14 Naval Staff Directorate, *British Maritime Doctrine*, 2nd edn., BR1806 (London: HMSO, 1999). A correction had been submitted by the author to this manual.
15 'Philosophical Ramblings', Doug McLean, email, 1 November 2003, 21:13:28 GMT.
16 N.A.M. Rodger, 'Image and Reality in Eighteenth-Century Naval Tactics', *The Mariner's Mirror*, Vol. 89, No. 3 (August 2003): 280–96.
17 'HMS *Conn*, Report of Proceedings, 11 January to 2 February 1945', Lieutenant Commander Raymond Hart, DSC, RN, Senior Officer 21st Escort Group, 5 February 1945, ADM 217/755.
18 Commander Richard Compton-Hall, interview, 26 February 2000.
19 John Mosse, 'Half a Lifetime', Part II, August 1986, IWM 90/23/1: 1–2.
20 An extract from a Canadian shanty written by an anonymous Surgeon-Lieutenant in the 9th ('Barber Pole') Escort Group quoted in Alan Easton, *50 North: An Atlantic Battleground* (London: Eyre & Spottiswoode, 1963): 268.
21 'HMUDE Summary of Progress', 1 December 1949, NAA(M): MP1049/5, 1968/2/800.
22 Moore, *The Royal Navy and Nuclear Weapons* (London: Frank Cass, 2001): 46–59 and 184–5; Grove, *Vanguard to Trident: British Naval Policy since World War II* (London: The Bodley Head, 1987): 3–4.
23 Andrew Lambert, *Nelson: Britannia's God of War* (London: Faber and Faber, 2004): 359.

1 Echoes from the past, 1917–40

1 'German Navy (Submarines)', CB1182S, [NID], April 1918, AL: 35 and 40.
2 'Remarks on Submarine Warfare', Operations Division, CB0259, January 1917, AL: 4.
3 'Tactics of Attack', in Appendix I to 'German Navy (Submarines)', CB1182S, [NID], April 1918, AL: 88.

Notes 179

4 'Remarks on Submarine Tactics against Convoys', Anti-Submarine Division, Naval Staff, Admiralty, CB620, October 1917, in 'Convoy Orders, 1917–1919', AL: 6–8.
5 'Mercantile Convoys: General Instructions for Port Convoy Officers, Ocean and Destroyer Escorts, and Commodores of Convoys', CB648(2), 18 October 1918, ADM 186/40.
6 Robert J. Urick, *Principles of Underwater Sound*, 3rd edn. (California: Peninsula Publishing, 1983): 334.
7 'Remarks on Submarine Tactics against Convoys, Protection of a Convoy by Extended Patrols, Instructions for Escorts and Patrols, 1919', Convoy Section Division, Naval Staff, CB648(2)A, 30 April 1919, in 'Convoy Orders, 1917–1919', AL: 19.
8 'Procedure when Hunted with Hydrophones', in Appendix II to 'German Navy (Submarines)', CB1182S, [NID], April 1918, AL: 91.
9 'Methods Recommended for Carrying out Searches for Hostile Submarines', CB1238, October 1916, ADM 186/373.
10 'Remarks on Protection of a Convoy by Extended Patrols', Anti-Submarine Division, Naval Staff, Admiralty, CB680, November 1917, in 'Convoy Orders, 1917–1919', AL.
11 'Employment of Aeroplanes for Anti-Submarine Work', Colonel Williamson, Commanding No. 18 Group, RAF, 14 August 1918, NA, AIR 1/642/17/122/252.
12 Martin Doughty, *Merchant Shipping and War: A Study in Defence Planning in Twentieth-Century Britain* (London: Royal Historical Society, 1982): 47.
13 Quoted in, 'The Defeat of the Enemy Attack on Shipping, 1939–1945: A Study of Policy and Operations, Vol. 1B (Plans and Tables)', Historical Section, Admiralty, BR1736(51)1B, [CB3304(1B)], 16 April 1957, ADM 234/579: 5.
14 'Home Waters – Part IX, 1 May 1917 to 31 July 1917', DTSD, Naval Staff Monographs (Historical) – Volume XIX, Monograph No. 35, CB917R, [OU 5528(H)], August 1939, NHB: 241–5.
15 'Home Waters – Part VIII, December 1916 to April 1917', DTSD, Naval Staff Monographs (Historical) – Volume XVIII, Monograph No. 34, CB917Q, [OU 5528(G)], May 1933, NHB: 471.
16 Maiolo, *The Royal Navy and Nazi Germany*: 126.
17 The narrative which follows is drawn, in part, from the many issues of 'Progress in Torpedo, Mining, Anti-Submarine Measures, and Chemical Warfare Defence', in ADM 186, and 'Progress in Tactics', AL.
18 'The Development of British Naval Aviation, 1919–1945', Naval Staff History, SecondWorld War, Vol. I, CB3307(1), BR1936(53)(1), 14 July 1954, NHB: 89.
19 Janet M. Manson, *Diplomatic Ramifications of Unrestricted Submarine Warfare, 1939–1941* (London: Greenwood Press, 1990): 109.
20 'Progress in Torpedo, Mining, Anti-Submarine Measures, and Chemical Warfare Defence, 1932', CB3002/32, 1933, ADM 186/500: 34.
21 Joseph Maiolo, 'Deception and Intelligence Failure: Anglo-German Preparations for U-boat Warfare in the 1930s', Paper delivered at the Military History Seminar, King's College, London, 23 February 1999: 15–16; 'Report on Methods of Submarine Location (Draft notes for reply to 1st Sea Lord enquiry dated October 1929)', [A.B. Woods, Admiralty Research Laboratory], 9 November 1929, and B.S. Smith, HMS *Osprey*, to Director, Scientific Research & Experimental Department, Admiralty, 14 August 1929, ADM 218/273.
22 'Defence against Submarine Attack', CID Paper 1318-B [Extract], March 1937, ADM 199/2365.
23 'Progress in Torpedo, Mining, Minesweeping Anti-Submarine Measures and Chemical Warfare Defence, 1937', CB3002/37, 1937, ADM 186/541: 33.
24 DNI, to Admiralty Librarian, 10 June 1937, and 'The Naval War, 1914–1918, Submarine War on Commerce', German Official History, Vol. III, Pt. 1, Chs. 1–12, AL: 118–19.

25 'Home Waters and the Atlantic, Volume I, September 1939–8 April 1940', Naval Staff History, Second World War, CB3301(1), 31 December 1954, NHB: 71.
26 'Progress in Tactics, 1937', Tactical Division, CB3016/37, December 1937, AL: 115.
27 '[Battle of the Atlantic], Chapter V, September 1939', [F. Barely and D.W. Waters], n.d., Box PT135, NHB: 23.
28 C.D. Howard-Johnston to J.D. Brown, NHB, 24 February 1980, CCAC, HWJN.
29 Grove (ed.), *The Defeat of the Enemy Attack on Shipping*: 4.
30 'Convoy on the Outset of War with Germany', Plans Division, 19 February 1938, ADM 1/9501.
31 Minute, Admiral Lord Chatfield, First Sea Lord, 8 March 1938, ADM 1/9501.
32 'Convoy on the Outset of War with Germany', Plans Division, 19 February 1938, ADM 1/9501.
33 'Protection British Shipping in the Vicinity of the British Isles during the first 14 days of an Emergency', Captain F.R Garside, Assistant D of P, 30 August 1938, in 'Naval War Memorandum (Germany)', Admiralty, 1937–1939, Case 00244, Vol. II, NHB.
34 'Movement of Advanced Air Striking Force and Field Force to France, Plan "W4"', Section IXA, 'Naval War Memorandum (European)', Admiralty Letter, M.00697/39, January 1939, Case 00244, Vol. III, NHB.
35 Maiolo, *The Royal Navy and Nazi Germany*: 120–1.
36 'Review of the Requirements of Trade Protection', Section III, 'Naval War Memorandum (European)', Admiralty Letter, M.00697/39, January 1939, Case 00244, Vol. III, NHB: 11.
37 'Trade Protection – Detailed Arrangements', Section VII, 'Naval War Memorandum (European)', Admiralty Letter, M.00697/39, January 1939, Case 00244, Vol. III, NHB: 49–50.
38 Geoffrey Budd, telephone interviews, 23–26 March 2003.
39 [Principles of Anti-Submarine Patrol by Aircraft], J. Lawson, Admiralty, M/NAD.398/37, 31 August 1937, AIR 15/38.
40 'Manual of Anti-Submarine Warfare, 1939', Tactical Division, CB3044, February 1939, NHB: 38.
41 Minute, DNAD, 15 May 1939, ADM 1/12141.
42 'Anti-Submarine Striking Forces, [Revised Form of Draft]', Memorandum by Tactical Division, Naval Staff, June 1938, ADM 1/12141.
43 Minute, D of P, 22 March 1939, ADM 1/12141.
44 Minute, Captain D.A. Budgen, RN, D of TD, 13 April 1939, ADM 1/12141.
45 'Review of Methods of Dealing with the U-boat Menace', ADM 1/10468: 42.
46 Jürgen Rohwer, *Axis Submarine Successes of World War Two: German, Italian and Japanese Submarine Successes, 1939–1945* (London: Greenhill Books, 1999): 1–5.
47 'Anti-Submarine Operations in North Atlantic, 12 to 16 September 1939', Pack No. 0556/0, BSR 522/1, NHB.
48 'Home Waters and the Atlantic, Volume I …', NHB: 69.
49 '[Battle of the Atlantic], Chapter V, September 1939' [F. Barely and D.W. Waters], n.d., Box PT135, NHB: 29–30.
50 Minute, G.M.B. Langley, for Director of Naval Air Division, 9 October 1939, ADM 199/137.
51 Minute, J.H. Edelsten, D of P, 25 October 1939, ADM 199/137.
52 '[Conduct of Aircraft Carriers and Destroyers when Engaged in Anti-Submarine Operations]', S.H. Phillips, Secretary, Admiralty, M.015382/39, 28 November 1939, ADM 199/124.
53 'Home Waters and the Atlantic, Volume I …', NHB: 70–1.
54 'The Development of British Naval Aviation, 1919–1945', Naval Staff History, Second World War, Vol. I, CB3307(1), BR1936(53)(1), 14 July 1954, NHB: 92; K.C. Baff, *Maritime is Number Ten: The Sunderland Era* (Privately Published, 1983): 35.

55 W.A.B. Douglas, Roger Sarty, Michael Whitby, *No Higher Purpose: The Official Operational History of the Royal Canadian Navy in the Second World War, 1939–1943*, Vol. II, Part 1 (St. Catherines, Ontario: Vanwell Publishing Limited, 2002): 115.
56 Commander G.A. Titterton, Historical Section, Admiralty, to Squadron Leader Mervyn Mills, AHB, Air Ministry, 29 March 1959, in 'Selected Convoys: Mediterranean, 1941–42, Revised Battle Summaries, Nos. 18, 32', Folder, NHB.
57 'Vice Admiral Binney's Committee, IDC.2', Vice Admiral T.H. Binney, Imperial Defence College, 21 September 1939, ADM 205/1 [emphasis supplied].
58 Pencil margin note in, 'Vice Admiral Binney's Committee, IDC.2', Vice Admiral T.H. Binney, Imperial Defence College, 21 September 1939, ADM 205/1: 2.
59 'Home Waters and the Atlantic, Volume I …', NHB: 70–1; Roskill, *War at Sea*, Vol. I: 134–5.
60 'Review of the Situation at Sea, December 1939, Vice Admiral Binney's Committee', Vice Admiral T.H. Binney, IDC.38, 8 December 1939, ADM 1/9793.
61 Note, Churchill to First Sea Lord, 20 November 1939, ADM 205/2.
62 Captain A.G. Talbot, Director of Anti-Submarine Warfare, to First Sea Lord, [M.013984/39], 23 November 1939, ADM 205/2.
63 Minute, Captain J.H. Edelsten, D of P, PD.08182/39, 26 November 1939, ADM 1/10084.
64 Ibid.
65 Minute, Captain M.J. Mansergh, DTD, 29 December 1939, ADM 199/124.
66 Minute, Admiral H.M. Burrough, ACNS, 7 March 1940, ADM 1/10468.
67 'Review of Methods of Dealing with the U-boat Menace', ADM 1/10468: 31.
68 Ibid.: 14–15.
69 'Review of Methods of Dealing with the U-boat Menace', ADM 1/10468: 16.
70 Minute, Captain C.S. Daniel, D of P, 20 March 1940, ADM 1/10468. See annotation on [Captain L.E. Holland], AHO to First Sea Lord, 12 March 1940, ADM 1/10468.
71 Draft Minute, DASW, 26 July 1945, ADM 1/17659.
72 'The Offensive Value of the Modern Submarine', 'Salvo' (Lieutenant I.L.M. McGeoch), May 1939, IWM P347: 8–9; 'Exercise "ZL", Combined Fleets, 7–15 March 1935', in 'Exercises and Operations 1935', CB1769/35(1) and (2), September 1937, ADM 186/157: 43.
73 'Anti-Submarine Training', Captain R. Kerr, Captain (D), Second Destroyer Flotilla, [13 June 1939], ADM 205/3.
74 'The Evolution of the *Osprey*', Lieutenant Commander F.M. Mason, Summer 1938 (issued 30 January 1942), P.1009, AL: 27.
75 'Anti-Submarine Training', ADM 205/3.

2 Mastering the submersible, 1939–43

1 High Command of the Navy, *The U-Boat Commander's Handbook, 1942, New Edition 1943*, (Gettysburg, PA: Thomas Publications, 1989): 17.
2 W.S. Chalmers, *Max Horton and the Western Approaches* (London: Hodder and Stoughton, 1954): 106.
3 Manson, *Diplomatic Ramifications*: 5–6 and 113.
4 'Progress in Tactics, 1948', DTSD, TSD.108/48, CB03016/48, 30 November 1948, ADM 239/144: 14.
5 Compton-Hall, 26 February 2000.
6 G.J. Kirby, 'A History of the Torpedo: Part 3', *Journal of the Royal Naval Scientific Service*, Vol. 27, No. 2 (1972): 85.
7 'Reports of Proceedings – Convoys ONS18 and ON202', Admiral Max Horton, Commander-in-Chief, Western Approaches, 31 December 1943, Captain M.J. Evans, RN, Papers, IWM 65/25/1.

8. 'Some Operational Implications of a Homing Torpedo', L. Solomon, Report 36/43, 1 June 1943, ADM 219/52.
9. 'Information on U-Boats', Part 13, 'Conduct of Anti-U-Boat Operations', CB4097(13)(44), June 1944, NHB: paragraphs 1472–3 and Table I.
10. 'U-boat Tactics', in 'Monthly Anti-Submarine Report, January 1941', DASW, CB04050/41(1), [February 1941], NHB: 6.
11. 'U-boat Methods of Combined Attack on Convoys, 1 February to 31 October 1941', Naval Section [GC&CS, Bletchley Park], ZIP/ZG/116, 10 November 1941, ADM 223/1: 15–16.
12. 'Report on anti-convoy activity by Kptlt. Topp (U-boat tactics by a German Commander)', 1942, AIR 40/1821: 3–4; Message DASW to various, 2024A/11 October, 11 October 1942, ADM 199/1732; 'Hints on Escort Work – Part III', A/ Captain J.D. Prentice, RCN, Captain (D) Halifax, Memorandum D.0-24-11, 21 May 1943, Folder CNA 7-6-5, Vol. 11023, RG 24, NAC.
13. 'United States Fleet Anti-Submarine Bulletin', R.S. Edwards, Chief of Staff, USN, Vol. I, No. 1, June 1943, NHB: 2.
14. Calculated from data in: Rohwer, *Critical Convoy Battles*: 219–23. The average of the 30 firing ranges calculated by Rohwer is 3,269 yards (standard deviation, σ, 2,090 yards), or if the exceptionally long and short ranges are excluded, 2,978 yards (σ 1,194 yards). The average firing range estimated by the U-boats was 2,152 yards (σ 937 yards).
15. High Command of the Navy, *The U-Boat Commander's Handbook, 1942, New Edition 1943* (Gettysburg, PA: Thomas Publications, 1989).
16. 'Grand Admiral Dönitz on the U-boat War', in 'The Anti-Submarine Report, September, October, November and December 1945', DTASW, CB04050/45(7), 19 December 1945, NHB: 24.
17. 'U-boat Methods of Combined Attack on Convoys, 1 February to 31 October 1941', Naval Section [GC&CS, Bletchley Park], ZIP/ZG/116, 10 November 1941, ADM 223/1: 5.
18. M. Llewellyn-Jones, 'A Clash of Cultures: The Case for Large Convoys', in Peter Hore (ed.), *Patrick Blackett: Sailor, Scientist, Socialist* (London: Frank Cass, 2003): 142; 'Pack Tactics by Submarines of the United States Navy', Section 5, 'Monthly Anti-Submarine Report, January 1945', Anti-U-Boat Division, CB04050/45(1), 15 February 1945, NHB.
19. 'Effect of High Submerged Speed on U-boat Tactics', W.H. McCrea, NORD, Report No. 20/45, 23 April 1945, ADM 219/225: 1.
20. 'Pack Tactics by Submarines (Summary)', E.J. Williams, JTS-C No. 10, 21 February 1944, ADM 219/631: 1.
21. 'Grand Admiral Dönitz on the U-boat War', in 'The Anti-Submarine Report, September, October, November and December 1945', DTASW, CB04050/45(7), 19 December 1945, NHB: 24.
22. 'Coastal Command Manual of Anti-U-Boat Warfare', May 1944, AIR 15/294: Article 1.
23. 'Visual Sighting of U-Boats', Wing Commander T.V. Stokes, RAAF, Overseas Headquarters, 12 December 1944, AWM 54, 81/4/81 [emphasis supplied].
24. Minute, Wing Commander R.N. Waite, Wing Commander Plans, to SASO, 10 February 1939, AIR 15/38.
25. 'Outline of Coastal Command's Anti-U-Boat Warfare 1939-August 1944', Wing Commander T.V. Stokes [20 September 1944], AWM 54, 81/4/81.
26. R. Compton-Hall to A. Hampshire [c. 1998].
27. H.P. Willmott, 'The Organisations: The Admiralty and the Western Approaches', in Stephen Howarth and Derek Law (eds.), *The Battle of the Atlantic 1939–1945: The 50th Anniversary International Naval Conference* (London: Greenhill Books, 1994): 184.

Notes 183

28 'Coastal Command Manual of Anti-U-Boat Warfare', May 1944, AIR 15/294: Article 21.
29 Bernard Lovell, *P.M.S. Blackett: A biographical memoir* (London: The Royal Society, 1976): 64; 'Note on Relation Between the Use of Aircraft to Give Cover to Convoys and in the Bay', P.M.S. Blackett, CAOR, 22 March 1943, ADM 205/30.
30 'A/S Operations against Snort U-boats Working Inshore', E.J. Williams, DNOR, Report No. 66/44, 29 August 1944, ADM 219/148.
31 'Note on Depth Charge Attacks by Aircraft' [L. Solomon], CAOR, 17 February 1944, CCAC, FWCT 2/4/5; 'Monthly Anti-Submarine Report, September 1944', ADM 199/2061.
32 'Progress in Underwater Warfare, 1949', DTASW, TASW.30/50, CB04050(49), 17 July 1950, ADM 239/274: 79.
33 'Admiralty Convoy Instructions to Escorts: General – Operation of Surface Escorts', Anti-U-Boat Division, CB04234(2)(44), August 1944, NHB: Article 93.
34 'Progress in Underwater Warfare, 1949', DTASW, TASW.30/50, CB04050(49), 17 July 1950, ADM 239/274: 79.
35 'The Asdic and its Associated Weapons', W.E. Dawson, ER30, HM Underwater Detection Establishment, Portland, February 1947, DERA, AN.15971: 4.
36 A.B. Wood, OBE, DSc, 'From Board of Invention and Research to Royal Naval Scientific Service', in *Journal of the Naval Scientific Service*, Vol. 20, No. 4 (July 1965): 16–97, CCAC, GOEV 3/7; 'Anti-Submarine Measures in World War I', Commander F. Barely, Historical Section, S.5659, Searches Vol. 29, 30 November 1960, NHB.
37 'The Asdic Beam', in 'Asdic Notebook', M. Walford, MLJ; H.W. Smith, 'Countering the Fast Conventional Submarine, 1946–1956', in 'Sonar Systems in the RCN, 1945–68', Partial Draft, 15 January 1997, DHH; Commodore (D) Western Approaches to DAUD, 16 July 1944, ADM 217/90; 'Monthly Anti-Submarine Report, October 1944', ADM 199/2061: 3.
38 'A/S Screening', Part 3, 'Conduct of Anti-U-Boat Operations', CB4097(3)(44), June 1944, NHB: Tables I and II.
39 'Type 144. Trials of Operating Procedure', HMA/SEE, Fairlie, Internal Report No. 159, December 1943, ADM 259/382: 7. For a full description see: M. Llewellyn-Jones, 'The Royal Navy and the Challenge of the Fast Submarine, 1944–1954: Innovation or Evolution?' in Richard Harding (ed.), *The Royal Navy, 1930–2000* (London: Cass, 2004): 138.
40 'Asdic Operating and Control: Supplementary Notes on Procedure and Control', CB4127(4)(45), ASW 304/45, July 1945, NHB: 9.
41 'Detection, Attacking, Hunting', CB4097(2)(41), December 1941, Box 468, RG 38, NARA2: paragraph 77.
42 The variation of ranges given reflects the alternate explosive fillings of the depth-charges. The Mark X depth-charge, fired singly from the torpedo tubes of a few escorts, contained a ton of explosive, but no successes were recorded with this weapon.
43 'Conduct of Anti-U-Boat Operations – Part 10 – A/S Weapons', DASW, CB4097(10)(44), July 1944, Box 468, RG 38, NARA2: paragraphs 1093 and 1044.
44 'Creeping Attack', Admiralty Message, DTG 181904A August 1943, NAA(M): MP1185/8, 1932/3/45.
45 'Asdic Notebook', MLJ: 54.
46 'Conduct of Anti-U-Boat Operations – Part 2 – Detection and Action', CB4097(2)(44), November 1944, Box 468, RG 38, NARA2: paragraphs 195 and 200.
47 'The Asdic and its Associated Weapons', DERA, AN.15971: 11.
48 Llewellyn-Jones, 'The Pursuit of Realism': 219–39.
49 Arnold Hague, *The Allied Convoy System, 1939–1945: Its Organisation, Defence and Operation* (Annapolis, Maryland: Naval Institute Press, 2000): 5, 10 and 25–6.

50 'Admiralty Convoy Instructions to Escorts: General – Operation of Surface Escorts', Anti-U-Boat Division, CB04234(2)(44), August 1944, NHB: Article 35; 'A/S Screening', Part 3, 'Conduct of Anti-U-Boat Operations', CB4097(3)(44), June 1944, NHB: paragraphs 401–3.
51 'A/S Screening', Part 3, 'Conduct of Anti-U-Boat Operations', CB4097(3)(44), June 1944, NHB: paragraphs 401–5 and Figure 1.
52 'Admiralty Convoy Instructions to Escorts: General – Operation of Surface Escorts', Anti-U-Boat Division, CB04234(2)(44), August 1944, NHB: Articles 30–4.
53 'Anti-Submarine Protection of Convoys', A/Commander Harvey Newcomb, A/S 121/1/3, 5 May 1943, NAA(M): MP1049/5, 2026/12/537. Newcomb, an interwar A/S specialist, drew his information from the Admiralty's *Monthly Anti-Submarine Report* (as well as personal contact with Admiralty staff).
54 'Admiralty Convoy Instructions to Escorts: General – Operation of Surface Escorts', Anti-U-Boat Division, CB04234(2)(44), August 1944, NHB: Article 38; 'Remarks on *Philante* Exercises, 29 July 1944', W.H. McCrea, DOR/44/60, 3 August 1944, ADM 219/142.
55 'Conduct of Anti-U-Boat Operations – Part 2 – Detection and Action', CB4097(2)(44), November 1944, Box 468, RG 38, NARA2: paragraphs 285–96; 'US Fleet, Anti-Submarine and Escort of Convoy Instructions (BUSCIs)', FTP 223A, January 1945, File 79/532, DHH: 1-60.
56 'Detection, Attacking, Hunting', CB4097(2)(42), December 1942, Box 468, RG 38, NARA2: paragraphs 193 and 308–9.
57 'Air and Surface A/S Searches and Striking Forces', Part 4, BR1679(4) [formerly CB4097(4)(44)], June 1944, NHB: 20.
58 'Conduct of Anti-U-Boat Operations – Part 2 – Detection and Action', CB4097(2)(44), November 1944, Box 468, RG 38, NARA2: paragraphs 343–4 and 375–8.
59 'Operation 'CW': Analysis for NW Approaches, 25 August – 17 October 1944', W.H. McCrea, DNOR, 1 December 1944, ADM 1/17653: 16.
60 Quoted in: D.A. Rayner, *Escort: the Battle of the Atlantic* (London, William Kimber, 1955): 155.
61 'Some Operational Implications of a Homing Torpedo', L. Solomon, Report 36/43, 1 June 1943, ADM 219/52.
62 'Conduct of Anti-U-Boat Operations – Part 2 – Detection and Action', CB4097(2)(44), November 1944, Box 468, RG 38, NARA2: paragraphs 380–1.
63 'Monthly Anti-Submarine Report, June 1944', ADM 199/2061: 27.
64 R. Whinney, *The U-boat Peril: An Anti-Submarine Commander's War* (Poole: Blandford, 1986): 127; Terrence Robertson, *Walker RN* (London: White Lion edn., 1975): 142.
65 Peter Gretton, *Convoy Escort Commander* (London: Cassell, 1964): 166.
66 Alan Burn, *The Fighting Captain: Frederick John Walker and the Battle of the Atlantic* (London: Leo Cooper, 1993): 113.
67 'Second Support Group Orders', Captain F.J. Walker, CB, DSO, 19 June 1943 (still extant, with amendments, 9 March 1944), File PGC 5, IWM P432: 2 [emphasis supplied].
68 Alan Burn, *The Fighting Captain: Frederick John Walker and the Battle of the Atlantic* (London: Leo Cooper, 1993): 142.
69 W.S. Chalmers, *Max Horton and the Western Approaches* (London: Hodder and Stoughton, 1954): 212.
70 'U-boat Methods of Combined Attack on Convoys, 1 February to 31 October 1941', Naval Section [GC&CS, Bletchley Park], ZIP/ZG/116, 10 November 1941, ADM 223/1: 20–1.
71 'The German Navy – The U-Boat Arm', Lieutenant H.M. Anderson, RNVR, Lieutenant Commander R.J. Goodman, RNVR and Commander A.M.S. MacKenzie, RNVR (ed.), GC&CS Naval History, Vol. XVII, c. December 1945, NHB: 219–20.

Notes 185

72 'A/S Warfare in Relation to Future Strategy, Memorandum by the First Lord of the Admiralty', War Cabinet, Anti-U-Boat Warfare, AU(43)1, 5 January 1943, ADM 1/14793: 10.
73 'Instructions for the Operation of Escort Carriers', Admiral Max Horton, Commander-in-Chief, Western Approaches, Memorandum No. WA.0756/36, 7 February 1943, ADM 1/13081.
74 'Analysis of U-boat Operations in the Vicinity of Convoy SC130, 18-21 May 1943', Anti-U-boat Division, Admiralty, 15 July 1943, ADM 199/2020.
75 'Notes on Support Group Operations, September, 1943 – January, 1944', [Leon Solomon], CAOR, OIC/SI.919, 6 April 1944, ADM 223/172.
76 'An Analysis of the Operation of Support Groups in the North Atlantic (Period 14 April – 11 May 1943)', Anti-U-boat Division, Admiralty, 15 June 1943, ADM 199/2020; 'An Analysis of the Operation of Support Groups in the North Atlantic (Period 5 May – 12 June 1943)', Anti-U-boat Division, Admiralty, 15 July 1943, ADM 199/2020.
77 Lieutenant Commander John Guest, RNVR, telephone interview, 14 May 2001.
78 'Admiralty Convoy Instructions to Escorts: General – Operation of Surface Escorts', Anti-U-Boat Division, CB04234(2)(44), August 1944, NHB: Article 1.
79 Julian Corbett, *Some Principles of Maritime Strategy* (Naval Institute Press, 1972): 172–3.
80 Corbett, *Some Principles*: 29–30 and 171–2.
81 'A Study of the Philosophy and Conduct of Maritime War...', MLJ: 20 [emphasis supplied].
82 D.A. Rayner, *Escort: the Battle of the Atlantic* (London: William Kimber, 1955): 87.
83 'Western Approaches Tactical Policy', Admiral Max Horton, Commander-in-Chief, Western Approaches, No. WA.0609/45, 27 April 1943, File 307-0, Vol. 11940, RG 24, NAC.
84 'Report of Committee on the Winter Campaign of 1941–1942 in the Battle of the Atlantic', in 'Monthly Anti-Submarine Report, April 1941', DASW, CB04050/41(4), [May 1941], NHB: 10.
85 'Western Approaches Tactical Policy', Admiral Max Horton, Commander-in-Chief, Western Approaches, No. WA.0609/45, 27 April 1943, File 307-0, Vol. 11940, RG 24, NAC; 'Anti-Submarine Measures', E.J. King, Commander in Chief, United States Fleet and Chief of Naval Operations, FF1/A16-3(9), 19 May 1943, Folder CNA 7-6-1, Vol. 11022, RG 24, NAC.
86 'Admiralty Convoy Instructions to Escorts: General – Operation of Surface Escorts', Anti-U-Boat Division, CB04234(2)(44), August 1944, NHB: Article 1.
87 'Western Approaches Tactical Policy', Admiral Max Horton, Commander-in-Chief, Western Approaches, No. WA.0609/45, 27 April 1943, File 307-0, Vol. 11940, RG 24, NAC.
86 'Battle of the Atlantic: Recent Changes in Enemy Tactics', CSO(M), C-in-C, WA, Hush Message, 142141A December 1943, ADM 217/358.

3 Elusive victory: countering the schnorkel, 1944–45

1 'Inshore U-Boat Operation', Admiralty Message, CASO No. 6, DTG 252307A October 1944, NAA(M): MP1185/8, 1932/3/45.
2 'U-boat Situation, Week Ending 11 September 1944', Captain Rodger Winn, RNVR, OIC/SI.1078, n.d., ADM 223/172; 'Schnorkel', Appendix 'A' to 'Report on German and Our Strategy and Tactics: Anti-Submarine Warfare (Section C, Sub-Sections 1-4)', Wing Commander T.V. Stokes, RAAF, Overseas Headquarters, London, 61/50/Air, 14 November 1944, AWM 54, 81/4/81.
3 'Notes on Two U-boat Cruises in the English Channel', DDIC, DAUD, DNOR, OIC/SI/1021, 24 July 1944, ADM 223/261.

4 'Report on Methods of Collection of Sound from water and the Determination of the Direction of Sound', Professor Sir Ernest Rutherford, FRS, Manchester University, BIR.10064/16, 30 September 1915, in 'Submarines, Mines, Electrical Acoustics, etc.', Section II, BIR Reports 1915–1917, NHB: 8.
5 'Detection of U-boats in the English Channel and Approaches (Rough analysis of the period D to D+10)', E.J. Williams and L. Solomon, Report No. 48/44, 19 June 1944, ADM 219/131.
6 'Report on Development in A/S Tactics in the United Kingdom, June 1944', AWM 54, 81/4/81: 12.
7 Captain C.D. Howard-Johnston, DAUD, and Captain N.A. Prichard, DASW, Ref: D.559 (Draft), 5 August 1945, ADM 1/17653.
8 'U-boat Situation, Week Ending 28 August 1944', Captain Rodger Winn, RNVR, OIC/SI.1062, n.d., ADM 223/172.
9 'Records of Warship Construction, 1939–1945. The History of DNC Department', Written 1945-46. Approved for issue by DSDE, 1981', RNSM Box 5: 39.
10 'Note on the value of "Snort" to U-boats', L. Solomon and E.J. Williams, DNOR, Report No. 62/44, 19 August 1944, ADM 219/144.
11 'Note on U-boats Fitted with Snort', DDIC and LS/EJW, DNOR, OIC/SI.1036, 11 August 1944, ADM 223/172.
12 'The Schnorkel Smoke Myth', Appendix V, in 'The RAF in Maritime War, Vol. V …', AIR 41/74: 1.
13 'Detection of Schnorkel Fitted U-Boats', Headquarters, Coastal Command, CC/S.17261 A/U Ops., 17 December 1944, AWM 54, 81/4/81.
14 'Note on the value of "Snort" to U-boats', L. Solomon and E.J. Williams, DNOR, Report No. 62/44, 19 August 1944, ADM 219/144.
15 'A/S Operations against Snort U-boats Working Inshore', E.J. Williams, DNOR, Report No. 66/44, 29 August 1944, ADM 219/148 [emphasis supplied].
16 Commander E.H. Mann (Ret), DASW, to DAUD, 6 September 1944, ADM 219/148.
17 Those still without schnorkel were severely handled by anti-submarine forces.
18 'Periodic Summary of the Anti-U-Boat Campaign, No. 37 – 4 December 1943', Captain C.D. Howard-Johnston, DAUD, 6 December 1943, File D 01-18-0, Vol. 11575, RG 24, NAC: 2-4.
19 'Standing Orders for U-boat Hunts off Northern Ireland (Short Title: Operation "CW")', Commander-in-Chief, Western Approaches, 24 February 1944, ADM 199/468: 2.
20 'Orders for Anti-U-boat Operations in Coastal Waters of the Western Approaches Command (Short Title: Operation "CE")', Admiral Max Horton, C-in-C, WA, WA.3036/020/7, [M.010815/44], 11 October 1944, ADM 199/501: 358.
21 'Operation "CW" …', ADM 1/17653.
22 'Survey of A/U Operations in UK Coastal Waters, July 1944 – May 1945', [W.H. McCrea], DNOR, 13 July 1945, ADM 1/17653: 4.
23 'Inshore U-Boat Operation', Admiralty Message, CASO No. 6, DTG 252307A October 1944, NAA(M): MP1185/8, 1932/3/45.
24 'Inshore Operations', Appendix (ii), to, 'Type XXI U-boat (A Provisional Appreciation)', E.J. Williams, DOR/44/68, 4 September 1944, ADM 219/150.
25 'Submarine Warfare in the Channel', Commander J.D. Prentice, RCN, Senior Officer EG11, HMCS *Ottawa*, to Commodore (D), Western Approaches, 17 July 1944, Folder CNA 7-6-1, Vol. 11022, RG 24, NAC.
26 'Anti-U-boat Operations Inshore', Captain C.D. Howard-Johnston, DAUD, Ref: D.218, 11 September 1944, ADM 223/20.
27 'Anti-U-Boat results inshore in Western Approaches Command for the period 1 September 1944 to 31 January 1945', C.D. Howard-Johnston, DAUD, D.353, 4 February 1945, ADM 205/44.

28 Minute, Commodore G.W.G. Simpson, RN, Commodore (D), Western Approaches, No.DW.40/603.OP, 26 July 1944, File D 01-18-0, Vol. 11575, RG 24, NAC.
29 'Choice of Weapons for "Opening-Up" U-boats', Section V, 'The Anti-Submarine Report, September, October, November and December 1945', DTASW, CB04050/45(7), 19 December 1945, NHB.
30 'U-Boat Tactics', Secretary, Navy Board, Melbourne, 22 September 1944, NAA(M): MP1185/8, 1932/3/45.
31 'Experience Gained during Anti-U-boat Inshore Operations', Captain C.D. Howard-Johnston, DAUD, Ref: D.218, 11 September 1944, ADM 223/20: 2 [emphasis supplied].
32 'A Model Anti-U-Boat Operation in the Indian Ocean – 5–14 August 1944', Section 6, 'Monthly Anti-Submarine Report, July 1944', DAUD, CB04050/44(7), 15 August 1944, NHB; 'Abstract 24, AHH', TSD/Historical Section, Abstract Volume 24, A.H. Haggard, n.d., NHB.
33 'Operation "Victual" Passage of Convoys JW59 and RA59A to and from North Russia', Captain C.D. Howard-Johnston, DAUD, 15 November 1944, ADM 199/351.
34 Michael Whitby, 'The Strain on the Bridge', in John Reeve and David Stevens (eds.), *The Face of Naval Battle: The Human Experience of Modern War at Sea* (Crows Nest, NSW, Australia: Allen & Unwin, 2003): 200–18.
35 Gretton to Howard-Johnston, 15 September 1980, 'H–J' File, Gretton Papers, MSS/93/008, NMM(G).
36 Commander P.W. Burnett to Captain C.D. Howard-Johnston, 12 November 1944, ADM 199/501. Burnett was referring to the operations of his Escort Group in mid-September 1944.
37 'Report of Proceedings, Tenth Escort Group, 26 December 1944 to 3 January 1945', Commander P.W. Burnett, RN, No. 1A/8, 4 January 1945, ADM 217/373.
38 Admiralty Message to AIG #2 359AZ, Repeated to Commander 12th Fleet, 26 August 1944, Folder CNA 7-6-1, Vol. 11022, RG 24, NAC.
39 'Admiralty Convoy Instructions to Escorts: General – Operation of Surface Escorts', Anti-U-Boat Division, CB04234(44)(2), August 1944, NHB: Article 56.
40 'DAUD 081734B to C-in-C, WA', in 'Friday, 8 September 1944, War Diary (Naval), 1–14 September 1944', NHB.
41 'C-in-C, WA, 092035 to Admiralty', in 'Saturday, 9 September 1944, War Diary (Naval), 1-14 September 1944', NHB; 'Monthly Anti-Submarine Report, October 1944', DAUD, CB04050/44(10), 15 November 1944, NHB.
42 'Survey of A/U Operations …', ADM 1/17653.
43 'Experience Gained during Anti-U-boat Inshore Operations', Captain C.D. Howard-Johnston, DAUD, Ref: D.218, 11 September 1944, ADM 223/20: 4.
44 'On a Ship in Convoy being Torpedoed in an Area where the U-boat can Bottom', Appendix IV (7 April 1945) to 'Orders for Anti-U-boat Operations in Coastal Waters of the Western Approaches Command (Short Title: Operation "CE")', Admiral Max Horton, C-in-C, WA, WA.3036/020/7, [M.010815/44], 11 October 1944, ADM 199/501: 371–4.
45 'Air Operations', in Appendix VII to, 'Orders for Anti-U-boat Operations in Coastal Waters of the Western Approaches Command (Short Title: Operation "CE")', Admiral Max Horton, C-in-C, WA, WA.3036/020/7, [M.010815/44], 11 October 1944, ADM 199/501: 377–9.
46 'Admiralty Convoy Instructions to Escorts: General – Operation of Surface Escorts', Anti-U-Boat Division, CB04234(44)(2), August 1944, NHB: Articles 34 and 35.
47 'Orders for Anti-U-boat Operations in Coastal Waters of the Western Approaches Command (Short Title: Operation "CE")', Admiral Max Horton, C-in-C, WA, WA.3036/020/7, [M.010815/44], 11 October 1944, ADM 199/501: 359–60.

48 'HMS *Conn*, Report of Proceedings, 11 January to 2 February 1945', Lieutenant Commander Raymond Hart, DSC, RN, Senior Officer 21st Escort Group, 5 February 1945, ADM 217/755; '5th Escort Group Narrative: 21 January – 12 March 1945', NHB.
49 'Survey of A/U Operations …', ADM 1/17653: 7.
50 'Convoy Protection in Inshore Waters', Admiralty Message, CASO No. 7, DTG 131737Z February 1945, NAA(M): MP1185/8, 1932/3/45.
51 'Inshore Operations', in 'Admiralty Convoy Instructions to Escorts (Short Title ACI), General Sections 1–6', Part XII, DAUD, CB04234(44), April 1945, ADM 239/345.
52 'Admiralty Convoy Instructions to Escorts (Short Title ACI), 1944', Part XII, 'Inshore Operations', Anti-U-Boat Division, August 1944, ADM 239/345: Article 163.
53 'Operation "CW": Analysis for NW Approaches, 25 August – 17 October 1944', W.H. McCrea, DNOR, 1 December 1944, ADM 1/17653: 16.
54 'Air and Surface A/S Searches and Striking Forces', Part 4, BR1679(4) [formerly CB4097(4)(44)], June 1944, NHB: 14–15.
55 'Minutes of Squadron Commanders' Conference held at Headquarters, Coastal Command on 29 November 1944', AWM 54, 81/4/81: 2.
56 'Anti-Snort Trials', E.J. Williams, DNOR, Report No. 70/44, 5 October 1944, ADM 219/152.
57 'Minutes of Squadron Commanders' Conference … 29 November 1944', AWM 54, 81/4/81: 3.
58 'Minutes of Squadron Commanders' Conference … 29 November 1944', AWM 54, 81/4/81: 7.
59 'Survey of A/U Operations …', ADM 1/17653.
60 '*Kriegstagebuch*, *U-247*, 18 May to 28 July 1944', NID, PG/30225/NID, FDS, NHB.
61 'Monthly Anti-Submarine Report, October 1944', DAUD, CB04050/44(10), 15 November 1944, NHB: 7–8.
62 See, for example: '25 June 1944', in 'Translation of PG/30349, BdU's War Log, 16–30 June 1944', FDS, NHB.
63 See, for example, the series of papers at NA in ADM 223/20, ADM 223/172, ADM 223/198, ADM 223/203, DEFE 3/732, DEFE 3/735 and HW 1/3191. For the later assessments, see: ADM 223/21.
64 'C-in-C, WA 031805B to Admiralty', in 'Sunday, 3 September 1944, War Diary (Naval), 1–14 September 1944', NHB.
65 'Admiralty, 021511B to C-in-C, WA …', in 'Saturday, 2 September 1944, War Diary (Naval), 1–14 September 1944', NHB.
66 'Inshore U-Boat Operation', Admiralty Message, CASO No. 6, DTG 252307A October 1944, NAA(M): MP1185/8, 1932/3/45.
67 'Survey of A/U Operations …', ADM 1/17653: 6.
68 Captain C.D. Howard-Johnston, DAUD, and Captain N.A. Prichard, DASW, Ref: D.559 (Draft), 5 August 1945, ADM 1/17653.
69 'Operation "CW": Analysis for NW Approaches, 25 August – 17 October 1944', W.H. McCrea, DNOR, 1 December 1944, ADM 1/17653: 15.
70 [Report of Proceedings of 9th Escort Group for period 7 October to 3 November 1944], Commander Layard, Senior Officer, EG9, 7 November 1944, ADM 217/728.
71 'Sunday, 3 September; 1944, War Diary (Naval), 1–14 September 1944', NHB.
72 Captain C.D. Howard-Johnston, DAUD, and Captain N.A. Prichard, DASW, Ref: D.559 (Draft), 5 August 1945, ADM 1/17653.
73 'A/S Training for Operations in Inshore Waters', W.H. McCrea, DNOR, Report No. 83/45, 8 January 1945, ADM 219/283.
74 Doug McLean, 'The U.S. Navy and the U-Boat Inshore Offensive', in William B. Cougar (ed.), *New Interpretations in Naval History: Selected Papers from the Twelfth Naval History Symposium* (Annapolis: Naval Institute Press, 1997): 310–24.

75 'U-boat Situation, Week Ending 11 September 1944', Captain Rodger Winn, RNVR, OIC/SI.1078, n.d., ADM 223/172.
76 W.S. Chalmers, *Max Horton and the Western Approaches* (London: Hodder and Stoughton, 1954): 212.
77 'Minutes of the Meeting held at 10, Downing Street, SW1 on Tuesday, 31 October, 1944, at 6.0 pm', AU(44) 3rd Meeting, War Cabinet Anti-U-boat Warfare, NA, CAB 86/6: 3–4.
78 'Prospects in the U-boat War', E.J. Williams, ADNOR, Report No. 81/44, 17 November 1944, ADM 219/161: 1.
79 'Review of U-boat Results in Inshore Waters, Period 1 July to 31 October', Captain C.D. Howard-Johnston, DAUD, Ref: D.294, 23 November 1944, ADM 223/20: 1–3.
80 'Monthly Anti-Submarine Report, August 1944', 15 September 1944, ADM 199/2061; 'Monthly Anti-Submarine Report, November 1944', 15 December 1944, ADM 199/2061.
81 'Review of U-boat Results in Inshore Waters', Admiral Edelsten, ACNS(UT), UT.37, 30 November 1944, ADM 205/36.
82 'A Forecast of the Results of the U-boat Campaign during 1945, Memorandum by the First Sea Lord', Admiral of the Fleet A.B. Cunningham, COS(45)14(0), 6 January 1945, NA, PREM 3/414/1.
83 Howard-Johnston, DAUD, to Fawcett, SNLO Coastal Command, Ref. D.327, 26 December 1944, CCAC, FWCT 2/4/5.
84 'Possibilities of the Coming U-boat Offensive [April 1945]', H.W. Fawcett, Naval Staff, Coastal Command, 1 December 1944, CCAC, FWCT 2/4/5: 1–2 and 5.
85 'Survey of A/U Operations …', ADM 1/17653: 7–8.
86 'Narrative and Remarks by Senior Officer', Section I, Part 1, 'Report of Proceedings', Commander P.W. Burnett, RN, HMS *Braithwaite*, Ref. No. 1A/10, 20 February 1945, ADM 199/198: 29–30.
87 C.D. Howard-Johnston to J.D. Brown, NHB, 24 February 1980, CCAC, HWJN [emphasis supplied].
88 Captain C.D. Howard-Johnston, DAUD, and Captain N.A. Prichard, DASW, Ref: D.559 (Draft), 5 August 1945, ADM 1/17653.

4 The dawn of modern anti-submarine warfare, 1944–46

1 Doenitz, *Memoirs*: 265.
2 M. Llewellyn-Jones, 'British Responses to the U-boat, Winter 1943 to Spring 1945' (MA, London, King's College, December 1997): 7–11.
3 'Deep and/or Fast U-boats', Captain HMA/SEE, Fairlie to DASW, 10 April 1944, ADM 1/16495.
4 'The Type XXI U-boat – A Provisional Appreciation', in 'Monthly Anti-Submarine Report, August 1944', 15 September 1944, ADM 199/2061: 17–19.
5 'Type XXI U-boat (A Provisional Appreciation)', E.J. Williams, DOR/44/68, 4 September 1944, ADM 219/150.
6 Professor Sir William McCrea, FRS, interview, 17 April 1998; 'Tactics against Fast Submerged U-Boats', A/Commander J. Plomer, RCNVR, Director of the Combined Tactical Unit to Captain (D), Halifax, 25 November 1944, Folder CNA 7-6-1, Vol. 11022, RG 24, NAC.
7 C.D. Howard-Johnston to J.D. Brown, NHB, 24 February 1980, CCAC, HWJN.
8 Llewellyn-Jones, 'Trials with HM Submarine *Seraph*', *passim*.
9 'Underwater Internal Combustion Propulsion – General Considerations', n.d., RNSM A1948/009.
10 'The Trend of Submarine Design', Lecture by RN Newton, RCNC, DNC Department, November 1945, RNSM A1991/058: 5; 'HMS *Seraph* (*P.219*) First of Class Trials, September 1944', Office of Admiral (S/M), RNSM A1991/250: 8.

11 Interview, Professor Sir William McCrea FRS, 17 April 1998; 'Monthly Log of HM Submarine *Seraph*, Month of September 1944', ADM 173/18701.
12 'Western Approaches Monthly News Bulletin, November 1944', 18 December 1944, Box 396, RG 38, NARA2.
13 David Syrett (ed.), *The Battle of the Atlantic and Signals Intelligence: U-Boat Situations and Trends, 1941–1945* (Aldershot: Ashgate, 1998): 423, fn. 624.
14 D.C.R. Webb, letter, 6 August 1997; Peter Evans, email, 22 December 1998.
15 'Dependence of Submarine Propeller Noise on Depth of Submarine', Director of Scientific Research, SRE/SM/7/0, 19 June 1944, ADM 283/13; Urick, *Principles of Underwater Sound*: 338.
16 Telephone interview, Rear Admiral J.H. Adams, CB, LVO, 2 March 1999.
17 'Conduct of Anti-U-Boat Operations – Part 2 – Detection and Action', CB4097(2)(44), November 1944, Box 468, RG 38, NARA2: paragraphs 188–9.
18 Hessler, *The U-boat War*, Vol. III: 86.
19 Quoted in 'Monthly Anti-Submarine Report, November 1944', 15 December 1944, ADM 199/2061: 21.
20 'Notes on A/S Trials with a Fast Submarine', W.H. McCrea, Report No. 72/44, 9 October 1944, ADM 219/154; 'Notes on A/S Trials with a Fast Submarine, 'Rockabill', 10–30 October 1944', [W.H. McCrea], Report No. 80/44, 11 November 1944, ADM 219/160; 'Asdic Trials with HM S/M *Seraph* as Target', J.A. Hakes, Research Note No. 53, HMA/SEE Fairlie, November 1944. DERA, AN 28144.
21 'Minutes of the Meeting ...', AU(44) 3rd Meeting, CAB 86/6: 24.
22 'The Use of Squid against the 25 knot U-Boat', [Captain N.A. Prichard], DASW, [ASW 945/45], 30 June 1945, ADM 1/17591: 3.
23 Paul Mallett, letter, 7 July 1999; 'EG2: D-Day to VE', Ron Curtis, June 1997, MLJ.
24 'Minutes of the First Meeting of DASW's Sub-Committee of ACNS(UT)'s U-boat Warfare Committee held at the Admiralty on Thursday, 30 November 1944, (Copy)' Folder NSS 1271-22, Vol. 8080, RG 24, NAC.
25 'Memorandum for the File', 28 November 1944, Enclosure (S) to 'High Speed Submarines – Report of Tests Against (Project No. 103)', T.A. Turner Commander Anti-Submarine Development Detachment, United States Atlantic Fleet, ASDD/A5-7 Serial: 0024, 6 April 1945, Box 4476, RG 313, NARA2.
26 'The Asdic and its Associated Weapons', DERA, AN.15971: 8.
27 'Notes on A/S Trials with a Fast Submarine, "Rockabill", 10–30 October 1944', [W.H. McCrea], Report No. 80/44, 11 November 1944, ADM 219/160: 4.
28 'Minutes of a Meeting held at ACHQ Liverpool on 3rd October 1944 to discuss a Programme of Schnorkel and other Trials and Practices', Admiral Horton, 4 October 1944, ADM 1/16121: 4.
29 Air Ministry, *The Origins and Development of Operational Research in the Royal Air Force* (London: HMSO, 1963): 96; '"High Tea" Range Tests with a Fast Submarine', ASWDU Report No. 45/16, 25 May 1945, AIR 65/175; 'Sonobuoy Range Tests', 15 July 1944, AIR 65/115; 'The Use of Sonobuoy Equipment', HQ Coastal Command Training Instruction No 28, dated 9 June 1944, AIR 15/584.
30 'Western Approaches Tactical Unit Annual Report – 1944', Captain Gilbert Roberts, 18 December 1944, ADM 1/17557; Milner, *U-boat Hunters*: 215; McLean, 'The Last Cruel Winter': 99.
31 Commander A.F.C. Layard, Diary, 3–6 February 1945, RNM.
32 'HE Listening versus Transmitting by Asdic – Operational Considerations', The Captain, HMS *Osprey*, to DASW, No. 636/86, dated 26 January 1945, ADM 1/17569.
33 Baker-Cresswell to Gretton, 5 October 1981, 'Battle of the Atlantic', Gretton, 23 Part 1, 1 of 2, MS93/008, NMM(G).
34 'Fast U-boats', Captain HMA/SEE, Fairlie to DASW, 28 March 1945, ADM 1/16495.
35 Captain R.J.R. Dendy, RN, Captain HMA/SEE, Fairlie, to Director of Miscellaneous Weapons, Admiralty, No. D.1802, 12 March 1945, ADM 1/17583; 'Hedgehog and

Squid Probabilities', J.R. Thompson, DMWD/20/61, 19 April 1945, ADM 1/17583; 'Hedgehog and Squid Probabilities (Addendum to DMWD/20/61)', J.R. Thompson, DMWD/20/61A, 16 May 1945, ADM 1/17583.
36 Llewellyn-Jones, 'British Responses to the U-boat ...', p. 7.
37 'Effect of High Submerged Speed on U-boat Tactics', W.H. McCrea, NORD, Report No. 20/45, 23 April 1945, ADM 219/225: 2.
38 Ibid: 2.
39 ZIP/ZTPGU/35546, TOI 1015 and 1435, 12 January 1945, DEFE 3/740.
40 'Life and Letters of Gilbert Howland Roberts', Book 1, '11 October 1900 – 4 August 1945' [c. mid-60s], Captain G.H. Roberts RN, Papers, IWM 66/28/1: 144.
41 Captain G.H. Roberts, RN, Western Approaches Tactical Unit, to C-in-C, WA, 30 May 1945, ADM 1/17561, *passim*; Erich Topp, letter, 7 July 1997; Peter Cremer, *U333: The Story of a U-boat Ace*, tr. Lawrence Wilson (London: The Bodley Head, 1984): 202.
42 The following narrative is based on the interrogations of Rear Admiral Godt, Commanders Cremer and Hessler, and Lieutenant Commander Mehl, in: Captain G.H. Roberts, 30 May 1945, ADM 1/17561.
43 Hessler, *The U-boat War*, Vol. III: 86; '*Kampfanweisungen fur Typ XXIII* (Battle Instructions for Type XXIII)', M.G. Saunders (tr.), DNI, NID.24, Ref: TR/PG/28986/NID, 24 April 1946, Box 270, FDS, NHB.
44 'Summary of Statements made by German Naval and Technical Personnel', NID 1/PW, Summary No. 133 for week ending 22 June 1945, 'P/W Summaries, 121–136' Vol. VII, NHB.
45 This is discussed in more detail in Chapter 5.
46 'Bergen', Gretton Papers, NMM(G).
47 W.S. Chalmers, *Max Horton and the Western Approaches* (London: Hodder and Stoughton, 1954): 228.
48 Minute, [Commander] I.M.R. Campbell for Director of Naval Intelligence, 15 March 1945, ADM 116/5202; Minute, G.B.H. Fawkes for Admiral (Submarines), 27 April 1945, ADM 1/16384.
49 'The Use of Squid against the 25 knot U-Boat', Captain N.A. Prichard, DASW, to Captain HMS *Osprey* and Captain HMA/SEE, ASW 945/45, 2 July 1945, ADM 1/17591.
50 'The Use of Squid against the 25 knot U-Boat', [Captain N.A. Prichard], DASW, [ASW 945/45], 30 June 1945, ADM 1/17591: 2.
51 'The Use of Squid against the 25 knot U-Boat', 30 June 1945, ADM 1/17591: 3.
52 'Surface Craft Tactical Countermeasures to Type XXI U-Boats', Research Report No. 93, ASWORG/206 (LO)1380-45, 4 May 1945, ADM 1/17588.
53 'The Use of Squid against the 25 knot U-Boat', 30 June 1945, ADM 1/17591: 4–5.
54 'Summary of DTASW's Investigation on A/S Warfare', Annex C to TASW.021/46, Revised Edition, 4 May 1946, ADM 1/20960: 4; 'Progress Report: Shipborne A/S Weapons', TASW.038/46, [5 September 1946], ADM 1/20960: 6–8.
55 Minute, Engineer-in-Chief, 30 January 1946, ADM 1/27774.
56 'Monday, 7 May 1945, War Diary (Naval), 1–15 May 1945', NHB.
57 'Search for three experimental U-boats, Type XVII, May 26th', Appendix X to Captain G.H. Roberts, 30 May 1945, ADM 1/17561; Chris Madsen, *The Royal Navy and German Naval Disarmament, 1942–1947* (London: Frank Cass, 1998): 112–113, 124, nn. 64 and 180.
58 'Submarine Development', DTASW, TASW.330/47, November 1947, ADM 1/27215: 4; 'HMS *Meteorite* Trials Report, 17 March to 30 April, 1949', RNSM A1994/097.
59 'Minutes of a Meeting held at Northways on 25 June 1945: Trials to be carried out in, and with, U-boats', n.d., ADM 1/18557.
60 Minute, G.B.H. Fawkes for Admiral (Submarines), 16 November 1945, ADM 116/5500.

61. 'Type of German U-boats Required for Post War Experiments and Tests', Admiral (Submarines), Northways, to Secretary of the Admiralty, 15 October 1944, ADM 1/16384.
62. 'Third Submarine Flotilla Monthly General Letter – July 1945', Captain (S/M), Third Submarine Flotilla, HMS *Forth*, to Admiral (Submarines), No. TSF.1230/3714, 8 August 1945, RNSM A1944/007.
63. 'Submarine Development: Lecture given to Senior Officers' Technical Course on Tuesday 6 May 1947', [A.J. Sims], RNSM A1990/083: 4 and 9.
64. 'Survey of A/U Operations …', ADM 1/17653: 2; Hinsley, *et al*, *British Intelligence*, Vol. III, Part 2: 633.
65. NID L.C. Report No. 999, H. Clanchy, DDNI(H), 16 June 1945, ADM 1/17653.
66. 'Submarine Warfare in the Pacific', Secretary, Naval Board, NSS. 11270-53 Vol. 1 (Staff), 13 June 1945, Folder CNA 7-5-9, Vol. 11022, RG 24, NAC.
67. Memoir, Mrs D. Coyne, [early 1990s], IWM 93/22/1: 170–2 and 183.
68. '*Osprey* Tactical Unit – Policy', [Captain] N.A. Prichard, DASW, to The Captain, HMS *Osprey*, ASW1044/45, 25 July 1945, ADM 1/17591.
69. 'Planning', [C.D. Howard-Johnston], 12 June [1945], ADM 1/17653.
70. DASW, to The Captain HMS *Osprey*, ASW/AUD.2018/45, 27 August 1945, ADM 1/17653.
71. [Captain] N.A. Prichard, DASW, to The Captain, HMS *Osprey*, ASW1044/45, 30 July 1945, ADM 1/17591.
72. 'Tactical Trials with Captured German U-boats', DASW, [28] August 1945, ADM 1/18557.
73. 'Appendix. Remarks on First of Class Trials and Deep Dive of *U-2326*', Enclosure No. 3 to Admiral (Submarines') letter No. 1681/SM.3530 of 24 November, 1945. ADM 1/18557.
74. 'First of Class Trials – Type XXI and Type XXIII U-boats', Admiral (Submarines) to the Secretary of the Admiralty, No.1311/SM.3530, 7 September 1945, ADM 1/18328.
75. 'Third Submarine Flotilla Monthly General Letter – July 1945', Captain (S/M), Third Submarine Flotilla, HMS *Forth*, to Admiral (Submarines), No. TSF.1230/3714, 8 August 1945, RNSM A1944/007.
76. 'Trials with Captured German U-boat – Type XXIII', Commander John Grant, Commander (D), Londonderry Flotilla, HMS *Fame*, D.14/21/1, 18 October 1945, ADM 1/18557: 2.
77. 'Enclosure C to Commander (D), Londonderry Flotilla, HMS *Flame*'s No: D.14/21/1 dated 18 October 1945', ADM 1/18557.
78. A similar point is made in Rodger, 'Image and Reality'.
79. 'HMS *Scotsman*: Conversion to Fast A/S Target', Section 27, DNC Department, October 1948, RNSM A1991/098.
80. 'Ingolin (Hydrogen Peroxide). Underwater Propulsion Development', 1945–6, ADM 1/27774; 'HMS *Meteorite* Trials Report, 17 March to 30 April, 1949', RNSM A1994/097.
81. 'Report of Operation "Thankful"', David J. Lees, German Naval Group, World Ship Society, 1 December 1991.
82. 'Third Submarine Flotilla Monthly General Letter – July 1945', Captain (S/M), Third Submarine Flotilla, HMS *Forth*, to Admiral (Submarines), No. TSF.1230/3714, 8 August 1945, RNSM A1944/007.
83. 'First of Class Trials – Type XXI and Type XXIII U-boats', Admiral (Submarines) to the Secretary of the Admiralty, No.1311/SM.3530, 7 September 1945, ADM 1/18328.
84. Enclosure to Admiral (Submarines) Letter No. 1415/SM.3577, 4 October 1945, covering the Report by Lieutenant J.S. Launders, DSO, DSC, RN, Commanding Officer of ex-German *U-3017*, 30 August 1945, ADM 1/18949; Board of Inquiry Report, HMS *Amphion* at Barrow-in-Furness, 3 September 1945, ADM 1/18949. No record of the loss of a Type XXI due to a battery explosion has been discovered.

Notes 193

85 Gary E. Weir, *Forged in War: The Naval-Industrial Complex and American Submarine Construction, 1940–1961* (Washington: Naval Historical Center, Department of the Navy, 1993): 104 and 114.
86 'Board of Inquiry to Investigate the Explosion Onboard *U-3017* on 29 August 1945 (Captain (S/m), Third Submarine Flotilla's No. 6306/3739 of 13 July 1945)', G.E. Creasy, Rear Admiral (Submarines), 1415/SM.3577, 4 October 1945, ADM 1/18949.
87 'Meeting held by VCNS on 28 December, 1945, to consider the number of submarines that could be kept in service in the Post-War Fleet', Head of Military Branch II, 5 February 1946, ADM 1/19301; 'Meeting held by Vice Controller at 1430 on 24 January 1946 to consider further the number of Submarines that could be kept in the Post-War fleet', M.023/46, M. Platt, Head of M. II, 18 February 1946, ADM 1/19301.
88 'First of Class Trials – Type XXI and Type XXIII U-boats', Admiral (Submarines) to the Secretary of the Admiralty, No.1311/SM.3530, 7 September 1945, ADM 1/18328.
89 'Proposal to refit and re-commission *U-2518* on return by the French Navy', [Captain] Ashbourne, DTASW, TASW.44/47, 7 February 1947, ADM 116/5500.
90 'First of Class Trials – Type XXI and Type XXIII U-boats', Admiral (Submarines), No.1311/SM.3530, 7 September 1945, ADM 1/18328.
91 Minute, L. Solomon, DNOR, 1 November 1945, ADM 1/18328.
92 Minute, Director of Operations Division, 2 November 1945, ADM 1/18328.
93 'Formation and Organisation of Naval Operational Research Department', CE.60648/1946, 1941–6, ADM 1/20113.
94 Minute, DTASW, 10 November 1945, ADM 1/18328; 'Proposal to refit and re-commission *U-2518* …', ADM 116/5500.
95 Minute, E.W. Pratt, for Director of Scientific Research, 18 December 1945, ADM 1/18328; Minute, R.C Boyle, for DTM, 4 January 1946, ADM 1/18328.
96 Moore, *The Royal Navy and Nuclear Weapons*: 19.
97 Viscount Cunningham of Hyndhope, *A Sailor's Odyssey* (London: Hutchinson & Co., 1951): 577.
98 N.A.M. Rodger, *The Admiralty* (Lavenham: T. Dalton, 1979): 154–5.
99 Minute, VCNS to First Sea Lord, 3 September 1945, ADM 1/17743.
100 Hackmann, *Seek & Strike*: 327; 'Report on Torpedo, Anti-Submarine, Ordnance and Electrical Branches by Rear Admiral H.C. Phillips', March 1944, ADM 116/5692; 'The Middleton Steering Committee: Report on the Torpedo Anti-Submarine Branch', Rear Admiral G.B. Middleton, CBE, Captain C.L. Robertson, John G. Lang, PAS(NP) and K. W. Matthews, Secretary, 22 December 1945, ADM 1/20207.
101 Mosse, 'Half a Lifetime': 76–7.
102 'Torpedo, Anti-Submarine and Mine Warfare Division – Institution', H.V. Markham, Office Memorandum No. 394, CE.58514/45, 24 September 1945, ADM 1/17743.
103 '[Battle of the Atlantic], Chapter III, Between the Wars', [F. Barely and D.W. Waters], n.d., Box PT135, NHB.
104 E. Maurice Chadwick, 'The Night the Gnats Bit', in *Starshell*, Vol. VI, No. 7 (Fall 1997): 11–12.
105 These included: Burnett – *U-744*, *U-989*, *U-1278*, *U-1279* (and probably two others); Ormsby – *U-198*, *U-386*, *U-406*; and Mosse – *U-354*, *U-394*.
106 'Asdic Trough the Ages', Section 6, 'Monthly Anti-Submarine Report, January 1945', Anti-U-Boat Division, CB04050/45(1), 15 February 1945, NHB: 18.
107 Gretton to Howard-Johnston, 15 September 1980, 'H–J' File, Gretton Papers, MSS/93/008, NMM(G).

5 Short-term problems, long-term solutions, 1946–47

1 Franklin, *Britain's Anti-Submarine Capability*: 190.
2 Richard J. Aldrich, *The Hidden Hand: Britain, America and Cold War Secret Intelligence* (London: John Murray, 2001): 235 and 237; Richard J. Aldrich, 'Secret

Intelligence for a post-war world: reshaping the British intelligence community, 1944–51', in Richard J. Aldrich (ed.), *British Intelligence, Strategy and the Cold War, 1945–51* (London: Routledge, 1992): 24–5.
3 Aldrich, *The Hidden Hand*: 237–8.
4 Ibid: 239.
5 Ibid: 243; 'Captain D4 *Agincourt*, 1951', Note by [M.J. Evans], Captain M.J. Evans, RN, Papers, IWM 65/25/1.
6 Aldrich, 'Secret Intelligence': 27; 'USSR General Report', CX Report, 10 October 1945, NA, WO 208/4566.
7 Aldrich, *The Hidden Hand*: 244–5.
8 Quoted from DO(47)44, see: Aldrich, 'Secret Intelligence': 16.
9 'Top Secret Annex to Study of Undersea Warfare', 22 April 1950, Command File, Post 1 Jan 46, CNO Studies 1950, Box 475, Operational Archives, Naval Historical Center, Washington, DC. The author's attention was drawn to this document by Dr Garry Weir.
10 'Operation 'Unthinkable', Report by the Joint Planning Staff', G. Grantham, G.S. Thompson, W.L. Dawson, Offices of the War Cabinet, Final, 22 May 1945, CAB 120/691.
11 'Russia's Strategic Interests and Intentions', Report by the Joint Intelligence Sub-Committee, JIC(46)1(0) Final (Revise), 1 March 1946, CAB 81/132.
12 'Russian Naval Tactics', NID/16, 10 October 1946, ADM 1/20030.
13 'Russia's Strategic Interests and Intentions', JIC(46)1(0) Final (Revise), 1 March 1946, CAB 81/132.
14 'Monthly Intelligence Report, August 1948', NID, 10 September 1948, DNH.
15 'USSR and Satellite Navies', Naval Intelligence Division, NID.06956/48, CB 03187, October 1951, NHB: 89–93.
16 Jürgen Rohwer and Mikhail S. Monakov, *Stalin's Ocean-Going Fleet: Soviet Naval Strategy and Shipbuilding Programmes, 1935–1953* (London: Frank Cass, 2001): 205.
17 Aldrich, 'Secret Intelligence': 27.
18 For example: 'Tactical Planning for High Speed U-boats', Captain Harry D. Hoffman, USN, US Naval Technical Mission in Europe: Report No. 287-45, File A9-16(3)(10/Hn), Serial 00284, 11 September 1945, NavTecMisEu, Box 30, Series IV, Technical Reports No. 268-45 – 289-45, Operational Archives, Naval Historical Center, Washington, DC.
19 'Guides to German Records Microfilmed at Alexandria, VA, No. 82 Records of Headquarters, German Army High Command (*Oberkommando des Herres* – OKH/FHO) Part IV', National Archives and Records Service, General Services Administration, Washington, 1982, NHB. For the full document, see: 'Operation of U-boat Type XXI (Document issued by Admiral Dönitz from Naval Staff Headquarters on 10 July 1944)', Department of Research Programmes and Planning, Admiralty, ACSIL Translation No. 542 (PG.18487), March 1952, FDS, Box 269, NHB.
20 'Proposed Paper for Policy and Plans Sub-Committee [Air Reconnaissance for Submarines of the Future]', [Captain A.N.C. Bingley, DNAW, 26 June 1947], ADM 1/20384; S.G. Gorshkov, *The Sea Power of the State* (Annapolis, Maryland: Naval Institute Press, 1976, translated 1979): 118.
21 'Proposal to Transfer the Foreign Documents Section of NID to DTSD (Historical Section)', E.W. Longley-Cook, DNI, NID.05172/48, 7 December 1948, in 'Personnel and Administration, 1 June 1948 to 31 December 1949', TSD/HS, NHB.
22 'Eleventh TAS Liaison Meeting: Minutes', Part 13, 'Paper I – Review of Soviet Naval and Air Forces and their TAS Roles; Paper II – Soviet Underwater Weapons: Discussion', 9–11 September 1952, ADM 189/235: 152–7.
23 'Russian Submarines in the Second World War: An Estimate of their Efficiency (Reference: NATO (Secret) ID 0940/1 of 4 January 1955)', Historical Section, Admiralty, Box PT135, NHB.

24 'USSR and Satellite Navies', Naval Intelligence Division, NID.06956/48, CB 03187, October 1951, NHB: 365.
25 'Joint Sea/Air Warfare Committee: Minutes of the Fourteenth Meeting of the Tactical and Training Sub-Committee, held in the Admiralty on Wednesday, 3 March 1948', Sub-SAWC/II/41/48, 9 March 1948, Box 102, RG 313, NARA2; 'Third Submarine Flotilla Monthly General Letter – March 1946', Captain W.J.W. Woods, Captain (S/M), Third Submarine Flotilla, HMS *Forth*, No. TSF.0817/A/13, 31 March 1946, RNSM A1946/001.
26 'Scale and Nature of Attack against Sea Communications', Joint Intelligence Committee, JIC(48)69(0)Final, 11 August 1948, CAB 158/4.
27 Minute, Philip Currey, for DTSD, 29 April 1947, ADM 1/20030.
28 'Soviet Interests, Intentions and Capabilities – General', Report by the Joint Intelligence Sub-Committee, JIC(47)7(Final), 6 August 1947, CAB 158/1.
29 'The Overall Strategic Plan, May 1947 (DO(47)44 (Also COS(47)102(0)) (Retained – Cab Off))', Appendix 7, in J. Lewis, *Changing Direction: British Military Planning for Post-war Strategic Defence, 1942–1947* (London: The Sherwood Press, 1988): 372.
30 'Appreciation of Russian Intentions: Memorandum by the First Sea Lord', Fraser [?], COS(49)161, 5 May 1949, DEFE 5/14.
31 Minute, E.M. Gollin, Director of Operational Research, 1 April 1947, ADM 1/20030; 'Large Type German Submarine', R.W.L. Gawn, Chief Constructor, Admiralty Experimental Works, Haslar, 20 July 1944, Folio 34, RNSM A1991/183; Minute, F. Brundrett, MA, DDSR, 17 December 1945, ADM 1/20113; Ewen Montague, *Beyond Top Secret U* (London: Peter Davies, 1977): 59–62.
32 'Joint Sea/Air Warfare Committee: Minutes of the 2nd meeting of the Committee held at the Admiralty on 27 August 1946', SAWC 2/46(12), 27 August 1946, AIR 20/6842; 'Joint Sea/Air Warfare Committee Report by the Joint Secretaries of the Sea/Air Warfare Sub-Committees on the Work carried out since – 5 February 1948', SAWC/I/49/2, 28 June 1949, AIR 20/6842.
33 See Chapter 4.
34 'Joint Sea/Air Warfare Committee: Report by the Joint Secretaries of the Joint Sea/Air Warfare Sub-Committees on the work carried out since 28 June 1949', SAWC/I/50/2, 21 July 1950, AIR 20/6842.
35 'The Development of A/S Warfare', TASW.021/46, Revised Edition, 4 May 1946, ADM 1/20960: 1 and Annex B.
36 'Policy Review of Methods of Attacking Submerged Submarines by Surface Vessels and (Appendix) by Aircraft', Annex B to TASW.021/46, Revised Edition, 4 May 1946, ADM 1/20960: 1.
37 'Progress in Underwater Warfare, 1946', DTASW, TASW.1453/46, CB04050(46), March 1947, ADM 239/420: 35.
38 'Annual Report of TAS Schools, 1946', UWD, CB4486, UW.05407/47, 24 October 1947, ADM 189/66: 37.
39 Minute, DASW, 2 April 1944, ADM 1/16495.
40 'Policy Review of Methods of Attacking Submerged Submarines …', ADM 1/20960: 2.
41 'Summary of DTASW's Investigation …', ADM 1/20960.
42 Unmarked Paper of Detailed Comments on Problems at HMA/SEE, [August 1942], 'Papers Re Resignation from HMA/SEE, Fairlie in 1942', KEYN 1, Correspondence: World War II and Radar, Acc. 23/667/669 (Keynes), Box 1, CCAC, KEYN; 'Example C: The Spit Beam Asdic', Draft, n.d., CCAC, GOEV 3/1; 'Half-Yearly Scientific and Technical Progress Report', HM Underwater Detection Establishment, Portland, 1946 (2), ADM 213/362.
43 'Progress Report: Shipborne A/S Weapons', TASW.038/46, [5 September 1946], ADM 1/20960: 6–9.

44 'Fourth Anti-Submarine Conference', J.D. Price, Vice Chief of Naval Operations, OP 312F/rh A19 Serial 00296P31, 18 August 1949, File 8100.5, Vol. 3734, RG 24, NAC.
45 'Policy Review of Methods of Attacking Submerged Submarines …', ADM 1/20960: 3.
46 'A Review of the Methods of Attacking Submerged Submarines by Aircraft', Appendix to Annex B to TASW.021/46, Revised Edition, 4 May 1946, ADM 1/20960; 'Magnetic Submarine Detector (MAD)', Admiralty.134/1942, 1942, ADM 1/11741; P.M.S. Blackett, 'Evan James Williams. 1903–1945', in *Obituary Notices of Fellows of The Royal Society*, 1945–1948, Vol. V (London: Morrison & Gibb for The Royal Society, 1945–1948): 396.
47 'A Review of the Methods of Attacking Submerged Submarines by Aircraft', ADM 1/20960.
48 'The Development of A/S Warfare', ADM 1/20960: 2.
49 'Development of the Submarine', Annex A to TASW.021/46, Revised Edition, 4 May 1946, ADM 1/20960: 6.
50 'Progress in Tactics, 1948', ADM 239/144: 24.
51 'The Development of A/S Warfare', ADM 1/20960: 3.
52 'Submerged Performance Tests on German Type XXI Submarines', William E. Schevill and Allyn C, Vine, Woods Hole Oceanographic Institution, 17 March 1947, File 3, Submarine/Undersea Warfare Division, Series III, Box 12, OA, NHC; 'Special Submarine Group – Prospective Operations Schedule (Revised)', W. R. Laughton, The Commander Special Submarine Group, FC5-2/S8, 1 March 1946, File 1, Submarine/Undersea Warfare Division, Series III, Box 12, OA, NHC.
53 'Submerged Performance Tests on Type XXI U-Boats', Staff Officer (Anti-Submarine) to Director of Torpedo, Anti-Submarine and Mine Warfare, Admiralty, A/S 230-1, 14 April 1947, RNSM A1991/076.
54 'Proposed Evaluation of Present Guppy Submarine Conversion and Equipment', L.R. Daspit, Commander Submarine Squadron Four, to Commander Submarine Force, US Atlantic Fleet, FC5-4/S1, 24 March 1948, Box 98, RG 313, NARA2.
55 Erich Topp, letter, 17 August 1997.
56 Hessler, *The U-boat War*, Vol. III: 86.
57 'Development of the Submarine', ADM 1/20960: 2.
58 'Notes on the "Kurier" System', Enclosure (A), in '"Kurier" System of U-boat Communication', 7 July 1945, Report No. 187-45, NavTecMisEu, Series III, Letter Reports #180-45 thru #205-45, Box 14, OA, NHC; 'On the Value of Squash in Pack Attacks', [Leon Solomon], DNOR, OIC/SI1254, [19 March 1945], ADM 223/261.
59 'Development of the Submarine', ADM 1/20960: 3.
60 Minute, Captain Lord Ashbourne, DTASW, TASW.214/[45], 18 October 1945, ADM 116/5853.
61 Minute, DNAW, 25 July 1946, ADM 1/20045.
62 Minute by D of P, 26 August 1945, ADM 1/20045.
63 'Third A/S Tactical Liaison Meeting held in HMS *Vernon* on 1st and 2nd May 1947', A.198/3/47, 17 May 1947, distributed by Op-32-F-45, n.d., Box 102, RG 313, NARA2.
64 'Joint Paper on Sea and Air Aspects of Search and Convoy Defence', P.W. Burnett, for DTASW, and F.J. Finnigan, Director of Operations, Sub-SAWC/II C.30414/D of Ops, [July 1946], Box 96, RG 313, NARA2.
65 'Minutes of the 1st Meeting of the Tactical and Training Sub-Committee and the 1st Meeting of the Technical Investigation Sub-Committee …', Cdr G.R. Carver and W/Cdr J.L. Crosbie, Sub-SAWC/II/2/46 and Sub-SAWC/III/2/46, 13 May 1946, AIR 15/786.
66 Minute, Group Captain V.C. Darling, RAF, DDOps(M), 30 September 1946, AIR 2/5950.

Notes 197

67 'German U-boat Strategy in the War', Appendix XVIII, to 'Some Weaknesses in German Strategy and Organisation, 1933–1945', Report by the Joint Intelligence Sub-Committee, JIC(46)33(Final), 20 October 1946, NHB.
68 'Joint Paper on Sea and Air Aspects of Fleet Defence against Submarines', F.J. Finnigan, Director of Operations, Air Ministry, Captain G. Willoughby, DNAW and Captain Lord Ashbourne, DTASW, Admiralty, TASW.4261/46, [1 November 1946], ADM 1/20936, Covering Letter.
69 'Joint Paper on ... Convoy Defence', Box 96, RG 313, NARA2.
70 'General Implications of Improved Submarine Performance', Section II, 'Joint Paper on ... Convoy Defence', Box 96, RG 313, NARA2: 5.
71 'Minutes of the Fourth Meeting of the Tactical and Training Sub-Committee of the Joint Sea/Air Warfare Committee ...', J.L. Crosbie and G.R. Carver, Joint Secretaries, Sub-SAWC/II/9/46, 19 July 1946, ADM 116/5614.
72 'Conduct of Anti-U-Boat Operations: Part IV, Air and Surface A/S Searches and Striking Forces' DASW, ASW 3078/43, BR1679(4), June 1944, ADM 234/293.
73 'Joint Paper on ... Convoy Defence', Box 96, RG 313, NARA2: 5.
74 'Summary of DTASW's Investigation ...', ADM 1/20960.
75 'Joint Paper on ... Convoy Defence', Box 96, RG 313, NARA2: 5.
76 'Conduct of Anti-U-Boat Operations: Part IV, Air and Surface A/S Searches and Striking Forces' DASW, ASW 3078/43, BR1679(4), June 1944, ADM 234/293: 23–5.
77 'Joint Paper on ... Convoy Defence', Box 96, RG 313, NARA2: 5–6; 'US Fleet, Anti-Submarine and Escort of Convoy Instructions (BUSCIs)', FTP 223A, January 1945, File 79/532, DHH: 1–5.
78 'Joint Paper on ... Convoy Defence', Box 96, RG 313, NARA2: 3.
79 'Report by DOR(E) on Sonobuoys – British/American Standardisation', Air Commodore G.W. Tuttle, DOR(E), C.34223/47 and Sub-SAWC/II/54/48, 4 August 1948, ADM 116/5819; 'First Commonwealth TAS Liaison Meeting [10–20 October 1949] – Report by RAN Representative', Lieutenant Commander I.K. Purvis, RAN, n.d., NAA(M), MP 1185/8, 1846/4/343.
80 'MAD, Question of Fitting in our A/S Aircraft', DACD, ACD.33/42, 12 September 1942, ADM 1/11741; 'Test of MAD Equipment for Detecting the Presence of Submerged Submarines from the Air', Coastal Command Development Unit, RAF Tain, Ross-shire, Report No. 87, CCDU/20/122/AIR, 3 December 1942, File S-28-1-4, Vol. 5271, RG 24, NAC; P.M.S. Blackett, 'Evan James Williams. 1903–1945', in *Obituary Notices of Fellows of The Royal Society*, 1945–1948, Vol. V (London: Morrison & Gibb for The Royal Society, 1945–1948): 396; Professor Westcott, letter, 28 June 1998; Flight Lieutenant Bell, letter, 1 July 1998.
81 'Joint Paper on ... Convoy Defence', Box 96, RG 313, NARA2: 6.
82 'Convoy A/S Escort', in 'Conduct of Anti-U-Boat Operations, 1940', DASW, ASW.2191/40, CB4097(11)(42), November 1940 [with amendments to 25 April 1945], Box 468, RG 38, NARA2: Plates 4–7.
83 Compton-Hall, 26 February 2000.
84 'Joint Paper on ... Fleet Defence ...', ADM 1/20936, *passim*; 'Joint Paper on ... Convoy Defence', Box 96, RG 313, NARA2, *passim*.
85 'Joint Paper on ... Convoy Defence', Box 96, RG 313, NARA2: 10.
86 'Joint Paper on ... Fleet Defence ...', ADM 1/20936: 6.
87 Memorandum by G.N. Oliver, ACNS, 31 December 1946, ADM 1/20384.
88 'Ability of the Submarine of the Future to Make Contacts', [Captain Lord Ashbourne, DTASW, 28 January 1947], ADM 1/20384.
89 'Proposed Paper for Policy and Plans Sub-Committee [Air Reconnaissance for Submarines of the Future]', [Captain A.N.C. Bingley, DNAW, 26 June 1947], ADM 1/20384.

198 *Notes*

90 'Prevention of Enemy Air Reconnaissance Co-operating with Submarines: Appreciation', [Captain E.H. Shattock, DNAW, 5 February 1947], ADM 1/20384.
91 Ibid.
92 Minute, G.N. Oliver, ACNS, 18 April 1947, ADM 1/20384.
93 'Proposed Paper for Policy and Plans Sub-Committee ...', ADM 1/20384.
94 Minute by F. Brundrett, MA, DDSR, 17 December 1945, ADM 1/20113.
95 Minute, E.M. Gollin, Director of Operational Research, 1 April 1947, ADM 1/20030.
96 Ibid.
97 Ibid; Llewellyn-Jones, 'A Clash of Cultures': 138–66.
98 Minute, Gollin, 1 April 1947, ADM 1/20030.
99 Minute, Peter Cazalet, for D of P, 22 April 1947, ADM 1/20030.
100 'Exercise "Spearhead"', in 'Progress in Tactics: 1947', DTSD, CB03016/47, 17 October 1947, ADM 239/143: 45–6.
101 Minute, Philip Currey, for DTSD, 29 April 1947, ADM 1/20030.
102 Minute, G.N. Oliver, ACNS, 5 May 1947, ADM 1/20030.
103 Minute [Vice Admiral Sir Rhoderick McGrigor, VCNS], 7 May [1947], ADM 1/20030.
104 Minute, D of P, 20 August 1947, ADM 116/5966; Minute, USS, 23 October 1947, ADM 116/5966; Eric J. Grove, 'The Post War "Ten Year Rule" – Myth and Reality', *Journal of the Royal United Services Institute*, Vol. 129, No. 4 (December 1984): 48–53.

6 New problems, old recipes, 1947–48

1 'Proceedings of Anti-Submarine Warfare Conference, 17 June 1946', Op-34H:jn (SC) A16-3(17) Serial: 00012P34, Forrest Sherman, Deputy Chief of Naval Operations, 25 June 1946, Post 1946 Command File, CNO Ser: Conferences, Anti-Submarine Warfare 1946–8, Box 325A, OA, NHC.
2 'Report of Coordinator of Undersea Warfare and Assistants' Visit to British Naval Activities, Jan. 19 – Feb. 12 1947', Forrest Sherman, Deputy Chief of Naval Operations (Operations), Op-31B:ch (SC) A16-3(17) Serial 003P31, 30 April 1947, Box 90, RG 313, NARA2: 2.
3 'Review of the Problems of Future A/S Warfare', TASW.2014/47, [December 1946], in 'Report of Coordinator of Undersea Warfare and Assistants' Visit to British Naval Activities, Jan. 19 – Feb. 12 1947', Forrest Sherman, Deputy Chief of Naval Operations (Operations), Op-31B:ch (SC) A16-3(17) Serial 003P31, 30 April 1947, Box 90, RG 313, NARA2: 5.
4 'Review ... Future A/S Warfare', Box 90, RG 313, NARA2: 6–8.
5 'Anti-Submarine Problems of the Future', TASW.4666/47:W. Burnett, for DTASW, 16 August 1947, AIR 20/6381: Summary.
6 Minute, Philip Currey, for DTSD, 29 April 1947, ADM 1/20030.
7 Grove (ed.), *The Defeat of the Enemy Attack on Shipping*, Plan 4.
8 'Cause of U-boat Sinkings – 2nd World War', Diagram 20 in 'Exercise 'Trident', Volume II', CB004521, April 1949 (issued 23 January 1950), ADM 239/490.
9 'Anti-Submarine Problems of the Future', AIR 20/6381: Part 2.
10 'Report of Proceedings', Commander P.W. Burnett, RN, HMS *Braithwaite*, Ref. No. 1A/10, 20 February 1945, ADM 199/198.
11 'Anti-Submarine Problems of the Future', AIR 20/6381, Part 1.
12 Ibid, Part 2.
13 'German Underwater Rockets', US Naval Technical Mission in Europe, Technical Report No. 500-45, October 1945, NHB; Eberhard Rössler, *The U-boat: The Evolution and Technical History of German Submarines*, tr. Harold Erenberg (London: Arms and Armour Press, 1981): 145.
14 'Anti-Submarine Problems of the Future', AIR 20/6381: Part 3.

15 'Maritime Radar for Search and Shadowing', Sub-SAWC/II/62/48, n.d., in 'Great Britain – Navy Anti-Submarine Warfare Doctrine', Commander F.A. Brock, USN, Undersea Warfare Section, CinCNELM, 1 November 1948, Box 96, RG 313, NARA2.
16 'Torpedo Mine Mk 24', Bernard Stephens, 30 April 1998.
17 'Report of Coordinator of Undersea Warfare …', Box 90, RG 313, NARA2: 2.
18 'Anti-Submarine Problems of the Future', AIR 20/6381: Part 4.
19 Ibid.
20 'Anti-Submarine Problems of the Future', AIR 20/6381, Part 5. These issues are discussed more fully in: M. Llewellyn-Jones, 'A Flawed Contender: The "Fighter" Submarine, 1946–1950', in Martin Edmonds (ed.), *100 Years of the Trade: Royal Navy Submarines Past, Present & Future* (University of Lancaster: Centre for Defence and International Security Studies, February 2001): 58–67.
21 'Rubber Covering of German Submarines Anti-Asdic (German code name 'Alberich')', 20 September 1945, Report No. 352-45, NavTecMisEu, Series IV, Technical Reports #351-45 thru #370-45, Box 35, OA, NHC.
22 'Anti-Submarine Problems of the Future', AIR 20/6381: Part 9.
23 'Progress in Underwater Warfare, 1946', ADM 239/420; Anthony Gorst, '"We must cut our coat according to our cloth": the making of British defence policy, 1945–48', in Richard J. Aldrich (ed.), *British Intelligence, Strategy and the Cold War, 1945–51* (London: Routledge, 1992): 157.
24 Note by Sir Henry Tizard to the Minister [of Supply], 24 August 1948, DEFE 9/12; 'Research and Development Priorities: Report by the Defence Research Policy Committee', H.T. Tizard, COS(49)220, 9 July 1949, DEFE 5/14.
25 'Anti-Submarine Problems of the Future', AIR 20/6381, Part 1 [emphasis added].
26 'HMUDE Summary of Progress', 1 December 1948, NAA(M): MP1049/5, 1968/2/800.
27 This had been a constant concern of the Americans during the latter stages of the Second World War. See: Philip K. Lundeberg, 'Operation "Teardrop" Revisited', in Timothy J. Runyan and Jan M. Copes (eds.), *To Die Gallantly: The Battle of the Atlantic* (Oxford: Westview Press, 1994): 210–30.
28 C.H. Waddington, *OR in World War 2: Operational Research against the U-boat* (London: Elek Science, 1973): 37.
29 'Anti-Submarine Problems of the Future', AIR 20/6381: Summary and Part 1.
30 Minute, [Captain] Ashbourne, DTASW, 1 November 1946, ADM 1/20030.
31 'The Evolution of the *Osprey*':1009, AL: 29–30.
32 'Minutes of the Seventh Meeting of the Policy and Plans Sub-Committee held in the Admiralty on 7 November 1947, Sub-SAWC 1/14/47, 13 November 1947, AIR 20/10176.
33 'A/S Problems of the Future – Attack-at-Source and Harbour Defence', G.N. Oliver, Office of the Chief of Naval Staff, 8 December 1947, ADM 1/21546.
34 Minute, G.N. Oliver, 8 December 1947, ADM 1/21546; Minute, D of P, 17 December 1947, ADM 1/21546; 'Small Battle Units', DTASW, TASW.4037/48, April 1948, DEFE 2/1660; Richard H. Allen, 'The Attack-at-Source and the Development of the British X-Craft Midget Submarine, 1945–1958' (MA, London, King's College, 2000).
35 The Intermediate (B) was the requirement which produced the *Porpoise* Class submarine.
36 Eberhard Rössler, *The U-boat: The Evolution and Technical History of German Submarines*, tr. Harold Erenberg (London: Arms and Armour Press, 1981): 204 and 273–4; Ships' Cover 746/A, Super-*Seraph* (*Scotsman*), Folio 4, NMM(W).
37 'USSR and Satellite Navies', Naval Intelligence Division, NID.06956/48, CB 03187, October 1951, NHB: 89–93.
38 'A Review of Past Submarine Tactics and a Forecast of Probable Future Enemy Submarine Tactics', DTASW, TASW.329/47, June 1948, ADM 1/30840: 7–8.
39 'A Review of Past Submarine Tactics …', ADM 1/30840: 8.

40 'Progress in Tactics: 1947', ADM 239/143: 11–13.
41 'Joint Sea/Air Warfare Committee: Minutes of the Tenth Meeting of the Policy and Plans Sub-Committee held in the Air Ministry on Wednesday 13 April 1949', Sub-SAWC/I/6/49, 26 May 1949, AIR 20/6383.
42 'Joint A/S School, HMS *Ferret*, Londonderry', Senior Canadian Naval Liaison Officer, London, to The Naval Secretary, Department of National Defence (Naval Service), Ottawa, NUK. 4915-1, 11 June 1947, File S-4973-30 Vol. 1, Vol. 1814, Acc. 83-84/167, RG 24, NAC; Rear Admiral J.H. Adams, CB, LVO, interview, 28 May 1998.
43 'ASW Training', Commander in Chief US Pacific Fleet to Chief of Naval Operations, A5-9 Serial: 00181, 12 July 1948, Records of the Naval Operating Forces: Commander in Chief Atlantic (CinCLant) Secret Administrative Files, 1941–1949, Box 96, RG 313, NARA2.
44 'A/S Warfare in Relation to Future Strategy', Cabinet War Room, 2 January 1943, ADM 1/14793.
45 'Joint A/S Warfare – Convoy Defence and Offensive Operations – A General Outline Lecture', Lieutenant Commander D.E.B. Field, RN, Wing Commander H.A.S. Disney, RAF, Commander A.W.F. Sutton, RN, Joint A/S School, Londonderry, Issued 28 May 1947, Revised 27 October 1947, File S-4973-30 Vol. 1, Vol. 1814, Acc. 83-84/167, RG 24, NAC: 1.
46 'Convoy Defence and Offensive Operations…Lecture', File S-4973-30 Vol. 1, Vol. 1814, Acc. 83-84/167, RG 24, NAC: 2.
47 'Convoy Defence and Offensive Operations…Lecture', File S-4973-30 Vol. 1, Vol. 1814, Acc. 83-84/167, RG 24, NAC: 4.
48 'Report by RAF Observer in HMS Viking during period 24 April – 6 May 1944', HQ No. 19 Group, 30 May 1944, AIR 15/557; 'The RAF in Maritime War, Vol. IV: The Atlantic and Home Waters, The Offensive Phase, February 1943 – May 1944', (First Draft) n.d., AIR 41/48: 477–88 and 488fn1.
49 'Monday, 7 May 1945, War Diary (Naval), 1–15 May 1945', NHB: 148.
50 'Report on Interrogation of Admiral Godt, German Navy, Admiral Commanding BdU Ops. and his Staff Officers, [May 1945]', Gretton Papers, MSS/93/008, NMM(G); 'Report of Proceedings', Commander P.W. Burnett, RN, HMS *Braithwaite*, Ref. No. 1A/10, 20 February 1945, ADM 199/198: 41.
51 'Progress in Tactics, 1948', ADM 239/144: 6.
52 'An Outline of the Conduct of Naval Air A/S Operations in Defence of Trade', Acting Commander A.W.F. Sutton, RN, Joint A/S School, Londonderry, 15 September 1947, File S-4973-30 Vol. 1, Vol. 1814, Acc. 83-84/167, RG 24, NAC: 3–4.
53 'RAF Staff College: Précis of Lecture on Surface Tactics', Lieutenant Commander D.E.B. Field, RN, Joint A/S School, Londonderry, File S-4973-30 Vol. 1, Vol. 1814, Acc. 83-84/167, RG 24, NAC.
54 'Report of Interrogation of German Prisoners of War by Captain Roberts RN', Admiral Max Horton, Commander-in-Chief, Western Approaches, WA 1947/00534/6, 11 June 1945, ADM 1/18670.
55 'Progress in Tactics, 1948', CB 03016/48, TSD 108/48, Tactical and Staff Duties Division, Admiralty, 30 November 1948, ADM 239/144: 11.
56 'Convoy Defence and Offensive Operations … Lecture', File S-4973-30 Vol. 1, Vol. 1814, Acc. 83-84/167, RG 24, NAC: 6.
57 'Remarks on Air Staff Paper on the Employment of Heavy Bomber Force against Enemy U-boat Organisation' [covered by First Lord's note, 15 December 1944], PREM 3/414/1.
58 'Convoy Defence and Offensive Operations … Lecture', File S-4973-30 Vol. 1, Vol. 1814, Acc. 83-84/167, RG 24, NAC: 3 and 6.
59 Admiral R. McGrigor, Commander-in-Chief, Home Fleet to Admiral of the Fleet Lord Fraser of North Cape, First Sea Lord, 24 November 1948, Section 5, ADM 205/70.

60 'Staff Meeting held in the Upper War Room on 13 September at 1030 am', in 'Staff Meetings in Upper War Room', Vol. 14, 1 September to 31 December 1944, NHB; 'Part IV – The Control and Operations of Aircraft and Surface Vessels in a CVE, April 1945', in 'Naval Air Anti-U-Boat Instructions (Short Title: NAUIs)', AWD 650/45, CB04405 (G.B.), Naval Air Warfare and Flying Training Division, April 1945, Box 147, RG 38, NARA2.
61 'An Outline of the Conduct of Naval Air A/S Operations in Defence of Trade', File S-4973-30 Vol. 1, Vol. 1814, Acc. 83-84/167, RG 24, NAC: 6; 'Convoy Defence and Offensive Operations ... Lecture', File S-4973-30 Vol. 1, Vol. 1814, Acc. 83-84/167, RG 24, NAC: 7.
62 'RAF Staff College: Précis of Lecture on Surface Tactics', File S-4973-30 Vol. 1, Vol. 1814, Acc. 83-84/167, RG 24, NAC.
63 'Précis: Command and Control of Joint A/S Operations', Wing Commander H.A.S. Disney, RAF, n.d., File S-4973-30 Vol. 1, Vol. 1814, Acc. 83-84/167, RG 24, NAC.
64 'Third A/S Tactical Liaison Meeting held in HMS *Vernon* on 1st and 2nd May 1947', A.198/3/47, 17 May 1947, distributed by Op-32-F-45, n.d., Box 102, RG 313, NARA2: 22–3.
65 'Trade Protection – Defence of Ocean Convoys', Oulton and Onslow, 17 October 1947, Box 102, RG 313, NARA2: 1.
66 M. Llewellyn-Jones, 'Preface', in *The Royal Navy and the Mediterranean Convoys to Malta in World War Two* (London: Cass, forthcoming).
67 'Minutes of the Fourth Meeting of the Tactical and Training Sub-Committee ...', ADM 116/5614; Reference Sheet, 'Defence of Fleet Units against Submarine Attack', C.E.E. Paterson for DTASW, TASW.380/48, 19 August 1948, AIR 2/5950; 'Trade Protection – Defence of Ocean Convoys (73/JAS/RAF/S.100/AIR), Wing Commander C.B. Gavin-Robinson, RAF, and Commander J.W. Hale, RN, Sub.SAWC/II/36/48, 18 February 1948, Box 102, RG 313, NARA2.
68 'Trade Protection – Defence of Ocean Convoys', Group Captain W.E. Oulton, Director (RAF) and Captain R.G. Onslow, Director (RN), Joint A/S School, Londonderry, No. 73/JAS/RAF/S.100/AIR, 17 October 1947, Box 102, RG 313, NARA2.
69 'Trade Protection – Defence of Ocean Convoys', Box 102, RG 313, NARA2: Part II.
70 'The Asdic and its Associated Weapons', DERA, AN.15971: 18.
71 'RAF Staff College: Précis of Lecture on Anti-Submarine Tactics – Shore Based Aircraft', Wing Commander H.A.S. Disney, RAF, Instruction Office, Joint A/S School, Londonderry, 12 September 1947, File S-4973-30 Vol. 1, Vol. 1814, Acc. 83-84/167, RG 24, NAC.
72 'Convoy Defence and Offensive Operations ... Lecture', File S-4973-30 Vol. 1, Vol. 1814, Acc. 83-84/167, RG 24, NAC: 5; 'Minutes of the 4th Meeting of the Technical Investigation Sub-Committee, 8 August 1946', Sub-SAWC/III/7/46, 12 August 1946, ADM 116/5614.
73 'The Experimental Four Square Asdic Set', HMA/SEE, Fairlie, Internal Report No. 230, 9 November 1945, ADM 259/429: 2; M. Llewellyn-Jones, 'The Royal Navy and the Challenge of the Fast Submarine, 1944–1954: Innovation or Evolution?' in Richard Harding (ed.), *The Royal Navy, 1930-2000* (London: Cass, 2004): 135–69.
74 'Progress in Underwater Warfare, 1946', ADM 239/420: 34.
75 'Minutes of the First Meeting of DASW's Sub-Committee of ACNS(UT)'s U-boat Warfare Committee held at the Admiralty on Thursday, 30 November 1944, (Copy)' Folder NSS 1271-22, Vol. 8080, RG 24, NAC.
76 'Progress in Tactics: 1947', ADM 239/143: 21–2.
77 'Progress in Underwater Warfare, 1947', DTASW, TASW.116/48, CB04050(47), 8 October 1948, ADM 239/421: 33.
78 'Third A/S Tactical Liaison Meeting held in HMS *Vernon* on 1st and 2nd May 1947', A.198/3/47, 17 May 1947, distributed by Op-32-F-45, n.d., Box 102, RG 313, NARA2: 22.

79 'Progress in Tactics, 1948', ADM 239/144: 28; and more particularly, 'Progress in Underwater Warfare, 1947', ADM 239/421: 33.
80 'Progress in Underwater Warfare, 1947', ADM 239/421: 34.
81 Ibid: 35.
82 'Semi-Annual Summary of US Naval Forces Eastern Atlantic and Mediterranean, 1 April 1948 – 1 September 1948', Commander-in-Chief, US Naval Forces Eastern Atlantic and Mediterranean, to Secretary of the Navy, 14 October 1948, LHCMA, MF 868.
83 Friedman, *U.S. Submarines*: 242.
84 'Conduct of A/S Operations by Ships and Aircraft', Admiralty and Air Ministry, CB04097(1/51) and SD 697(1/51), TASW.196/50, 3 October 1951, Box 468, RG 38, NARA2, Part 4: 43–9.
85 'Aircraft and Aircraft Carriers', Part 4 of 'Conduct of A/S Operations...', Box 468, RG 38, NARA2: 46–7.
86 'Exercises with USS *Trumpetfish*', Captain E.A. Gibbs, 11 June 1948, Box 96, RG 313, NARA2: 5.
87 'Exercises with USS *Trumpetfish*', Box 96, RG 313, NARA2: 4 [emphasis in the original].
88 Ibid: 8.
89 'Progress in Tactics, 1949', DTSD, TSD.109/49, CB03016(49), 29 September 1949, ADM 239/565: 61.
90 'Progress in Underwater Warfare, 1948', DTASW, TASW.53/49, CB04050(48), 10 September 1949, ADM 239/422: 40.
91 'Progress in Underwater Warfare, 1948', ADM 239/422: 40.

7 Future uncertainties, 1948–49

1 Norman Friedman, *The Fifty Year War: Conflict and Strategy in the Cold War* (Annapolis: Naval Institute Press, 2000): 60.
2 C.R. Attlee, *As it Happened: His Autobiography* (London: Heinemann, 1954): 170.
3 Michael Dockrill, *The Cold War, 1945–1963*, (London: Macmillan, 1988): 34–51.
4 'Certain Assumptions for Planning Purposes', Report by the Joint Intelligence Sub-Committee, JIC(46)19(0)(Final), 6 March 1946, CAB 81/132.
5 Peter Hennessy, *The Secret State: Whitehall and the Cold War* (London: Allen Lane, 2002): 18.
6 Percy Cradock, *Know Your Enemy: How the Joint Intelligence Committee Saw the World* (London: John Murray, 2002): 29.
7 'Assumptions as to Risk of Future War and Target Date for Re-equipment of the Fleet', 1947–1948, ADM 116/5966.
8 Moore, *Royal Navy and Nuclear Weapons*: 42; A.B. Birnie to M.M. Low, A/M.01938/46, 1 March 1948, AIR 2/12249.
9 'Joint Sea/Air Warfare Committee: Minutes of the 2nd meeting of the Committee held at the Admiralty on 27 August 1946', SAWC 2/46(12), 27 August 1946, AIR 20/6842.
10 The Naval Staff History dealing with these aspects in the Mediterranean, Indian and Pacific Oceans, reached the final draft stage but was never issued. 'History of Naval Aviation', Vol. III, Draft Chapters I-XXV and Appendices, NHB, Box T.21164-T.21190.
11 Minute, Captain E. Shattock, DNAW, 14 July 1948, ADM 1/24518.
12 'Guidance on Future Tactical Problems for Naval Aircraft', Captain G. Barnard, RN, The Director, RN Tactical School, TC No. 166/1/5, 18 June 1948, ADM 1/24518.
13 Minute, Captain H.G. Dickinson, for D of P, 20 July 1948, ADM 1/24518.
14 'Policy and Fleet Tactical Training', R. Dick, DTSD, TSD.4580/48, 14 July 1948, ADM 205/69.

Notes 203

15 'Maritime Policy as it affects Exercise 'Trident'':L. Vian, Fifth Sea Lord, 10 September 1948, ADM 205/69.
16 'Maritime Policy as it affects Exercise 'Trident'', Fraser, First Sea Lord, 14 September 1948, ADM 205/69.
17 'Maritime Policy':L. Vian, Fifth Sea Lord, 15 September 1948, ADM 205/69.
18 'Maritime Operations', T.M. Brownrigg, D of P, 28 September 1948, ADM 205/69.
19 'The Proposed Policy for Build-up of Naval Aviation after the Outbreak of War', Appendix II to 'Maritime Operations', T.M. Brownrigg, D of P, 28 September 1948, ADM 205/69.
20 'Maritime Policy', Fraser, First Sea Lord, 29 September 1948, ADM 205/69.
21 'Conduct of A/S Operations ...', Box 468, RG 38, NARA2; 'ATP1 [Allied Naval Maneuvering Instructions], Change 1: January 1952', Box 4, RG 38, NARA2.
22 'Plan "Galloper"', Chiefs of Staff Committee, Joint Planning Staff, JP(49)134(Final), 1 March 1950, DEFE 6/11: 7.
23 'Strategic Guidance from the Standing Group to the Regional Planning Groups on the North Atlantic Treaty Organisation', Chiefs of Staff Committee, Joint Planning Staff, JP(49)149(Final), 21 November 1949, DEFE 6/11.
24 Eric Grove and Geoffrey Till, 'Anglo-American Maritime Strategy in the Era of Massive Retaliation, 1945–60', in John B. Hattendorf and Robert S. Jordan (eds.), *Maritime Strategy and the Balance of Power: Britain and America in the Twentieth Century* (Basingstoke, Hants.: Macmillan Press, 1989): 276.
25 Admiral R. McGrigor, Commander-in-Chief, Home Fleet to Admiral of the Fleet Lord Fraser of North Cape, First Sea Lord, 24 November 1948, Section 5, ADM 205/70: 3.
26 'Remarks by Commander-in-Chief, Home Fleet', Enclosure No. 6 to 'Exercise "Sunrise"', Admiral McGrigor, Commander-in-Chief, Home Fleet, No.393/940/105/10, 28 March 1949, ADM 116/5779.
27 'Monthly Intelligence Report, July 1949', NID, 10 August 1949, DNH.
28 'Exercise "Trident", Volume I', CB004520, April 1949, ADM 239/489: iii.
29 'Exercise "Trident"', ADM 239/489: xiv.
30 Grove (ed.), *The Defeat of the Enemy Attack on Shipping*: xvi; 'Historical Section of TSD – Review of Narrator Posts, Roger M. Bellairs, 11 November 1949, T.27309, NHB.
31 'The Defence of Ocean Shipping in 1957', Vice Admiral G.N. Oliver, CB, DSO, President RN College, Greenwich, Item 17, in 'Exercise "Trident"', ADM 239/490: 85.
32 'The Convoy System: "Offensive or Defensive"?' Commander F. Barley and Lieutenant Commander D.W. Waters, Historical Section, Admiralty, December 1954, NHB.
33 'Exercise "Trident"', ADM 239/489: xiv.
34 'A Survey of the Tasks of the Maritime Forces in Support of the Three Pillars of Our Strategy', Item 13, in 'Exercise "Trident"', ADM 239/489: 25.
35 'A Joint Planning Staff Conference before the Outbreak of War', Item 28, and 'The Defence of a Convoy against Submarine Attack: Demonstration by the RN Tactical School', Item 30, in 'Exercise "Trident"', ADM 239/490.
36 'Torpedo, Anti-Submarine and Mine Warfare Division – Institution', H.V. Markham, Office Memorandum No. 394, CE.58514/45, 24 September 1945, ADM 1/17743.
37 Minute by Captain V.D'A. Donaldson, DTASW, 13 October 1952, ADM 1/24139.
38 'Historical Research Memorandum No. 1: Surface and Air Anti-Submarine Escort of Shipping in Convoy, and Anti-Submarine Transit Area Patrols in Two World Wars', Historical Section, Admiralty, May 1953, ADM 1/24962, Table V.
39 This Lofar technology developed into the Cold War SOSUS acoustic arrays.
40 Norman Friedman, email, 17 May 2002, 16:26:11 GMT; 'Sub-sonic Hydrophone Investigation', Admiralty Research Laboratory, Teddington, ARL/N.5/95.27/D, 31

August 1949, ADM 204/2841; 'Long Range Detection of Submarines using VLF Hydrophone Equipment', DTASW, 20 June 1952, ADM 1/24506.
41 'Defence of Ocean Convoys against Submarine Attack', DTASW, TASW.397/48, August 1948, AIR 20/6384; 'Defence of Fleet Units against Submarine Attack', DTASW, TASW.380/48, August 1948, AIR 2/5950.
42 'The Tactical Employment of Patrol Groups', Sub-SAWC/II/63/48, [TASW.404/48], [30 September 1948], AIR 2/5950.
43 'Joint Sea/Air Warfare Committee: Report by the Joint Secretaries of the Joint Sea/Air Warfare Sub-Committees on the work carried out since 28 June 1949', SAWC/I/50/2, 21 July 1950, AIR 20/6842.
44 'Anti-Submarine Tactical Papers', Naval Secretary, Naval Service, Department of National Defence, NSS 8100-5 (Staff), 3 February 1949, File 8100.5, Vol. 3734, RG 24, NAC.
45 Peter Hennessy, *The Secret State: Whitehall and the Cold War* (London: Allen Lane, 2002): 19-20; 'USSR General Report', CX Report, 10 October 1945, WO 208/4566; 'Top Secret Annex to Study of Undersea Warfare', 22 April 1950, Command File, Post 1 Jan 46, CNO Studies 1950, Box 475, OA, NHC.
46 'Top Secret Annex to Study of Undersea Warfare', 22 April 1950, Command File, Post 1 Jan 46, CNO Studies 1950, Box 475, Operational Archives, Naval Historical Center, Washington, DC.
47 Reference Sheet, 'Defence of Fleet Units against Submarine Attack', C.E.E. Paterson for DTASW, TASW.380/48, 19 August 1948, AIR 2/5950.
48 'Defence of Ocean Convoys …', AIR 20/6384: 4.
49 'The Problem Confronting Enemy Submarines', TASW.396/48, August 1948, AIR 20/6384.
50 'Progress in Tactics: 1947', ADM 239/143: 15–16; 'Trade Protection – Defence of Ocean Convoys', Box 102, RG 313, NARA2, Appendix VI; Reference Sheet, 'Defence of Fleet Units against Submarine Attack', C.E.E. Paterson for DTASW, TASW.380/48, 19 August 1948, AIR 2/5950.
51 Ibid: 1–6; 'Defence of Fleet Units …', AIR 2/5950: 1–6.
52 Gorshkov, *Sea Power*: 118.
53 Mahan, *Influence* (c.1889): 196; A.T. Mahan, *The Influence of Sea Power upon the French Revolution and Empire, 1793–1812*, Vol. I (Boston: Little, Brown & Co., 1895): 179–80.
54 'German U-boat Strategy in the War', Appendix XVIII, to 'Some Weaknesses in German Strategy and Organisation, 1933-1945', Report by the Joint Intelligence Sub-Committee, JIC(46)33(Final), 20 October 1946, NHB: 180 and 183.
55 'Defence of Ocean Convoys …', AIR 20/6384: 5–7; 'Defence of Fleet Units …', AIR 2/5950: 5–6.
56 'Tactical Employment of Patrol Groups', AIR 2/5950: 1.
57 Ibid: 3.
58 'Item 6 – The Anti-Submarine Problem', Captain R.G. Onslow, DSO, RN, Naval Director of the Joint Anti-Submarine School, in 'Minutes of Naval Air Tactical Conference held at RNB, Lee-on-Solent, 31 May to 3 June 1948', AWD.394/48, n.d., NAA(M): MP1049/5, 1874/2/63.
59 'Fifth Partial Report (Part I) on Project Op/V32/A16-3(17)(Revised): Development of Air and Coordinated Surface Tactics for use Against the Medium Speed Deep-Diving Submarines (Hunter-Killer Groups)', R.P. Biscoe, Commander Operational Development Force, 30 June 1948, Box 96, RG 313, NARA2.
60 'Composition of Hunter-Killer Groups', W.R. Edsall, Assistant Chief of Staff to Commander in Chief US Atlantic Fleet, FF13/A4-3(00189), 14 December 1949, Box 103, RG 313, NARA2.
61 'Proceedings of Anti-Submarine Warfare Conference, 17 June 1946', Op-34H:jn (SC) A16-3(17) Serial: 00012P34, Forrest Sherman, Deputy Chief of Naval Operations, 25 June 1946, Microfiche F3642-1, Sheet 001, OA, NHC: 28–9.

62 'Annual Report of TAS Schools, 1948', UWD, CB4486(48), UW.05088/1949, January 1949, ADM 189/68: 23.
63 'The First Experience of A/S Actions with Intermediate (B) Submarines', in 'Progress in Underwater Warfare, 1949', CB04050(49), 17 July 1950, ADM 239/274: 53 and 64.
64 Llewellyn-Jones, 'The Pursuit of Realism': 234.
65 'The First Experiences of A/S Actions with Intermediate (B) Submarines: Addendum to CB04050(48) – Progress in Underwater Warfare, 1948', DTASW, TASW.312/49, CB04050(48)(N), 1 December 1949, ADM 239/423: 6.
66 'Progress in Underwater Warfare, 1948', ADM 239/422: 37.
67 Ibid: 114; Hackmann, *Seek & Strike*: 338; 'First Commonwealth TAS Liaison Meeting …', NAA(M): MP1185/8, 1846/4/343.
68 'HM Submarine *Scotsman*. Report of First of Class Trials', Flag Officer S/M, Fort Blockhouse, n.d., RNSM A1991/104.
69 'Super *Seraph* – Submerged Control Preliminary Report. Report No. 25/46', Superintendent, Admiralty Experiment Works, Haslar, to DNC, 11 November 1946, and 'HMS *Scotsman*: Conversion to Fast A/S Target', Section 27, DNC Department, October 1948, RNSM A1991/098; 'HM Submarine *Scotsman* – First of Class Trials', G. Bryant, DNC Department to Flag Officer (Submarines), [5] November [1948], and '*Scotsman* Trials', G. Bryant to DNC, Memo dated 5 November 1948, RNSM A1991/104.
70 'Echo and HE Characteristics of the Submarine *Scotsman*', J.W. McCloy, HM Underwater Detection Establishment Report No. 95, October 1951, ADM 259/29: 10.
71 'The First Experience of A/S Actions with Intermediate (B) Submarines', ADM 239/274: 54.
72 'A/S Practices of HMS *Battleaxe*, *Crossbow*, *Scorpion* and *Broadsword* with HM Submarine *Scotsman* in the North Channel in January and February, 1949', in 'Progress in Underwater Warfare, 1949', CB04050(49), 17 July 1950, ADM 239/274: 71.
73 'Conduct of Anti-U-Boat Operations: Part IV, Air and Surface A/S Searches and Striking Forces', DASW, ASW 3078/43, BR1679(4), June 1944, ADM 234/293; 'TAS Warfare Springback', Lieutenant Commander J.H. Adams, Royal Navy, Commanding Officer [HMS *Creole*], 1 June 1950, Adams Papers.
74 'The First Experiences of A/S Actions with Intermediate (B) Submarines …', ADM 239/423: 19-28.
75 'A Model Anti-U-Boat Operation in the Indian Ocean – 5–14 August 1944', Section 6, 'Monthly Anti-Submarine Report, July 1944', DAUD, CB 04050/44(7), 15 August 1944, NHB; 'Report of Proceedings for Period 30 July – 17 August 1944', Commander G.A.G. Ormsby, RN, Senior Officer 60th Escort Group, HMS *Taff*, STA/B/19, 17 August 1944, ADM 199/498.
76 'Conduct of A/S Operations …', Box 468, RG 38, NARA2, Part 6: 9–12.
77 'A/S Practices of HMS *Battleaxe*, *Crossbow*, *Scorpion* and *Broadsword* with USS *Dogfish* in the North Channel in February and March, 1949', in 'Progress in Underwater Warfare, 1949', CB04050(49), 17 July 1950, ADM 239/274: 74–5.
78 'Progress in Underwater Warfare, 1948', ADM 239/422: 39.
79 'The First Experience of A/S Actions with Intermediate (B) Submarines', ADM 239/274: 56.
80 'The First Experiences of A/S Actions with Intermediate (B) Submarines …', ADM 239/423: 2 [emphasis in original].
81 Leo Marriott, *Royal Navy Destroyers since 1945* (London: Ian Allan, 1989): 87.
82 Vice Admiral Sir Lancelot Bell Davies, KBE, email, 6 January 2001.
83 'Progress in Underwater Warfare, 1948', ADM 239/422: 41.
84 'Progress in Tactics, 1949', ADM 239/565: 27.
85 'Progress in Underwater Warfare, 1948', ADM 239/422: 40–1.
86 'Underwater Detection Establishment – Research and Development – Progress Report Number 2', DTSR, 17 November 1947, NAA(M): MP1049/5, 1968/2/663;

'Half-Yearly Scientific and Technical Progress Report', ADM 213/362; 'Fitting of High Speed Dome to Destroyers', Ship Design Policy Committee, SDPC(49)14, 25 May 1949, ADM 116/5632.
87 ACNS to First Sea Lord, ACNS/263, 20 October 1948, ADM 205/69.
88 'Fitting of High Speed Dome to Destroyers', ADM 116/5632.
89 'HMUDE Summary of Progress', 1 December 1948, NAA(M): MP1049/5, 1968/2/800.
90 'Report on 10th TAS Liaison Meeting – HMS *Vernon* – 18–20 September 1951', Lieutenant Commander M.S. Batterham, RANVR, 9 October 1951, NAA(M): MP1049/6, 5036/32/140.
91 'Underwater Weapons and Equipment – Research Reports – Summary', DTSR, 28 April 1949, NAA(M): MP1049/5, 1968/2/780.
92 Mosse, 'Half a Lifetime': 76; 'Joint Anti-Submarine School, Londonderry. Progress Report – Summer Term, 1952', C-in-C, Plymouth, M.024475/52, ADM 1/23733: 7–10.
93 'Eleventh TAS Liaison Meeting: Minutes', Part 4, 'Evaluation of Fast A/S Frigate Conversions', paper read by Captain M. Le Fanu, DSC, RN, Captain (D), Third Training Squadron, 9–11 September 1952, ADM 189/235: 37; M. Llewellyn-Jones, 'The Royal Navy and the Challenge of the Fast Submarine, 1944–1954: Innovation or Evolution?' in Richard Harding (ed.), *The Royal Navy, 1930–2000* (London: Cass, 2004): 135-69.
94 'Admiralty Research Laboratory and Admiralty Gunnery Establishment, Teddington: Statement of Work in Hand – August 1945', NAA(M): MP1049/5, 1968/2/577.
95 Llewellyn-Jones, 'British Responses to the U-boat': 17.
96 'Summary of Operations Aircraft Development Squadron Four Detachment in the United Kingdom during the Period 26 May to 17 June 1948', F.E. Bardwell, Commanding Officer, Aircraft Development Squadron Four, to Chief of Naval Operations, VX-4/A4-3 Serial: 005, 1 September 1948, Box 97, RG 313, NARA2; 'Joint A/S School Exercises', The Commanding Officer, 19 Carrier Air Group to The Commanding Officer, HMCS *Magnificent*, 28 May 1948, File S-4973-30 Vol. 1, Vol. 1814, Acc. 83-84/167, RG 24, NAC.
97 'The Application of Lofar Techniques to Sonobuoys', D.A. Hanley, UDE Pamphlet No. 293, September 1953, ADM 259/205.
98 'Anti-Submarine Tactics and Training', Squadron Leader R.J. Wilcock, RCAF, for Air Member, Canadian Joint Staff, London, S25-28 (Armament), 3 April 1951, File S-28-1-4, Vol. 5270, RG 24, NAC.
99 'Transit Offensives and the Inshore U-boat', I.E. Tweedie, Department of Operational Research, Report No. 29, August 1953, ADM 219/607.
100 R.A. Brie, 'Rotary-wings at Sea', *The Aeroplane* (6 July 1951): 25 'Third A/S Tactical Liaison Meeting held in HMS *Vernon* on 1st and 2nd May 1947', A.198/3/47, 17 May 1947, distributed by Op-32-F-45, n.d., Box 102, RG 313, NARA2.
101 'HMS *Venturer* – Report of Eleventh War Patrol', Lieutenant J.S. Launders, RN, No. SC 4110, 15 February 1945, ADM 199/1815.
102 Vice Admiral Sir Arthur Hezlet, KBE, CB, DSO*, DSC, telephone interviews, 22 and 23 September 2000; *Navy List* (3), January 1946.
103 'Anti-Submarine Problems of the Future', AIR 20/6381, Part 5.
104 M. Llewellyn-Jones, 'A Flawed Contender': 58–67.
105 N. Abercrombie to Commanders-in-Chief and Flag Officer (Submarines), etc., M.TASW.289/47, 8 January 1948, ADM 1/24407.
106 'Requirements for an HTP Operational Submarine', Flag Officer Submarines 705/S/M.068 dated 8 September 1952 with Notes by Admiralty Divisions and Departments', [DTSD, 12 November 1952], ADM 1/23729.

Conclusion: Joining up the dots, 1944–49

1 'Anti-Submarine Training', ADM 205/3.
2 'HM Submarine *U-1407* – Trials', 23 May 1947, RNSM A1977/043.
3 'Exercises with USS *Trumpetfish*', Box 96, RG 313, NARA2.
4 Cunningham, *Odyssey*: 577.

Bibliography

A note on sources

Where quotations are given, or citations made, they have been taken verbatim from the original sources, except where – occasionally – odd spellings were used, or where, for example, dates are expressed in different formats. These have been silently corrected. Other additions by the author are denoted, as usual, by square brackets.

Sources were gleaned from a number of archives. Often the source is available in a number of these institutions, but the citations given in the notes are those where the particular document was first found by the author.

Primary sources

AL	Admiralty Library, Ministry of Defence	
	Confidential Books (CBs)	
	Technical Histories	
	Miscellaneous Files	
AHB	Air Historical Branch	
AWM	Australian War Memorial, Canberra	
BRNC	Britannia Royal Naval College, Dartmouth	
CCAC	Churchill College Archives Centre, Cambridge	
	GOEV	Goodeve Papers
	KEYN	Keynes Papers
	FWCT	Fawcett Papers
	HWJN	Howard-Johnston Papers
DERA	Defence Evaluation and Research Agency, Winfrith	
DHH	Directorate of History and Heritage, Ottawa	
DNH	Directorate of Naval History, Canberra	
IWM	Imperial War Museum, London	
	IWM P347	I.L.M. McGeoch Papers
	IWM P432	P.G. Cazalet Papers
	IWM 65/25/1	M.J. Evans Papers
	IWM 66/28/1	G.H. Roberts Papers

Bibliography 209

	IWM 90/23/1	J.P. Mosse Papers
	IWM 93/22/1	Mrs D. Coyne Papers
LHCMA	Liddell Hart Centre for Military Archives, King's College, London	
NA	National Archives (formerly Public Record Office), Kew	
	ADM 1.	Admiralty and Secretariat Papers
	ADM 116.	Admiralty and Secretariat Cases
	ADM 137.	Admiralty, Historical Section, Records used for Official History, First World War
	M 173.	Submarine Logs
	ADM 186.	Admiralty: Publications
	ADM 189.	Torpedo and Anti-Submarine School Reports
	ADM 199.	War History Cases and Papers
	ADM 204.	Admiralty Research Laboratory: Reports and Notes
	ADM 205.	First Sea Lord Papers
	ADM 213.	Admiralty Centre for Scientific Information Liaison: Reports
	ADM 217.	Station Records: Western Approaches
	ADM 218.	Royal Naval Scientific Service: A.B. Woods Papers
	ADM 219.	Directorate of Naval Operational Studies: Reports
	ADM 223.	Admiralty: Naval Intelligence Division and Operational Intelligence Centre: Intelligence Reports and Papers
	ADM 229.	Admiralty: Department of the Director of Naval Construction: Directors' Papers
	ADM 234.	Navy Reference Books: BR [Books of Reference] Series
	ADM 239.	Navy Reference Books: CB [Confidential Books] Series
	ADM 259.	Underwater Detection Establishment
	ADM 283.	Department of Scientific Research and Experiment: Reports
	AIR 1.	Air Historical Branch Records, First Series
	AIR 2.	Air Ministry: Registered Files
	AIR 15.	Coastal Command, 1936–65
	AIR 20.	Air Ministry, and Ministry of Defence: Air Historical Branch: Unregistered Papers
	AIR 40.	Directorate of Intelligence Files
	AIR 41.	Air Historical Branch: Narratives and Monographs
	AIR 65.	Air/Sea Warfare Development Unit: Reports
	CAB 81.	Chiefs of Staff Sub-Committees, 1939–45
	CAB 86.	Battle of the Atlantic Committee, 1941–2 and Anti-U-Boat Warfare Committee, 1942–5
	CAB 120.	Cabinet Office: Minister of Defence Secretariat: Records
	CAB 158.	Ministry of Defence. Joint Intelligence Sub-Committee later Committee. Memoranda (JIC Series)
	DEFE 2.	Combined Operations Headquarters, and Ministry of Defence, Combined Operations Headquarters later Amphibious Warfare Headquarters: Records

210 *Bibliography*

	DEFE 3. Intelligence from Enemy Radio Communications, 1941–5
	DEFE 5. Chiefs of Staff Committee Memoranda
	DEFE 6. Joint Planning Committee
	DEFE 9. Ministry of Defence: Papers of Sir Henry Tizard, Chairman of Defence Research Policy Committee
	HW 1. Government Code and Cypher School: Signals Intelligence Passed to the Prime Minister, Messages and Correspondence
	PREM 3. Prime Minister's Papers
	WO 208. War Office: Directorate of Military Operations and Intelligence, and Directorate of Military Intelligence
NAA(C)	National Archives of Australia, Canberra
NAA(M)	National Archives of Australia, Melbourne
	MP1049/5
	MP1049/6
	MP1185/8
NAC	National Archives of Canada, Ottawa
	RG 24. A/S Warfare Files
NARA2	National Archives and Records Administration 2, College Park, Maryland
	RG 38. Records of the Office of the Chief of Naval Operations: Registered Publications Section: US Navy and Related Operational, Tactical & Instructional Publications, 1918–70 and Records of the Office of the Chief of Naval Operations: Registered Publications Section, Foreign Navy and Related Foreign Military Publications, 1913–60
	RG 313. Records of the Naval Operating Forces: Commander in Chief Atlantic (CinCLant) Secret Administrative Files, 1941–9
NHB	Naval Historical Branch, Ministry of Defence
	Biographical Files
	Confidential Books (CBs)
	F. Barley and D.W. Waters Papers
	Foreign Documents Section (FDS)
	Naval War Memorandum (European)
	Searches
	Staff Histories
	U-boat Assessment Committee
	War Diaries
	Miscellaneous Files
	5th Escort Group Narrative
NMM(G)	National Maritime Museum, Greenwich
	MSS/93/008 Gretton Papers (since these papers were used, they have been catalogued)
NMM(W)	National Maritime Museum, Woolwich
NHC(OA)	Naval Historical Center, Navy Yard, Washington (Operational Archives)

Personal Papers
        Rear Admiral J.H. Adams (now held in CCAC)
        Electrical Sub Lieutenant M. Walford, RNVR
RNM   Royal Naval Museum, Portsmouth
        Commander A.F.C. Layard, Diary
RNSM Royal Naval Submarine Museum, Gosport
RS   The Royal Society
        BP Blackett Papers

Interviews and correspondence

Geoffrey Budd, telephone interviews, 23–6 March 2003
Commander Richard Compton-Hall, interview, 26 February 2000
Professor R.D. Keynes, interview, 30 July 1999
Professor Sir William McCrea, FRS, interview, 17 April 1998
Rear Admiral J.H. Adams, CB, LVO, interview, 28 May 1998 and telephone interview, 2 March 1999
Lieutenant Commander John Guest, RNVR, telephone interview, 14 May 2001
Vice Admiral Sir Arthur Hezlet, KBE, CB, DSO*, DSC, telephone interviews, 22 and 23 September 2000
Flight Lieutenant Bell, letter, 1 July 1998
R. Compton-Hall, letter to A. Hampshire [c. 1998]
Paul Mallett, letter, 7 July 1999
D.C.R. Webb, letters, 6 August 1997 and 9 June 1998
Bernard Stephens, letter 'Torpedo Mine Mk 24', 30 April 1998
Erich Topp, letters, 7 July and 17 August 1997
Professor Westcott, letter, 28 June 1998
Vice Admiral Sir Lancelot Bell Davies, KBE, email, 6 January 2001
Richard Compton-Hall, emails, 20 June 2000
Peter Evans, email, 22 December 1998
Norman Friedman, email, 17 May 2002
Doug McLean, 'Philosophical Ramblings', email, 1 November 2003

Unpublished private papers

Adams Papers (since lodged at Churchill College Archives Centre, Cambridge)
World Ship Society
SOCA – Submarine Old Comrades Association, Gatwick Archive
MLJ – Author's Collection

Secondary sources

Theses

Richard H. Allen, 'The Attack-at-Source and the Development of the British X-Craft Midget Submarine, 1945–1958' (MA, London, King's College, 2000).

Tim Benbow, 'The Impact of Air Power on Navies: The United Kingdom, 1945–1957', (DPhil, St. Anthony's College, 1999).
Michael Shawn Cafferky, 'Uncharted Waters: The Development of the Helicopter Carrying Destroyer in the Post-War Canadian Navy, 1943–1964' (PhD, Carleton University, Canada, 1996).
William James Crowe Jr., 'The Policy Roots of the Modern Royal Navy, 1946–1963' (PhD, Princeton University, 1965).
George Durnford Franklin, 'British Anti-Submarine Tactics, 1926–1940' (MPhil, University of Glasgow, June 2001).
William Glover, 'Officer Training and the Quest of Operational Efficiency in the Royal Canadian Navy, 1939–1945' (PhD, London, King's College, 1993).
M. Llewellyn-Jones, 'The Royal Navy on the Threshold of Modern Anti-Submarine Warfare, 1944–1949' (PhD, London, King's College, February 2004).
M. Llewellyn-Jones, 'British Responses to the U-boat, Winter 1943 to Spring 1945' (MA, London, King's College, December 1997).
D.M. McLean, 'The Last Cruel Winter: The RCN Support Groups and the U-Boat Schnorkel Offensive' (MA, Royal Military College of Canada, March 1992).
John Simpson, 'Understanding weapon acquisition processes: a study of naval anti-submarine aircraft procurement in Britain, 1945–55' (PhD, University of Southampton, 1976).

Books

Air Ministry, *The Origins and Development of Operational Research in the Royal Air Force* (London: HMSO, 1963).
Air Ministry, Pamphlet No. 248: *The Rise and Fall of the German Air Force (1933 to 1945)* (Issued by the Air Ministry (A.C.A.S.[I]), 1948).
Richard J. Aldrich, *The Hidden Hand: Britain, America and Cold War Secret Intelligence* (London: John Murray, 2001).
Richard J. Aldrich (ed.), *British Intelligence, Strategy and the Cold War, 1945–51* (London: Routledge, 1992).
Chris Ashworth, *RAF Coastal Command, 1936–1969* (Sparkford: Patrick Stephens, 1992).
C.R. Attlee, *As it Happened: His Autobiography* (London: Heinemann, 1954).
K.C. Baff, *Maritime is Number Ten: The Sunderland Era* (Privately Published, 1983).
Arthur Banks, *Wings of the Dawning: The Battle for the Indian Ocean, 1939–1945* (Malvern Wells: Images, 1996).
Correlli Barnett, *Engage the Enemy More Closely: The Royal Navy in the Second World War* (London: W. W. Norton & Co., 1991): 854.
Clay Blair, *Silent Victory: The US Submarine War Against Japan* (New York, 1975).
D.K. Brown (ed.), *The Design and Construction of British Warships, 1939–1945. The Official Record: Submarines, Escorts and Coastal Forces* (London: Conway, 1996).
Alan Burn, *The Fighting Captain: Frederick John Walker and the Battle of the Atlantic* (London: Leo Cooper, 1993).
W.S. Chalmers, *Max Horton and the Western Approaches* (London: Hodder and Stoughton, 1954).
Julian Corbett, *Some Principles of Maritime Strategy* (Naval Institute Press, 1972).
Percy Cradock, *Know Your Enemy: How the Joint Intelligence Committee Saw the World* (London: John Murray, 2002).

Peter Cremer, *U333: The Story of a U-boat Ace*, tr. Lawrence Wilson (London: The Bodley Head, 1984).

John Creswell, *British Admirals of the Eighteenth Century* (London: Allen & Unwin, 1972).

John Creswell, *Naval Warfare: An Introductory Study* (London: Sampson Low, Marston & Co., 1942).

Viscount Cunningham of Hyndhope, *A Sailor's Odyssey* (London: Hutchinson & Co., 1951).

Thurston Dart, *The Interpretation of Music* (New York: Harper, 1963).

Michael Dockrill, *The Cold War, 1945–1963*, (London: Macmillan, 1988).

Karl Doenitz, *Memoirs: Ten Years and Twenty Days*, tr. R.H. Stevens, intro. Jürgen Rohwer (London: Greenhill Books, 1990).

Martin Doughty, *Merchant Shipping and War: A Study in Defence Planning in Twentieth-Century Britain* (London: Royal Historical Society, 1982).

W.A.B. Douglas, Roger Sarty, Michael Whitby, *No Higher Purpose: The Official Operational History of the Royal Canadian Navy in the Second World War, 1939–1943*, Vol. II, Part 1 (St. Catherines, Ontario: Vanwell Publishing Limited, 2002).

W.A.B. Douglas, Roger Sarty, Michael Whitby, *No Higher Purpose: The Official Operational History of the Royal Canadian Navy in the Second World War, 1943–1945*, Vol. II, Part 2 (forthcoming).

W.A.B. Douglas, *The Creation of a National Air Force: The Official History of the Royal Canadian Air Force*, Vol. II (Toronto: University of Toronto Press, 1986).

David Edgerton, *England and the Aeroplane: an Essay on a Militant and Technological Nation* (Basingstoke: Macmillan, 1991).

Dwight D. Eisenhower, Crusade in Europe (London: William Heinemann, 1948).

Giuseppe Fioravanzo, *A History of Naval Tactical Thought*, tr. Arthur W. Holst (Annapolis: United States Naval Institute, 1979).

George Franklin, *Britain's Anti-Submarine Capability, 1919–1939* (London: Frank Cass, 2003).

Norman Friedman, *The Fifty Year War: Conflict and Strategy in the Cold War* (Annapolis: Naval Institute Press, 2000).

Norman Friedman, *U.S. Submarines Since 1945: An Illustrated Design History* (Annapolis: U.S. Naval Institute Press, 1994).

Norman Friedman, *The Postwar Naval Revolution* (London: Conway, 1986).

Norman Friedman, *Submarine Design and Development* (London: Conway, 1984).

Michael Gannon, *Black May: The Epic Story of the Allies' Defeat of the German U-Boats in May 1943* (London: Aurum Press, 1998).

W.J.R. Gardner, *Decoding History: The Battle of the Atlantic and Ultra* (London: Macmillan, 1999).

F.N. Goodwin, *Castle Class Corvettes (Frigates): An Account of the Service of the Ships and their Ships' Companies* (Castle Class Corvette (Frigate) Association (forthcoming)).

S.G. Gorshkov, *The Sea Power of the State* (Annapolis, Maryland: Naval Institute Press, 1976, translated 1979).

Christina J.M. Goulter, *A Forgotten Offensive: Royal Air Force Coastal Command's Anti-Shipping Campaign, 1940–1945* (London: Frank Cass, 1995).

William Granville, *Sea Slang of the Twentieth Century* (London: Winchester Publications, Ltd., 1949).

Peter Gretton, *Crisis Convoy: The Story of HX231* (London: Peter Davies, 1974).

Peter Gretton, *Convoy Escort Commander* (London: Cassell, 1964).

Eric J. Grove (ed.), *The Defeat of the Enemy Attack on Shipping, 1939–1945*, revised edn. (Aldershot: Ashgate for The Navy Records Society, 1997).

Eric J. Grove, *Vanguard to Trident: British Naval Policy since World War II* (London: The Bodley Head, 1987).

Willem Hackmann, *Seek & Strike: Sonar, Anti-submarine Warfare and the Royal Navy 1914–54* (London: HMSO, 1984).

Arnold Hague, *The Allied Convoy System, 1939–1945: Its Organisation, Defence and Operation* (Annapolis, Maryland: Naval Institute Press, 2000).

Paul G. Halpern, *A Naval History of World War I* (London: UCL Press, 1994).

Peter Hennessy, *The Secret State: Whitehall and the Cold War* (London: Allen Lane, 2002).

Günther Hessler, *The U-boat War in the Atlantic, 1939–1945*, Vol. III: *June 1943–May 1945* (London: HMSO, 1989).

High Command of the Navy, *The U-Boat Commander's Handbook, 1942, New Edition 1943* (Gettysburg, PA: Thomas Publications, 1989).

F.H. Hinsley, E.E. Thomas, C.F.G. Ransom & R.C. Knight, *British Intelligence in the Second World War: Its Influence on Strategy and Operations*, Vol. III, Part 1 (London: HMSO, 1984).

F.H. Hinsley, E.E. Thomas, C.A.G. Simkins and C.F.G. Ransom, *British Intelligence in the Second World War: Its Influence on Strategy and Operations*, Vol. III, Part 2 (London: HMSO, 1988).

D. Howse, *Radar at Sea. The Royal Navy in World War 2* (London: Macmillan for The Naval Radar Trust, 1993).

Michael T. Isenberg, *Shield of the Republic: The United States Navy in an Era of Cold War and Violent Peace, 1945–1962* (New York: St. Martin's Press, 1993).

Admiral of the Fleet, Viscount Jellicoe of Scapa, *The Crisis of the Naval War* (London: Cassell, 1920).

F.A. Kingsley (ed.), *The Development of Radar Equipments for the Royal Navy, 1935–1945* (London: Macmillan Press, for the Naval Radar Trust, 1995).

Andrew Lambert, *Nelson: Britannia's God of War* (London: Faber and Faber, 2004).

M. Llewellyn-Jones (ed.), *The Royal Navy and the Mediterranean Convoys to Malta in World War Two* (London: Cass, forthcoming).

M. Llewellyn-Jones (ed.), *The Royal Navy and the Arctic Convoys to Russia in World War Two* (London: Cass, forthcoming).

Bernard Lovell, *P.M.S. Blackett: A biographical memoir* (London: The Royal Society, 1976).

Edward N. Luttwak, *Strategy: the Logic of War and Peace* (Cambridge, Mass.: Harvard University Press, 1987).

A.T. Mahan, *The Influence of Sea Power upon the French Revolution and Empire, 1793–1812*, Vol. I (Boston: Little, Brown & Co., 1895).

A.T. Mahan, *The Influence of Sea Power upon History, 1660–1783* (*London*: Sampson Low, Marston, Searle & Rivington, c.1889).

Joseph A. Maiolo, *The Royal Navy and Nazi Germany, 1933–39: A Study in Appeasement and the Origins of the Second World War* (London: Macmillan Press, 1998).

Chris Madsen, *The Royal Navy and German Naval Disarmament, 1942–1947* (London: Frank Cass, 1998).

Janet M. Manson, *Diplomatic Ramifications of Unrestricted Submarine Warfare, 1939–1941* (London: Greenwood Press, 1990).

Arthur J. Marder, *From the Dreadnought to Scapa Flow: The Royal Navy in the Fisher Era, 1904–1919*, Vol. IV: *1917: Year of Crisis* (London: Oxford University Press, 1969).

Leo Marriott, *Royal Navy Destroyers since 1945* (London: Ian Allan, 1989).
Leo Marriott, *Royal Navy Frigates since 1945*, 2nd edn. (London: Ian Allan, 1990).
Dwight R. Messimer, *Find and Destroy: Antisubmarine Warfare in World War I* (Annapolis, Maryland: Naval Institute Press, 2001).
Marc Milner, *The U-boat Hunters: The Royal Canadian Navy and the Offensive against Germany's Submarines* (Annapolis, Maryland: Naval Institute Press, 1994).
James L. Money (ed.), *The Dictionary of American Naval Fighting Ships*, Vol. VI, Historical Sketches – Letters R through S (Washington, DC.: United States Government Printing Office, 1976).
Ewen Montague, *Beyond Top Secret U* (London: Peter Davies, 1977).
Richard Moore, *The Royal Navy and Nuclear Weapons* (London: Frank Cass, 2001).
Naval Staff Directorate, *British Maritime Doctrine*, 2nd edn., BR1806 (London: HMSO, 1999).
Navy List, various.
Henry Newbolt, *History of the Great War: Naval Operations*, Vol. V (London: Longmans, 1931).
Axel Niestlé, *German U-boat Losses during World War II: Details of Destruction* (London: Greenhill, 1998).
D.P. O'Connell, *The Influence of Law on Sea Power* (Manchester: Manchester University Press, 1975).
Richard Overy, *The Battle* (London: Penguin, 2000).
Richard Overy, *Why the Allies Won* (London: Pimlico, 1996).
Michael A. Palmer, *Origins of the Maritime Strategy: The Development of American Naval Strategy, 1945–55* (Annapolis: Naval Institute Press, 1990).
Kenneth Poolman, *Escort Carrier, 1941–1945: An Account of British Escort Carriers in Trade Protection* (London: Ian Allan, 1972).
D.A. Rayner, *Escort: the Battle of the Atlantic* (London: William Kimber, 1955).
Terrence Robertson, *Walker RN* (London: White Lion edn., 1975).
N.A.M. Rodger, *The Admiralty* (Lavenham: T. Dalton, 1979).
Jürgen Rohwer and Mikhail S. Monakov, *Stalin's Ocean-Going Fleet: Soviet Naval Strategy and Shipbuilding Programmes, 1935–1953* (London: Frank Cass, 2001).
Jürgen Rohwer, *Axis Submarine Successes of World War Two: German, Italian and Japanese Submarine Successes, 1939–1945* (London: Greenhill Books, 1999).
Jürgen Rohwer, *The Critical Convoy Battles of March 1943: The Battle for HX.229/SC.122* (London: Ian Allan, 1977).
S.W. Roskill, *Naval Policy Between the Wars*, Vol. II: *The Period of Reluctant Rearmament, 1930–1939* (London: Collins, 1977).
S.W. Roskill, *The Strategy of Sea Power: It Development and Application* (London: Collins, 1962).
Stephen Roskill, *The War at Sea 1939–1945*, Vol. I: *The Defensive* (London: HMSO, 1954).
Stephen Roskill, *The War at Sea 1939–1945*, Vol. III, Part II: *The Offensive 1st June 1944–14th August 1945* (London: HMSO, 1961).
Eberhard Rössler, *The U-boat: The Evolution and Technical History of German Submarines*, tr. Harold Erenberg (London: Arms and Armour Press, 1981).
Jon Tetsuro Sumida, *Inventing Grand Strategy and Teaching Command: The Classic Works of Alfred Thayer Mahan Reconsidered* (London: The John Hopkins University Press, 1997).
Robert C. Stern, *Type VII U-boats* (London: Arms and Armour Press, 1997).

David Syrett (ed.), *The Battle of the Atlantic and Signals Intelligence: U-Boat Situations and Trends, 1941–1945* (Aldershot: Ashgate, 1998).
David Syrett, *The Defeat of the German U-Boats: The Battle of the Atlantic* (Columbia: South Carolina University Press, 1994).
John Terraine, *Business in Great Waters: The U-Boat Wars 1916–1945* (London: Leo Cooper, 1989).
Robert J. Urick, *Principles of Underwater Sound*, 3rd edn. (California: Peninsula Publishing, 1983).
Jordan Vause, *Wolf: U-boat Commanders in World War II* (Shrewsbury: Airlife, 1997).
C.H. Waddington, *OR in World War 2: Operational Research against the U-boat* (London: Elek Science, 1973).
D.W. Waters, *Convoy as a Mine Countermeasure in Two World Wars* (Admiralty: Historical Section, 1953).
Anthony J. Watts, *The U-Boat Hunters* (Abingdon, Oxon.: Purnell Book Services, 1976).
Gary E. Weir, *Forged in War: The Naval-Industrial Complex and American Submarine Construction, 1940–1961* (Washington: Naval Historical Center, Department of the Navy, 1993).
D.E.G. Wemyss, *Walker's Groups in the Western Approaches* (Liverpool: Daily Post and Echo Ltd., c. 1948).
R. Whinney, *The U-boat Peril: An Anti-Submarine Commander's War* (Poole: Blandford, 1986).
Mark Williams, *Captain Gilbert Roberts RN and the Anti-U-Boat School* (London: Cassell, 1979).
John Winton, *Convoy: The Defence of Sea Trade 1890–1990* (London: Michael Joseph, 1983).
Who's Who, various.
Kenneth Wynn, *U-Boat Operations of the Second World War*, Vol. 2: *Career Histories, U511–UIT25* (London: Chatham Publishing, 1998).
William T. Y'Blood, *Hunter-Killer: US Escort Carriers in the Battle of the Atlantic* (Annapolis, Ma.: Naval Institute Press, 1983).

Articles

Richard J. Aldrich, 'Secret Intelligence for a post-war world: reshaping the British intelligence community, 1944–51', in Richard J. Aldrich (ed.), *British Intelligence, Strategy and the Cold War, 1945–51* (London: Routledge, 1992): 15–49.
P.M.S. Blackett, 'Evan James Williams. 1903–1945', in *Obituary Notices of Fellows of The Royal Society*, 1945–1948, Vol. V (London: Morrison & Gibb for The Royal Society, 1945–1948).
R.A. Brie, 'Rotary-wings at Sea', in *The Aeroplane* (6 July 1951).
E. Maurice Chadwick, 'The Night the Gnats Bit', in *Starshell*, Vol. VI, No. 7 (Fall 1997): 11–12.
David Edgerton, 'From Innovation to Use: Ten Eclectic Theses on the Historiography of Technology', *History of Technology*, Vol. 16, No. 2 (1999): 111–36.
David Edgerton, 'The Prophet Militant and Industrial: the Peculiarities of Correlli Barnett', in *Twentieth Century British History*, Vol. 2 (1991): 360–79.
Ralph Erskine, 'Kurier', n.d., Paper kindly supplied by author, 7 December 1999.
G.D. Franklin, 'A Breakdown in Communications: Britain's Over Estimation of Asdic's Capabilities in the 1930s', in *The Mariner's Mirror*, Vol. 84, No. 2 (May 1998): 204–14.

W.J.R. Gardner, 'Blackett and the Black Arts', in Peter Hore (ed.), *Patrick Blackett: Sailor, Scientist, Socialist* (London: Frank Cass, 2003): 126–37.

Andrew Gordon, 'The Doctrine Pendulum', in Peter Hore (ed), *Hudson Papers*, Vol. 1 (Ministry of Defence, 2001): 73–102.

Anthony Gorst, '"We must cut our coat according to our cloth": the making of British defence policy, 1945–48', in Richard J. Aldrich (ed.), *British Intelligence, Strategy and the Cold War, 1945–51* (London: Routledge, 1992): 143–65.

P. Gretton, 'Why Don't We Learn From History', in *The Naval Review* (January 1958).

Eric Grove and Geoffrey Till, 'Anglo-American Maritime Strategy in the Era of Massive Retaliation, 1945–60', in John B. Hattendorf and Robert S. Jordan (eds.), *Maritime Strategy and the Balance of Power: Britain and America in the Twentieth Century* (Basingstoke, Hants.: Macmillan Press, 1989).

Eric J. Grove, 'The Post War "Ten Year Rule" – Myth and Reality', in *Journal of the Royal United Services Institute*, Vol. 129, No. 4 (December 1984): 48–53.

John B. Hattendorf, 'Maritime conflict', in Michael Howard, George J. Andreopoulos and Mark R. Shulman (eds.), *The Laws of War: Constraints on Warfare in the Western World* (London: Yale University Press, 1994).

Holger H. Herwig, 'Innovation Ignored: The Submarine Problem, Germany, Britain, and the United States, 1919–1939', in Williamson Murray and Allan R. Millett (eds.), *Military Innovation in the Interwar Period* (Cambridge: Cambridge University Press, 1996): 227–64.

Wayne P. Hughes, Jr., 'The Strategy-Tactics Relationship', in Colin S. Gray and Roger W. Barnett (eds.), *Seapower and Strategy* (Maryland, Annapolis: Naval Institute Press, 1989).

G.J. Kirby, 'A History of the Torpedo: Part 3', in *Journal of the Royal Naval Scientific Service*, Vol. 27, No. 2 (1972).

Andrew Lambert, 'Seapower 1939–1940: Churchill and the Strategic Origins of the Battle of the Atlantic', in Geoffrey Till (ed.), *Seapower: Theory and Practice* (Essex, Ilford: Frank Cass, 1994).

'The Overall Strategic Plan, May 1947 (DO(47)44 (Also COS(47)102(0)) (Retained – Cab Off))', Appendix 7, in J. Lewis, *Changing Direction: British Military Planning for Post-war Strategic Defence, 1942–1947* (London: The Sherwood Press, 1988).

M. Llewellyn-Jones, 'The Royal Navy and the Challenge of the Fast Submarine, 1944–1954: Innovation or Evolution?', in Richard Harding (ed.), *The Royal Navy, 1930–2000* (London: Cass, 2004): 135–69.

M. Llewellyn-Jones, 'The Pursuit of Realism: British Anti-Submarine Tactics and Training to Counter the Fast Submarine', in John Reeve and David Stevens (eds.), *The Face of Naval Battle: The Human Experience of Modern War at Sea* (Crows Nest, NSW, Australia: Allen & Unwin, 2003): 219–39.

M. Llewellyn-Jones, 'A Clash of Cultures: The Case for Large Convoys', in Peter Hore (ed.), *Patrick Blackett: Sailor, Scientist, Socialist* (London: Frank Cass, 2003).

M. Llewellyn-Jones, 'A Flawed Contender: The "Fighter" Submarine, 1946–1950', in Martin Edmonds (ed.), *100 Years of the Trade: Royal Navy Submarines Past, Present & Future* (University of Lancaster: Centre for Defence and International Security Studies, February 2001): 58–67.

M. Llewellyn-Jones, 'Trials with HM Submarine *Seraph* and British Preparations to Defeat the Type XXI U-Boat, September–October, 1944', in *The Mariner's Mirror*, Vol. 86, No. 4 (November 2000): 434–51.

M. Llewellyn-Jones, 'Clay Blair Jr., *Silent Victory: The US Submarine War Against Japan*', Book Review in *The Northern Mariner* (forthcoming).

Philip K. Lundeberg, 'Operation "Teardrop" Revisited', in Timothy J. Runyan and Jan M. Copes (eds.), *To Die Gallantly: The Battle of the Atlantic* (Oxford: Westview Press, 1994): 210–30.

Joseph Maiolo, 'Deception and Intelligence Failure: Anglo-German Preparations for U-boat Warfare in the 1930s', Paper delivered at the Military History Seminar, King's College, London, 23 February 1999.

Douglas M. McLean, 'Confronting Technological and Tactical Change: Allied Antisubmarine Warfare in the Last Year of the Battle of the Atlantic', in *Naval War College Review*, Vol. 47, No. 1 (1994): 87–104.

Doug McLean, 'The U.S. Navy and the U-Boat Inshore Offensive', in William B. Cougar (ed.), *New Interpretations in Naval History: Selected Papers from the Twelfth Naval History Symposium* (Annapolis: Naval Institute Press, 1997): 310–24.

Marc Milner, 'The Dawn of Modern Anti-Submarine Warfare: Allied responses to the U-boats, 1944–45', *RUSI Journal* (Spring 1989): 61–8.

W. Murray, 'Neither Navy was Ready', in *United States Naval Institute Proceedings*, No. 107 (1981).

T.H. Pratt, 'A Rose by Any Other Name: An Outline of Operational Analysis in Admiralty HQ, 1947–1970', in *Journal of Naval Science*, Vol. 7, No. 1 (January 1981): 2–9.

Henry Probert, 'Allied Land-Based Anti-Submarine Warfare', in Stephen Howarth and Derek Law (eds.), *The Battle of the Atlantic 1939–1945: The 50th Anniversary International Naval Conference* (London: Greenhill Books, 1994).

Robin Ranger, 'The Anglo-French Wars, 1689–1815', in Colin S. Gray and Roger W. Barnett (eds.), *Seapower and Strategy* (Maryland, Annapolis: Naval Institute Press, 1989).

N.A.M. Rodger, 'Image and Reality in Eighteenth-Century Naval Tactics', in *The Mariner's Mirror*, Vol. 89, No. 3 (August 2003): 280–96.

David Syrett, 'The Battle for Convoy OG69, 20–29 July 1941', in *The Mariner's Mirror*, Vol. 89, No. 1 (February 2003): 71–81.

Michael Whitby, 'The Strain on the Bridge', in John Reeve and David Stevens (eds.), *The Face of Naval Battle: The Human Experience of Modern War at Sea* (Crows Nest, NSW, Australia: Allen & Unwin, 2003): 200–18.

H.P. Willmott, 'The Organisations: The Admiralty and the Western Approaches', in Stephen Howarth and Derek Law (eds.), *The Battle of the Atlantic 1939–1945: The 50th Anniversary International Naval Conference* (London: Greenhill Books, 1994).

R.E. Woolven, 'Coastal Command's Early ASV Radars', in *Air Clues: The Royal Airforce Magazine*, Vol. 24, No. 5 (February 1970).

David Zimmerman, 'Tactics and Technology', in Stephen Howarth and Derek Law (eds.), *The Battle of the Atlantic 1939–1945: The 50th Anniversary International Naval Conference* (London: Greenhill Books, 1994).

Index

'A' Class submarine 48
Action Information Organization (AIO) 124
Admiralty 2, 3, 91–2, 175–6
Admiralty Convoy Instructions (ACI) 42
ahead throwing weapons *see* ATW
aircraft 6; carrier-based 135, 148; depth-charges 30; fighters 114, 138; First World War 10, 11; limitations 19; Patrol Groups 160; patrols 13, 16, 29, 54–5, 59–60, 120, 137; reconnaissance 28, 113–15, 138; schnorkel detection 49, 58, 60, 108; searching 54; shore-based 157–8; submarine detection 100, 108–9, 110–11, 124, 134, 167; surveillance 29, 39, 76; weapons 100
aircraft carriers *see* carriers
Allied tactical doctrine 150–5
Amberjack, USS 162, 165
America 119, 150, 161
Amphion, HMS 165
Anderson, J. 30
anti-submarine vessels *see* escorts
anti-submarine warfare 3–4, 90, 170–2; specialist school 14, 24
Anti-Submarine Warfare Manual 16, 17
Ark Royal 17
asdic: distinguishing echoes 24; fast submarines 82; First World War 10; future 124, 126–7; inter-war years 13; limitations 166; performance 47; *Seraph* trials 71–2, 74; Type 144: 30–3, 162; Type 170: 166, 173
asdic-absorbing anechoic rubber coating 127
Ashbourne, Captain Lord: DTASW 92; future submarines 112, 113, 119; investigations 102; SAWC 105; submerged submarines 98; true submarine 99, 101; Type XXI 103, 104; U-boat trials 85, 87, 89, 90

Atlantic, Battle of the 2, 39–45
atomic weapons 6, 150, 151, 172
attack-at-source 78, 117, 129, 136, 154
attacks (by A/S forces) 11–12, 32–4, 37–9, 52, 73, 98–104
attacks (by U-boats): daytime 27; dived 9; firing range 27; inshore operations 51; long range 25; night 9, 23, 27, 135; submerged 26, 27, 68; surface 23, 27
Attlee, Clement 147
ATW (ahead throwing weapons) 33–4, 45, 171, *see also* Hedgehog; Squid

Barley, Commander 153
Barnard, G. 148
Battleaxe 162, 165
Binney, T.H. 19
binoculars 28–9
Blackett, P.M.S. 64
British Maritime Doctrine Manual 3
Broadsword 162
Brownrigg, T.M. 149, 150
Budgen, D.A. 16, 17
Burnett, P.W.: career 5; doctrine papers 98, 105, 106, 109, 118, 170; doctrine re-assessment 67; DTASW 92, 120; future problems 123, 125, 126, 127, 168; Gnats 26; searching 52, 53, 66; strategic assumptions 128; Type 15 Frigate 167

carriers 17–18, 19, 41, 136–7, 148
Cazalet, P.G. 117
Churchill, Sir Winston 20
Coastal Command 58–60
Cochino, USS 89
Cold War 4, 7, 147
Convoy SC130 41
convoys 2–3, 151; aircraft 54–5, 59–60, 120; attacking 26–7, 39; defence 106–9, 137; doctrine papers 161; First

220 *Index*

World War 9–10; future 115–16, 128; introduction 10–11; nature of strategy 42; planning 14–16; protection 12–13; reinforcement of threatened 40; station-keeping 34; *see also* aircraft; escorts; Patrol Groups; support groups
Corbett, Julian 42
Courageous 17, 18
Cradock, Sir Percy 147
Creasy, G.E. 84, 85, 87, 88, 89
Cremer, Commander 78, 79
Crossbow 162, 165
Cunningham, A.B. 65, 91
Cunningham, J. 150
Currey, H.P. 117, 121

Danckerts, V.H. 17
Daniel, C.S. 17, 22
Darling, V.C. 105
defensive operations 3, 16, 42, 43, 149, 152, 173–5
Dendy, R.J.R. 76
depth-charges 10, 11, 30, 32–4, 171
detection (of U-boats) 28–32, 56
Dick, R. 148
Dickinson, H.G. 148
doctrine papers 104–12, 155–61
Dogfish, USS 162, 163–4
Donaldson, V.D'A. 154–5
Dönitz, Karl 68, 78
DTASW (Torpedo, Anti-Submarine and Mine Warfare Division) 91–2
Dunoon, Captain 86

Edelsten, J.H. 18, 20–1, 40, 64, 65
Ellwood, A.B. 59
Emmerman, *Kapitänleutnant* 79
Endymion, SS 14
enemy documents, captured 95–6, 103
Enigma 93
escort carriers (CVE) 41
escorts: disposition 34–5, 49, 54–6; fast submarines 101, 116, 157; First World War 9, 11–12; future requirements 123–4; inter-war years 13; planning 15, 16, 121; radar 30; U-boat casualties 154, 155; *see also* Patrol Groups; support groups
Excalibur, HM Submarine 95
exercises 5, 12, 23, 140–7, 152–4, 162–5
Explorer, HM Submarine 95

Fame, HMS 87, 98
fast submarines 4, 7, 97–100, 162–5
fast U-boats 68–9, 72

Fawcett, H.W. 65
fighters 114, 138
finance 6
Fleet, defence 157, 158
Fleet Air Arm 150
foxers 26, 38, 49–50, 72
Fraser, Lord 149, 150, 153
French, G. 104–5
future submarines 112–18, 119–29

Gates, Group Captain 78, 80
German U-boat officers 78–9
Gibbs, E.A. 143, 144, 145, 146, 173
Gnat (German Naval Acoustic Torpedo) 25–6
Godt, Rear Admiral 78, 79, 80
Gollin, E.M. 97, 115–16
Goodeve, Dr 69
Gorshkov, S.G. 158
Grant, J. 83, 87, 88
Graph, HMS 76
Gretton, P. 38, 42, 78
Guppy 162, 163

Haines, R.G.C. 102
Hakes, J.A. 70
Hart, Raymond 56
Hedgehog 33, 34, 45, 99
helicopters 140, 167
Hermes 17, 18
Hessler, Commander 78, 79
Hezlet, A.R. 168
HMA/SEE (Her Majesty's Anti-Submarine Experimental Establishment, Fairlie) 83
Horton, Max: fast submarines 80; Gnat 39; 'Gooseberry' 54, 55; *Seraph* trials 70, 73; 'sub-convoy' tactic 135; submarines 25; task 63
Hotspur, HMS 98
Howard-Johnson, C.D.: fast U-boats 73; and Fawcett, H.W. 65; Gnat 38, 54; inshore operations 52, 60, 62, 63, 66–7, 86; *Osprey*, HMS 14; tactics 42–3; Type XXI 69; U-boat tactics 37; and Winn, R. 64
hydrophone effect (HE) 9, 71–2, 76, 112

inshore operations: control 54; escorts 51–2; lessons from 66–7, 86; reinforcements 60; tactics 49, 56, 57; U-boat tactics 61, 122
intelligence: detection of U-boats 22, 43, 60, 122; future submarines 113;

Index

integrated 98; Russia 93–4, 95; Type XXI 69
Intermediate (B) submarine 130, 132, 135, 157, 158, 160, 161, 165
Intermediate submarine 130–1

Japan 86
Joint Anti-Submarine School (JASS) 104, 109, 111, 131–40
'Joint Paper on Sea and Air Aspects of Fleet Defence against Submarines' 105, 109–12
'Joint Paper on Sea and Air Aspects of Search and Convoy Defence' 105, 106–9
Joint Sea/Air Warfare Committee (SAWC) 98, 105, 111, 159

Kerr, R. 23, 24
Kingfisher, HMS 70, 71

Le Fanu, M. 167
Lillicrap, Charles 69
Limbo mortar 124, 166
'look' zone 111
lost-contact procedures 36–7, 53
Low, F.S. 94

McCormick, Admiral 151
McCrea, W.H.: demobilization 78; detection 63, 66; fast submarines 76–7; packs 28; searching 62; *Seraph* trials 70; sonobuoys 74; support groups 51, 54, 58, 61; Type XXI 73
McGrigor, Sir Rhoderick 117–18, 151, 152
Mackenzie, H.S. 96
Madden, Sir Charles E. 162, 163, 164
Magnetic Anomaly Detector (MAD) 100, 125
Mansfield, J.M. 173
manuals, tactical 3, 4–5, 16, 17, 34, 150
Mermaid, HMS 52
Meteorite, HMS 84, 102
mine warfare 6, 21, 22, 120
Mitchell, D.R. 70, 73, 74
modern submarines 157
Mosse, J.P. 5, 24, 52, 92, 106, 120, 170

night attacks 9, 23, 27, 135
Norfolk, HMS 1
nuclear submarines 131, 168
nuclear weapons 6, 150, 151, 172

ocean operations 56, 60, 61, 79, 122

offensive operations: air strike policy 150; America 161; Budgen, D.A. 16; Currey, H.P. 117; and defensive 3, 42, 152, 173–5; First World War 121–2; JASS 136; policy 20–2; Roberts, G.H. 43; Vian, P. 149
Oliver, G.N. 112, 117, 129, 153–4
Oliver, R.D. 105
Onslow, R.G. 132, 136, 139, 161
Ormsby, G.A.G.: career 5; doctrine papers 106, 170; DTASW 92, 120; helicopters 140; Type 15 Frigate 167; *U-198* 52
Osprey, HMS 14, 24, 83, 86
Oulton, W.E. 132, 136, 139

pack tactics 27, 28, 76, 79
pair-ship tactics 141–2
Paterson, C.E.E. 129, 137; doctrine papers 155, 156, 157, 159, 160, 161
Patrol Groups 159–60, 161, *see also* escorts; support groups
periscopes 8, 112
Peyton-Ward, Captain 58, 65
Phillips, T.S.V. 14–15
pouncers 55, 57
Pound, Sir Dudley 20, 23
Prentice, J.D. 51
Prichard, N.A.: fast U-boats 68, 73–4, 81, 82, 83, 86; inshore operations 62, 66–7; night attacks 23

R-1, USS 75
radar 29, 30, 100, 112–13, 114, 125, 167
radio 8, 27–8, 39, 156
Red Navy, submarines 95
Relentless 167
research 127
Ring tactic 142–3, 144–5, 164
Roberts, G.H. 43, 69, 78–9, 80, 81, 84
Rocket 167
Roland Morillot 131, 152
Roskill 19
Royal Navy 2, 3, 11
Russia: assessment of threat from 85–6, 93–7, 117, 128, 130, 172; Cold War 147; shadowing 114, 116

S-Class submarine 87, 88, 91, 98, 102, 131
SAWC (Joint Sea/Air Warfare Committee) 98, 105, 111, 159
Sceptre 98
Schnee, Adalbert 1, 78, 79
schnorkel 4, 46–9; aircraft 6, 108; countermeasures 50–8, 60–3, 64–5,

171; inshore operations 122; North-West Approaches 50
Scorpion, HMS 162, 166
Scotsman, HMS 102, 162–3
sea/air cooperation 109, 111, 131, 135
Sea/Air Warfare Committee (SAWC) 98, 105, 111, 159
searching 52–5; doctrine papers 106–9, 160; for fast submarines 72–3, 163; lost-contacts 36–7; systematic 57–8, 62
searchlights 10
Selene 162
Senior Officers, escort groups 44, 138
Seraph trials 69–71, 73, 74, 75, 141
shadowing 114
Shattock, E.H. 113, 114, 148
Sherman, Vice Admiral 161
Simpson, G.W.G. 52
Sims, Admiral 42
Sims, A.J. 85
Slatter, L.H. 120
Solomon, Leon 26, 47, 48, 49, 65, 90
sonobuoys: air-dropped 47–8, 100, 108, 124, 134; development 124; fast submarines 74–5; limitations 167; Patrol Groups 160; tactics 144; training 134
Soviet Union *see* Russia
'Special Operations' 129
Squid 33, 34, 45, 81–3, 99
striking forces 13, 17, 22, 137–8, 160
Styer, C.W. 118, 119, 120
'sub-convoy' tactic 135
submarines: as anti-submarine vessels 126, 168; technical development 129–31
submerged operations 98–104
support groups 19, 40; 1944: 61; dispositions 55–6, 138; future 110, 132; mopping-up operations 44; offensive sweeps 50; surface 39; value of 41, 132; *see also* escorts; Patrol Groups
surface operations 8, 77
surface patrols 11, 110

T-Class submarine 162
tactics: adaptation 173; Atlantic, Battle of 39–45; contact, on gaining 35–9; development 6, 129–31; inshore operations 49; schnorkel countermeasures 50–8, 60–3, 64–5; U-boats 8

Talbot, A.G. 17, 20, 21–2
targets, finding (by submarines) 25, 112–16
TASW (Torpedo, Anti-Submarine and Mine Warfare Division) 91–2
Taylor, Group Captain 59–60
threat assessment 93–7, 105
Titteron, G.A. 19, 153
Tizard, Sir Henry 120
Topp, Erich 79, 103
Torpedo, Anti-Submarine and Mine Warfare Division (DTASW) 91–2
torpedoes 25; active 125; anti-submarine 140, 167; firing ranges 109; homing 77, 109, 125, 126; pattern-running 25, 77, 109
trade protection 15, 17, 18, 109, 111
training 44, 62–3, 73, 75
'Trident' exercise 152–4
true submarine 99, 101, 131
Trumpetfish, USS 143–5
Turpin 167
Type VII U-boat 26, 46, 76, 84, 95
Type IX U-boat 46, 95
Type XVII Walter-boat 80, 84, 85
Type XXI U-boat: assessment 72, 75–8; captured 84–5, 102; commanders 78, 79; development 68, 70; first patrol 1; future problem of 63–4; post-war trials 72, 88, 89, 90; Russia 7, 95; tactics 58, 79, 80, 103–4; *see also* Intermediate (B) submarine
Type XXIII U-boat 79, 85, 87, 89, 95, 98
Type XXVI Walter-boat 80, 81, 95, 130, *see also* Intermediate submarine
Type XVIIB U-boat 81

U-39 17
U-198 52
U-247 60
U-264 47
U-448 46
U-570 26
U-864 168
U-1105 84, 127
U-1171 84
U-1406 84
U-1407 84, 88, 102
U-2326 85, 87, 88, 89, 90, 98
U-2501 70
U-2502 85, 89
U-2511 1, 70, 78
U-2513 79, 102

U-2518 90, 131
U-2519 78
U-3008 102
U-3017 89, 90
U-Boat Commanders Handbook, The 27
U-boats: attacks *see* attacks (by U-boats); casualties 30, 54, 121, 154, 155; defensive power 25; fast 68–9, 72; firing positions 35; First World War 8–9, 10, 11, 121; numbers pre-war 15; performance 26; submerged operations 68, 76; surface operations 8, 77; tactics 1939–43: 25–8, 40, 44, 122; trials by British 84–5, 87, 88, 89, 90, 98; *see also specific U-boats*; Types; Walter high-speed U-boats
United States Navy (USN) 2

Venturer, HMS 168
Vian, Sir Philip 148–9
visual contact 28–9

Walker, Frederick John 38, 38–9, 92
Walter high-speed U-boats 63, 80, 81, 84, 95, 130
Walter turbine 68, 80, 81
Warne, R.S. 120
Waters, Lieutenant Commander 153
weaknesses, enemy's 133
Western Approaches Tactical School (WATU) 43, 44, 69
Williams, E.J. 29, 47, 48, 49, 50, 64, 69
Willoughby, G. 105
Winn, R. 48, 64
Woods, W.J.W. 87

eBooks – at www.eBookstore.tandf.co.uk

A library at your fingertips!

eBooks are electronic versions of printed books. You can store them on your PC/laptop or browse them online.

They have advantages for anyone needing rapid access to a wide variety of published, copyright information.

eBooks can help your research by enabling you to bookmark chapters, annotate text and use instant searches to find specific words or phrases. Several eBook files would fit on even a small laptop or PDA.

NEW: Save money by eSubscribing: cheap, online access to any eBook for as long as you need it.

Annual subscription packages

We now offer special low-cost bulk subscriptions to packages of eBooks in certain subject areas. These are available to libraries or to individuals.

For more information please contact webmaster.ebooks@tandf.co.uk

We're continually developing the eBook concept, so keep up to date by visiting the website.

www.eBookstore.tandf.co.uk

Printed in Great Britain
by Amazon